D0836453

WITHDRAWN
TORONTO PUBLIC LIBRARY
OFFERS THIS ITEM FOR SALE

Canada and the United States

John Herd Thompson
and Stephen J. Randall

Canada and the United States: Ambivalent Allies Fourth Edition

McGill-Queen's University Press

Montreal & Kingston

© 1994, 1997, 2002, 2008 by the University of Georgia Press

ISBN 978-0-7735-3398-1

Legal deposit second quarter 2008
Bibliothèque nationale du Québec

Published simultaneously in the United States by the University of
Georgia Press

Printed in the United States of America

McGill-Queen's University Press acknowledges the support of the
Canada Council for the Arts for our publishing program. We also
acknowledge the financial support of the Government of Canada
through the Book Publishing Industry Development Program (BPIDP)
for our publishing activities.

Library and Archives Canada Cataloguing in Publication
Thompson, John Herd, 1946–
   Canada and the United States : ambivalent allies / John Herd
Thompson and Stephen J. Randall. — 4th ed.

Includes bibliographical references and index.
ISBN 978-0-7735-3398-1

   1. Canada—Relations—United States. 2. United States—Relations—
Canada. I. Randall, Stephen J., 1944– II. Title.
FC249.T48 2008   303.48′271073   C2008-902104-5

Set in 10 on 14 Palatino by Newgen
Printed and bound by Maple-Vail

To the Canadian and U.S. servicepeople who lost their lives
on the UN-sanctioned NATO mission in Afghanistan

Contents

Maps

Preface to the Fourth Edition

Nation-states have no friends, only interests. Historians are much luckier; this fourth edition of *Canada and the United States: Ambivalent Allies* is the work of two friends of thirty-five years. But many others in addition to the two men credited on the cover participated in the creation of this and previous versions. Lester Langley conceived the *United States and the Americas* series and decided that Canada was sufficiently of the Americas to merit a place in it. Nancy Grayson, Jon Davies, and the staff of the University of Georgia Press remain supportive, patient, gentle, and, when necessary, firm with the authors. Student research assistants tracked down material; colleagues too numerous to cite individually offered insight and guidance. Andrea Ramsey helped prepare the index. In 1992, cartographer Bill Mills drew the maps for the first edition the old-fashioned way with pen and ink; in 2007, Jillian Dowding, assistant director of the U.S. Institute at Calgary, created the tables on binational trade with Microsoft Excel.

We thank purchasers of the first, second, and third editions for buying enough copies to give us the opportunity to create a fourth edition. The broad theses of *Ambivalent Allies* stand the tests of critical assessment and of time. But although its central arguments remain unchanged, the fourth edition of *Ambivalent Allies* is virtually a new book, from the Introduction to the Epilogue and the Bibliographical Essay. We rewrote and retitled chapter 1 to reflect new scholarly arguments about the origins of U.S.-Canadian differences that de-emphasize the role of the American Revolution in establishing these differences. Chapter 2 fully incorporates the "New Western History" and cutting-edge scholarship on binational migration. Chapter 3 integrates new arguments about international transmission of progressive reform ideas. In chapters 4 and 5, which discuss the period from 1919 to 1947, we have found a place for new scholarship but have compressed what were three chapters in earlier editions. Chapters 7 through 10 were chapters 8 through 11 in the third edition. Chapter 8 benefits from Stephen Randall's primary research in the Jimmy Carter presidential library, but we significantly rewrote all four chapters to bring them up to date with new historical literature. The authors owe particular appreciation to the archivists at the presidential libraries for the creative searches in their files. A fresh concluding chapter, "Playing by New American Rules, 2001–2007," describes the dramatic changes in the U.S.-Canadian relationship during George W. Bush's presidency and sets them into their transformed international context.

Reviewers and readers were kind enough to bring mistakes of fact and interpretation in the first three editions of *Ambivalent Allies* to our attention. We offer our appreciation in anticipation that they will do the same with this fourth edition. Our concluding profound thanks belong to our fellow scholars Janet Ewald and Annie Katzenberg, our partners not in research but in life.

John Herd Thompson, Durham, North Carolina, USA
Stephen J. Randall, Calgary, Alberta, Canada
October 2007

Canada and the United States

Introduction

The first edition of *Canada and the United States: Ambivalent Allies*, published in 1994, began with our comment that "the inclusion of a volume on Canada in a series on *The United States and the Americas* is an ironic reflection of changing international realities." Since we wrote that sentence, the justification for discussing Canada as an "American" nation has become much more obvious. Canada's manifest ties to the Western Hemisphere grew more evident with the 1987 Free Trade Agreement between Canada and the United States, with Canada's decision to join the Organization of American States, and most particularly with the North American Free Trade Agreement (NAFTA) encompassing Canada, the United States, and Mexico.

For more than two hundred years, the relationship between the United States and what gradually emerged from the Second British Empire as the Canadian nation-state has been intense. Substantial and minor conflicts, bilateral and multilateral institution building, tranquility and turbulence have marked those two centuries. Since the terrorist attacks on the United States on 11 September 2001, the term "undefended border" has fallen from favor. Many scholars and politicians however, stoutly maintain that a "special relationship" links Washington and Ottawa. They assert that the U.S.-Canadian relationship is unlike any other international interaction, and that the fundamental maxim of international relations—that nations have no friends, only interests—does not apply to the United States and Canada.

These platitudes belie the dissonance of the nineteenth century and exaggerate the harmony of the twentieth; as the twenty-first century unfolds, they seem archaic. We argue in *Ambivalent Allies* that the notion of a special relationship is more useful for after-dinner speeches than for historical analysis. What is most important for historians who would understand the binational relationship is to appreciate the shifting international context in which it evolved and continues to evolve.

The central fact of the U.S.-Canadian relationship has been similar to the U.S. relationship with the countries of Latin America: its essential one-sidedness. One may speak of a relationship in which influence flows in both directions, as indeed it sometimes has; but the essential reality has been the imbalance in power. "Canada" until it became a unified dominion in 1867 was a series of colonies of the British Empire. Those colonies and the nascent nation-state of Canada would not have survived as a political entity distinct from the United States without that British connection. In the twentieth century, as the United States emerged as a major power, Canada evolved within the British Empire into a not-quite independent international actor. As the United States became a global power, Canada styled itself a "middle" power. Even that term exaggerates the political, economic, and especially military power of Canada in the world arena. Measured by other than its membership in the G8, by what criteria could contemporary Canada be considered a "middle" power in comparison to, for example, India or Iran?

The asymmetry in the bilateral relationship is reflected in the imbalance between the relative attention Canadian and U.S. scholars give to it. An observer of the professional literature in history or political science would be struck by the prodigious industry Canadian scholars devote to the study of what they call "Canadian-American relations" and by the prevailing neglect of the subject by U.S. academics. Scores of Canadian professors have built careers in the field, but only a few senior U.S. scholars have reached the front ranks of the academy by writing about Canada. The leading historians of U.S. foreign policy in the twentieth century, from Samuel Flagg Bemis and Thomas Bailey to Robert Farrell, Robert Divine, Thomas Paterson, and Walter LaFeber, mention Canada only when it intrudes dramatically into the U.S. narrative: the War of 1812, the boundary settlements of the nineteenth century, the Washington Treaty of 1871, the Alaska boundary dispute of 1903. Thereafter Canada vanishes, in spite of the facts that it was a critical member of America's cold war alliances, and that the two nations developed the largest bilateral trade in the history of the world.

Canada has been a matter of similarly consuming disinterest to the

U.S. public. Between 1920 and 1950, Hollywood formed America's image of Canada as a frozen wilderness inhabited by aboriginal trappers, red-coated Mounted Policemen, and a few beautiful women to sustain the interest of Hollywood's leading men. As Gary Cooper told his costar in *Northwest Mounted Police* (1940), "before I came to Canada I thought the women would be like the mountains—cold and distant." In twenty-first-century America, a stereotype of a Canada obsessed with ice hockey has partially supplanted this older stereotype of a Canada covered with ice. Stuart Elliott, the *New York Times* columnist on media and advertising, mused in May 2007 that "As pollsters in Canada seek to determine which of the country's hockey teams can be deemed 'Canada's team,' how many Americans, if asked the same question, would reply, 'What's hockey?' and how many would reply, 'What's Canada?'"[1]

Most U.S. leaders understood Canada's strategic significance, however. Until the 1870s, they worried about Canada as a base for a British assault on the young republic; during the cold war they appreciated that Canada stood between the USA and USSR. Despite this awareness of Canada's geopolitical importance, some American leaders nonetheless have failed to comprehend Canada's economic significance. Presidents Richard Nixon, Gerald Ford, and Ronald Reagan, for example, each learned to his surprise that Canada, not Japan, was the United States' largest trading partner. Jeffrey Simpson, national columnist of the *Toronto Globe and Mail*, Canada's most influential English-language newspaper, speaks for his countrypeople when he regularly deplores "Americans' general lack of interest in Canada"; Americans, Simpson once claimed, "know and care the square root of squat about Canada."[2]

Simpson's bitterness reflects deep-rooted Canadian anxiety. To every generation of Canadians, the U.S. presence has been an unavoidable fact of everyday life. Canadian, especially English-Canadian, nationalism has been shaped largely in reference to the United States. Canada came to exist only in reaction to the United States, assembled from those British (former French) North American colonies that did not take part in the American War of Independence. America's most despised traitors became Canada's mythical founding fathers; one country's Tory was the other's "United Empire Loyalist." It would have been unimaginable, as political parties came into being in the course of the nineteenth century, for the United States to have spawned a "Tory" party, even if many of the "Tory" values have been adopted by the Republican Party.

The British North Americans who became Canadians were not a colonized people who struggled to be free and then claimed uniqueness among the community of nations; rather, English Canadians chose to retain a parliamentary constitution and to remain a constitutional monarchy within the British Empire. French Canadians in 1776 chose the lesser of two threats—British imperialists seemed less dangerous than would-be American liberators. At the very least, they were farther away. In 1867, English and French Canadians together chose the confederation of their colonies in part as a defense against the perceived ambitions of the United States expressed in the Anglo-American conflicts that the Civil War engendered. Canadian Conservatives explicitly designed their "National Policy" for economic development to create a transcontinental Canada in defiance of the United States. In subsequent generations fear of American domination continued to feed Canadian nationalism. Significantly, the abandonment of that National Policy with the free trade agreement with the United States in the 1980s produced a backlash from those who held a different vision of Canada. Canadians take the occasional U.S. musings about political union far more seriously than do the Americans who propose them. Behind Canada's anxiety over the possibility of Quebec independence, for example, is fear of how vulnerable the English-speaking remnant would be to the United States—despite the fact that the United States has showed not the slightest sign of malevolent intent.

Since there was no other external threat to Canadian autonomy and identity save the United States, it was against Americans that Canadians repeatedly pledged to "stand on guard" in the English-language lyrics of their national anthem. Historians S. F. Wise and Robert Craig Brown suggest that "The average Canadian . . . appears to have leaped from the womb fully equipped with a lifetime's antagonism toward the United States."[3]

The obvious fact that the United States has always been far more important to Canada than Canada is to the United States exacerbates this antagonism. Canada takes up more space on the map, but its population, huddled within a hundred miles of the border, has been consistently about one-tenth that of its southern neighbor. Since the mid-nineteenth century, the United States has been a magnet pulling Canadians south. Except for brief periods of unusual circumstance, such as the aftermath of the American War of Independence, the Fraser and Yukon river gold rushes, the opening of the Canadian west, or the Vietnam War resistance, comparatively few Americans have migrated to Canada. The United States has had by far the richer geographical endowment when measured in terms of accessible arable land. Americans have been the "people of plenty"; Canadians have been a people of relative scarcity, despite their forest, ocean, and mineral resources. French mariner Jacques Cartier was too harsh when he described the rugged granite that covers half of Canada as "the land God gave to Cain," but he understood the inhospitable northern environment. The Canadians who extracted its natural resources have become dependent upon markets in the United States; trade with the United States accounted for one-fifth of Canadian gross national product (GNP), while only 2 percent of U.S. GNP depended on trade with Canada. But in the twenty-first century, this dependency has become mutual. By the end of the 1990s, Canada had become the largest single source of imported energy to the United States.

The historical development of U.S.-Canadian relations must be understood both in bilateral context and in the context of the evolving international system and the vast expansion of America's role within it. *Ambivalent Allies* thus continues to situate the U.S.-Canadian relationship in the broad framework of American foreign policy more fully than does the traditional historical literature. The American War of Independence, the Haitian revolution, and then the Latin American wars for independence left Canada, along with the British West Indies, Cuba and Puerto Rico, among the few remaining outposts of European colonialism in the Western Hemisphere. Canada's British colonial connection isolated it from the larger concerns of the Americas, especially with the articulation of the Monroe Doctrine in the 1820s and its subsequent modifications over the next two centuries. Britain and the United States were the only real powers in the Western Hemisphere in the nineteenth century, although many others—from Russia and France to Germany and Italy—at times claimed a presence. Bilateral Anglo-American tension made Canada a pawn in great power rivalry.

The rise of the United States and Germany to great power status in the late nineteenth and early twentieth centuries gradually altered the relative importance of Canada in the Anglo-American relationship. Britain, facing both a shift in the balance of power in Europe and problems within its own empire by the 1890s, thus needed a friendly United States on its western flank. Canadian interests could in large measure be sacrificed to those larger geopolitical goals. By the end of World War I, the financial capital of the world had shifted from London to New York, and the United States had become a military power. With Britain in evident decline and its powerful neighbor on the rise, Canada had to strive for an American policy, and in turn the United States had to give at least fleeting thought to its Canadian policy. The result was the emergence in the first thirty years of the twentieth century of a more independent, distinct, and mature Canadian foreign policy and of a truly bilateral U.S.-Canadian relationship.

Had there been any doubt after World War I of the preeminence of U.S. power, there could be none by the end of World War II. With Britain and France sapped by their struggle with the Third Reich, Germany's dismemberment left the United States and the Soviet Union as two self-consciously distinct political systems, glowering at one another over a prostrate Europe. The decline of Britain, the intensity of the cold war, the hegemony of the United States, and the impossibility of nonalignment pushed Canada into an American orbit. If it was important to the United States to ensure that insignificant countries in Central America, East Asia, and the Pacific remained in the capitalist, "free world" camp, it was even more imperative that no significant deviation be tolerated from the United States' closest neighbor. Canada showed little inclination to deviate, however. Allied with the United States in the North Atlantic Treaty Organization (NATO) and the North American Air Defense Agreement (NORAD), Canada became an integral player in the cold war. The slow process that transformed Canada from a European to an American nation is arguably not yet complete. Certainly the trilateral North American Free Trade Agreement has not completed the process. Yet this shift has profoundly altered U.S.-Canadian defense, political, and economic relationships, just as the sheer weight of U.S. cultural presence pressed constantly upon Canadians.

Canada and the United States: Ambivalent Allies emphasizes the years of "America's rise to world power." Between 1903 and World War II, Canada moved toward the establishment of an independent foreign policy; in this period the two countries erected many of the bilateral institutions and mechanisms that governed their relationship in the twentieth century. From their wartime alliance after 1941 through the end of the 1950s, the two countries united in a world war and cold war alliance based on economic interest and shared assumptions about the nature of the world and their responsibilities within it. The years from 1960 until 1984 most merit our subtitle *Ambivalent Allies*, as this binational consensus fragmented, and the two countries moved apart in their approaches to the cold war, defense relations, trade, foreign investment, and cultural policy. Division escalated as Canada sought a global "'Third Option'" by which it could increase its independence from the United States.

In 1984, Brian Mulroney's Conservative Party—the "Tory" Party/"les Tories" in the political slang of both Canada's official languages—fervently proclaimed a renewal of the continental harmony of the 1950s. The ultimate irony in the relationship had occurred: the Tories, named out of the legacy of an American Revolution rejected in 1776, embraced the United States with a never-before-displayed ardor. Nurtured on anti-Americanism, many segments of traditional Canadian society protested; but the Conservatives won reelection in 1988, as the issue of free trade with the United States figured more prominently than any single issue ever has in a Canadian national election. The massive rejection of the Conservative Party in 1993, and its replacement with a Liberal government under Prime Minister Jean Chrétien, in part reflected the Canadian electorate's judgment against Mulroney's attempted new intimacy with the United States.

In spite of its rhetorical commitment to reverse the pro-American policy of its predecessors, the Chrétien government altered little in the bilateral relationship. Perennial bilateral irritants persisted, but nothing that is fundamental in the relationship was transformed at Canadian initiative. Chrétien and his colleagues had loudly proclaimed that they would redraft NAFTA to protect Canadian sovereignty; once in office they came to embrace it. Those Canadians who feared that NAFTA was the stalking horse for a U.S. integrationist agenda were mistaken, however. Increased economic integration has not yet brought about the feared political and social harmonization.

The contested election that installed conservative Republican George W. Bush in the White House in January 2001, and the terrorist attacks on the United States that September, set in motion a process that severely strained the U.S.-Canadian relationship. Canada offered the United States the strongest possible support after the terrorist attacks, but the rapid military escalation of President Bush's "war on terror" alarmed Canadians and their government. Prime Minister Chrétien, reelected with a third consecutive parliamentary majority in the same month that a minority of Americans chose George W. Bush, refused to make Canada a member of the "coalition of the willing" for the U.S.-led invasion of Iraq in March 2003. The fourth edition of *Ambivalent Allies* explores the unprecedented tension that arose between the two countries, as actions of the Bush administration appeared to challenge fundamental values that Canadians imagined they shared with Americans. The election of a minority Conservative government led by Prime Minister Stephen Harper in January 2006 brought to power individuals with a closer ideological affinity to those who dominate the Bush administration, but the U.S.-Canadian relationship has yet to be rebuilt. We conclude this introduction as we concluded that in the third edition: the saga of the ambivalent alliance will have no ending, happy or otherwise. Its history makes clear that the U.S.-Canadian relationship in the future cannot be other than intense, close, usually cooperative, yet conflictual in both its details and its fundamentals.

1   Building North American
Nation-States, 1774–1871

Between 1774 and 1783 the American War of Independence fragmented the North American centerpiece of the first British Empire. From the turmoil two countries eventually emerged: with no little irony, the war that created the United States also created Canada. Twice in one generation, from 1776 to 1781 and again from 1812 to 1815, the American colonies and then the fledgling United States fought the world's most powerful nation-state in two wars that determined the fate of the continent. As Canadian historian A. R. M. Lower wrote melodramatically: "Of greater moment than the boundary settlement was the parting itself. Here surely was the profoundest depth of the Revolution. For the parting had been in bad blood." What transpired in North America during and immediately following American independence led to the creation of the two nation-states that have since shared the northern half of the continent. Was the division a conscious choice, a "revolution rejected" by "Canadians" and those "Americans" who sought refuge in British North America and pledged continued loyalty to the British Crown? Did the split between what became Canada and the United States derive from fundamentally different political orientations or from the pragmatic military realities of the moment?[1]

Breaking Up the First British Empire

When the American colonists turned their muskets against British imperial authority at Lexington and Concord, Britain controlled four colonies to the north that became part of nineteenth-century British North America and eventually modern Canada: Newfoundland, Prince Edward Island (called St. John's Island until 1799), Nova Scotia, and Quebec. As among the thirteen colonies to the south, differences among these colonies were profound. Tiny Prince Edward Island, with a population of perhaps three thousand farmers and fishers, and Newfoundland, with a population of fifteen thousand scattered in fishing villages along its rugged coast, were remote from the ideological and military conflicts of the Revolution. Nova Scotia, which geographically included both modern Nova Scotia and New Brunswick, had an economy based on agriculture, the fishery, shipbuilding, and international trade. In language, religion, and ethnicity, Nova Scotia was more akin to Massachusetts than to Quebec. More than half of its twenty thousand people who circled the Bay of Fundy shore were Yankee migrants, many who had come to appropriate the farms of the French Acadians deported by the British in the 1750s. But Halifax, the colonial capital on the Atlantic coast, was an important harbor for the Royal Navy.

Quebec, the official name for what was usually called "Canada," had been taken from France by force on the Plains of Abraham during the Seven Years' War, 1756–63. Quebec was the most populous of these northern colonies, and the largest geographically after the Quebec Act of 1774 expanded the colony into the interior almost to the boundaries of preconquest New France. Montreal was the entrepôt of the fur trade of this vast western territory, and the garrison town of Quebec was the colony's administrative capital. Four-fifths of Quebec's European-descended population of one hundred thousand were peasant families who farmed under the seigneurial system, the feudal system of landholding left untouched by their British conquerors. Except for the Montreal merchants who controlled the fur trade and the British soldiers and administrators, Quebec was French-speaking, Roman Catholic, and without the elective political institutions in place in every other colony of British America save Newfoundland. Britain had confirmed all of these peculiarities—Roman Catholicism, seigneurialism, non-elective government—in the Quebec Act of 1774. This act enraged those colonials to the south suspicious of imperial designs: its real object, wrote Alexander Hamilton, was "to encircle the Thirteen Colonies in a ring of British steel." Such fears precipitated the aggrieved American colonists toward independence. Historians have demonstrated that their anxiety was unfounded, and that the Quebec Act should not be considered among the "Intolerable Acts"; but the authors of the Declaration of Independence, with the benefits of neither hindsight nor archival access, may be forgiven the conclusion to which they jumped.[2]

The concentration of British military power to the north of the thirteen colonies made Nova Scotia and especially Quebec of substantial strategic importance to the Continental Congress, the fledgling American government. The Revolutionary leadership was profoundly ambiguous about both colonies. In his study of the thirteen colonies' resistance to the Stamp Act in 1765 and 1766, the first concerted colonial resistance to British authority, historian Edmund S. Morgan notes that Nova Scotia and Quebec (along with Florida, Barbados, Grenada, and Jamaica) "consistently made use of the stamps—to the great disgust of the other colonies." Nonetheless, many Nova Scotians had blood ties to New England, and French Canadians had little reason for loyalty to Britain, so that they could be regarded as potential Revolutionary patriots. In 1775, Thomas Jefferson believed that "the delegates of Canada will join us in Congress and complete the American union," and Article XI of the Articles of Confederation provided that on application "Canada shall be admitted into and entitled to all the advantages of the union." Yet both northern colonies threatened American military security as bases for potential British blows against the independence movement. "I hope we shall secure to the United States Canada [and] Nova Scotia by our arms," wrote Samuel Adams in 1778; "we shall never be on a solid footing till Britain cedes to us what Nature designs we should have, or till we wrest it from her." This ambivalence was demonstrated in letters from the Congress that circulated in Canada and Nova Scotia, inviting the "oppressed inhabitants" to share "the Transcendent Nature of Freedom" but threatening severe reprisals if they dared to support British authority. Two American forces under Generals Richard Montgomery and Benedict Arnold invaded Quebec in November and December 1775 in an attempt to deny control of the St. Lawrence River by the British and to eliminate Quebec as a staging ground for a British invasion of the thirteen colonies. Montgomery's soldiers captured Montreal and joined Arnold and his men in a siege of the fortified town of Quebec. The siege failed in large part because smallpox ravaged the American army and left it unable to resist a Royal Navy fleet with British reinforcements; in the words of historian Elizabeth Fenn, "a tiny virus had proved far more ferocious than the British troops these men had come to fight." The British counterstroke was equally ineffective, however: General Burgoyne's defeat in 1777 at Saratoga brought France into the war as a formal ally of the American colonists. Britain had the naval capacity to contain the rebellion within the thirteen colonies, but not to defeat it.[3]

Internal Canadian considerations also militated against any general uprising in Quebec in support of Montgomery and Arnold, although American officers reported that the local populations were (wisely) friendly. The Quebec Act was not universally popular among the English merchants of Montreal, who received a delegation from the Boston Committee of Correspondence in 1775; one of them, James Price, traveled to Philadelphia as an unofficial representative to the Continental Congress. The minority of English merchants who supported the Revolution, however, did so because of personal ties to the thirteen colonies; those who were involved in the fur trade were commercially connected to Britain and would have lost their livelihood if Americans came to control the fur trade in the Ohio and Mississippi river valleys. The Quebec Act promised political and economic stability to the French-Canadian elite of landholders, the legal profession, and the Roman Catholic Church, making them the most enthusiastic supporters of British authority. They appealed to their tenants and parishioners to oppose the Americans. Nonetheless, when Montgomery's army arrived at Montreal in 1775, French Canadians would not fight in support of British governor Guy Carleton, forcing him to flee upriver to Quebec. The *habitants* may have been hostile to the Quebec Act, which restored their ecclesiastical tithes and seigneurial economic obligations. Hostile to the Quebec Act or not, most of the local population showed no inclination to fight for either side. French-Canadian peasant grievances fit poorly with political models and ideals imported from revolutionary America, and the invading American soldiers were poor emissaries of colonial solidarity against the British. Although George Washington's circular to the people of Quebec assured them that the American army came "not to plunder, but to protect you," one American general dismissed the French-Canadian peasants as "but little removed from savages." Such attitudes, another general admitted, led to "scandalous excesses" by the American volunteers, so that "few of the inhabitants escaped abuse" at their hands. Thus although Quebec remained loyal to the Crown, it cannot be classified in any real sense as Loyalist or "Tory," to the extent that areas of anti-Revolution sentiment existed in New York, Georgia, and the Carolinas, where individuals made conscientious decisions to oppose the Revolution. As French-Canadian nationalist Henri Bourassa put it a century later, French Canadians had to choose between two evils—the British or their English colonists to the south—and the English in London seemed further away and less imminently threatening. Thus, though there were loyalists and rebels scattered throughout Quebec, self-interest dictated caution and neutrality.[4]

Neutrality is perhaps also the best word to describe Nova Scotia's response to the American Revolution. There was no doubt discontent against British authority, but there was no revolt, apart from some pro-Patriot feeling in western Nova Scotia revealed by a comic-opera Patriot invasion from northern Maine. Several communities of transplanted Yankees around the Bay of Fundy and in the South Shore fishing villages petitioned the governor not to require them to bear arms against their New England neighbors and relatives. But despite this demographic connection to Massachusetts, historian Elizabeth Mancke has argued persuasively that Nova Scotia "lay outside" the "constitutional and ideological formulation" of the thirteen colonies. Mancke points out that Nova Scotia (like Quebec and Prince Edward Island) joined the British Empire as a new "conquered colony" in the eighteenth century and as a result "had been under tighter metropolitan control" than the older colonies "chartered and settled in the seventeenth century." Nova Scotia's elective assembly had been established only in 1758, and because British policy explicitly proscribed municipal governments in new colonies, Nova Scotia could not develop the "vibrant tradition of town government" reflected in the assemblies of the American colonies. The reformist inclinations of ordinary Nova Scotians burned more brightly in the Great Awakening, a religious revival that swept the colony during the 1770s and 1780s, than they did in revolt against British imperial authority. British sea power made any serious Patriot attack unlikely to succeed if it had been undertaken, and marauding American privateers who made hit-and-run raids on Nova Scotia undermined whatever revolutionary sympathies their victims might have held before they were robbed at pistol point. For the Halifax merchant elite that provisioned the Royal Navy and that was linked to London with ties of credit, the balance sheet decreed loyalism. Colonial institutional divergence, economic interest, and British sea power determined the fate of Nova Scotia.[5]

Thus, as General Cornwallis surrendered his British army at Yorktown to combined French and American troops in 1781, the colonies that would become Canada were firmly under British control. The envoys that the Continental Congress sent to France to negotiate peace—John Jay, John Adams, and Benjamin Franklin—were instructed to request Canada as reparations for war damage caused by British military operations. Despite their best diplomatic efforts, however, Canada remained British when the Treaty of Paris was concluded in 1783. The fate of Quebec and Nova Scotia had been perhaps determined less by ideology and political preference than by geography and the realities of the balance of military power between Great Britain and the thirteen American colonies. But for whatever reasons, the American War of Independence had not spread and could not be carried into the northern colonies, and that failure eventually gave birth to Canada and permanently shaped the subsequent U.S.-Canadian relationship.

From War of Independence to the War of 1812

The Treaty of Paris in 1783 resolved the issue of independence for the thirteen colonies: the treaty declares that "His Britanic [sic] Majesty acknowledges the said United States . . . to be free, sovereign, and independent states." British negotiators eagerly sought a rapprochement with the new nation-state, however, and the treaty accordingly made concessions beyond those that the military situation would have dictated. Thus for the British colonies to the north, American independence brought substantial territorial loss: the U.S.-Canadian boundary was set at the forty-fifth parallel, cutting off the vast interior hinterland that had been reconnected to Quebec in 1774. The St. Croix River was fixed as the U.S.–Nova Scotia boundary, but cartographical error left disagreement about precisely which river was, in fact, the St. Croix; the result was several generations of border disputes. Equally serious for the Atlantic colonies was the loss of the anticipated exclusive access to the fisheries off their coasts. Samuel Adams loudly insisted that "God Almighty . . . gave the people of America a right" to them, and threatened to "enkindle a new war" over Newfoundland and Nova Scotia to obtain them for the new United States. Britain thus conceded the New Englanders the "liberty" of continued access, but the issue remained as a contentious legacy of the treaty.[6]

The most momentous heritage for the northern colonies from American independence was political and ideological: it launched them on a divergent political path that led to the evolution of the modern Canadian nation-state and provided Canada with its founding myth. An estimated half-million of the 2.5 million residents of the thirteen colonies remained loyal to Britain during the War of Independence. This estimate is surely low. An overwhelming majority of the half-million African-American slaves in the colonies, who were promised freedom by the British in return for their allegiance, hoped, worked, and often fought for British victory. Sixty to one hundred thousand of these Loyalists, black and white, committed, in Roger Daniels's words, "the most profoundly un-American act that one can imagine": they left America. Forty thousand of these émigré Loyalists—"Tories" in the American narrative—went north, thirty-five thousand of them to Nova Scotia and the remainder to Quebec, where they settled in the Gaspé Peninsula to the east and along the north shore of Lake Ontario. Who were these anti-Americans, and why did they come? The plethora of Loyalist studies defies easy summarization, but historian Neil MacKinnon's conclusion about those who came to Nova Scotia will serve as a generalization: "the motives of these immigrants . . . ranged all the way from pathetic necessity to naked opportunism [and] their origins were as mixed as their motives." The Loyalists came from every one of the thirteen colonies, although New York predominated, and were "not simply an upper-class fragment [but] cross-sections of the American social pyramid." A disproportionate number were members of religious or ethnic minorities. More than three thousand were African-American freedmen and former slaves. One thousand were Native Americans who had fought as British allies. One thing united them, a bond that they shared with the French Canadians. "Almost all the loyalists," writes historian W. H. Nelson, were "in one way or another, more afraid of America than they were of Britain."[7]

These Loyalists exercised a remarkable influence on British North America. Their arrival forced Britain to create two new colonies. In 1784 the western shore of the Bay of Fundy was detached from Nova Scotia to become New Brunswick, and in 1791 Britain divided the old province of Quebec into Lower and Upper Canada, which later became Canada East and Canada West, and ultimately Quebec and Ontario. With Loyalists as their founding parents, Upper Canada and New Brunswick became bastions of a British North American identity built on the precepts of Loyalism: strong support for the Crown and British institutions, and a rejection of American republicanism. For many Loyalists, the United States was "Satan's Kingdom," a "land of banditti" doomed to be destroyed by the "Tyrannic power of a republican Government." The Loyalist goal—at least that of the Loyalist elite—was to build a superior society in the provinces to which they had fled, a society in which, said New York–born Upper Canadian Richard Cartwright, "under the epitome of the English constitution, we enjoy the greatest practical political freedom." As an important link within a worldwide empire, British North America would be, in the words of Massachusetts-born New Brunswicker Edward Winslow, "the envy of the American states."[8]

This sense of mission and the extravagant anti-Americanisms replete in Loyalist writings were the products of an elite; several thousand ordinary Loyalists abandoned Nova Scotia to return to the United

States in the 1790s. The Loyalist myth built up around them in Canada in the nineteenth century (like all national myths, America's included) is only tangentially linked to the historical reality of the eighteenth century. Sociologist Seymour Martin Lipset exaggerates when he ascribes the differences between Canada and the United States to the Continental Divide of "Revolution and Counterrevolution." But the Loyalist myth, though never uncontested or static, did become sufficiently hegemonic to form the base of the "extremely constricting ideology" (to use historian S. F. Wise's words) from within which British North Americans would view the United States.[9]

There was, however, an inescapable ambivalence in this evolving colonial ideology: as much as British North Americans criticized America, they were simultaneously obsessed with it. The United States became the standard against which they measured not only the moral purity of their own society but also its material progress. Until 1812 the border was wide open to commerce, and transborder travel was heavy enough that one Burlington, Vermont, tavern keeper painted George Washington's portrait on the south side of his sign and Admiral Horatio Nelson's likeness on the north. British North America imported agricultural and transportation techniques from the United States. The Canadas also imported people: between 1791 and 1812, fifteen thousand New Englanders moved north to the Eastern Townships of Lower Canada, and fifty thousand New Yorkers and Pennsylvanians settled the lands of Upper Canada, granted almost free by the British Crown. Historians George Rawlyk and Jane Errington have pointed out that even the Loyalist elite's anti-American critique was copied directly from the writings of American Federalists, who were similarly alarmed with what they saw as the democratic excesses of the Jeffersonian Republicans. British North Americans drank to George III's health on 4 June, the king's birthday, instead of to American independence a month later, but if the colonials were developing a society that was spiritually British, they were also building one that was materially American, or at least North American.[10]

Day-to-day interaction among peoples ran more smoothly than the relationship between the British and U.S. governments; between 1783 and 1812, Anglo-American tensions made the future of British North America uncertain. For the new United States the post-Revolutionary period was one of economic growth, political experimentation, and uncertainty and weakness in international affairs. Hemmed in on the seaboard, with Britain, Spain, and France still colonial powers in the hemisphere, a sense of vulnerability and isolation shaped U.S. foreign policy in this generation and influenced the course of Anglo-American relations and, by default, those with British North America. U.S. leaders were compelled to come to terms with the continued dominance of Britain to the north and on the seas. It seemed, as historian H. G. Nicholas has put it, that the treaty of 1783 "had bought peace largely by imprecision and omission" and left "not a clean break, but a line of ragged connections" between Britain and the United States. The border of New England and Nova Scotia remained in dispute, as did U.S. commercial rights in the British West Indies. During the wars of the French Revolution and the Napoleonic Wars chronic friction developed over neutrality of the seas and the impressment of American merchant seamen into the British navy. A critical issue that directly affected Canada was the continued presence of British troops in forts in the Ohio Valley a decade after the Treaty of Paris had required them to withdraw. This allowed Montreal merchants to steal the profits of the fur trade and enabled the British to supply their Indian allies in the area to resist American settlers. In 1794 the Washington administration dispatched John Jay to London to resolve this question as well as the tensions over British seizures of U.S. ships and men on the high seas. Jay won no concessions on British maritime policy but made a breakthrough on the question of the western forts. In Jay's Treaty the British confirmed their abandonment of their Indian allies that began in the peace treaty of 1783, an abandonment made evident when British troops refused to assist the Indian Confederacy when it was defeated by U.S. forces led by General Anthony Wayne at the Battle of Fallen Timbers in August 1794. Ratified in 1795, Jay's Treaty provided for British withdrawal from the Ohio Valley and made legal the extensive intercourse already going on across the forty-fifth parallel. The claim of some historians that Jay's Treaty established the tradition of "exceptionalism" in U.S.-Canadian relations is exaggerated, but the treaty did assure, as Alexander Hamilton put it, "good neighborhood between the United States and the bordering British Territories." It created what historian Bradford Perkins refers to as "the first rapprochement" between Britain and the United States, and although it left the most irritating Anglo-American disputes unresolved, it delayed for two decades their explosion into war between Britain and the United States—a war with Canada as the scene of battle and the potential prize.[11]

The War of 1812

Historians continue to debate the causes of the War of 1812. The most recent interpretations describe the war as "the Second War of Independence" and "the War that forged a nation" and emphasize the desire of the young republic to vindicate the American Revolution, to strengthen republican institutions, and to enhance the political fortunes of the Republican Party of Jefferson, James Madison, and James Monroe. However the origins of the war are explained, taking Canada is dismissed as (in historian Reginald Horsman's words) "a useful side benefit of a war that had become necessary largely because of British maritime policy." British seizure of U.S. ships engaged in trade with French-controlled Europe and the continued searching of U.S. ships for deserters from the British navy, symbolized by HMS *Leopard*'s attack on USS *Chesapeake* in 1807, undoubtedly damaged both America's economy and its national pride. President Jefferson's controversial and narrowly approved embargo act of that year, and the Non-intercourse Act that replaced it in 1809, dramatically reduced U.S. trade (and correspondingly increased domestic manufacturing), with serious dislocation for those U.S. merchants who exported agricultural products to European markets. But neither act could solve the maritime problems so long as Britain feared Napoleonic France infinitely more than American enmity. To John C. Calhoun in 1812, Britain left Americans "an alternative only between the base surrender of their rights, and a manly vindication of them [by] an immediate appeal to arms."[12]

American Migration
to Canada
1783-1918

African-American Freedom-Seekers 1814 2,000

United Empire Loyalists 1783 30,000

Post-Loyalist Migration 1791–1812

7,500

15,000

50,000

40,000

African-American Freedom-Seekers 1840–1860

Agricultural Migration 1896–1914 162,000

8,000

1,800 Hutterites 1917–1918

67,000

70,000

17,000

Mormons 1887 (2,000) and a continuing migration to 1905

Atlantic Ocean

500 km
300 mi
250
150
0

NOVA SCOTIA

NEW BRUNSWICK

MAINE

N.H.

VERMONT

QUEBEC

Montreal

Ottawa

N.Y.

MASS.

CONN.

R.I.

N.J.

PENNSYLVANIA

DEL.

MD.

WEST VIRGINIA

VIRGINIA

NORTH CAROLINA

SOUTH CAROLINA

Toronto

Detroit

MICHIGAN

OHIO

KENTUCKY

TENNESSEE

INDIANA

ILLINOIS

Chicago

WISCONSIN

IOWA

MISSOURI

KANSAS

COLORADO

UTAH

NEBRASKA

SOUTH DAKOTA

WYOMING

MONTANA

IDAHO

NEVADA

CALIFORNIA

San Francisco

OREGON

WASHINGTON

Seattle

Vancouver

Victoria

BRITISH COLUMBIA

YUKON TERRITORY

NORTHWEST TERRITORIES

ALBERTA

SASKATCHEWAN

N.D.

MINNESOTA

MANITOBA

ONTARIO

Hudson BAY

Pacific Ocean

wm

The "land hunger" explanation of the War of 1812—the thesis that maritime rights were simply "righteous pretexts" for Americans such as Calhoun who coveted Canada's "rich bottom land"—has been largely dismissed by historians, if not by subsequent generations of Canadian schoolteachers. But difficulties on the western frontier did contribute to the escalation of British-American conflict and had implications important for understanding subsequent U.S.-Canadian relations. Western Americans continued to claim, inaccurately, that only British support allowed Tecumseh and Tenskwatawa ("The Prophet"), leaders of the Algonquian Confederacy, to continue to resist U.S. traders and settlers who sought their lands. Although the Indians bought their weapons from British merchants, they were, in the words of historian Richard White, "independent political agents" who needed no British incitement to continue their century-long war against American expansion. But this perception fueled demands from such westerners as Henry Clay of Kentucky that Canada be invaded, as did the deaths of two hundred Americans killed when General William H. Harrison won a fiercely fought battle with the Indian Confederacy at Tippecanoe Creek in November 1811. Hezekiah Niles's *National Intelligencer*, founded that same year, demonstrated the increase in U.S. interest in British North American affairs that marked the eve of war. Niles shared with many of his countrymen the belief that Upper Canada could and should be captured, but that this should be done not for territorial expansion but to expel the British, who manipulated the Indians and imposed authoritarian European values and institutions upon British North America. Niles agreed with Michigan territorial governor William Hull that conquest would bring "civil, political and religious liberty" to the Canadians. As they had been forty years earlier, however, Americans were ambivalent about the colonies and the colonials to their north. John Randolph of Virginia and John Stanley of North Carolina dismissed Canadian lands as of little use, the climate as inhospitable, and the people as unenlightened. Niles's newspaper reflected this ambivalence: it would be easier to "manufacture the Devil into a christian," he editorialized, than "to make a republican of a Canadian Frenchman or an imported Scotchman."[13]

In June 1812, President Madison asked Congress for a declaration of war against Great Britain. The president emphasized maritime issues, relegating British incitement of the "savages" to an afterthought, but the congressional votes that carried the war declaration came from the West and the South, with a reluctant commercial New England—the region to which maritime issues should have been most important—pulled along in the wake of nationalist pro-war sentiment. For the "war hawks" of the West and the South, an attack on Canada seemed not only a logical way to defeat the Indian confederacies and open the way for westward expansion, but also the only strategic means by which the United States could counter British naval supremacy. Canada was to be seized as a hostage rather than captured as a prize of war.[14]

The large numbers of American-born in the Canadas made American leaders confident of easy victory. Thomas Jefferson, in a prediction often quoted derisively by Canadian historians, thought that victory would be "a mere matter of marching." As from 1775 to 1776, however, most Canadians showed little interest in the unique brand of liberty offered to them by their potential conquerors. Instead, they identified the Americans with Napoleonic France, "the greatest tyranny that ever oppressed the world," as an Upper Canadian newspaper put it. At every invasion point U.S. forces met firm resistance from British regulars, from Britain's Indian allies, and, eventually, from the Canadian militia. The Canadian militia's resistance toughened as the war went on because the invading U.S. Army did not behave like liberators: after their first advance into Upper Canada was repelled, General George McClure's New York militia put the Niagara peninsula village of Newark to the torch, turning residents out into a subzero December night. But although every American invasion of Canada faltered, the United States did not "lose" the War of 1812. U.S. captains embarrassed the Royal Navy on the high seas, on the Great Lakes, and on Lake Champlain, thwarting British counter-invasions, and U.S. troops repelled British amphibious assaults on coastal cities. In this sense, the War of 1812 was a decisive dead heat that confirmed the post-Revolutionary military stalemate.[15]

As the end of the Napoleonic Wars in Europe threatened British escalation of the war in North America, President Madison welcomed negotiations to resolve the conflict. Britain's initial hard line—demands for American recognition of a distinct Indian buffer state, boundary adjustments south of the Great Lakes, and nullification of U.S. fishing rights in British North American waters—softened with military reverses at Plattsburgh and Baltimore. The price for continued war weighed too high against the prospective gain, so that as 1814 drew to a close Britain consented to the Treaty of Ghent, ending the war without territorial gain for either combatant. The War of 1812's real losers were the Native peoples who had fought as Britain's allies; it was a cruel outcome for them, given their critical contribution to turning back the American invasions of Canada. Instead of a state of their own, they were left to choose between the charity of the British Crown and an American Indian policy made increasingly brutal by memories of the war.[16]

The Treaty of Ghent and the Rush-Bagot agreement of 1817 together set the terms for Anglo-American, and thus U.S.-British North American, relations for the next generation. As on other occasions when Britain negotiated with the United States, British North American interests were secondary to imperial considerations. The treaty established boundary commissions to settle territorial disputes, particularly over lands occupied by British forces during the war, but it was ominously silent on the main issues Madison had identified as the causes of war: neutrality on the seas and impressment of U.S. seamen. The subsequent Rush-Bagot agreement saved both the United States and Britain from a potentially costly arms race to protect their respective borders. The naval limitation provisions applied only to the Great Lakes and limited the number of armed vessels on Lake Champlain and Lake Ontario to one each and to two on each of the other Great Lakes. There were no limits on land fortification, on the other hand, and both Britain and the United States built extensively. True to the spirit of the Treaty of Ghent, the two parties also concluded a convention in 1818 in which they agreed to a boundary between U.S. and British territory that ran from Lake of the Woods to the Rocky Mountains along the forty-ninth parallel, leaving the sensitive Pacific boundary unresolved. In the interim, the Oregon territory was considered open to both American citizens and British subjects. By the same agreement, U.S. fishers gained the "liberty" to use the fisheries off the Newfoundland and Labrador coasts, a "right" the U.S. fishers felt that they already possessed, with the result that this too would return to trouble later generations.[17]

The battles and diplomacy of the War of 1812 quickly became less relevant than the new social realities they bequeathed. By neutralizing the military power of the Native peoples and ending liberal British land policies for immigrants from the United States, the War of 1812 deflected American migration away from Upper Canada and westward to Ohio and Michigan. The War of 1812's most substantial legacy was its imprint on the public historical memory of the United States and Canada. It retaught the lessons of the War of Independence and further inculcated separate national identities into the minds of ordinary folk on each side of the border. Nationalist mythmakers rewrote weary survival into glamorous victory. For Canadians, the War of 1812 eventually became chapter 2 in their rejection of American republicanism, a chapter with a happier ending and with gallant heroes who were winners, not losers: Sir Isaac Brock, dead defender of Queenston Heights, the Canadian militiamen, and Laura Secord, who crept through the American lines to warn of the Yankee attack at Beaver Dams. (The history primers never mentioned that British regulars and Indian allies won most of the battles, or that Laura Secord was Massachusetts-born, the daughter of a major in the Massachusetts militia!) In the United States, every schoolchild memorized Oliver Hazard Perry's laconic summation of his victory on Lake Erie: "We have met the enemy and they are ours." Andrew Jackson—a *Symbol for an Age*, historian John William Ward has called him—won his national fame with his "brilliant and unparalleled victory at New Orleans [which] has closed the war with a blaze of Glory [and] placed America on the very pinnacle of fame." It is entirely appropriate that the War of 1812 provided both the setting for "The Star-Spangled Banner" and the inspiration for "We stand on guard for thee" in the English-language chorus of "O Canada."[18]

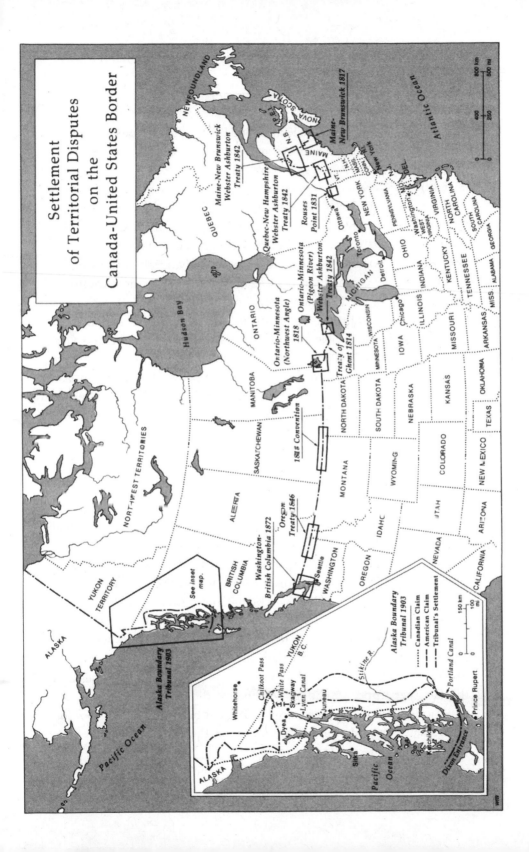

Settlement
of Territorial Disputes
on the
Canada-United States Border

Manifest Destiny and Imperial Rivalry

In the decades between 1820 and 1860 British North America and the United States continued to move away from their earlier common colonial heritage, but they did so at very different rhythms. For the United States the 1820s brought the first stirring of sectionalism over the westward expansion of slavery, which Thomas Jefferson worried was a "fire bell in the night." Political power shifted from the Massachusetts-Virginia establishment that had dominated the first half-century of the young nation to new leaders from the expanding regions of the country, men such as Andrew Jackson, symbol of the more-mythical-than-real age of the common man. Stimulated first by Jefferson's embargo and then by protective tariffs, the first factories rose against the pastoral landscape of New England. Irish Roman Catholic and German immigrants crowded the nation's cities, providing a labor force for an American industrial revolution. Culturally, although European intellectual currents swept through the East, American intellectuals attempted to demonstrate that the United States was not English; James Fenimore Cooper's novels, for example, "struck a responsive chord in American readers." One modern survey of U.S. history entitles the period "the Creation of the American National Character," and another as the making of "An American Culture." Agitation for change on a broad range of issues confronted established traditions and institutions: religious revivalism, temperance, women's rights, abolitionism—all had their spokespersons.[19]

The United States and British North America were so close geographically and so similar ethnically (save for the French Canadians of Lower Canada and New Brunswick) that many American ideas spilled north. The stirrings of *Democracy in America* that fascinated Alexis de Tocqueville during his stay in the United States in the 1830s seemed to be reflected in rebellions in Upper and Lower Canada. Religious revival found a Canadian analog, not surprising given kinship ties and the fact that Upper Canadian Methodists did not separate from the American Methodist Church until 1828. On both sides of the border, Protestant men and women railed against the evil of liquor; in 1836,

British North American temperance societies began to affiliate with the American Temperance Union. The movement for common schools and curriculum reform in British North America paralleled similar developments to the south. The Anti-Slavery Society of Canada cooperated actively with American abolitionists.[20]

Similarities there were; but it is critical not to confuse these affinities with fundamental agreement. The antislavery movement in Canada owed at least as much to British as to U.S. influence. In the area of educational reform Upper Canadian Methodist school promoter Egerton Ryerson shared the U.S. goal of an educated citizenry but denounced textbooks published in the United States as "anti-British" and pronounced that the purpose of the common school was to make "this country British in domestic feeling." British North America at midcentury was emphatically that—British. Between 1820 and 1860, the colonies welcomed almost one million immigrants from the British Isles; in the first Canadian census of 1851, the British-born made up more than 20 percent of the population and outnumbered the American-born seven to one. In Upper Canada in particular, where they were overrepresented among the colony's political leaders, there was a conscious emulation of British traditions. After Britain allowed the colonies to assume virtual autonomy in local affairs in the 1840s, French-Canadian elites came to admire their British system of government almost as fervently. "We will never forget our allegiance," vowed E. P. Taché, "till the last cannon which is shot on this continent in defence of Great Britain is fired by the hand of a French Canadian." For those who rejected this Loyalist consensus, British North America had a safety valve: they could simply walk across the open border to the United States. Beginning in the 1840s, substantial numbers of British North Americans did exactly that—250,000 in total by 1860—but their motivation seems more to have been economic betterment rather than political discontent.[21]

British North America confronted the same agonies and pleasures in the nineteenth-century transition to industrial capitalist society, but it did so at a slower pace and within the bosom of the British Empire. Trade across the border was brisk, especially after the completion in 1825 of the Erie Canal linking Albany on the Hudson River with Buffalo on Lake Erie. But Canadian merchants pressed for the completion of the Welland Canal to bypass Niagara Falls between Lakes Ontario and Erie, strengthening the Great Lakes–St. Lawrence route and firming the ties between Upper and Lower Canada that historian Donald Creighton has labeled "The Commercial Empire of the St. Lawrence." As part of a competing world system, British North America shared its mother country's clash with the United States over economic opportunity, trade, resources, and territory. For U.S. foreign policy, the period was marked by the pretense to hemispheric domination expressed in Monroe's statement of 1823, later enshrined as the Monroe Doctrine, and by the burst of youthful nationalist chauvinism embodied in John L. O'Sullivan's concept of "Manifest Destiny." The defensive expansionism of America's first half-century gave way to what historian William Goetzmann aptly calls the years "when the eagle screamed,". as the United States consolidated its borders to the north, west, and south against potential competing empires and began to people the continent between Mexico and British North America.[22]

In an era in which the United States took half of Mexico in a short but bloody war, and U.S. privateers filibustered in Central America and the Caribbean, Anglo-American disputes over boundaries, over border violations after the rebellions of 1837, over fugitive slaves seeking sanctuary, and over control of western territories and resources were without exception resolved without further war. Such settlements reflected caution on the part of both parties after the costly stalemate of 1812–14, growing political and international maturity in the United States, and the skill of individual diplomats. But war remained a very real possibility: the eventual peaceful resolution of these conflicts should not mask their intensity. Nor should peaceful resolution be interpreted as preordained or cited (as some historians and many politicians have subsequently cited it) as evidence of a "special relationship" between Canada and the United States from 1818 to the present day. British North America was the pawn—and the hostage—in Anglo-American disputes.[23]

Heated tensions surrounded the 1837 rebellions in Upper and Lower Canada, for example. The rebellions were the product of maturing societies with groups that neither shared the values nor accepted the dominance of the established order; to that extent they mirrored what took place in electoral politics in Jacksonian America. In the Upper Canadian case, radical reformers identified with William Lyon Mackenzie, who advocated political democratization along lines that they believed emulated the United States. For Mackenzie, the American influence was very direct. He had met President Jackson in 1829, had subsequently described him as the best of "these modern Romans," and had been impressed by what he saw in U.S. politics. Yet his pro-American position evolved slowly and remained ambivalent. Like virtually all British North Americans, he was appalled by slavery, the basic contradiction between the rhetoric of liberty and the reality of American life. U.S. politicians, he wrote in 1827, "mock the ear with the language of freedom in a capital polluted with Negro slavery." Yet he admired the U.S. representative system of government, the use of nominating conventions to choose candidates for office, the election of higher officials and (he imagined incorrectly) the Senate. He attributed America's economic progress and entrepreneurial spirit to republican institutions and pressed those virtues on his countrymen. Mackenzie's ignorance about the technique of selecting U.S. senators is less significant than his ideological isolation. The majority among Upper Canadian reformers were moderates committed to the imperial connection, who sought to emulate British, not U.S., electoral and economic reformers.[21]

In Lower Canada ethnic divisions exacerbated the conflict, as a French-Canadian majority in the elected legislature contested an English-Canadian oligarchy based in an appointed executive grouped around the British governor. French-Canadian *patriotes* echoed arguments heard in Virginia and Massachusetts a half-century earlier and marched as *les fils de la liberté*—the sons of liberty. Their principal spokesman, Louis-Joseph Papineau, Speaker of the Assembly, evolved from an anti-American to an advocate of annexation to the United States, praising republican institutions rather than English radicalism as "our model and our study." Closer examination of Papineau's political program, however, reveals his profound misconceptions about what statehood would portend for French Canadians. His assumption that the French language, laws, and institutions of Lower Canada would be forever protected by the principle of state's rights is remarkably naive. Alexis de Tocqueville understood the United States better: "if the [French] Canadians united with the United States," he wrote, "their population will be soon absorbed." John L. O'Sullivan's *Democratic Review* urged support for "the cause of the Canadian rebellion," an Albany newspaper headlined "Hurra for Papineau and Freedom," and a half-dozen Vermont towns voted small sums for the Canadian patriots. With U.S. support the rebels might have succeeded, but no U.S. intervention was ever contemplated, and the rebels were crushed; "the American government's determination to preserve peace with Great Britain," concludes historian Allan Greer, "sealed the fate of revolution in Canada."[25]

What involved the United States was not the exportation of American ideals but the flight of the defeated rebels—Mackenzie and Papineau among them—to the United States. Mackenzie established a provisional rebel government on American soil, and his followers, reinforced by a handful of American sympathizers, made minor incursions into Canada that provoked Anglo-Canadian retaliation. In December 1837, the Upper Canadian militia crossed the border at Navy Island in the Niagara River and burned an American ship, the *Caroline*, which was being used to provision the rebels. One American was killed in the fighting, but it might well have been one hundred given the vociferous reaction that swept northern U.S. border cities and communities. Sir George Arthur, lieutenant governor of Upper Canada, feared war was imminent; President Martin Van Buren and his cabinet wanted peace, Arthur believed, "but how are they to help if the People will it?" Van Buren acted quickly: General Winfield Scott went to New York to prevent reckless military ventures against Canada that would have provoked a full-scale Anglo-American war—the rebels' goal. Mackenzie and others were taken into custody, and the crisis was deferred until November 1840, when a Canadian named Alexander McLeod was arrested in Lewiston, New York, as the self-proclaimed killer of the single American casualty of the destruction of the *Caroline*. British foreign secretary Lord Palmerston warned the U.S. minister in

London that "McLeod's execution would produce war . . . frightful in its character," and both sides prepared for its outbreak. Fortunately for the United States, Britain, the Canadas, and especially McLeod, the jury believed his plea that his exploit at Navy Island had been nothing more than a drunken boast. McLeod escaped the gallows, and Americans and Anglo-Canadians avoided looking at each another through gunsights yet again.[26]

Conflict between Maine and New Brunswick lumbermen over access to timber exacerbated the tensions built by the McLeod trial. The so-called Aroostook War illustrated a unique problem of Anglo-American diplomacy created by American federalism: the governor of Maine sent the state militia to the long-disputed border to rattle its sabers in support of Maine timber barons. As in New York, Winfield Scott intervened to hold the state government in check until diplomats set the machinery in motion to reach a settlement. By 1842 Secretary of State Daniel Webster and the British minister to Washington, Lord Ashburton, had come to terms on a Maine–New Brunswick boundary. Their success illustrates the sometimes determinant role of individuals in international relations. Webster was a strong Anglophile, highly regarded in England; Ashburton was married to an American and was connected to Baring Brothers Bank, which had loaned millions of pounds in the United States. The Webster-Ashburton Treaty was a sound compromise. It drew the boundary far enough south to enable the British to construct a military road linking Quebec to New Brunswick and divided the disputed forests almost equally, much to the chagrin of Maine. The agreement also explicitly defined the boundary from Lake Superior to the Lake of the Woods, and a separate exchange of notes made verbal amends for the *Caroline* affair.[27]

No such graceful compromise characterized the resolution of the Oregon question. In the 1840s five thousand American settlers followed the missionaries and fur traders into the area to challenge the Hudson's Bay Company, Britain's instrument of indirect rule. Whig secretary of state John C. Calhoun offered in 1844 to simply extend the forty-ninth parallel to the coast to divide the region, but Democratic presidential candidate James K. Polk vowed to take all of the territory to fifty-four degrees, forty minutes—effectively cutting British North America off from the Pacific. Given the tenuous U.S. presence in and claim to the area, Polk's "Fifty-four, Forty or Fight" was campaign rhetoric, but once victorious, it became his campaign promise. Polk's secretary of state, James Buchanan, more realistically renewed the forty-ninth parallel proposal, but this time Richard Pakenham, British minister to Washington, rejected the compromise. Polk escalated the dispute into the Oregon Crisis by reiterating the Monroe Doctrine's assertion that the United States would not tolerate "any European interference on the North American continent," a claim so absurd given the British colonial presence in North America that it raised doubts about Polk's capacity for higher office. Publicly the president refused British offers to discuss the boundary, but a U.S. war with Mexico loomed, and British foreign minister Lord Aberdeen was deadly serious in mobilizing a British fleet and land forces in Canada for war. The Democratic administration eventually saw the wisdom of negotiation, the Senate concurred, and in 1846 the boundary was set at the forty-ninth parallel to the Strait of Juan de Fuca, precisely where it could have been before Polk's irresponsible bellicosity.[28]

If there was interest in the United States in acquiring Britain's North American possessions peaceably, there was none at all in taking them by force, and Great Britain had demonstrated that force would be necessary. But if Britain stood firm against wholesale concessions of territory to the United States, the 1840s nonetheless brought important changes to imperial economic policies: Parliament dismantled the mercantilist tariff preferences that had created protected British markets for colonial grain and timber. Outraged merchants in Montreal sought economic salvation in the United States. In October 1849, the Annexation Manifesto called for "Friendly and peaceable separation from British connexion, and a union upon equitable terms with the great North American confederacy of sovereign States." Given that the Montreal business community had been politically Tory and traditionally inclined to see the United States as an "insatiable democracy" guilty of "dreadful crimes," some Americans misinterpreted the manifesto as sincere rejection of monarchy and an embrace of U.S. republicanism. The *New York Tribune* rushed a special correspondent north to report on the impending annexation. But by 1850, support for annexationism had become ephemeral on both sides of the border. Some in the northern free states believed that the acquisition of Canada would shift the political balance in their favor on the issue of the extension of slavery, but as William Lloyd Garrison reminded abolitionists, Canada would never wish to be annexed to the United States "while a slave remains on our soil." Slavery was only one star in the constellation of ideological reasons for which the majority of British North Americans rejected annexation to the United States. Without strong support in New Brunswick, Nova Scotia, or Canada West, the Annexation Manifesto drew a dozen angry denunciations for every expression of support. The initiative it began died of natural causes four years before it was rendered irrelevant by the reciprocity treaty.[29]

In 1854, the U.S. Congress and the colonial legislatures of British North America endorsed a ten-year reciprocity agreement negotiated in Washington between Canadian governor general Lord Elgin and U.S. secretary of state William Marcy. The accord provided for free movement of products of "land, mine and sea": grain, coal, livestock, timber, and fish. American fishers were formally allowed unrestricted access to coastal fisheries north of the thirty-sixth parallel—legal recognition of the de facto practices of the New England fleet—and shippers were granted mutual access to U.S.-controlled Lake Michigan and the Canadian-controlled St. Lawrence canals. Although greeted with mixed feeling in the Maritime colonies because of the fishery concessions, the accord was eagerly welcomed by the Canadas as evidence that the threat of American aggression had diminished. In the United States, southern senators rationalized support for reciprocity as insurance against annexation, a guarantee that British North Americans "will not undertake to join the North to disturb the political balance," was how one senator put it. North-south trade had always been significant, and the treaty accelerated it (although econometric historians debate the precise dimensions of its contribution). American capital and expertise moved north in what historian Arthur Lower calls a "North American assault on the Canadian forest" to cut the lumber to construct the U.S. Middle West. The interconnections of commerce were symbolized by the engineering marvel of the age, the great international railway suspension bridge that spanned the Niagara River. For the moment, economic reciprocity reflected public will on both sides of the border and the growing Anglo-American accord in the Western Hemisphere in the 1850s. In less than a decade, however, the same sectional strains that had expedited the Senate's passage of reciprocity had abruptly severed this arrangement.[30]

Civil War Reshapes North America

The two momentous events in the history of the United States— the War of Independence and the Civil War—have equal significance in the history of Canada. Born in the War of Independence, modern Canada federated into a nation-state as the United States disintegrated into Civil War. America's forty-year sectional contest over slavery, the contest of two very different political economies and cultures—capitalist and neofeudal, Yankee and cavalier—burst into the bloodiest war of the nineteenth century at Fort Sumter in 1861. Britain and its North American colonies were not disinterested bystanders. British and British North American sentiment had long been strongly anti-slavery. Britain had led the international movement against the slave trade since the beginning of the century and had formally abolished slavery within its empire in 1834, thus acquiring the self-righteous certitude of a former sinner about America's "peculiar institution." Nova Scotia, New Brunswick, and the Canadas shared this tradition. Asked by U.S. abolitionists about settlement possibilities for former slaves in Upper Canada, Lieutenant Governor Sir John Colborne told them to "tell the Republicans on your side of the line that we do not know men by color." Black communities began to be founded in southwestern Upper Canada in the 1820s. The province became "Glory Land," the northern terminus of the Underground Railroad, after a landmark legal case in 1833 in which an Upper Canadian court refused to extradite fugitive slaves Thornton and Ruthie Blackburn. About thirty-five thousand more émigrés had followed the Thorntons to "Glory Land" by 1861. Some historians point to the fact that the refugees were received with racism only slighted less virulent than in the northern United States as evidence that Euro-Canadians were as prejudiced against blacks as Euro-Americans were. But as one of the African Americans who chose Canada put it, "I have enjoyed more pleasure here in one month than in all my life in the land of bondage." Prominent abolitionists Frederick Douglass, Harriet Tubman, Levi Coffin, and John Brown visited their communities and lectured in Canadian cities; Brown's disastrous assault on the federal arsenal at Harper's Ferry was conceived near Chatham, Canada West, in 1858. One of his coconspirators, Samuel Gridley Howe, pronounced Canada a "reliable ally" and "immense moral aid" in the antislavery cause.[31]

British North American opinion on the Civil War defies easy categorization. Opposition to slavery did not lead to automatic support for the Union. *Harper's Weekly* warned against "the singular delusion" held by some Americans that "in the event of a separation between the Northern and the Southern States, Canada would leap into the arms of the former. . . . Canadians are intensely loyal to their Sovereign; and intensely hostile to Americans and American institutions." But this anti-Americanism did not translate to support for the Confederacy. Until Lincoln's Emancipation Proclamation in September 1862, the British North American consensus was that the war had been caused by economic differences between North and South rather than humanitarian concerns over slavery. Civil conflict thus represented the preordained failure of U.S. republicanism, brought about by an excess of democracy, overly strong state governments, and a weak central government. As in Britain, there was cynical speculation about the advantages to be gained at the expense of a dis–United States. Advocates of a broad federation of the British North American colonies saw long-term opportunity: "In consequence of the fratricidal war," said Canadian co-premier John A. Macdonald, "Canada had every prospect of being the great nation of this continent." Canadian leaders also saw immediate danger. "The shot fired at Fort Sumter," wrote Thomas D'Arcy McGee, "told the people of Canada to sleep no more, except on their arms, unless in their sleep they desire to be overtaken and subjugated."[32]

The combination of British North American proximity and British international ambitions meant that "the fratricidal war" would not be contained within purely domestic bounds. Britain quickly issued a proclamation of neutrality and refused to recognize the Confederacy, but it could hardly ignore the fact of Southern belligerency. Three battalions of infantry and an artillery battery rushed ostentatiously across the Atlantic to reinforce the British North American garrisons. The British cabinet feared Abraham Lincoln's secretary of state, William Seward, whom British prime minister Lord Palmerston described as a "vapouring, blustering, ignorant man." They had good reason to do so, for Seward seriously contemplated a diversionary war with Britain as a tactic to reunite North and South. Lincoln stopped such madness but did not countermand Seward's appointment of a secret emissary to Canada in an attempt to ensure that Canadian actions and opinions were consistent with northern desires. News of this appointment soon leaked to the press, a revelation that appropriately angered British authorities, since all U.S. diplomatic representation with Canada had to be channeled through the British ministry in Washington. The incident underlined a larger problem that plagued British North American–U.S. relations throughout the war: the U.S. determination that British territory not be used as a base for Confederate operations or a source of Confederate weapons. That issue arose early, with a diplomatic note from Seward protesting the sale of the lake steamer *Peerless* to "rebel" agents for use as a privateer to attack northern shipping. The allegations were groundless—the purchasers were New Yorkers—but the heated exchange of notes illustrated how delicate the Canadian position would be throughout the Civil War.[33]

Most incendiary of the border incidents was the raid on St. Albans, Vermont, by some twenty Confederate sympathizers in October 1864. The raiders terrorized the small community, murdered one man and wounded others, and looted the banks of two hundred thousand dollars before returning to the Canadian side of the border. There they were arrested, but Canadian and British authorities refused Seward's demand that they be extradited to the United States. Canada's sincere efforts to bring the raiders to justice were confounded by a Montreal magistrate who defined them as belligerents, rather than criminals, and thus beyond his jurisdiction. The raiders went free. The Canadian legislature at once enacted an alien act that provided for deportation of aliens who engaged in hostilities against a friendly country, but U.S. anger was not assuaged. Instead, it was compounded by Canadian refusal to return the fifteen thousand Union "skedaddlers"—deserters and draft dodgers—who fled to Canada and by the depredations of the *Alabama,* a Confederate warship that was built in a British shipyard and that preyed with deadly success on Union merchant vessels.[34]

In turn, the Union naval blockade of the Confederacy revived the Anglo-American dispute over neutrality of the seas. In November 1861 the British mail ship *Trent* was stopped and searched in international waters off Cuba by the USS *San Jacinto.* Union captain Charles Wilkes arrested two Confederate envoys en route to London, James Mason and John Slidell. An outpouring of chauvinistic anti-British nationalism awaited Wilkes in port, but President Lincoln and Charles Sumner, chairman of the Senate Foreign Relations Committee, both understood the diplomatic and military consequences of his rash decision. Britain prepared immediately for war with the United States. The North American garrisons were tripled with fourteen thousand reinforcements, and British strategists planned preemptive strikes along the border to forestall the U.S. invasion. The strategists held out little hope of holding Canada against concerted American attack. Instead, the Royal Navy would force an American retreat: one cabinet minister spoke of "the regrettable necessity of having to burn New York and Boston." Lord Palmerston assured Queen Victoria that her forces were ready "to inflict a severe blow upon and to read a lesson to the United States which will not soon be forgotten." Britain's cautiously drafted ultimatum, however, left the United States space for a face-saving de-escalation. Seward asserted the U.S. right to stop and search on the high seas, but he disavowed Wilkes's actions and, most importantly, freed Mason and Slidell.[35]

The defeat of the Confederacy, symbolized by Robert E. Lee's surrender at Appomattox Court House in April 1865, did not resolve these Civil War stresses to Anglo-American relations. Some American voices, none of them significant, echoed the *Chicago Tribune'*s call for the Union to retaliate against Britain by devouring its North American colonies "as quickly as a hawk would gobble a quail." The contentious atmosphere led Britain, and especially British North America, to take such threats too seriously. Henry Adams wrote from London that it was "whispered about that with the . . . Union restored, and a great army is left in our hands, the next manifestation will be one of hostility to this country. The various steps to rescind old treaty obligations, especially relating to Canada, . . . are cited as proof of our intentions to attack that country at once." The "old treaty obligations" were the 1817 Rush-Bagot agreement on Great Lakes armament, which Seward threatened to abrogate but did not, and the Reciprocity Treaty of 1854, which became the final casualty of the Civil War. John Potter, U.S. consul in Montreal, publicly boasted that "in two years from the abrogation . . . the people of Canada themselves will apply for admission to the United States." [36]

Several thousand Irishmen living in the United States seemed disinclined to wait even that long. The Irish Republican Brotherhood—the Fenians—hoped that military action against British North America would somehow achieve their goal of an independent Ireland. Demobilization of the Union Army swelled the movement with Irish-born veterans and enabled the Fenians to launch a series of forays northward between 1866 and 1871. The Fenian grand strategy was convoluted: it was never clear if these attacks were simple terrorism, serious attempts to capture hostage territories, or provocations to an Anglo-American war that might create an opening for rebellion in Ireland. Their tactics, on the other hand, were all too apparent to the British North American militiamen who were killed or wounded repelling the raids. Although some Fenian leaders believed they had secret support from Secretary of State Seward, there was no U.S. complicity in Fenian incursions. But the reluctance of U.S. politicians to alienate an ethnic group growing in electoral importance contributed to a lack of official enthusiasm for serious U.S. action to control the Brotherhood's activities. [37]

Thus the Civil War and its aftermath steered Britain's North American colonies toward union as the Dominion of Canada. There was a complex agenda of domestic reasons for the union, but the external threat represented by the United States—economic, military, and Fenian terrorist—provided essential momentum to the movement to Confederation. The U.S. challenge persuaded those who made the decision—the British government and the colonial elites of Nova Scotia, the Canadas, and especially New Brunswick—that in union lay the hope, if not the promise, of future strength. Defensive expansion against the United States motivated the incorporation of Manitoba in 1870 and British Columbia the following year; with the exception of the island provinces of Newfoundland and Prince Edward Island, Canada by 1871 had expanded to its present boundaries. W. L. Morton, a conservative-nationalist historian of Canada, has described the *Trent* crisis as "the Canadian Lexington and Concord, the definite initiation of Canadian independence." Frank H. Underhill offered a more iconoclastic summation. "Somewhere on Parliament Hill," he suggested, "there should be erected a monument to this American ogre who has so often performed the function of saving [Canada] from drift and indecision."[38]

Lingering post–Civil War disputes and some long-standing issues were resolved in 1871 in the Treaty of Washington. The northern triumph and the emergence of unified nation-states in Germany and Italy made Britain conscious of the need to keep a relatively cooperative United States on its Western Hemispheric flank; even more than in 1783, American goodwill was more important than a defense of seemingly narrow and less significant (at least to Britain) Canadian interests. Yet the discussions on the treaty were a tiny first step toward Canadian-American, as opposed to Anglo-American, relations, for Prime Minister John A. Macdonald of Canada served as one of five British members of the Joint High Commission that conducted the negotiations. The British government was more eager for Macdonald to participate than he was; it was, he knew, inevitable that he offend Britain, the United States, or the Canadian electorate. Macdonald anticipated a recurring complication of mutual British and Canadian conduct of the relationship with the United States—British and Canadian interests would not always be compatible.

In 1871, the contentious matter was the inshore fishery. The abrogation of reciprocity meant that American fishers were excluded from the waters of the Maritime Provinces. The Macdonald government's fisheries protection cruisers enforced the exclusion vigorously, seizing interlopers and fining their captains. The United States was sufficiently annoyed that President Grant complained in his 1870 message to Congress of "the colonial authority known as the Dominion of Canada," a "semi-independent but irresponsible power [that] has exercised its delegated power in an unfriendly way." Macdonald hoped to win renewed reciprocity in exchange for fishing rights, but Republican secretary of state Hamilton Fish was adamantly protectionist. Under British pressure, Macdonald capitulated. The Anglo-American Treaty of Washington granted the United States access to an ocean resource they had long coveted. In return, Canadian fishers obtained the right to sell their catch duty-free in U.S. markets and to navigate on the mostly frozen rivers of the new U.S. territory of Alaska. The United States disclaimed responsibility for the Fenian raids and refused to consider compensation for them. The other provision of the treaty that directly concerned U.S.-Canadian relations was the agreement to submit the unresolved section of the Pacific coast boundary to arbitration by the emperor of Germany (how better to draw a boundary than with a German ruler, wags observed) who awarded to the United States the disputed island of San Juan south of Vancouver Island.[39]

For Canada the treaty provided little tangible reward for a century of loyalty to the Crown; yet on another level the Treaty of Washington was a preliminary phase in confirming U.S. acceptance of Canadian borders and the reality of the Canadian Confederation. Legally, emotionally, and especially in U.S. eyes, Canada remained a British colony for generations to come. Along with the remaining Spanish colonies in the Western Hemisphere, the Dominion's existence as a "semi-independent power" reminded the United States that it was neither omnipotent nor alone on the continent. By 1871, it was clear that Canada had joined the United States and Mexico as the nation-states of North America.

2   Canada in the Shadow of Industrial America, 1871–1903

The triumph of Union nationalism and industrialism over Confederate decentralization and agrarianism in the United States coincided not only with the Canadian Confederation but also with movements of national unification elsewhere in the world. Germany, Italy, Argentina, and—most significant to the United States and Canada—Mexico all emerged from mid-nineteenth-century turmoil as unified nation-states and passed into periods of rapid economic growth and development. Confronted in Europe, Africa, and Asia by Germany as a rival imperial power, Britain disengaged from the Western Hemisphere. The Treaty of Washington signaled the withdrawal of the Royal Army from North America, despite Canadian protests. By 1872, the only red-coated regiments left in Canada were the garrisons at the naval bases of Halifax and Esquimalt, British Columbia. The United States was suddenly close to the principal objective of its Canadian policy: it no longer needed to actively fear British military power on its northern border. Britain remained the ultimate guarantor of Canadian security, however. "The true defence of our colonies," Colonial Secretary Edward Cardwell warned the world, was "that war with them is war with England." But if Canada was any less a hostage in Anglo-American relations, Canadians felt that they had not been released so much as abandoned to their own resources in North American relations.[1]

Canada's view of "the Great Republic" was encapsulated in the Canadian editorials recognizing America's centennial in 1876. "Every well-wisher can rejoice in progress as steady as it has been remarkable," began the *Toronto Globe*, "even though he may hold by a very different political system, and may render allegiance to a very different, and in his estimation greatly preferable, political power." "Let us rejoice that so much good has been accomplished, not that so much evil is still manifest." A list of "symptoms of degeneracy among our neighbors" followed, little changed from Loyalist critiques: "the increasing unscrupulousness of public men, . . . the murders, the frauds, the failures, the falsehood, the immoralities." Comparing the speeches on Dominion Day—July first—with the "spread-eagle" rhetoric on the Fourth of July, the editor noted that Canadians "may have little talk about fighting and dying for the Dominion, but let them be put to the test and they will show satisfactorily what they are able to do." The *Globe* was among the least anti-American newspapers. The almost universal Canadian assumption was that the United States coveted its northern neighbor and plotted annexation. In Canadian political caricature, the United States was "Brother Jonathan," a skinny, avaricious version of Uncle Sam who invariably pressed his unwanted attentions on fair "Miss Canada."[2]

No corresponding caricature of Canada ever appeared in political cartoons in the United States: in fact, few Americans paid much attention to Canada at all. After a visit to Washington, a Canadian cabinet minister was shocked by "the crass ignorance of everything Canadian among leading public men." Who would want to know anything about a "bleak, arid and provincial . . . frigid colony?" asked Henry James. President Andrew Johnson had pointedly not congratulated Canada on the first Dominion Day; on the Confederation's birthdays thereafter, U.S. editorialists continued the tradition. "The average American," writes historian Lester B. Shippee, "ignored the fact that a colony was disappearing and a nation was rising in its place." Active annexationism was passé, replaced by the assurance that the continental fulfillment of America's Manifest Destiny would not require recourse to arms. As Representative William Munger of Ohio told the House in 1870, now that "England's star has passed its zenith, . . . Canada will fall into our lap like a ripe apple." To help shake the tree, throughout the late nineteenth century the United States tested Canadian national sovereignty in boundary, fisheries, and sealing disputes. Important as these issues were—especially to Canada—they were matters of local

"Coming Home from the Fair," *Canadian Illustrated News* (1876). Courtesy Metropolitan Toronto Reference Library. "Brother Jonathan," a skinny, avaricious version of Uncle Sam, invariably pressed his unwanted attentions on innocent "Miss Canada." Although Brother Jonathan has evolved into "Uncle Sam," and Miss Canada's dress and demeanor have changed with the times, Canadian editorial cartoonists continue to use this trope.

rather than national interest to the United States and of indifference to Britain, until the Venezuela and Alaska boundary disputes at the end of the century. No one yet spoke of an "undefended border" between Canada and the United States, and each country planned for the possibility of war with the other. But by century's end, armed conflict became increasingly improbable, and there was gradual movement toward an actual direct bilateral U.S.-Canadian relationship.[3]

Westward the Course of Empires

This gradual movement is more apparent to historians in retrospect than it was to contemporary decision makers who lived during the period. Canadians were bent on extending their new country to the Pacific, an expansion they justified with their own northern vision of "maintaining the honor of the British Flag" westward. The *Montreal Star* caught this vision: "The Dominion has an opportunity . . . of showing the world what can be achieved by a people living under free institutions, and whose constitution is based upon the principle of right and justice to all men." There was considerable concern in Ottawa and some in London that this western patrimony would be usurped by Americans unless Canada acted decisively to claim it. Prodded by the Andrew Johnson administration's purchase of Alaska from Russia, the infant Dominion had made an emulous acquisition of its own. In 1869, Canada bought the vast northwestern empire of the Hudson's Bay Company for $1.5 million and passed the Act for the Temporary Government of Rupert's Land to extend the formality of Canadian colonial authority over the region from the U.S. border on the south and the Ontario border on the east to the continental divide in the west and the Arctic to the north. Effective control proved more difficult to establish. The people of the Red River Settlement, the largest community in the region, demanded better terms for the transfer to Canada, turned back the new lieutenant governor, and established its own provisional government at Fort Garry. The focal point of the Red River Resistance was the Métis, the mixed-blood descendents of French traders and Native mothers, but Métis spokesman Louis Riel had significant support in his negotiations with the Macdonald government.[4]

The resistance created an opening for Americans anxious to assist Canada's new northwest to fulfill its "manifest destiny," among them the businessmen of St. Paul, Minnesota, and Jay Cooke, promoter of the Northern Pacific Railroad. Control of Red River, the geographic gateway to the Pacific, would strangle their northern commercial rival in its cradle. As Representative Ignatius Donnelly, one of their congressional spokespersons, explained: "If the revolutionists of the Red River are encouraged and sustained by the avowed sympathy of the American people, we may . . . see the Stars and Stripes wave from Fort Garry, from the waters of Puget Sound, and along the shores of Vancouver." About two hundred of the two thousand white residents of Red River were like-minded Americans, who formed an active annexationist group around Oscar Malmros, the saloon keeper who served as U.S. consul. Two of them—Colonel Enos Stutsman, a U.S. treasury agent, and W. E. B. O'Donoghue, an Irish-American adventurer—infiltrated Riel's provisional government. They kept the State Department informed of the situation and urged support for the resistance, as did another U.S. secret agent in Red River, James Wickes Taylor. But the annexationists faced an insurmountable obstacle: Her Majesty's subjects at Red River did not want to become Americans. Riel's provisional government flew the British Union Jack over its headquarters at Fort Garry and rejected at gunpoint O'Donoghue's attempt to replace it with a rebel flag of his own design. However dissatisfied they were with the original terms of their union with Canada, no group in the settlement other than the Americans saw joining the United States as an attractive alternative.[5]

Annexation also failed because Washington refused to help Malmros and his fifth column further destabilize Red River. The American ambassador in London, J. L. Motley, warned Secretary of State Hamilton Fish that U.S. intervention would provoke a British response, and Fish and President Grant were loathe to trade a long-term U.S. objective—British withdrawal from Canada—for an uncertain prospect of territorial expansion. Lest they be tempted to do so, the Macdonald government sent a joint Anglo-Canadian military expedition west in 1870 to show the United States that Britain intended Canada to inherit the northwest. Fish briefly denied the expedition's supply vessel passage through a U.S. canal at Sault Ste. Marie but on reflection relented. Once in Red River, the troops accomplished their purpose without firing a shot. It was the last British military action in North America—"a long way to come," remarked a lieutenant, "to have the band play *God Save the Queen*." Riel won most of the better terms that he sought (although not a personal amnesty), and Manitoba became a Canadian province in July 1870.[6]

The incorporation of the western interior into the Confederation left British Columbia as the last piece of Canada's transcontinental puzzle. The Pacific coast colony had immense commercial and strategic value to the British world system. Beyond the potential of its coal, mineral, and forest resources, the ports at Victoria and Esquimalt linked North America to extensive British interests in the Pacific and Indian oceans. At the height of the British Columbia gold rush, from 1858 to 1862, annexation to the United States had seemed a probable future for the colony. Forty thousand of the fifty thousand miners who panned the rivers for placer gold were U.S. "forty-niners," hardened veterans of the California rush. They poled their skiffs up the Fraser River with grunted choruses: "Soon our banner will be streaming / Soon the Eagle will be screaming / And the Lion, see, it cowers / Hurrah Boys! The river's ours!" The colony's trade ties ran largely north-south, and with a transcontinental railroad in progress in the United States, closer political integration along the same economic axis carried considerable logic. The California legislature certainly thought so: it resolved that all "fair and honorable means" be used to detach British Columbia from its "Kingly Empire" and attach it to the American Union.[7]

British governor James Douglas moved quickly to make certain that this did not happen, and his superiors in London sent four warships and companies of Royal Marines to help Douglas maintain control. And like the would-be expansionists in Minnesota, the Californians lacked the support they needed in that part of British North America that they coveted. In British Columbia, the U.S. miners ran out at the same time that the placer gold did. The American consul in the colonial capital of Victoria assured Washington that the British Columbians were "restless and dissatisfied" and thus eager for annexation, but only forty-eight men signed an 1869 petition asking President Grant for annexation, and only three of those were British subjects. Even during the gold rush, the British minority had controlled the political institutions on Vancouver Island and on the mainland; in combination with the British navy this proved formidable. Lieutenant Governor Anthony Musgrave made clear that Britain's will was that British Columbia confederate with Canada, and economic self-interest confirmed the decision. Canada promised a rail link to eastern markets within ten years (a promise unkept), and businessmen in Victoria knew that as part of the United States, their city would be a satellite of San Francisco instead of the British imperial entrepôt en route to Asia. There was little love for the Canadian federation, as an anonymous poet explained in verse: "True loyalty's to Motherland / and not to Ca-na-da. / The love we bear is second-hand / To any step-mama." Whatever reason tipped the balance in favor of the British Empire and Canada, British Columbia became Canada's Pacific province in March 1871. Now, like the United States, Canada stretched from sea to sea. The arbitration of the Strait of Juan de Fuca boundary in 1872 completed (with the significant exception of the Alaska boundary) the diplomatic process begun ninety years before.[8]

But this western boundary existed only in a diplomatic sense; in terms of human and economic geography, national perimeters remained undefined. The Great Plains and the mountain ranges were oblivious to the political ambitions of men and women, and it was thus inevitable that problems would spill over the dividing lines men drew in the dust and rocks of the frontier. Miners, ranchers, farmers, and corporations poured into the American West, bringing with them railroads and repeating rifles, barbed wire and boomtowns, and sometimes violent conflict. Historian Richard Maxwell Brown calls the process by which the West was integrated into a national capitalist economy the "Western Civil War of Incorporation." Particular forms of violence and lawlessness characterized this conflict: clashes between Indians and whites, range wars, stagecoach robbery, vigilantism, lynching, and gunfights. The simultaneous Canadian westward movement was, historians allege, very different. The occupation of western Canada, writes historian Paul F. Sharp, was "orderly [and] well-planned," in contrast to the "violence and hatred south of the forty-ninth parallel." The North-West Territories, adds historian Stan D. Hansen, were "free from the more lurid episodes associated with the American frontier." The contrast between a "wild" and a tranquil West is an article of faith among Canadians. In historian Desmond Morton's words, it became "one of those self-congratulatory myths which bind a nation together." Like all myths, it has some foundation in reality. Canadian mining camps in British Columbia and the Klondike seem to have been less disturbed by crime and disorder. The Canadian ranching frontier was not a northern extension of its competitive U.S. counterpart, but an Anglo-Canadian cattle oligopoly. Ranchers' cartels replaced range wars, and rustlers met a magistrate and a prison cell rather than vigilantes and a rope. The starkest divergence was the temper of relations between Indians and whites. *Harper's Weekly* lamented after the Battle of the Little Big Horn in 1876 that "over the Canadian line the relations between Indians and whites are so tranquil, while on our side they are summed up in perpetual treachery, waste and war." Between 1866 and 1895, the U.S. Army fought 943 military engagements with Native peoples; Canadian troops fought 7, all but one of them a battle of the 1885 North-West Rebellion.[9]

Why were the two Wests different? There are circumstantial explanations: slower settlement, fewer Native people, and fewer white settlers. And all parties learned from the U.S. example. America's bloody Indian wars taught the Plains tribes in Canada the futility of confronting white weaponry, and the Assiniboine, Cree, and Blackfoot knew that the Canadian government could call upon the same weapons to destroy them. In 1885, the Gatling Machine Gun Company of Chicago provided the Canadian militia with two Gatling guns and crews to help suppress the Cree. The Gatlings were not all that Canada borrowed: most of the institutional framework for western expansion was copied directly from the United States, most obviously the railway land grant policy and the free homestead system. As *The Nation* observed in 1877, even in Indian administration "the general form and professed objects of the two systems are almost identical." Both countries used similar bureaucracies, signed treaties, and confined Indians on reservations ("reserves" in Canada) with the avowed goal of assimilating them into white society. What made the difference, concludes historian Hana Samek, was that "the settlers who arrived in the [Canadian] territories brought with them a tradition of respect for 'Queen's Law' and a deference to authority, traits that many Americans are proud to note were absent from their frontier population." Canada's minister of the interior David Mills sanctimoniously explained to his U.S. counterpart Carl Schurz that America's western disorder stemmed not from its inability to control Indians, but from its unwillingness to control white men.[10]

Canada had to control its settlers because the country simply could not afford a "wild" West, militarily or monetarily. Instability along the border that threatened U.S. lives or property, such as the 1873 Cypress Hills Massacre, would have brought U.S. expeditions into Canada as it later did into Mexico. Killing Indians was also expensive: in 1869, the U.S. government spent more on Indian wars than the entire revenue of the Canadian government! Ottawa kept tight control over the North-West Territories, granted representative government to the white settlers glacially, and extended provincial status much more slowly than the United States extended statehood. Alberta and Saskatchewan became provinces only in 1905 and were denied full provincial status, with control of the natural resources, until 1930. Canadian Indian policy was similar in legal form to U.S. policy, but the officials who administered it lacked the American zeal to force Indians to accept private land ownership, so that reserves in Canada were not broken up into individual allotments as they were in the United States.[11]

The most significant institutional divergence between the U.S. and Canadian Wests was the North West Mounted Police (NWMP). It should be noted that the Macdonald government's decision in 1873 to establish the force was greeted with the hearty approval of Secretary of State Hamilton Fish and that the second contingent of the NWMP went west on U.S. railroads to Fargo, Dakota Territory, before they rode north to Manitoba. The Mounties, concluded an American Indian affairs expert in 1911, were Canada's "one great advantage in dealing with her Indians over the United States." In the Canadian West they filled not only the role played in the United States by the U.S. Army, but also the role of the locally elected sheriffs and judges who had no interest in protecting Indians from the white electorate. As historian Wallace Stegner melodramatically phrases it, the scarlet Norfolk jackets worn by the NWMP made "the International Boundary . . . a color line: blue below, red above, blue for treachery and unkept promises, red for protection and the straight tongue." The United States made three treaties with the Blackfeet in Montana and because of settlers' demands for Blackfeet land respected none of them; Canada made one treaty with the Blackfoot (as they were called in Canada) and in general lived up to its terms. Canadians, searching as ever for the Republic's feet of clay, denounced U.S. Indian policy as "white savagery." In this they simply echoed domestic U.S. critics such as Helen Hunt Jackson, who held up Canada in her book *A Century of Dishonor* (1884) as an example for the United States to emulate. Even defenders of U.S. policy admitted that "in the Dominion . . . the plighted faith . . . once made to the Indian tribes, has never been violated. The red men can trust the Crown . . . and are therefore as loyal as any other British subjects."[12]

The most written-about comparison between the U.S. and Canadian Wests is the case of Sitting Bull and the Sioux. In the 1870s, gold miners moved into the Black Hills of the Dakota, Wyoming, and Montana territories, guaranteed to the Sioux by an 1868 agreement. The U.S. government sought revision of the agreement to remove the Sioux from the area, but Chief Sitting Bull and his people rejected all attempts to buy their hunting grounds and sacred places. In the spring of 1876, the U.S. Army moved to force the issue. On 25 June, Colonel George Armstrong Custer and his regiment of the Seventh Cavalry stumbled onto 2,500 Sioux warriors on the Little Bighorn River. It was the greatest Indian triumph of the long Plains War. In death, Custer and his 264 troopers became America's most celebrated martyrs; in victory, Sitting Bull became a Native Napoleon, the most dangerous Indian that America had ever confronted. More important for U.S.-Canadian relations, the chief and three thousand Sioux evaded capture and fought a strategic retreat north into Canadian territory.[13]

Sitting Bull remained on Canadian soil for five years, a constant worry to Assistant Superintendent James Walsh of the NWMP and the small detachments he assigned to watch them. The Sioux situation became the subject of a considerable triangular diplomatic correspondence among Canadian and U.S. authorities. The Sioux hunted across the border and occasionally raided white settlements and Crow reservations in Montana. Secretary of State William Evarts protested "these propensities for murder and plunder" and claimed that Canadian merchants were arming the Indians. These accusations notwithstanding, the Mounted Police monitored Sitting Bull's movements with much better success than the Seventh Cavalry had been able to. The Indians needed some ammunition, for they had to hunt the dwindling buffalo herds to feed themselves. Although the *New York Herald* wished "the Great Mother joy of her new subjects," the Sioux were consistently denied status as "British Indians," however much loyalty Sitting Bull professed to the "Great Mother," Queen Victoria. Canadian Indian administrators were unwilling to share the meager allotment for "Canadian" Indians with refugees from the United States, and the Sioux controlled no land of their own to exchange for support. In 1881, impending starvation forced the Sioux to reluctantly retrace their path to Montana. In their five years in Canada, noted a Montana editor with admiration, "these Sioux . . . have behaved themselves well, comparatively speaking." Sitting Bull was killed a decade later during a final act of defiance against American authority.[14]

"Annexing Canadians": Patterns of Migration

Extensive transborder migration has been an ever-present fact of the U.S.-Canadian relationship. Historian Marcus Lee Hansen's term for it—"The Mingling of the Canadian and American Peoples"—is singularly inapt, however. "Mingling" implies reciprocity, a numerical equivalence that has never existed. Despite Canada's much smaller population, the southward flow of Canadians has been a torrent compared to the trickle of American residents who moved north. To further vitiate the "mingling" concept, the Canadian and U.S. emigrants have been strikingly different. Sitting Bull and his people were typical of U.S. migrants to Canada. Like the exiled Tories after the War of Independence and the fugitive African-American passengers on the Underground Railroad, the Sioux saw Canada as a refuge from the United States that was nonetheless enough like America to be familiar. In 1887, a similar search for sanctuary propelled members of the Church of Jesus Christ of Latter-Day Saints—Mormons—from Utah Territory to the North-West Territories of Canada. The Mormons had moved west to escape America, only to have America move west to engulf them. The Senate insisted that the Latter-Day Saints renounce their practice of polygamy as the price of Utah's admission as a state. Church elders decided that statehood was worth a monogamous marriage, but not all church members accepted this decree as divine revelation. Led by Charles Ora Card, Brigham Young's son-in-law, two thousand Mormons trekked to the District of Alberta. The Canadian government welcomed these experienced dryland farmers with more enthusiasm than it had the Sioux, overlooking their conjugal idiosyncrasies for a time in favor of the skills and capital they brought with them. This Canadian pattern of making concessions to religious minorities was repeated with German Mennonites, who were granted land together in block settlements in Manitoba, and with Russian Doukhobors in Saskatchewan. Twentieth-century Canadians would later cite this as an example of the tolerant cultural pluralism of their "multi-cultural mosaic." In the late nineteenth century, however, concessions to religious and ethnic minorities were a confession of the inability of the Canadian West to compete for population with its U.S. analogue.[15]

In their national anthem "O Canada," English Canadians pledge to love their "home and native land" and French Canadians to honor the "terre de nos aïeux"—the land of our ancestors. Between 1870 and 1900 more than a million Canadians broke that pledge, including Calixa Lavallée, the composer of the song. U.S. census takers counted 1,179,922 Canadian-born residents in the United States in 1900, 785,461 English-speaking Canadians and 394,461 French-speaking. This was almost a quarter of Canada's 1900 population. "The Americans may say with truth," observed Toronto essayist Goldwin Smith, "that if they do not annex Canada they are annexing the Canadians." Although diverse in

Net Canadian Migration
to the United States
1840-1900

427,000 Emigrants
from the Maritimes

582,000 Emigrants
from Quebec

521,000 Emigrants
from Ontario

408,000

58,000

130,000

116,000

287,000

104,000

Atlantic Ocean

NFLD

PRINCE EDWARD I.

NOVA SCOTIA

Halifax

NEW BRUNSWICK

MAINE

QUEBEC

N.H.

VT.

MASS.

Boston

R.I.

CONN.

New York

NEW JERSEY

DEL.

MARYLAND

Washington

Montreal

Ottawa

NEW YORK

PENNSYLVANIA

Toronto

WEST VIRGINIA

VIRGINIA

ONTARIO

James Bay

MICHIGAN

OHIO

KENTUCKY

WISCONSIN

INDIANA

Chicago

ILLINOIS

MINNESOTA

IOWA

MISSOURI

St. Paul

Minneapolis

MANITOBA

NORTH DAKOTA

SOUTH DAKOTA

NEBRASKA

KANSAS

500 km

300 mi

250

150

0

wm

origins and destinations, these emigrants shared an economic motivation for migration southward: underemployed Maritimers found work in the "Boston States," French-Canadian day laborers and their families moved to the "facteries" of industrial New England, and Ontarians farmed the Middle West or clerked in Chicago. Sitting Bull had a Canadian counterpart in Big Bear, a Plains Cree chief who led his band from Saskatchewan to Montana in search of the disappearing northern herd of buffalo. Big Bear was refused a reservation by the United States just as Sitting Bull had been by Canada.[16]

Euro-Canadians were more welcome. Their migration was the continuation of a movement that had begun in the 1840s but that was amplified and altered after the Civil War. Before 1870, many of the migrants had been seasonal workers such as lumbermen or fishers, who returned after a season in the woods or on the banks. After 1870, sojourning turned to settlement, and more became permanent residents. Canadians were ambivalent about their countrypeople in the Republic. Quebec orators denounced the emigrants as "deserters, cowards, loafers, and delinquents." Ontarians agreed that "we have kept the winnowed grain while the chaff has gone to them." Canadians in the United States had traded "comfort and plenty" for "privation and misery," another journalist-patriot assured his readers. "They remain only because they are too poor or too proud to return in rags to their Canadian friends." Realists worried that "Uncle Sam absorbs the bone, sinew and youth of British America," that Canada was losing the flower of its younger generation. Both optimists and pessimists took pride in the achievements of individual Canadians in "the States": railroad entrepreneur James J. Hill, or the five chaired Harvard professors born in Nova Scotia or New Brunswick, or the twenty-eight Canadians who played U.S. major league baseball in 1884—among them outfielder "Tip" O'Neill, who recorded a .435 batting average in 1887, second-highest in the history of the game. In the late nineteenth century, however, most of the migrants were unskilled; the expression "Brain Drain" would not become part of the Canadian vocabulary until the 1920s.[17]

How did these expatriate Canadians—the second largest immigrant group in the United States—behave, and how did Americans react to their presence? We know much more about French-Canadian than English-Canadian immigrants because their language and religion set them farther apart from the U.S. mainstream and made the Roman Catholic Church, the Quebec government, and state governments sufficiently anxious about them to commission investigative studies. They faced the same virulent nativism as European immigrants, but nineteenth-century French-Canadian immigrants in New England fiercely resisted the "melting pot" of assimilation. "The Canadian French are the Chinese of the Eastern States," concluded a much-quoted Massachusetts report in 1881. "They are a horde of industrial invaders, not a stream of stable settlers. . . . Rarely does one of them become naturalized." This last accusation was accurate. Sustained by clerical and lay elites in Quebec who saw them as an "advance guard" of French Canada, the immigrants re-created "little Canadas," complete with schools, newspapers, and voluntary institutions, and battled with the Irish-American Catholic episcopacy for control of their own French-language parishes.[18]

English-Canadian immigrants to the United States have received relatively little attention from historians, who assume too easily that they left "scarcely a ripple" as they assimilated into an American milieu. They did what other émigrés did: published newspapers, joined social clubs, and celebrated distinctive holidays. The *Canadian-American* of Chicago reported on "the many social organizations" made up of immigrants who "wished not to forget their Dominion birth," and after a boisterous Dominion Day in 1880, a Michigan newspaper complained that it seemed as if "about half the population of Canada has arrived here during the month past." Unlike French Canadians, who were concentrated in factory work, English Canadians spread across the occupational spectrum. Historian Nora Faires has found that in Detroit in the late nineteenth century, they "spanned the hierarchy from extreme poverty to spectacular wealth," with most "occupying the working-class rungs of the city's occupational ladder." Like French Canadians, English Canadians often returned home for visits and had very low rates of naturalization relative to other immigrant groups or delayed becoming U.S. citizens until late in life. James Naismith, Canadian inventor of what George Will has called the "uniquely American" sport of basketball, left Montreal's McGill University for Massachusetts at age thirty but remained a subject of Their Majesties until he was sixty-five. These Canadian Americans were, it seemed, almost as ambivalent about the United States as were the families they left behind.[19]

Tariffs, Trade, and Economic Integration

The hemorrhage of Canadians to the United States painted the backdrop against which Canadian governments played out their tariff and trade strategies. The promise of economic growth to rival America's, explicit in Confederation, proved elusive—thus the exodus southward. Remembering the prosperity of the 1850s, both the Macdonald Conservative (1867–73) and the Alexander Mackenzie Liberal (1874–78) governments sought reciprocal trade agreements with the United States. Neither government succeeded in persuading Washington that renewed reciprocity held any advantage for the United States. Civil War tariff increases that had stimulated manufacturing continued in force, and the victorious Republicans remained a resolutely high-tariff protectionist party; the Democrats, tied more to agriculture than industry, sought reduction of the tariff but never its abolition. The negotiations in 1874 between Republican secretary of state Hamilton Fish and Canadian finance minister George Brown revealed another stumbling block to freer U.S.-Canadian trade. Fish shocked Brown with the demand that Canada maintain a higher tariff against British goods as a condition for lower tariffs within North America. The draft treaty that emerged from their discussions met a barrage of criticism in both Congress and Parliament and died without a decision in either legislature, largely because, as historian Allan Nevins concludes, "the selfish special interests were too strong." Canadian import duties remained lower than American, so that during the recession of the mid-1870s, U.S. manufacturers used Canada as a "slaughter market," dumping excess inventory north of the border. Canadian producers of everything from shoes to stoves appealed to Ottawa for tariffs of their own.[20]

The Macdonald Conservatives, returned to office in 1878, finally absorbed the message. Resolved upon "paying [the] U.S. in their own coin," the prime minister and his cabinet introduced the National Policy, a comprehensive system of protective tariffs designed to promote Canadian manufacturing in steel, textiles, coal, and petroleum products, and, via a Canadian Pacific Railway, to facilitate the internal exchange of agricultural and industrial products between western and eastern Canada. "We have no manufacturers here [and] our working people have all gone off to the U.S. . . . , adding to the strength, to the power and to the wealth of a foreign nation instead of adding to ours," Macdonald told Parliament. Without the National Policy, Canadians were condemned to be "hewers of wood and drawers of water." Macdonald's development strategy has been hailed as the foundation of Canadian autonomy, the masterstroke of nation building. In reality, Washington dictated that Canada would have high tariffs through its persistent disinterest in lower tariffs. The *Canadian Monthly and National Review* answered critics of "high tariff walls" bluntly: "Those who talk idly of a 'Chinese Wall' seem to forget that it has been already erected by our neighbors." The National Policy was not only made necessary by U.S. trade intransigence: it was the mirror image of U.S. policy, and as such was quietly protected by the British government. Its architects looked to the U.S. experience of commercial nationalism, concluding that the protectionist American tariffs were the cause of the all-too-obvious emergence of American industrial might in the course of the nineteenth century. Finance Minister Leonard Tilley went so far as to import an assistant from the U.S. Bureau of Statistics to advise him on drawing up the new Canadian tariff schedule![21]

The further paradox of the National Policy as economic nationalism was its role in the continental integration of the U.S. and Canadian economies. As soon as the tariff was raised in 1879, U.S. capitalists began to invest directly in Canada to leap over the protective tariff wall. As historian Michael Bliss has trenchantly observed, protection sowed "the Roots of the Branch Plant" and led to the presence of large numbers of wholly owned subsidiaries of U.S. corporations in Canada. One of the earliest of American multinationals in Canada was the Singer Manufacturing Company, which had sold its sewing machines through franchised dealers since the 1860s; now the tariff forced Singer to manufacture them in Montreal. A wide range of U.S. companies followed: International Harvester, National Cash Register, Westinghouse, James B. Duke's American Tobacco Company; the *Monetary Times* reported sixty-five such branch plants by 1887. In 1886, the American capitalist Samuel Ritchie incorporated the Canadian Copper Company to develop the rich nickel deposits of the Sudbury region of Ontario, a metal that became in high demand for its military application in armor plating. By 1890, Sudbury was the world's center of nickel production, and in 1902, the American-based giant International Nickel Company of Canada (INCO) emerged from a consolidation of a smaller number of competing firms. Other U.S. companies expanded by taking over Canadian ones: Standard Oil moved into Canada with its acquisition of a controlling interest in Imperial Oil. In 1900, direct and portfolio U.S. investment in Canada was 14 percent of total foreign investment, still well behind the 85 percent represented by British capital. But U.S. investment climbed steadily, exceeding 23 percent by 1914 in comparison with Britain's declining share of 72 percent. By 1913, one-quarter of all U.S. overseas investment was in Canada, in comparison to the one-half that was in all of the Latin American countries combined. The result of this activity was that between 1897 and 1908 Canada passed Mexico as the most important single target of U.S. direct and portfolio investment.[22]

Canadian tariff policy alone cannot explain the significant movement of U.S. capital into Canada in these years. Companies such as Western Union and New York Life Insurance operated in Canada with no obvious need for tariff protection. American Bell Telephone, later AT&T, bought its one-third interest in Bell Canada in order to forestall the growth of a Canadian rival that might one day threaten its virtual monopoly. Geographic proximity was an obvious factor enticing U.S.

investment north, and Canada was a relatively stable market for U.S. goods and capital, with a common language, at least in English Canada. Canada also had specific raw materials required by American industry. And as elsewhere in the Western Hemisphere (including the United States itself), as British economic influence declined, that of the United States emerged to replace it. Classic Marxist explanations of U.S. imperial expansionism stress the primacy of the search for markets and for secure investments. John A. Hobson contended in 1902 that American capitalism could not find adequate domestic markets for its goods and capital, an argument refined in Lenin's *Imperialism: The Highest Stage of Capitalism*. Such revisionist historians of U.S. foreign policy as Walter LaFeber and William A. Williams stress the critical importance of the 1890s depression in the United States as a catalyst in combining a complex range of strategic, intellectual, political, and economic forces to stimulate American expansion. Debate continues among scholars over these arguments, but there can be no doubt that both U.S. business and government placed considerable importance on foreign markets and access to raw materials. By the end of the nineteenth century, capital expansion had become a goal in U.S. foreign policy, which influenced relations with Canada just as it did those with other countries.[23]

A Renewed Critique of the Republic

Canadians made no complaint about U.S. economic imperialism; bringing foreign capital into the country was an explicit goal of the National Policy. But because it brought no sudden solution to Canada's economic problems, the National Policy shortly had critics. The goal of the Commercial Union movement that surfaced in the 1880s was the establishment of a common market between the United States and Canada, with a mutual protective tariff against the rest of the world. Promoted by men such as Erastus Wiman, a Canadian-born New York businessman whose Great Northwest Telegraph Company operated in both countries, the concept was popularized by Commercial

Union clubs on both sides of the border. Unlike more limited Canadian proposals for freer trade, the wholesale economic merger explicit in Commercial Union attracted support in Washington—"Brother Jonathan," observed a Liberal member of Parliament to party leader Wilfrid Laurier, "wants all or nothing." Despite such misgivings within the party, the Liberals built a form of Commercial Union into their platform in 1888 that they called "Full and Unrestricted Reciprocity." The Liberals—most of them, at least—did not seek political union with the United States. Commercial Union clubs in Canada concluded their meetings with cheers for Queen Victoria. As Sir Richard Cartwright told the New York Board of Trade, "we have our history, our traditions, our aspirations, just as you have yours"; unrestricted reciprocity was a simple business deal, to be "dealt with on business principles."[24]

But if not all the supporters of unrestricted reciprocity were annexationists, all the annexationists supported unrestricted reciprocity. Most outspoken among them was Goldwin Smith, a former Oxford Regius Professor of History who taught briefly at Cornell University before marrying a wealthy Toronto widow and settling into a career as an independent commentator on virtually everything. Smith had preached annexation since 1878, launched the idea of Commercial Union in 1880, and regularly reminded Canadians that their destiny lay as part of the American Republic. His sharp wit and quick pen contributed intellectual respectability to the first strong expression of continentalism since 1849. Smith lampooned Canada's hopelessly ambivalent feelings about the United States: Canadians enjoyed their economic relationship with America and wanted it to be close, but not too close. Despite the high tariffs, in per capita terms Canada was America's largest trading partner: 38 percent of Canada's exports went to the United States (53 percent to Britain), and 60 percent of its imports came from the United States (24 percent from Britain). In 1890, fears of losing that U.S. market intensified the debate about unrestricted reciprocity. In 1890, Congress passed the highly protectionist McKinley Tariff, which threatened to devastate Canadian agricultural exports. The Republican administration of Benjamin Harrison, in particular

Secretary of State James G. Blaine, had no desire to be gentle with Canada. A former senator from Maine, Blaine thought of Canada only as a competitor for fish and timber, a competitor best annexed. He rejected the overtures of the Canadian Conservative government toward the easing of tariffs on natural products. Publicly, Blaine declared himself "teetotally opposed to giving the Canadians the sentimental satisfaction of waving the British Flag . . . and enjoying the actual cash remuneration of American markets. . . . I do not mean that they shall be Canadians and Americans at the same time." Privately, he told President Harrison that by refusing any reciprocity short of Commercial Union, Canada would be forced to "ultimately, I believe, seek admission to the Union."[25]

Prime Minister Sir John A. Macdonald turned Blaine's rebuff to spectacular political advantage. He made the Canadian election of 1891 a national referendum on the relationship with the United States, describing the Liberal policy of unrestricted reciprocity as "veiled treason," a synonym for annexation. A Conservative majority, he told crowds, "will show to the Americans that we prize our country as much as they do, that we would fight for our existence." In industrial areas of the country the Tories warned of idle workers and idle capital if the Americans were granted unrestricted access to Canadian markets, but the appeal was more emotional than economic. Conservative editors summoned up images of a "crisis not less momentous" than the American invasions of 1775–76 and 1812–14. "Is Canada to be wiped out?" screamed the *Regina Standard:* "Shall the Union Jack droop and the British lion cower while the eagle screams and the stars and stripes wave triumphantly from Alaska to the Gulf of Mexico?" In Quebec, the Roman Catholic clergy warned against the evils of encroaching American cultural values. The loyalty campaign worked: the Conservatives won a renewed majority in Parliament and increased their share of the popular vote.[26]

The Conservative election victory did not end the sensitive debate over closer economic links with the United States. For a century after 1891, support for the tariff became a prerequisite for national political success in Canada. The Liberals had to adopt the essence of the National Policy before the electorate would entrust them with power. The "specter of annexation" honed the blades of anti-Americanism and sharpened the Canadian critique of the Republic. The public schools, complained Goldwin Smith, were turned "into seedplots of international enmity by implanting hatred of the Americans into the breasts of our children." Their parents read in anti-reciprocity polemics that in the United States "criminals go unpunished, and life and property are insecure; . . . lawless lynchings are of almost hourly occurrence; . . . Sunday is devoted to dissipation: drinking, dancing, gambling [and] vulgar rowdyism of men and women." In 1892, business and political elites in New York and Toronto, including Goldwin Smith, Andrew Carnegie, and Theodore Roosevelt, established a Continental Union League. It was an idea whose time was yet to come. Although it anticipated the important role that binational elite organizations would eventually play in propagandizing the idea of continentalism, it lasted barely two years. In the 1890s, interest in such links within U.S. political circles was too feeble, and Canadian antagonism to the United States much too strong. In July 1892, the *New York Times* reported two incidents in which "excited Canadians" tore down (and tore up) American flags flown in Canada on Dominion Day.[27]

Resources and Boundaries

More than the anger aroused by reciprocity prompted these attacks on the Stars and Stripes. The headline of the same page of the *Times* that described the desecrations of Old Glory reported "25 'British' Sealers Seized in Alaska." The sealing vessels flew the Union Jack, but they were in fact from British Columbia, evidence that the perennial diplomatic quarrels over boundaries and resources continued to mark the trilateral British-Canadian-American relationship between 1871 and 1903. The reconciliation over fishing rights contained in the Washington Treaty of 1871 did not endure. By 1885, the United States had abrogated the section of the treaty that pertained to fishing rights, and tensions mounted between Canadian and U.S. fishers. In the 1890s, quarrels over access took on a new environmental dimension, as conservationists in both countries expressed alarm at the rapid decline of fish stocks in the Great Lakes brought about by commercial overfishing and industrial pollution. In 1892, a joint investigative commission, established by the United States and by Britain acting on Canada's behalf, began a four-year study of the contiguous fisheries. The inquiry produced reams of evidence but no regulatory results. Each country suggested different solutions; neither country acted.[28]

Sovereignty and self-interest engendered conflict on the Pacific coast as well. The dispute over pelagic sealing (that is, sealing in the open seas) was the most emotional ocean-resource conflict of the late nineteenth century. On the surface the issues seemed clear enough. The United States controlled the Pribilof Islands in the Bering Sea, where the fur seal herds in the region concentrated; but even the Americans could not control the migratory, mating, and fishing habits of the seals, and it was the killing of seals on the high seas that posed the main problem. Within U.S. territorial waters, policy prohibited the slaughter of females and young seals and placed limits on the seal harvest as a whole The immutable problem was how to deal with the high-seas harvest. American officials claimed that killing seals in the open sea resulted in a disproportionate kill of females and threatened the long-term viability of the herd. In 1889, President Benjamin Harrison brought the issue officially to Canadian attention, warned of U.S. action against violators, and followed the cautionary warning with the seizure of several Canadian vessels. The British government, so often accused by Canadians of "apparent indifference to . . . the young Dominion across the sea," did not hesitate: warships moved into the sealing waters to protect Canadian sealers against American coast guard cutters. The two parties reached a temporary accommodation in 1891, halting sealing for that season, and the following year the British and Americans assented to arbitration by an international tribunal on which the U.S. delegates were outvoted. The tribunal determined that pelagic sealing within limits should continue and also awarded more than four hundred thousand dollars in compensation to Canadians.

The resulting destruction of the herds in the next two decades, however, led to a more determined resolve to end the problem. In 1911, the United States obtained British, Russian, and Japanese cooperation in establishing strict regulations over the industry. The 1911 agreement rejected U.S. claims to jurisdiction outside the three-mile limit and established a conservation agreement between Canada and the United States that provided for catch limits on a shared basis.[29]

In environmental terms, the United States held the better argument on the issue of pelagic sealing; the Russians also prohibited the kill except on land. But the symbolic importance of Canadian access to the seal fishery in the Bering Sea was as vital to the dispute as the economic question, with the result that the conflict assumed greater proportions than "the actual value of the seals involved." Domestic politics also played a role in shaping U.S. foreign policy positions. The Republican Party was the party of commercial expansionism, and the North American Commercial Company, which controlled the U.S. hunt, had important Republican connections, including D. O. Mills, the father-in-law of Whitelaw Reid, editor of the *New York Tribune,* and S. B. Elkins, a financial adviser to Secretary of State James G. Blaine. As much as "humanitarian" and environmental considerations shaped U.S. policy toward pelagic sealing, so too did the desire of Republican businessmen to contain foreign competitors.[30]

The issue of U.S. access to Canadian fisheries and to fisheries in Newfoundland (which did not become a Canadian province until 1949) paralleled the dispute over sealing. The tribunal established by the Washington Treaty offered a ruling that placed such a high price on U.S. access to Canadian fisheries that President Chester Arthur abrogated the agreement in 1885, thus leaving the two countries in the same state of uncertainty as had prevailed since the War of 1812. Efforts by the Harrison administration in the 1890s to circumvent the Canadian government and obtain a separate agreement with Newfoundland, including reciprocity, ran aground on the shoals of Canadian leverage in London, with the result that the British government overruled the Newfoundland initiative. The fisheries issue lingered as a nagging reminder of the basic competition between the two countries, until re-solved by an international arbitration ruling in 1910.[31]

The fur seal controversy, with its naval threat and counterthreat, was a minor aberration in what historian H. G. Nicholas has called the "longest period of amicable inanition that Anglo-American relations have ever known." In this context, the dispute between Britain and the United States over the boundary between British Guiana and Venezuela erupted with astonishing suddenness. In July 1895, Secretary of State Richard Olney blustered his way into the history of American foreign policy with an aggressive defence of the Venezuelan claim and a blunt demand that Britain agree to arbitration. Olney based his command on the Monroe Doctrine: the United States would not let European powers push around small nations in the Western Hemisphere. America was "master of the situation and practically invulnerable; . . . on this con-tinent . . . its fiat is law." At the same time, Olney noted that as long as European powers were "permanently encamped on American soil," the United States had no alternative but to be "armed to the teeth." When the British government stalled, Democratic president Grover Cleve-land announced that he would personally arbitrate the boundary and enforce his decision with U.S. arms. The threats and fears of previous war scares were immediately disinterred by military planners and the popular press. Britain would launch amphibious attacks on the U.S. Atlantic coast, the United States would capture Canada. Canadians pretended to believe that their "resistance would be a hard nut for the invader to crack" and that "the American spread eagle . . . will find him-self pretty light poultry." This, too, was bluster. Neither side wanted or was prepared for war, and British prime minister Lord Salisbury even-tually accepted binding neutral arbitration (which went in Britain's favor). The Venezuela crisis, writes historian C. P. Stacey, "was the last occasion when active military preparations were made in Canada for defence against the United States."[32]

The Venezuela crisis spurred Britain to renewed efforts to placate the United States and was thus a turning point in America's rise to world power. The crisis, concluded Captain Alfred Thayer Mahan, champion of U.S. sea power, "indicates the awakening of our countrymen to the fact that we must come out of our isolation . . . and take our share in the turmoil of the world." The Spanish-American war demonstrated America's strength. Canada maintained a neutrality that helped the United States more than the Spanish, who would have purchased Canadian coal for their fleet. Canadians prickled at the self-satisfactions of "l'impérialisme yankee," such as when U.S. editors compared Dewey's victory at Manila Bay to Nelson's at Trafalgar. In rapid succession the United States gained effective control over the Philippines, Cuba, Puerto Rico, Hawaii, and Panama. At century's end, the Republican McKinley administration copied Britain's Open Door policy toward China, while in Latin America the Anglo-American Hay-Pauncefote Treaty of 1901 paved the way for a U.S. canal across the isthmus. The United States was on its way to becoming a world power. Neighbors to the north could only watch with their usual combination of envy and tense expectation.[33]

Conflict on the Alaska Frontier

The last section of what was to become the "undefended border" was the boundary between Alaska and British Columbia. Beyond simple lines on a map, much more was at stake: harbors, minerals, and, not least, prestige. The conflict can only be understood in the contexts of the emergence of the United States as an imperial power and British concern about changes in the balance of power in Europe and the Far East with the rise of Germany and Japan. Canada was not an innocent bystander in turn-of-the-century imperialism and militarism, of course. Canadian involvement in the Anglo-Boer War in South Africa gave Canadians a taste of the jingoism that ran through parts of American society during the Spanish-American War. Like the United States, Canada looked to expand its economic horizons. As an example, because it was illegal before 1914 for U.S. banks to operate international branches, their Canadian competitors carved a dominant niche in the Caribbean.[34]

The discovery of gold in 1897 on Bonanza Creek in Canada's unsettled Yukon Territory meant that the Alaskan boundary question could be deferred no longer. Fifty thousand prospectors rushed for the gold. Most of the miners—and, according to Canadian authorities, all of the prostitutes, gamblers, and gunmen—were U.S. citizens. Interpreting this presence as a threat, the Canadian government promptly organized a territorial government and dispatched a "Yukon Field Force" of two hundred regular troops overland from British Columbia to assist the North West Mounted Police to maintain order and assert Canadian sovereignty. Their task was exacerbated by the near impossibility of reaching the gold fields by any route that passed entirely through Canadian territory. Most migrants came by sea, landed at the U.S. port of Skagway in the Alaska Panhandle, and trekked through the White or Chilkoot Pass into Canadian territory. The riches of the region—more than a million ounces of gold in 1900—made jurisdiction over coastal access points contentious. Although a lengthy border was in question, the principal issue was which country controlled the mouth of the Lynn Canal, the strait that joined Skagway to the North Pacific. Both sides took extreme positions at the outset. Canada claimed the boundary followed a line along the mouths of the ubiquitous inlets that ran into the mountains from the Pacific, thus incorporating the Lynn Canal, including Skagway, into Canada. The United States conversely claimed a line that would have brought under U.S. jurisdiction a significant portion of northern British Columbia and the Yukon.[35]

In May 1898, an Anglo-Canadian-American conference in Washington had established a trilateral Joint High Commission to settle all unresolved boundary questions, but the commission dissolved in dissension in less than a year, unable to agree upon a formula for Alaskan arbitration. In the Hay-Pauncefote Treaty of 1901, Britain relinquished its right to participate in the Panama Canal and thus lost a potential bargaining chip on the Alaska boundary. Given the British desire for U.S. friendship, the mother country likely would not have supported the more extreme boundary demands of its North American colony, regardless of which party had the stronger legal claim. Because legal opinion favored the United States, the Canadian cause was hopeless.

Nineteenth-century Russian and British maps confirmed the area in question had been Russian prior to 1867 and had become American with the purchase of Alaska. Nor, in subsequent years, had Anglo-Canadian authorities protested the development of Skagway.

Although the United States granted Canada temporary use of the head of the Lynn Canal in 1899, and the Liberal government of Sir Wilfrid Laurier accepted, jurisdiction remained unsettled in 1901 when an assassin's bullet killed William McKinley in Buffalo and brought Vice President Theodore Roosevelt into the White House. Roosevelt added his aggressive personality to an already difficult situation in U.S.-Canadian relations. Roosevelt's vision of U.S. national security involved the linking of the Atlantic and the Pacific, and Alaska represented an important strategic stepping-stone to the Far East. Even if national honor had not been at stake, control of the approaches to Alaska was simply too important to leave to chance, the Canadians, or third-party arbitration. Instead, Roosevelt deployed several hundred American troops as a sign of U.S. resolve to control the area against both international interlopers and the unruly local population. Roosevelt adamantly refused arbitration, arguing that the Canadian case was too weak to be taken seriously. "There are cases where a nation has no business to arbitrate," he told an English friend. "If we suddenly claimed a part of Nova Scotia you would not arbitrate." British desire not to alienate the United States contributed to an agreement early in 1903 to submit the boundary dispute to a mixed commission of six "impartial" jurists, three to be appointed by each party. President Roosevelt showed his disregard for the spirit of the agreement and his understanding of the need for Senate approval of his actions by appointing strong partisans: Secretary of War Elihu Root, prominent Massachusetts Republican senator Henry Cabot Lodge, and a former Republican senator from Washington, George Turner. In fairness to Roosevelt, there is no evidence that the two Canadians among the British appointees—Sir Louis Jetté, lieutenant governor of Quebec, and Allen B. Aylesworth, a Toronto lawyer, approached their assignments without prior assumptions about the merits of the case. The third British representative, Lord Alverstone, Chief Justice of England, was a man not to be envied. Roosevelt belligerently issued private warnings to the British through Associate Justice Oliver Wendell Holmes Jr. that if the commission failed to sustain the U.S. position, he would use U.S. military forces to achieve the same end.[36]

The outcome of the commission's enquiry is infamous in Canadian historical mythology. Lord Alverstone, this version runs, sold out Canada in the interest of Anglo-American accord, and the two Canadians on the panel accordingly refused to sign the decision. The commission awarded the critical control of the head of the Lynn Canal and the vital coastal strip north from fifty-six degrees forty minutes north latitude to the United States. There were minor concessions to Canada, such as the award of several islands in the Portland Channel, but these were of little consequence. Any fair assessment of the merits of the case, however, indicates that Lord Alverstone would have been remiss to find otherwise, and that the Canadian members of the panel were in a political dilemma that made it virtually impossible for them to have acted differently in the emotional drama of the moment. The Alaska boundary dispute was a decisive moment in Anglo-Canadian relations with the United States. Its resolution removed what Theodore Roosevelt referred to as the last serious point of friction between the United States and Great Britain. The appointment of a majority of Canadians to the boundary commission proved useless in guarding Canada's interests but by its failure was part of the emergence of an independent Canadian tradition in foreign policy. For Canadians, the boundary dispute was a spur to Canadian nationalism, anti-Americanism, and more than a tinge of resentment against British authority, a sentiment that tended to give English and French Canadians common cause. The *Montreal Herald* editorialized that "no Canadian government will be again likely to lay itself open to such treatment as meted out to Canada, whose ministers were tricked and deluded from first to last."[37]

The boundary dispute also underlined the stark asymmetry of power between Canada and the United States. No Canadian accepted this disparity as permanent, however. In the thirty-five years since Confederation, Canada had crossed the continent, and the original four provinces had become nine. "The Americans have 100 years the

start of us. The United States cannot go on making the same progress,"
Dominion Day speakers assured Canadians. Canada, with its superior political inheritance from Britain, would catch up, and Canadians
would build a country materially equal to America and morally superior to it. "As the nineteenth century was the century of the United
States," said Prime Minister Laurier from innumerable platforms, "so
shall the twentieth century belong to Canada."[38]

3   Beginning a Bilateral
       Relationship, 1903–1918

The first two decades of the twentieth century witnessed dramatic changes in the world context of U.S.-Canadian relations. Britain and its European rivals—France, Germany, Austria, and Russia—declined in relation to an emergent America. During the Republican presidencies of Theodore Roosevelt and William Howard Taft, the United States came to terms with its newly won status as a world power, built a battleship navy, and consolidated its political and economic influence in the Caribbean and in Central and South America, and extended it in the Pacific. The upheavals of World War I made the United States an international creditor and a military force able to compete with Britain even at sea, where the Royal Navy had ruled for a century. The temporary eclipse of Germany, the Bolshevik Revolution that reduced Russia's international influence, the rise of Japan: all tilted the world strategic balance to the advantage of the United States. At home, a diverse range of reform movements grouped under the umbrella of the Progressive Movement prohibition of alcohol, women's suffrage, the labor movement, civil rights, consumer protection, social work—attempted to transform U.S. society in response to the massive economic changes of the last quarter of the nineteenth century. Virtually all progressives proposed a larger role for government in the activities of the private sector and in foreign trade and overseas investment.

Because Canada underwent the same industrial capitalist revolution, albeit at its own pace, the reforms of this "Progressive Age" that shook the Republic had counterparts in the Dominion and (with the notable exception of Prohibition) echoed elsewhere in the British Empire and Western Europe. But no country was more affected than Canada by the global emergence of the United States and the relative decline of Great Britain. Trade relations with the United States contin-

71

ued to preoccupy Canadian domestic politics as well as cross-border relations, as did the growing cultural influence of the United States upon Canadian society. Canadians were much less concerned about the increasing levels of American investment in Canadian resources and manufacturing. In its relations with Canada, however, the United States neither employed the heavy-handed dollar diplomacy nor played the role of international policeman that it did in the Caribbean in the early twentieth century. The many points of friction were smoothed without resort to any force more violent than political rhetoric. On the formal diplomatic front, the Canadian government quietly explored an increasing autonomy from Great Britain in the conduct of its affairs with the United States. The new realities of international economic and military power dictated the growing bilateralism in U.S.-Canadian relations. British strategic planners viewed war with the United States as "a contingency which, however improbable, is not impossible," but they secretly conceded that a successful defense of Canada was impossible. First Sea Lord Sir John Fisher privately suggested that Britain "not spend one man or one pound in the defence of Canada." Given this military forecast, maintaining troops and a naval presence in Canada had lost even symbolic value to Britain, or at least a symbolic value that equaled the cost to the exchequer of keeping them there. In 1906 the last British garrisons withdrew from Halifax, Nova Scotia, and Esquimalt, British Columbia, and were replaced by infantry from Canada's minuscule army. The establishment of a tiny Canadian Department of External Affairs in 1909 was another of the only slightly more than symbolic gestures of growing Canadian autonomy from Great Britain in the international sphere. The department was a small step toward a Canadian foreign policy, even if the real decisions were still made by in London and in the British embassy in Washington. Prime Minister Sir Wilfrid Laurier did not look on the creation of the department as the launching of an independent Canadian foreign policy. The impetus came from British ambassador James Bryce in Washington, who complained that Canadian-U.S. relations tied up three-quarters of the embassy's attention and who demanded "a sort of Foreign Office" in Ottawa through which Canadian affairs in Washington could be coordinated. Britain remained a significant political presence in the Canadian-American relationship, however, and the British Empire remained a potent emotional presence. London gently resisted independent Canadian representation in Washington, which might interfere with imperial designs, but ultimately conceded it to the Dominion in the 1920s.[1]

The Beginnings of Bilateral Relations

As in the previous century, shared boundaries, fisheries, and natural resources were the staples of U.S.-Canadian relations. What was significant about the twentieth-century Canadian-American approach to the outstanding points of contention was the effort to institutionalize and depoliticize the mechanisms of conflict resolution, an approach that the United States also pursued, although with less success, with Mexico. This preference to avoid diplomatic disputes that might become hotly debated public issues paralleled the emergence of a more bureaucratic and "scientific" approach to conflict management during the years of progressive reform. Whether it was the creation of a Bureau of Corporations under Theodore Roosevelt, the establishment of a U.S. Tariff Commission under Woodrow Wilson, or the attempts by John D. Rockefeller Jr. to develop a new industrial relations system that would eliminate strikes, the thrust of the Progressive Era was toward organization, systematization, stability, and conflict reduction. This approach found a harmonious echo in Canada: Rockefeller's expert consultant on industrial relations was William Lyon Mackenzie King, former Canadian minister of labor and future prime minister. It was thus not surprising that the United States and Canada sought to establish bilateral bureaucratic institutions to deal with contentious common problems.[2]

The first important initiative was the establishment of the International Boundary Commission in 1908. Stripped of their military implications in the new atmosphere of Anglo-American harmony, boundary questions became suddenly less intractable. As James Bryce commented about an obscure island on the Maine–New Brunswick boundary, "a century ago, it might conceivably have been . . . a spot on which to construct a small fort. . . . Today no use could be made of it except to erect a tiny summer cottage or perhaps an afternoon tea house." The IBC's mandate was to clarify the international boundary between Canada and the United States, with the exception of the Great Lakes and St. Lawrence boundary, which was surveyed and reported on by the International Waterways Commission under the 1908 treaty. There were several main projects: settle the boundary in the perennially difficult area of the St. Croix River and Bay of Fundy though Passamaquoddy Bay; determine the boundary from the mouth to the source of the St. Croix River; survey the boundary from the source of the St. Croix River to the St. Lawrence River; and "ascertain and re-establish accurately" the location of the international boundary from its intersection with the St. Lawrence River near the forty-fifth parallel to the mouth of the Pigeon River on the western shore of Lake Superior. From there the commissioners had the task of clarifying the boundary to the Lake of the Woods, on to the Rocky Mountains, across the mountains to the Gulf of Georgia, and finally across the boundary between Vancouver Island and the United States. They also set the boundary along the 141st Meridian from the Arctic Ocean to Mount St. Elias.

The IBC's mandate has always been reasonably specific and technical in nature, a fact that kept its operation relatively free of controversy and public debate. In theory, each commissioner appointed to the IBC has been "an expert geographer or surveyor," as stipulated by Article II of the 1908 treaty, although among United States appointments there have been such exceptions as John Illinski, an insurance broker and beer distributor appointed by Harry Truman. Some of the commissioners have served sufficiently lengthy terms to provide important continuity. O. H. Tittman, appointed by Theodore Roosevelt, served from 1909 until 1915, and E. Lester Jones, appointed by Harding, served under three presidents until his death in 1929. On the Anglo-Canadian side W. F. King served for the first decade (1906–1916), with J. J. McArthur beginning his appointment in 1917 and remaining until 1924.[3]

The IBC could not resolve everything—a separate Passamaquoddy

Bay Treaty was negotiated as a "diplomatic sideshow" in 1910—but the commission cut a new and nonconfrontational pattern for U.S.-Canadian relations. The commission produced results on the Arctic–Mount St. Elias boundary by 1918. In the 1952 report, the commissioners were still looking at the boundary between Tongass Passage and Mount St. Elias; by 1925, the more controversial St. Croix–St. Lawrence River boundary report was complete. Not until 1934 did the IBC produce its fifth report, this one on the boundary from the source of the St. Croix River to the Atlantic Ocean. That boundary had been under review since at least 1794. Resolution of that border with minimal controversy and technical expertise, in keeping with the entire ethos of the Progressive Era and the increasingly "professional" and technical nature of U.S.-Canadian bilateral relations, was no small accomplishment. Anyone inclined to make political mileage from the commissioners' reports would have had first to wade through volumes of charts, "geodetic datum," and "triangulation and traverse stations"! The age of Taylorism and scientific management had come to bilateral relations.[4]

The second and more significant bilateral mechanism was the International Joint Commission, established 11 January 1909, when British Ambassador James Bryce and Secretary of State Elihu Root signed the Boundary Waters Treaty. This permanent commission, working outside diplomatic channels to resolve water use problems, was a more broadly conceived successor to the International Waterways Commission. The Boundary Waters Treaty was in fact negotiated by two members of the International Waterways Commission, George Clinton for the United States and George Gibbons for Canada. The only British contribution to the discussion—other than Bryce's advice to the Canadians to settle for less than they eventually achieved—was the ambassador's signature. Composed of three U.S. and three Canadian appointees, the IJC was to advise both governments about water levels, pollution, power development, the impact of dams on fisheries and other downstream activities, and irrigation. Its establishment was a diplomatic victory for Canadian prime minister Sir Wilfrid Laurier, who had pressed vigorously for the establishment of a commission that would take thorny boundary water issues out the public eye and, he hoped, beyond political logrolling. He did so against the advice of Ambassador Bryce, who preferred ad hoc solutions to problems as they arose, and over the opposition of Secretary of State Root. Because the Boundary Waters Treaty was an Anglo-American agreement, high-level support was essential to diplomatic success; Laurier received it from Governor General Earl Grey and from President Theodore Roosevelt. Grey regarded Anglo-American friendship as the primary goal of British foreign policy. Accordingly, on his appointment to Ottawa in 1904 he made the settlement of U.S.-Canadian differences his personal project. Roosevelt was recruited to the boundary waters cause through his conservationist background. The American Civic Association warned him that without an international agreement the scenic beauty of Niagara Falls would be lost to unregulated water diversion for hydroelectric development. The president's confidant on conservation matters, Gifford Pinchot, was able to bend Root away from his opposition to a bilateral commission. The less-political approach to the bilateral relationship, the major achievement of the Boundary Waters Treaty, also conformed precisely to Roosevelt's progressive perception of how reform should be managed.[5]

The importance of a bilateral commission between two countries whose border is one-third water and whose rivers flow into one another's territory should be self-evident. The pressing problems of 1909 increased as power generation, industrialization, and water pollution intensified. By 1929, the IJC had dealt with twenty-seven cases, either submitted by private citizens or referred to it by the Canadian or U.S. governments. Cases ranged from the 1913 approval of the construction of the St. Mary's River Dam by the Michigan Northern Power Company to the 1928 recommendations on fumes generated by the Trail, British Columbia, smelter, recommendations that were rejected by the United States. The commission's decisions touched the lives of ordinary Canadians and Americans: its correspondence reveals their concerns about flooding, soil erosion, pollution, and property damage.[6]

The IJC has never deserved the fulsome praise heaped on it after World War I, when it was described as "the memorial dome to Anglo-American peace," and offered as a model for resolving the boundary between France and Germany. But the commission provided an institutional mechanism within which Canada and the United States could, in the words of international lawyer P. E. Corbett, "deal with matters . . . before they get to the stage of national bitterness." It signified, concludes Canadian scholar-diplomat John Holmes, "the triumph of the tradition of restraint . . . in quiet contradiction to the noisier thrust of Manifest Destiny." Yet leading university textbooks in Canadian history ignore the IJC, as does the leading textbook in U.S. foreign policy. Historians J. L. Granatstein and Norman Hillmer contend that the impact of the IJC has been exaggerated because its actual powers have been advisory, and its ability to invoke binding arbitration has been restrained by Congress and the executive in the United States, and by the Senate and Cabinet in Canada. One of the major failings of the treaty, according to both contemporary and later analysts, was its application only to waters that actually straddled the border, thus excluding, for instance, rivers that flowed into boundary waters or across the borders. However short they fall of their most idealistic descriptions, the Boundary Waters Treaty and the International Joint Commission represent the development of depoliticized decision making outside the boundaries of formal diplomacy in U.S.-Canadian relations. If the oft-proclaimed "special relationship" between the United States and Canada has any substance, the IJC is its essence. Whatever one decides about the "special relationship," the Boundary Waters Treaty was negotiated by Canadians, and thus represented a significant step on the road to formal bilateral diplomatic relations between North American neighbors.[7]

The difference between the official text of a treaty and the reality of its implementation was further evident in violations of the spirit and letter of the Rush-Bagot Treaty of 1817, which had theoretically demilitarized the Great Lakes. Rush-Bagot had been breached during the Civil War and was breached again in the 1890s, when the Harrison, Cleveland, and McKinley administrations began a serious naval building program, inspired by the writings of Alfred Thayer Mahan and the realities of U.S. imperial expansion. The United States sought the convenience of naval crews on the Great Lakes and of sending warships, with their weapons dismounted, to the lakes via the Canadian canal system, the only one deep enough to accommodate larger vessels. The United States punctiliously requested permission for these voyages, and Canada never refused, although Laurier's acquiescence was condemned as "madness" by Canadian patriots, who feared that the Americans might launch surprise attacks en route. Several of the U.S. ships that violated the Rush-Bagot agreement were built by Great Lakes shipyards eager for their share of the naval construction bonanza. The State Department explained away the *Gresham*, nine hundred tons and armed with modern guns, on the technical grounds that it was a "revenue cutter" and not a warship. British support for Canada on the naval issue was limited, and Canada lacked the military clout to deter the United States and feared that an open confrontation might only make Washington more belligerent. Both London and Ottawa conceded reality, agreeing that although warships were forbidden on the lakes, two armed training vessels and six revenue cutters would not add up to a warship! Between 1900 and 1910, the American inland navy exceeded these agreed limits, a point emphasized in 1909 with the USS *Nashville*, a modern fighting ship whose four-inch guns could launch a thirty-pound shell five miles. The niceties of formal diplomacy were observed: the *Nashville*'s guns were dismounted in Canadian waters, and after complaints from the Laurier government, the Taft administration graciously promised Ambassador Bryce that in the future it would adhere to the spirit of Rush-Bagot. One historian has referred to the diplomatic meanderings as an "invisible revision of the Rush-Bagot Agreement."[8]

Fisheries disputes remained the thorniest perennial in U.S.-Canadian relations, and in U.S.-Newfoundland relations. American access to Canadian and Newfoundland fisheries had been contentious since 1784, because the 1818 agreement continued to mean different things to each party. Only about two thousand New Englanders actually fished these waters, but the case took on greater importance because the fishers were represented in the U.S. Senate by Henry Cabot Lodge, the most powerful member of the Foreign Relations Committee. Thus a final interpretation became part of the larger effort of the Laurier government and the Roosevelt-Taft administrations to "clean the slate." As with boundary waters, the preferred method of resolution was to remove the problem from the vagaries of the political arena. In 1908, the United States and Great Britain agreed to establish the International Fisheries Commission. Early in Taft's presidency in 1909, the Laurier and Taft administrations agreed to submit outstanding claims over the fisheries to a tribunal formed from among the members of the Permanent Court of Arbitration at The Hague. That arbitration process produced a North Atlantic Coast Fisheries Agreement that clarified the terms of the ancient accord—and clarified them in language that satisfied Canada's Maritime Provinces and Newfoundland yet allowed New Englanders to fish subject to "equitable and fair" regulation. In 1911, further trilateral discussions followed in Washington over the details of Canadian fisheries regulations. Canada agreed to amend or repeal a number of Canadian regulations that U.S. captains contended disadvantaged them. Negotiators further agreed that any additional differences over the fisheries that could not be resolved through diplomatic channels would be referred to the Permanent Mixed Fishery Commission, as recommended by The Hague tribunal.[9]

Diplomacy lacks the drama of the wars and near-wars that marked the nineteenth century—one reason, no doubt, why relations with Canada almost vanish from the pages of U.S. diplomatic history after the Alaskan Boundary Dispute. Historian C. P. Stacey notes, for example, that only seventeen pages of the two volumes of Philip C. Jessup's *Elihu Root* (New York, 1938) are devoted to Root's remarkable accomplishments in U.S.-Canadian relations. Between 1905 and 1911, with Britain's considerable cooperation, the two countries concluded eight treaties or agreements and "cleaned the slate" of long-standing quarrels. Historian Peter Neary's description of these six years as a "new departure in Canadian-American relations" seems appropriate. The most significant departure was that there were now de facto direct relations between Ottawa and Washington, with only minimal British supervision. Things went more smoothly with "John Bull" on the sidelines, concluded Canadian diplomat Sir George Gibbons. With Great Britain "out of the game," he noted to Laurier, "there will be little prestige in tackling a little fellow." The United States had indeed resisted the temptation to bully its small neighbor and assert the obvious asymmetry of power between the two countries. In the shadow of the Alaska debacle, Laurier had gained substantial diplomatic ground. Who suspected that the government that had managed relations with the United States so competently was soon to be electorally crucified on the altar of Canada's anti-Americanism?[10]

The Americanization of Canada?

One reason for Laurier's bold assertion that the new century would "belong to Canada" was that the torrent of emigrants to the United States finally decelerated. Between 1896 and 1914, the number of American residents moving north came closer to equaling the number of residents of Canada heading south. The exact dimensions of these migrations remain elusive, because contemporary statistics of annual immigrant arrivals collected by the Canadian and U.S. governments disaccord dramatically with the decennial censuses. The most extravagant Canadian figures claim that 785,000 Americans came north, but Canadian census figures for the American-born are much more modest. Some migrants who came to Canada were born outside North America and are counted as Europeans; others were Canadians returning from sojourns in the United States; others, however, were Americans who came, saw, and returned south. The most convincing estimate sets the total number of Americans who came to Canada at 243,000, leaving a net out-migration of slightly fewer than 200,000 Canadians between 1896 and 1914. This was a spectacular improvement over the preceding half-century. What reshaped the pattern of Canadian out-migration was not so much that Americans moved to the Canadian West, but that English Canadians who left the Maritimes and Ontario now chose the Canadian West as their destination rather than the United States.[11]

The inexpensive farmland beneath the short grass prairie of Saskatchewan and Alberta that attracted these eastern Canadians also persuaded Americans to join the trek to the "last, best West." The Canadian government actively recruited farm families in the midwestern states, and railroads cooperated by offering special rail rates for the emigrants, their livestock, and their equipment. Others made the journey overland by prairie schooner from states bordering Canada. Once there, the newcomers found a familiar land survey and distribution system, which Canada had adapted from the U.S. Homestead Act: every adult male could claim a quarter-section, 160 acres, if he and his family were hardy enough to survive on it. A few of the American migrants became successful agribusinessmen, such as "Wheat King" A. J. Cotton, or Charles Noble, who employed 160 workers to till his 30,000 acres of southern Alberta. The majority, however, were simple farm families moving up the "agricultural ladder" from tenant farming to independence on a modest homestead of their own—fulfilling their "American dream" in Canada. One critical element, however, was missing: the southern parts of the Canadian prairies received much less rain than Minnesota, Nebraska, or even the Dakotas. For a third of the American migrants, the Canadian sojourn dissolved in the blowing dust of the droughts from 1917 to 1926.[12] (See the map of American migration to Canada on page 20.)

Minority groups continued to prefer Canada to the United States, as had the Mormons in 1887. Canadian land regulations permitted transplanted cultural communities to settle in close proximity, Canada promised exemptions from military service, and provincial governments provided minority language public schools. Attracted by these assurances that they could preserve their distinctiveness, Jewish homesteaders abandoned North Dakota to found six agricultural colonies in Manitoba and Saskatchewan, and seventeen hundred Hutterites left South Dakota for Manitoba and Alberta. Despite Canada's eagerness for farmer-settlers, and its greater official tolerance of ethnic minorities, African Americans were unwelcome. Immigration bureaucrats did their best to deny admission to blacks secretly, by limiting recruiting in states with large African-American populations, by refusing African Americans the inducements available to Euro-Americans, and by stringently applying medical regulations. When W. E. B. Du Bois complained of this discrimination in *Crisis*, the newspaper of the National Association for the Advancement of Colored People, the official response was blunt: "There is nothing in the Canadian immigration law which disbars any person on the ground of color, but since colored people are not considered as a class likely to do well in this country all other regulations respecting health, money etc., are strictly enforced, and it is quite possible that a number of your fellow countrymen may be rejected on such grounds." Had this form of restriction failed, however, Canada was ready to apply more overt racism: a federal order barring black immigrants was passed, but never implemented, in 1911.[13]

One group of Americans was always welcome in Canada: capitalists with money to invest. U.S. investment in Canada multiplied twelvefold between 1900 and 1920, from $167 million to $2.1 billion (U.S.). Most of the new investments went into resource extraction and into secondary manufacturing. Separate patterns developed in each sector. To avoid paying U.S. tariffs against manufactured products, the resource companies tried to do as little secondary processing in Canada as possible and to ship their wood, ore, or asbestos back to the United States in unrefined form. After 1900, the provincial governments of Ontario and Quebec began to confound these attempts by banning or taxing the export of unprocessed logs and ore. U.S. secondary manufacturing companies had been blackmailed since 1879 into opening branch plants by the Canadian protective tariff and by Canadian patent law, which denied patent protection to manufacturers without a domestic factory. These companies sold their products almost exclusively in the Canadian market, exporting almost nothing. Canadians seemed unconcerned that a large percentage of their economy belonged to Americans. Two critical sectors of the Canadian economy, transportation and banking, were almost untouched by U.S. capital. As large as American investment in Canada was, a far larger percentage of foreign investment—three times as much in 1914—belonged to British investors; in Canada, British investment was scarcely considered "foreign" investment at all.[14]

In Canada's trade union movement, the relationship between British and American participation was the reverse: few British unions had locals in Canada, but many American unions had affiliates there. U.S. craft unions—iron molders, coopers, railway engineers, typographers, shoemakers—first appeared in Canada in the 1850s, and for the next century the history of the Canadian trade union movement followed many of the contours of the American. In the 1880s, the craft unions were joined by the Knights of Labor. Founded in Philadelphia in 1869 as a fraternal organization dedicated to labor reform, the Knights erupted in the 1880s into almost a national industrial union, organizing semi-skilled and unskilled workers ignored by craft unions, fighting strikes when necessary, and working to create a "co-operative commonwealth" to replace U.S. industrial capitalism. The Knights reached their apex in the massive industrial conflict of the mid-eighties and thereafter perished in the face of employer resistance, economic depression, and conflict with the craft unions affiliated with the American Federation of Labor (AFL) established in 1886. The AFL's agenda for the American workers was defined by its president Samuel Gompers as "pure and simple" craft unionism aimed at improving wages and working conditions. Independent political action was anathema: American workers were to accept the world as it was, rather than "dream of what might be," as the Knights would have it. Paradoxically, the Knights of Labor lived on vigorously in Canada for two decades after they became moribund in the United States. In Ontario and Quebec, local assemblies of the Knights were the vanguard of a nascent working-class movement in both its industrial and its political struggles. Knights guided the Trades and Labor Congress (TLC), Canada's national labor federation, for the first decade after its birth in 1886.[15]

But it was craft unions affiliated with the American Federation of Labor that assumed the leadership in the prosperous years at the beginning of the new century, as union membership began to grow rapidly. Craft workers who crossed the international boundary wanted an American union card so as to be able to work in the United States. Canadian unions sometimes sought affiliation with an experienced U.S. union with money for organizational work. U.S. unions came to Canada in order to guarantee that U.S. employers could not use it as a northern nonunion sanctuary. There was also an element of internationalist idealism in this North American focus: "There is no 49th parallel of latitude in Unionism," declared one British Columbia miner.

"The Canadian and American workingmen have joined hands across the Boundary line for a common cause against a common enemy." Samuel Gompers appealed to such idealism in more restrained language: "We are more than neighbors; we are kin . . . our labor problem with all its ideals, aspirations and ambitions is alike for both of us." Lest any Canadian worker challenge the official AFL definition of those "ideals, aspirations and ambitions" (and perhaps encourage American workers to question them as well), after 1900 Gompers and his Canadian colleagues moved quickly to establish their authority within the Trades and Labor Congress of Canada. Their targets were the Knights of Labor and "dual" unions—autonomous Canadian or British unions whose membership included craftsmen (and they were virtually all crafts-*men*) for whom a competing AFL union already existed. Their victory was swift: at the Trades and Labor Congress convention in Berlin, Ontario, in 1902, Gompers's candidate John Flett became TLC president. The Canadian Congress then expelled the remaining Knights of Labor delegates and all those representing "dual" unions, and granted the AFL the ultimate authority in jurisdictional disputes—to determine, in other words, which unions would be allowed to become members of Canada's most important labor federation. Samuel Gompers, said the *Montreal Herald*, was now "the Napoleon of Labor, with a continent for his kingdom." Like branch plant industry, branch plant unions became the norm within the Canadian labor movement; the United Brotherhood of Carpenters and Joiners or the United Mine Workers of America were similar to Gillette or General Motors in this regard.[16]

What difference did this make for Canadian workers? The immediate effect of the Berlin decision of 1902 was increased fragmentation of the Canadian working-class movement by region, as most of the groups expelled were from Quebec. It was difficult for AFL unions operating in English to make up these losses, and the way was cleared for the Roman Catholic church to establish a system of Catholic unions within the province. The longer-term effect, writes historian Robert Babcock, was that "the international craft unions brought to Canada structural characteristics and policy predilections that were products of the America environment [:] craft union organization, short-term economic goals, apolitical unionism." Under AFL tutelage, the Canadian labor movement grew in the direction of a narrow business unionism preoccupied with the immediate interests of its members, rather than that of social movement unionism, dedicated to broader working-class objectives. Samuel Gompers's dictum to support individual "friends of labor" in the Republican and Democratic parties might have been sound advice in a congressional system, but it was structurally unsuited to a parliamentary system, in which individual Conservatives and Liberals had no legislative autonomy from their party's position.[17]

But it would be too simple to attribute all the limitations of the Canadian labor movement to the malevolent influence of what critics called the American "Separation" of labor, and to use the United States as a convenient scapegoat for Canadian problems. Canadian craft workers voluntarily chose U.S. unions to represent them, and by 1915 these unions spoke for 119,000 workers, 90 percent of the organized workers in Canada. Craft unionists in Canada practiced Labourist politics in spite of the AFL interdiction against them. And if there is a conservative binational labor heritage, there is also a "radical heritage" of binational challenges to AFL/TLC hegemony: the Western Federation of Miners, the American Labor Union, and the Industrial Workers of the World. Canadian employers were sufficiently alarmed by U.S. union organizers that a bill passed the Canadian Senate in 1903 calling for two years of imprisonment for any U.S. citizen who came to Canada to support striking workers. There had been "no difficulty in settling the labour disputes in our factories" before American organizers came north, argued one senator during the debate; Samuel Gompers should never "be allowed to come to Canada . . . to destroy our peace and harmony."[18]

Trade unionism was the worst of a series of objectionable importations from the United States that troubled Canadian elites. Immigrants to the Canadian West might bring America's Wild West along with them: "Alberta," worried a member of Parliament, "might be regarded as a typical American state." College fraternities, baseball leagues, and business associations were integrating the continent on north-south lines. "Our theatres, sports, magazines, newspapers, are all more or less of the Yankee sort," lamented Rodolphe Lemieux, Canada's post-master general. The tracts of Canadian social reformers cited U.S. rather than British examples, beseeching Canada to "listen to a warning voice from the Republic to the South." It seemed, concluded Sir Andrew MacPhail, as if "the American spirit" was "at war for the possession of Canada's soul." In his Columbia doctoral thesis published in 1907, Samuel E. Moffett described *The Americanization of Canada* with an air of satisfaction inappropriate to a social scientist. "The Americans and the English Canadians have been welded into one people. Canadians . . . are already Americans without knowing it." Canada had survived into the twentieth century, Moffett concluded, only because of "a long series of American mistakes"; it would soon be absorbed into the United States.[19]

Moffett proved not only a poor political scientist but also a poor prognosticator. Others who studied Canadian society reached very different conclusions. French sociologist André Siegfried recognized "American ideas, habits, and tendencies" but found these superficial: "at bottom, by taste and tradition, English Canadians are very English still." Siegfried might have added Scottish, Irish, and Welsh: between 1901 and 1921, 752,000 immigrants came to Canada from the British Isles, three times as many as from the United States. A German journalist touring the Canadian West, supposedly the most "Americanized" region of Canada, remarked that "the Canadians belong to the British Empire not merely out of habit, not for practical considerations, but from a warm feeling of kinship." He found "no trace whatsoever of leaning toward the United States." Scottish travel writer John Foster Fraser assumed that the tobacco-chewing Albertan in overalls he interviewed standing beneath a sign for "The Beer That Made Milwaukee Famous" would be a U.S. immigrant. Appearances aside, Fraser's subject proved a passionate British Canadian, whose "dislike of the States almost equal[ed his] loyalty to the Empire." Asked about the possibility of commercial union with the United States, he told Fraser that "we're not frightened of those Yankees and their tariffs. It ain't us wants reciprocity with Uncle Sam, but Uncle Sam who'd like to get a smile from Miss Canada."[20]

Reciprocity Repulsed

Nothing better illustrates all the dimensions of Canada's ambivalent relationship with the United States than the never-ending issue of reciprocal trade. The Canadian craving for a reciprocal trade agreement never really went away, however much it was dulled by the prosperity of the first decade of the new century. Even as Canadian voters rejected unrestricted reciprocity in 1891—an agreement that the United States had never formally offered—Sir John A. Macdonald had made clear that a "fair" reciprocity agreement remained a Canadian goal. On assuming the prime ministership in 1896, Wilfrid Laurier announced that there would be "no more pilgrimages" to Washington for trade agreements. The Liberals won four consecutive majority governments (1896, 1900, 1904, and 1908) with a protective tariff policy that seemed a carbon copy of that of the Macdonald Conservatives. Yet Laurier admitted that should the United States "come and knock on our door," he was ready to negotiate a free trade agreement. There were pragmatic economic reasons for this ambivalence between tariff protection against, and freer trade with, the United States. As intended, the high tariff attracted U.S. branch plants to Canada, but the counterargument in favor of reciprocal tariff reductions was Canada's chronic trade deficit with the United States: 1910 figures showed an imbalance of $242 million to $97 million. During the North Atlantic fisheries negotiations, Canada had repeated its offer to exchange access to the inshore fisheries for U.S. tariff concessions on Canadian primary exports, but the offer was rebuffed as it had been previously. It was thus a surprise when Finance Minister W. S. Fielding came home from discussions in Washington in 1910 with a bigger catch than Ottawa had anticipated— a large-scale trade agreement that satisfied most of the conditions Canadians had sought since the United States abrogated the Elgin-Marcy Reciprocity Treaty in 1866. There was to be near free trade in natural products, which made up virtually all Canadian exports to the United States: the draft agreement removed all tariffs on pulpwood, most minerals, and unprocessed agricultural products, and lowered tariffs on processed farm products. To the delight of the Laurier gov-

ernment, there would be only limited reductions in the tariffs on manufactured goods, which made up about three-quarters of U.S. exports
to Canada. Most Canadian tariffs against U.S. manufactured goods
remained in place, including the "imperial preferences" that permitted British manufactures into the Canadian market at rates lower than
those from the United States. "Making allowance for changed conditions," said the *Manitoba Free Press*, the new agreement was "the treaty
of 1854 all over again." There was one important difference: the agreement was to be enacted not by treaty but by concurrent legislation of
Congress and Parliament, so that neither two-thirds approval in the
U.S. Senate nor British diplomatic participation would be necessary.[21]

Historians debate why an agreement so favorable to Canada suddenly originated from Washington. Albert K. Weinberg, echoing
the fears of Canadian critics of the accord, interpreted reciprocity
in the tradition of Manifest Destiny, as "the tinder which set into flame
the expansionist impulse, inactive recently but still combustible." The
most generally accepted explanation is that the United States had no
thought of annexation, that Taft hoped an agreement would shore up
Republican electoral fortunes. After promising in the 1908 campaign
that the Republican party was "unequivocally for revision of the tariff," his administration was feeling political heat generated by the 1909
Payne-Aldrich tariff, which had indeed revised tariff rates—upward.
Without a reciprocity agreement with Canada, Payne-Aldrich would
have required the United States to apply new maximum penalty rates
to Canadian exports, the first shot in a possible trade war. President
Taft was also pushed toward reciprocity, historian L. E. Ellis suggests,
by the eagerness of the American Newspaper Publishers' Association to have untaxed access to cheaper Canadian newsprint. Richard
Gwynn argues that Taft made his "offer of almost unbelievable generosity" because of his affection for Canada, a love nurtured by years of
happy vacations and hearty meals at his summer home in Murray Bay,
Quebec. A more comprehensive explanation of U.S. motivation for reciprocity has been offered by Robert E. Hannigan and by Paul Wolman,
who interpret the agreement as part of a broader attempt by a group
of political and industrial "tariff revisionists" to chart new directions

for U.S. capitalism. Reciprocity was evidence, writes Hannigan, of "a new American continentalism, distinct from the annexationist variant prominent during the nation's first century," one with "very significant global implications." Its goal was to prevent Canada from developing into a "core" industrial state (the term is from Immanuel Wallerstein's *Capitalist World Economy*, discussed in chapter 2), which could compete with the United States, and "to guarantee for the American economy a cheap and continuous supply of Canadian natural products." Some of the tariff reductions in the reciprocity agreement did indeed run counter to the short-term interests of some U.S. industries, but this was not U.S. benevolence to Canada. Taft and the tariff revisionists, Wolman points out, thought "not only in terms of immediate self-interest but in terms of the collective future of their nation as the world's dominant economic power." Other than among those who would specifically be hurt by its provisions, the deal had widespread support in the United States. A month after Taft announced the agreement to Congress on 26 January 1911, the *New York Times* reported that reciprocity was "backed by such a force of public sentiment as we do not recall behind any measure in our political history," and that America's business leaders were "eager for Canadian reciprocity." [22]

Initial reaction in Canada to the announcement of the agreement was incredulous enthusiasm at the Liberal government's coup of improved access to U.S. markets at little apparent cost to Canada. The Conservative opposition was shocked into silence, and its crestfallen leader Robert Borden reported "the deepest dejection in our party." But resistance to the agreement mobilized rapidly outside Parliament. Eighteen prominent Toronto businessmen, all of them Liberals, denounced reciprocity as a threat to "Canadian autonomy and Canadian nationality." It would, said their manifesto, prevent Canadian development of "her own resources in her own way and by her own people, . . . weaken the ties which bind Canada to the Empire, . . . and make it more difficult to avert political union with the United States." Buoyed—and bankrolled—by new business supporters, the Conservatives regained their composure and fought reciprocity throughout the country and in Parliament as a Trojan horse for Americanization, or worse, for annexation. "I fear the Greeks when they are bearing gifts," said Conservative spokesman George Foster; reciprocity would be "the conquest of Canada by peaceful means and large gifts." By July, exasperated by Conservative filibusters, Laurier despaired of forcing the agreement through Parliament and asked the governor general for an election.[23]

Reciprocity's U.S. advocates unwittingly handed its Canadian opponents the tools they needed to win the election and pry the deal apart. The alacrity and the large majorities by which the reciprocity agreement sped through Congress (268 to 89 in the House of Representatives, 53 to 7 in the Senate) frightened Canadians. Could anything about which the United States was so unanimous possibly be good for Canada? American politicians had no idea of the intense scrutiny with which their every utterance on the subject would be analyzed and reanalyzed in Canadian newspapers. The congressional debates on reciprocity featured several old-fashioned spread-eagle annexationist speeches, the most quoted of which was by the Speaker of the House of Representatives. "I hope to see the day when the American flag will float over every square foot of the British North American possessions clear to the North Pole," said Missouri Democrat James Beauchamp "Champ" Clark. "I do not have any doubt whatever that the day is not far distant when Great Britain will see all her North American possessions become a part of this Republic." President Taft himself made the impolitic remark that Canada was at the "parting of the ways," which Canadian opponents of the agreement claimed meant that Canada had to choose between the United States and Britain, rather than between reciprocity and protection. "The talk of annexation is bosh," he told the press. "The United States has all it can attend to with the territory it now has." But the president's private assessment of the agreement, confided in a letter to Theodore Roosevelt on 10 January 1911, painted a different portrait. The agreement, Taft explained, "would produce a current of business between Canada and the United States that would make Canada only an adjunct of the United States. It would transfer all their important business to Chicago and New York, with their bank credits and everything else, and it would increase greatly the demand of Canada for our manufactures. I see this is an argument made against reciprocity in Canada, and I think it is a good one." Several historians cite this letter as a second Taft indiscretion that undermined the agreement. The letter, however, was not made public until April 1912 and therefore played no role in the defeat of reciprocity by the Canadian electorate in 1911.[24]

Taft's private analysis suggests, however, that the extravagant discourse that surrounded the 1910–11 reciprocity issue was more than simple America-bashing. The eighteen Toronto businessmen and the other Canadian capitalists who opposed reciprocity shared with Robert Borden the belief that Canada's "marvelous material resources" destined the country for "the highest position within this mighty Empire." They were determined, in other words, that within a British world system, Canada could become a "core" nation and need not be relegated to a peripheral role as America's "hewer of wood and drawer of water." The campaign—as much as any election campaign in a parliamentary democracy can revolve on a single issue—became a referendum on reciprocity. Familiar anti-American themes were revived. "Reciprocity means Annexation," warned the Montreal Woman's Anti-Reciprocity League, and annexation would mean "injury to home life and the marriage tie, |and| a lessening of national religion and morals." The newspaper *Le Devoir* pointedly asked French Canadians if they would enjoy the same religious and linguistic guarantees if Quebec became a state of the U.S. union. The choice, said a Conservative candidate, was between "the Union Jack and British connection as opposed to the Stars and Stripes and Yankee domination—the domination of a flag . . . conceived in treason and born in rebellion."[25]

The election's result echoed more emphatically Canada's 1891 rejection of the United States. It was a Liberal disaster—seven cabinet ministers, including the architect of the agreement, W. S. Fielding, lost their parliamentary seats—as the Conservatives won a comfortable majority of 134 to 87 in the House of Commons. Theodore Roosevelt attributed the defeat of reciprocity to "ill-judged remarks" by "three or four prize idiots, including the Speaker of the House," but the Canadian election of 1911 tells us much more than that about the relationship between the United States and Canada. Champ Clark struck the match, but the Canadian forest he set ablaze had been dried to tinder by a century and a half of anti-Americanism. "The man in the street [and only men could vote in Canada in 1911]," wrote a political science professor, voted against reciprocity "in order to show his resentment of long years of United States hostility and condescension." The *Varsity*, the student newspaper of the University of Toronto, put it more pithily: "Canada was indignant, and wiped America's eye." New prime minister Robert Borden tried to disavow the chauvinistic symphony he had conducted so skillfully during the campaign. "In rejecting reciprocity," he said in a post-election statement, "Canada has simply affirmed her adherence to a policy of national development which she has pursued for many years." That much was true. "The verdict was in no way dictated by any spirit of unfriendliness to the great neighboring republic," he continued, for "no such spirit exists." This was a convenient fiction by which Borden admitted a larger truth: that Canada had now to get on with everyday life next door to imperial America.[26]

"America Counted Her Profits; Canada Buried Her Dead"

Borden and his government matched his conciliatory words with equally conciliatory actions. Finance Minister Thomas White (one of the eighteen Toronto businessmen who had opposed reciprocity) journeyed to New York to assure Wall Street that Canada remained "a fine field for investment of their surplus funds," and the Conservatives gave final approval to the North Atlantic fisheries agreement that Laurier had hesitated for two years to confirm. To William H. Taft, this agreement summarized the new relationship he had worked to achieve among the United States, Canada, and Britain. In his last annual message in December 1912, the "lame duck" president—Taft had been defeated in November by Democrat Woodrow Wilson—noted with pride the "final conclusion" to the "century-old controversy."[27]

Intoxicated by Anglo-American amity, Prime Minister Borden expounded a new vision of the trilateral relationship in which Canada would play a unique mediating role in assuring harmony between the United States and Britain. As he explained to a New York audience, it was "the duty of Canada to become more and more of a bond of goodwill and friendship between this Great Republic and our Empire." There is no evidence that the Department of State or the British Foreign Office noted Borden's offer, which he repeated on several occasions to U.S. audiences, and nothing to suggest that it would have been taken seriously had it been noted. But this "linchpin" theory rapidly became a fundamental conviction of Canada's infant foreign policy, enduring even into the 1960s. An example was the remarkable rapidity with which Canadian leaders turned from manipulating the anti-Americanism of their countrypeople to memorializing the centenary of the end of the War of 1812. In August 1913, with Secretary of State William Jennings Bryan at the head table, Thomas White reminded a New York audience that "next year we celebrate a hundred years of peace." It would, he predicted, be the first century of "a thousand more years of peace between the two great English-speaking races." A trinational British-Canadian-U.S. committee set to work to plan the celebration of "the 100th Anniversary of peace between the United States and the British Empire." Their celebrations were cut short by the cannons of August 1914.[78]

As a British colony, Canada entered World War I (the "Great War," as it was universally known until the 1940s) automatically with King George V's declaration of war against Germany. Canada was "ready, aye ready" to "answer to the call of duty," promised Sir Wilfrid Laurier; few disagreed—in part because Canadians thought their empire would win a speedy victory. Instead, the war stalemated into appalling carnage between the trenches on the Western Front, with casualties counted in the hundreds of thousands. Borden and his government committed Canada, with a population of fewer than eight million, to maintain an army of half a million men in France, a commitment that meant the imposition of a military draft that split the country profoundly along French-English lines. To English Canadians, who by and large supported this commitment, the war became more than an exercise in British Empire solidarity. Long before the United States entered the war, they came to understand it as a crusade for democracy, a struggle to rescue tiny Belgium from ruthless German oppression.[29]

Because the United States had long and loudly professed such values (and had twice invaded Canada to save it from ruthless British oppression) President Wilson's declaration of neutrality seemed to Canadians to be hypocrisy. Wilson asked that Americans be "impartial in thought as well as in action" and went so far as to ask audiences in movie theaters not to cheer either side during newsreels of the war. His refusal even to lend moral support to the Allies (with whom Wilson personally sympathized) was incomprehensible to Canadians, and Secretary of State William Jennings Bryan's frequent criticism of Britain outraged them. European purchases of food, raw materials, and munitions in the United States stimulated both the U.S. economy and Canadian resentment. "America waxed richer and stronger," complained a bitter Canadian, while "Canada suffered, fought and sacrificed her prosperity and her sons." Official expressions of resentment were muted—like the British government, the Canadian government prayed for U.S. intervention—but private expressions were scathing. "The United States made its big mistake in allowing the Belgian tragedy . . . without lifting its voice in protest," wrote a Montreal lawyer to a friend serving overseas in the Canadian army. "Our big neighbor is big no longer. . . . The true American hangs his head in shame. . . . He is not a citizen of a nation, but belongs to a conglomeration of races undigested and undigestible; how he envies us our British citizenship and curses the spirit that has made his country a by-word and reproach among men with red blood in their veins."[30]

"Conglomeration of races" referred to Irish Americans and German Americans, whose antipathy to Britain was assumed to be one of the sources of Wilson's policy of neutrality. The possibility that German agents would recruit border raiders within these ethnic communities troubled the Canadian military and the Canadian public. The German Foreign Office seriously considered several plans for such attacks, but their military attaché in Washington achieved virtually no results in implementing them. The total damage from his campaign of sabotage was one slightly damaged New Brunswick railway bridge. It was evident, Canadians conceded, that "the conspirators were well watched from Washington." The most frustrating Canadian-U.S. wartime problems, as in the nineteenth century, stemmed from the issue of neutral rights at sea, an issue exacerbated by the development of the submarine. The Royal Navy commanded the surface of the Atlantic, so that Britain's trade with the United States could continue, but the Wilson administration forbade the sale of warships to belligerent nations. The British Admiralty secretly contracted with an American company to assemble "clandestine submarines" and coastal patrol vessels in Canadian shipyards, in defiance of both U.S. neutrality and Canadian customs and labor laws. In 1916, a German submarine freighter, the *U-Deutschland*, surfaced in Baltimore to load a cargo of nickel mined at Sudbury, Ontario. Canadians were outraged that metal mined by an American branch plant in Canada might be used in Europe against Canadian soldiers, sailors, and airmen. The submarine incident that most aroused Canadians was "the day's worth of havoc" of the *U-53* in October 1916. The first German combat submarine to cross the Atlantic, the *U-53* paid a courtesy call on the U.S. naval base at Newport, Rhode Island. U.S. naval officers and their families toured "the long gray visitor," the *New York Times* reported, and brought gifts to the German commander and his men. The *U-53*'s crew declined the many invitations to dinners ashore in Newport; instead they returned to sea to sink five Allied merchant ships just outside the three mile limit. One was the British-registered *Stephano*, a liner bound from New York to Halifax, sent to the bottom while two U.S. Navy destroyers waited compliantly to rescue the *Stephano*'s passengers. To have intervened would have been to "violate their duty of neutrality," Assistant Secretary of the Navy Franklin D. Roosevelt told the press; the U.S. captains had acted in "absolute accordance with international law." But to Canadians, the U.S. Navy was an accomplice in an act of piracy; these protestations of even-handedness infuriated them all the more. "The time will come when American Democracy will need to explain," editorialized the *Toronto Globe*.[31]

Submarines ultimately brought the United States into the war on the side of the Allies in April 1917. Germany's announcement that its

U-boats would torpedo all merchant ships trading with Britain without warning and without regard for their nationality put Wilson in Madison's position of 1812, and he made the same decision for war. The United States fought, he told Congress, because "the world must be made safe for democracy." Canadians welcomed their mighty neighbor to the Allied ranks. "Uncle Sam . . . definitely sets the scales of conflict in favor of democracy," wrote an Alberta editor, even if the United States was likely to be "no great force in the war." The most ironic evidence that Canada and the United States were fighting on the same side was the Canadian government's invitation to AFL president Samuel Gompers to visit Ottawa to address Parliament, which fifteen years earlier had debated forbidding him entry to the country. In April 1918, Gompers was no longer an "alien agitator" but a "sane, masterful leader"; in a series of speeches he told Canadian trade unionists that "this War is a people's war—labour's war," and urged them to show their support by pledging not to strike for the duration of the war effort. Although they now shared a common enemy, there was little military cooperation between the U.S. and Canadian armed forces. In France, their armies fought under separate commands. In the North Atlantic approaches, relations between the two navies were cordial, but the U.S. Navy was too preoccupied with shepherding U.S. merchant ships to coordinate antisubmarine defense with the Royal Canadian Navy. Nor did World War I substantially increase economic integration of the newfound allies. In both countries the demands of total war brought about an unprecedented degree of government intervention into economic affairs, intervention accomplished by parallel federal wartime bureaucracies. Canada's food controller W. D. Hanna visited U.S. food administrator Herbert Hoover, and the Imperial Munitions Board of Canada and the U.S. Ordnance Department signed an agreement to coordinate production of artillery shells. But so little real binational coordination took place before the war ended in November 1918 that the contacts had more symbolic than practical significance. Continental integration for total war lay twenty-five years in the future.[32]

The war did, however, accelerate the de facto development of independent Canadian representation in Washington. In October 1917, Borden cabled the Canadian high commissioner in the United Kingdom, stressing that it was urgent that a special Canadian representative be appointed in Washington, a position supported by Lord Northcliffe, head of the British War Mission in the United States. Borden argued that "the multiplicity of departments and commissions at Washington leads to disastrous delay if negotiations are conducted through the Embassy which is overwhelmed with a multitude of important matters not directly concerning Canada." The proposal was to appoint a Canadian official who would serve in the British embassy but would communicate directly with the U.S. government in matters concerning Canadian affairs. Before the end of World War I, Canada enjoyed a very distinct position as a British Dominion in its representation in Washington. Most negotiations between the Canadian Department of External Affairs and the U.S. State Department were conducted directly, with the consent of the British embassy, and this also became the practice with other government departments as well. As British ambassador Cecil Spring Rice observed to the governor general of Canada in early 1918, "the part that the Embassy plays is merely to inform the State Department and to stand aside until the negotiation is completed." Nonetheless, such arrangements were informal and at the indulgence of the British and U.S. governments. This suggests the importance of Borden's success in having established in February 1918 a formal Canadian War Mission in Washington, headed by businessman Lloyd Harris. Borden followed a few weeks later with an official visit to President Wilson. By the end of the war, Canada was in practice well on the road to formal, independent relations with the United States.[33]

But twenty months as comrades in arms could not reverse the resentment Canadians felt at three years of U.S. neutrality. Historian Michael Bliss concludes that Canadian and U.S. businessmen "were experiencing different wars"; given that Canada fought for three years longer and had ten times the proportional casualties, it was "a more profound experience for Canadians than it was for the Americans." Allying to fight the Kaiser did not change the Canadian stereotypes of the United States ingrained by a century and a half of anti-Americanism. Canadian reporters noted that during the 1918 Fourth of July parade in New

York, William Randolph Hearst, the "malignant figure" who published ten "anti-British" newspapers, had "remained seated with his hat on" as Canadian troops marched past carrying the Union Jack. When William Jennings Bryan spoke at a prohibition rally in Toronto in 1918, he was greeted by war veterans wearing gas masks and shouting "Go Home, You Pro-German" and "Shut the Sauerkraut Up." The former secretary of state protested that "My country raised an army of one and a half million," but the veterans' choruses of "God Save the King" and "The Maple Leaf Forever" forced Bryan from the platform without finishing his speech. Prime Minister Borden, just back from his visit to Washington, described the incident as "no doubt a misunderstanding" but concluded his curious apology by calculating that "to equal Canada's record [the United States] would have to place 5,500,000 men in the field." Canadian sensitivity about their country's contribution to defeating Germany was compounded after the Armistice, when the U.S. press, Hollywood, and Tin Pan Alley bragged that America had won the war. During the 1920s and 1930s, no Canadian forgot that Canada, with one-tenth the population, had more killed and wounded than the United States. In a study of U.S.-Canadian relations published in 1929, H. L. Keenleyside suggested that, as a result of such memories, "Canadian dislike for the United States was definitely increased . . . and time has not yet entirely healed the wound." A few pages later, he provided an unintentional example: "America," wrote the young Canadian historian, "counted her profits while Canada buried her dead." [34]

4 A Relationship Matures, 1919–1938

World War I was a watershed for both Canada and the United States. In the interwar decades Canada took its tentative first steps into the international community with a seat in the new League of Nations. The British Statute of Westminster in 1931 made Canada technically autonomous within the empire, but Britain remained a significant third presence in Canadian calculations about the United States. In these same decades, the United States affirmed its world power. U.S. foreign policy in the postwar decades seemed paradoxical: a trend toward political isolationism, best exemplified by U.S. rejection of the League of Nations, at the precise moment at which America achieved global military and economic reach. Yet there was no contradiction in this policy of "independent internationalism," argues historian Joan Hoff Wilson; U.S. government and business cooperated to gain foreign markets and raw material in a way that allowed business to retain maximum freedom of action. With Republicans ascendant in Congress and Warren Harding, Calvin Coolidge, and Herbert Hoover in the White House, the United States remained highly protectionist until 1933, a protectionism expressed in the Fordney-McCumber tariff of 1922 and in the Smoot-Hawley tariff in 1930. Canadian governments retaliated with their own tariff increases. As in the past, the Canadian protective tariff encouraged increased U.S. direct investment in the Canadian economy. As U.S. money came north, Canadians went south. The 1920s saw the renewal of the southward migration of the nineteenth century. Other issues from the past reasserted their importance in the bilateral relationship: the fisheries of both coasts, the development of the hydroelectric potential of boundary waters, and the transportation possibilities of the St. Lawrence waterway. During the 1920s, the International Joint Commission quietly disposed of a dozen

99

potentially thorny issues; during the 1930s, it would resolve two dozen more. Like their economies, U.S.-Canadian relations follow cycles; the early 1930s marked a simultaneous interwar nadir for both. After the relative prosperity of the 1920s, the Great Depression struck the United States and Canada more severely than any other countries on the globe, causing new problems and exacerbating old ones. The inauguration of President Franklin D. Roosevelt in 1933 brought new hope to a United States mired in despair; although it went unnoticed at the time, Roosevelt's presidency also offered an opportunity for bold new directions in the U.S.-Canadian relationship.[1]

A Formal Diplomatic Relationship

By the 1920s, an Anglo-American war involving Canada was universally described as "unthinkable," even though soldiers on both sides of the border still thought about it. Canada's Defence Plan No. 1 called for the use of "flying columns" to capture "key invasion bases" such as Seattle and Minneapolis in order to stall an American drive northward until the British Army arrived. The U.S. Army's Strategic Plan Red hypothesized a conquest of Canada in the event of war with Britain, after which the "territory gained . . . will become states and territories of the Union [and] the Dominion government will be abolished." Not even the soldiers, however, took these plans very seriously; the U.S. War Department obtained the maps of western Canada it needed for invasion planning by writing to the Canadian government and requesting them![2]

The Canadian bureaucrat who sent the maps to the War Department was flattered that the Americans had shown an interest; Canada's biggest diplomatic difficulty was to persuade the United States that the country to the north could be simultaneously a British Dominion and a world citizen with an independent role on the international stage. The United States opposed Canadian membership in the Pan American Union of western hemispheric states on the grounds that it was still a European colony—although Canada did not want to join in any event.

Along with a fear of being drawn into war through the League-imposed collective security, U.S. antagonism toward a separate Canadian seat in the League of Nations was one of the most frequent reasons for the U.S. Senate's hostility toward the Treaty of Versailles. In his defense of the League, President Woodrow Wilson urged that Canada have full membership. Canada occupied a position of "considerable importance in the industrial world," he told American Federation of Labor president Samuel Gompers, and because the "problems of the chief British Colonies and Dominions are much more like our own than like Great Britain's," Canada would be inclined toward the United States. During his 1919 tour to build public support for the League, he asked an audience in Colorado, "is not Canada more likely to agree with the United States than with Great Britain? Canada has a speaking part." But the Senate won out; Wilson lost his League, and his Democratic party lost the White House in 1920.[3]

Canadian leaders were profoundly disappointed by the U.S. rejection of the League of Nations and the apparent trend to isolationism under new president Warren G. Harding. Canadians were, however, equally unwilling to participate in military or economic actions to enforce collective security, as required under Article X of the League of Nations Covenant. Both countries blamed Europe as the source of the world's problems (although Canadians made a clear distinction between Britain and Europe) and moralized about how much better North Americans got along together than did European neighbors such as Germany and France. In Europe, anti-League senator William E. Borah liked to say, "there's not a square foot that hasn't been ankle-deep in blood"; Canadian delegate N. W. Rowell said the same thing to the League of Nations assembly at Geneva, blaming "European statesmen, European policies and European ambitions" for having "drenched the world in blood." The United States avoided collective security by refusing to join the League; Canada became a member and bored (in both senses of the verb) from within with long-winded speeches about the lessons the world could learn from "three thousand miles of undefended frontier" between the United States and Canada. Canada's first major international achievement was to amend and redefine the League

Charter to disable its collective security provisions. By 1925, Canadian delegates at Geneva had reshaped the League along exactly the lines Senator Henry Cabot Lodge had proposed in the Senate debate over the League six years earlier! To Canada's disappointment, however, this did not persuade the United States to change its mind.[4]

After the Senate repudiated President Wilson's treaty and thus the League, Canadian leaders concluded that U.S. politicians were infantile, unaware, and afraid of their responsibilities to the postwar world. "The U.S. has simply got to get back into the international game," *Manitoba Free Press* editor John W. Dafoe wrote to his publisher Clifford Sifton in 1921. Whatever their reservations about the U.S. nonparticipation in the League of Nations, Prime Minister Robert Borden and his colleagues had built their hopes for the postwar world in part on the continued blossoming of the Anglo-American alliance. Such cooperation would insulate Canada from U.S. hostility and allow the country to bask in a glorious Pax Anglo-Americana.[5]

Arthur Meighen's short-lived Conservative government made the Canadian desire to strengthen the Anglo-American relationship evident at the London Imperial Conference of 1921. Meighen strongly pressed Britain to abrogate the 1902 Anglo-Japanese naval alliance in the interest of Anglo-American solidarity. President Harding and Secretary of State Charles Evans Hughes were determined to sever the British-Japanese alliance, fearing that Japanese expansionism in the Pacific would provoke a regional war in which Japan could require British support. When delegates gathered later that year in Washington for the naval disarmament conference summoned by Secretary of State Hughes, former prime minister Robert Borden represented Canada in the British delegation; Japan was cut adrift in the interest of Anglo-American solidarity. The Washington treaties doomed the Anglo-Japanese alliance. Yet there were problems with this strategy unforeseen by Borden and the Americans. Without the Anglo-Japanese alliance, Japan became more isolated and more insecure in the Pacific; it was not surprising that it came into conflict with British and U.S. interests. The U.S. and British positions had also been compromised. The

United States was neither capable of nor committed to maintaining stability in China and the Far East; Australia and New Zealand were more vulnerable, and Canada could make no naval contribution at all in the Pacific. This was but one of the reasons that Canada's military dependency on the United States increased in the interwar period.[6]

Canada's relationship with the United States had become almost as important as that with Britain, in practical if not in emotional terms. In 1917 and 1918, Canada had set out on the road to formal independent relations with the United States, but the ad hoc wartime arrangements ended with the peace, and so the Canadian government pressed for the appointment of a Canadian minister in Washington. The British Colonial and Foreign offices feared a precedent that would end with imperial disintegration, but Secretary of State Bainbridge Colby and Senator Gilbert M. Hitchcock, chairman of the Foreign Relations Committee, anticipated "good results" would follow from putting "us in direct relation with the Canadian Government." After negotiation among Ottawa, Washington, and London, the Borden government announced in 1920 that a separate Canadian minister would be appointed. In keeping with Canada's continued desire for a degree of British Empire unity, the new minister would serve in the additional capacity of second-in-command of the British embassy and "also speak as a representative of the Empire though primarily as a Canadian." The Conservative government was defeated before such a hybrid ambassador could be appointed.[7]

When Liberal prime minister William Lyon Mackenzie King took office in December 1921, he rejected a dual assignment for a Canadian representative in Washington; better, he suggested, to "let British diplomatists manage British affairs and let us manage our own affairs." Greater Canadian autonomy was a consistent theme of King's long prime ministerships (1922–30, 1935–48). King appointed Queen's University political economist O. D. Skelton as undersecretary of the Department of External Affairs. Even more than King, Skelton sought a Canadian external policy autonomous of Britain. Their approach was critical to the emergence of an independent, bilateral, U.S.-Canadian relationship. But because public opinion and his own cabinet were divided on the matter, King waited five years to establish separate formal Canadian representation in Washington.[8]

Instead, Mackenzie King's first trip to Washington in July 1922 had the ostensible purpose of revising the Rush-Bagot agreement of 1817 on Great Lakes naval armament. The *New York Times* pointed out that "there has been no suggestion formally from this [Harding] administration that modification was considered necessary," and no new agreement came about. King dropped in on Secretary of State Charles Evans Hughes, chatted with President Harding, and issued a statement to the press that Canadian-U.S. friendship was "an object lesson to the continents of Europe and Asia of New World methods in the maintenance of international peace." The trip exemplified what would become King's favorite technique for conducting Canadian-U.S. relations: during twenty-three years as prime minister he was to make twenty-four such visits for "summit diplomacy" with Presidents Coolidge, Roosevelt, and Truman.[9]

King demonstrated the real and symbolic significance he attached to the United States in Canada's external policy again in March 1923 when he chose Washington as the place to establish a historic precedent, the signing of a treaty between a dominion and a foreign state without the co-signature of a representative of the British government. King seized on the renegotiated Pacific Halibut Treaty as a step toward a broader diplomatic goal of an independent Canadian voice in Washington. Charles Evans Hughes signed for the United States; with the acquiescence of the British government, Canadian minister of marine and fisheries Ernest Lapointe ignored the objections of the British ambassador and signed the treaty alone. "This may turn out to be a very significant day in the history of relations between Canada and the United States," Hughes is alleged to have commented, but discussion in the U.S. Senate contained no hint of any recognition of Canada and instead described the treaty as a "convention between the United States and Great Britain." The only extensive news coverage the agreement received was in British Columbia and Washington State, where fishers cared more about the halibut than the constitutional precedent.[10]

A more portentous constitutional moment came three years later, when the report of the Imperial Conference of 1926 defined Canada and the other British Dominions as "autonomous Communities within the British Empire, in no way subordinate [to Britain], . . . though united by a common allegiance to the crown." Mackenzie King waited for this declaration to announce that there would at last be formal Canadian representation in Washington. To demonstrate that Canada still valued its British connection, the terms "minister" and "legation" were used instead of "ambassador" and "embassy," and the new minister, Toronto industrialist Vincent Massey, was appointed via London through appropriate Privy Council and Royal channels. Massey was chosen in part for his Oxford training and his anglophilia—he and his wife, Alice, went to England to purchase all the furnishings for the new Canadian legation house—and he worked closely with British ambassador Sir Esme Howard to create in practice the sort of British-Canadian cooperation in Washington that Borden had once envisaged. Massey soon voiced the Canadian lament that Americans were ignorant about their northern neighbor. When he presented his credentials in February 1927 to Calvin Coolidge—who had been born and raised in the border state of Vermont and spent his entire political career in Massachusetts—the president asked if Massey's home town of Toronto were anywhere near Lake Ontario! Coolidge initially dismissed the idea of a U.S. legation in Ottawa, arguing that the diplomats would have nothing to do, but Massey's arrival prompted reciprocal action. In June 1927, William Phillips, a career foreign service officer and former American ambassador to Belgium, arrived as the first U.S. minister to Canada. This exchange of diplomatic representatives culminated two decades of gradual transition to truly U.S.-Canadian relations, and the energy, abilities, and commitment of Massey and Phillips cemented ties of state between the two neighbors during their three years in office. The varying circumstances of their appointments, however, showed how much more important the U.S.-Canadian relationship was to the smaller neighbor than it was to the larger one.[11]

The most contentious issues that the two legations faced were the ongoing problems created by Prohibition, the last legacy of the vanished idealism of progressive reform. Both Canada and the United States attempted it. In Canada, however, prohibition of liquor was entirely a provincial responsibility. Quebec never declared itself dry, and seven of the other eight provinces returned to varying degrees of moisture during the 1920s. The United States imposed Prohibition on a national scale in 1919 by the Eighteenth Amendment to the Constitution. The "noble experiment" was a disaster from the outset, for the Volstead Act that Congress passed to implement the arid millennium was virtually unenforceable. Instead U.S. Prohibition became an economic windfall for Canada, as entrepreneurs on both sides of the boundary immediately understood that vast profits awaited those who connected legal Canadian liquor with thirsty American throats. Prohibition Era earnings launched Canadian distillers to North American dominance in the industry. Some of the profits were made legally from increased tourism, as Canadian cities attracted U.S. vacationers and convention-goers. Winnipeg, Manitoba, advertised itself in the U.S. Midwest as "the city of snowballs and highballs." Much greater profits were made when Canadian "rum-runners" exported liquor to American "bootleggers." Canada, reported the *Ladies' Home Journal,* was "the headwaters of the Niagara of booze"—a million gallons of spirits a year—that was drowning Prohibition in the Republic. Prohibition enforcement was the largest single subject in U.S.-Canadian diplomatic correspondence during the fourteen years of the Eighteenth Amendment. U.S. officials requested that Canada deny shipping clearances to cargoes of alcoholic beverages that might wind up in the United States. Canada admitted no wrongdoing: it was legal to distill whisky and brew beer in Canada, and legal to export them. What happened to the exported liquor was not Canada's concern. "I don't even know what street Canada's on," gangster Al Capone told a Chicago grand jury curious about the origins of the alcohol in his speakeasies. After informal bilateral discussions in 1929 (informal so that the United States could avoid looking like a bully and Canada avoid appearing to give in), Prime Minister King grudgingly introduced legislation to ban liquor exports to countries under prohibition.[12]

Both before and after the ban, however, high-speed automobile chases and high-seas pursuits of Canadian rumrunners by U.S. law enforcement agencies led to diplomatic disputes between Canada and the United States. Overzealous U.S. Coast Guard captains went well beyond the twelve-mile limit: in 1929 the USS *Dexter* sank the Canadian rum-running schooner *I'm Alone* two hundred miles from the Louisiana coast in the Gulf of Mexico. U.S. newspapers praised the Coast Guard for standing up to "foreign bootleggers"; Canadian editors derided the United States as "the bully of the high seas." The State Department at first officially informed the British embassy in Washington before being firmly redirected to the Canadian legation. If nothing else, Prohibition gently reminded the U.S. government that Canada was no longer a British colony to be dealt with through London. More provocative than attacks on Canadian ships were U.S. prohibition agents who in "hot pursuit" chased rumrunners north of the international boundary. When Ontario bootlegger Arthur "Muskrat" Laframboise took a bullet on the Canadian side of the Detroit River, newspapers chorused outrage at "United States patrolmen [who] stalk their prey on Canadian soil and shoot to kill." Canadian policemen, one editorial noted, could "catch rumrunners without firearms."[13]

Economic Continentalism

The U.S. and Canadian economies followed parallel tracks after World War I. Thirty percent inflation in 1919 was followed by sudden contraction in 1920 and by the sharpest short-term economic downturn either country had yet experienced. Recovery came in 1922 in the United States and followed more slowly in Canada because the U.S. Fordney-McCumber tariff impeded Canadian exports. The recovery heralded an unprecedented economic expansion that in both countries lasted until 1929, long enough for President Herbert Hoover to declare that the United States was close to "the final triumph over poverty." The way in which Canada's business cycle echoed that of its larger trading partner was a pattern accentuated during the 1920s. When the United States was in good economic health, said commentators, so was

Canada; if the U.S. economy caught cold, they quipped, the Canadian economy developed pneumonia.[14]

A 1920s Canadian resource boom was inspired by U.S. demand and carried out in large part with imported American capital. Growth of Canada's newsprint paper industry, for example, was tied to increased circulation and size of the American newspapers: the Sunday *Chicago Tribune* required fifty thousand tons of newsprint a year from the *Tribune* corporation's Quebec mill. Canadian provincial governments refused to allow the export of unprocessed pulpwood to make newsprint in the United States. Unrestricted access for Canadian newsprint to the U.S. market was guaranteed by the 1913 Underwood Tariff Act, and American publishers used the power of their newspapers to protect this privilege; even in the protectionist atmosphere of the 1920s, Republican Congresses never dared to restore the duty. So U.S. papers bought newsprint from Canadians, or, like Colonel John McCormack's *Tribune*, came to Canada to manufacture it. By 1929, American capital controlled over a third of Canada's pulp and paper industry. Demand for Canadian base metals also came from the United States; the automobile, electrical, and radio industries used copper, nickel, lead, and zinc. The capital to create a large-scale mining and smelting enterprise was imported from the United States. The two largest copper-gold deposits opened during the 1920s were both controlled by the United States: Hudson Bay Mining and Smelting, in Manitoba, by the H. P. Whitney Company of New York, and Noranda Mines, in Quebec, by a syndicate that included a Rockefeller and a Du Pont. By 1930, 40 percent of mineral production in Canada was in the hands of U.S. companies. Canadian politicians, national and provincial, welcomed foreign capitalists and assisted them with the necessary infrastructure of railways and hydroelectric power plants. The generating potential of Canada's northern rivers was one of the attractions to U.S. investment; hydropower inspired American multimillionaires James B. Duke and Andrew W. Mellon to bring the Aluminum Company of America to Quebec in 1924.[15]

American capital went into Canada's secondary manufacturing sector as well, in particular into the rapidly expanding auto industry. Next to the United States, Canada had the highest per capita registration of motor vehicles in the world. Canadian automobile ownership would have been even greater had there not been an ad valorem Canadian protective tariff of 35 percent on imported passenger cars. But the tariff did what it was intended to do: encourage American automakers to establish branch plants in Canada. The president of Studebaker bluntly explained that his company assembled cars in Canada "purely because of the tariff." Studebaker, Packard, Willys-Overland, and the small U.S. manufacturers only assembled cars in Canada; Ford, General Motors, and Chrysler established factories that actually built automobiles. This enabled them to take advantage of the preferential duties allowed by Canada's membership in the Empire-Commonwealth to export cars to Britain, Australia, New Zealand, South Africa, and the West Indies. The auto industry was unusual among Canadian manufacturing industries in that almost one-third of its products were sold outside the domestic market. As a "miniature replica" of the U.S. auto industry, Canadian automobile production concentrated into a small number of very large corporations. Every independent Canadian automaker vanished. By 1930, three of every four cars made in Canada were Ford, GM, or Chrysler products. Hundreds of small U.S. manufacturers also failed to survive, but "automotive amalgamation" illustrated the particular problems of Canada's manufacturing economy. As the owner of a Canadian company absorbed by General Motors explained, "in Canada . . . the problems of distribution are so severe on account of the tremendous distance over which a product must be scattered to meet the market of a small population. . . . The successful companies of Canada have found it necessary to affiliate themselves with American interests, because with our small and limited outputs it is impossible to carry the tremendous burden of engineering expenses."[16]

American business had no fears about Canada as a source of supply for raw materials or as a market; it was also a place to carry out monopolistic activities that would have been illegal in the United States because of stronger U.S. antitrust laws. By the 1918 Webb-Pomerene Act, Congress made it legal for U.S. corporations to violate those laws in their operations abroad. Canada scarcely seemed alien to Ameri-

can capitalists accustomed to a more difficult Latin American investment environment. As historian Mira Wilkins puts it, "governments
were stable and friendly . . . people, institutions, values, and customs
were similar . . . risks [were] minimal." Food processors such as Swift,
Borden, Kellogg, and Kraft even found that "tastes seemed similar to
those in the United States." Coca Cola discovered that "climatic . . . and
racial factors"—cold weather and French Canadians—didn't hurt the
sales of Coke. Canadians actually enjoyed "the pause that refreshes"
more often per capita than Americans did, and Canadian sales more
than doubled between 1926 and 1929, until the Montreal bottling plant
became the second largest in the world.[17]

Canadian development had always been financed in part by foreign investment, and in relative terms, Canada was actually somewhat
less reliant on foreign investment in the interwar period than it had
been before 1914; during the 1920s, however, foreign capital was extremely important in absolute terms in the four industries that grew
dramatically: pulp and paper, mining and smelting, hydroelectricity,
and automobile manufacturing. What was most significant about foreign investment in the twenties was that both its source and its nature
changed. Great Britain, Canada's "mother country," was displaced by
the United States as Canada's principal creditor sometime in 1922; the
American advantage widened thereafter. U.S. investment in Canada
also differed from British in that a greater proportion of it was *direct*
investment ("subsidiaries and branch plants controlled by externally-
based parent corporations") than *portfolio* investment ("the import of
foreign capital by the sale of bonds or debentures or non-controlling
equity stock.") In 1921, the *Journal of the Canadian Bankers' Association*
explained the difference to its readers with a concrete example: "the
capital for Canadian railways has come chiefly from England, and the
lenders remained at home; the capital for mining . . . has come largely
from the United States, and the investors have often come with it in
person to see it put into the ground." British capital rarely established
branch plants; U.S. capital owned 466 branch plants in 1918 and established 641 more in the next twelve years. British portfolio investments
in the form of bonds or common stock could expire or be patriated;

American direct investments remained and grew larger from the profits earned in Canada. The expansion of the U.S.-owned automobile industry, for example, was financed primarily by reinvested earnings in Canada, not by actual exports of American capital; thus U.S. control increased even if the international flow of investment slackened. As of 1930, one-fifth of the "book value" of Canadian industry and more than two-fifths of mining, smelting, and petroleum was controlled by U.S. firms.[18]

A half-century later, economists began to suggest that heavy reliance on U.S. direct investment had stunted the development of the Canadian economy. They argued that the U.S. companies that came to Canada exported raw materials with little processing in Canada and frustrated Canadian attempts to expand their country's secondary manufacturing industries: U.S. capital put U.S. interests first. As historian José Igartua has put it, "resource regions of Canada were simple pawns on the continental, even global, chessboard of American corporate capitalism, . . . [and] Canadian capitalists were not very formidable knights." But during the 1920s, serious criticism of the growing U.S. economic presence in Canada was seldom heard. The most persistent critique of American investment came from French-Canadian nationalists, concerned about the effects of urbanization and industrialization upon Quebec society. No critic offered Canadians a serious alternative path to economic development; instead, textbook descriptions of the Canadian economy assured students that the importation of capital from the United States was but a temporary phase in Canada's rise to its predestined industrial might. Annexation no longer frightened anyone. "The [American] flag," concluded the *Regina Leader*, "does not follow cash." The owners of the branch plants, far from advocating continental economic unity, became the most vociferous defenders of the protective tariff; that, after all, was why they had come to Canada in the first place. Canada raised no barriers to continued U.S. investment and expressed less concern about it than any other country in which U.S. corporations did business. In July 1923, Warren G. Harding made the first visit to Canada by a president in office. Before a crowd of 40,000 in Vancouver, he praised Canada's cooperativeness. "We think the same thoughts, live the same lives and cherish the same aspirations. . . . Since the Armistice . . . approximately $2,500,000,000 has found its way from the United States into Canada for investment. That is a huge sum of money and I have no doubt it is employed safely for us and helpfully for you."[19]

Cultural "Imperialism" and Cultural Sovereignty

Cultural forces also drew Canada closer to the United States after World War I. The middle-aged members of the Imperial Order of Daughters of the Empire worried because "hundreds of energetic young women" were joining the "Junior League" rather than the IODE. Thousands of their husbands attended the weekly luncheon of a Canadian chapter of an American "service" club. Rotary had been the first to come north in 1920; by 1928, it had eighty-five Canadian chapters. During the twenties Rotary was joined by the Lions, Kiwanis, and Gyro clubs, each of which expanded rapidly throughout Canada. Clubs in Canadian provinces linked with those in adjoining American states; a Gyro pamphlet proudly proclaimed that the club "recognizes no boundary between the United States of America and the Dominion of Canada." Every summer at binational conventions, Rotarians, Gyros, Lions, and Kiwanians met in happy celebration of the "invisible border" and babbled about "the harmonious relationship that has always existed between the United States and Canada." More alarming than the service clubs to Canadian cultural nationalists were American radio programs, spectator sports, magazines, and movies. American mass culture touched every nation-state on the planet to some degree, but Canada's situation was unique. First, 70 percent of Canada's population shares a language with the United States. Second, English Canadians had no long separate history upon which to build a national identity: like Americans, they trace their ideological roots back to seventeenth-century England. Finally, Canadian exposure to U.S. mass culture was not mitigated by distance: 80 percent of the Canadian population lived within sixty miles of the U.S. border.[20]

This explains why Canada has been in quest of "cultural sovereignty" almost as long as the United States has been exporting popular culture. Prodded by a nationalist intelligentsia and by Canadian cultural industries seeking the same protected market enjoyed by other Canadian manufacturers, successive governments have groped to cope with American mass culture. The invariable first step has been to investigate. After royal commissions or parliamentary committees have issued weighty reports, one of two types of legislation usually follows: attempts to *protect* Canadian cultural industries with regulatory or tariff barriers, and attempts to *promote* indigenous Canadian mass culture through subsidies or government-sponsored creation of cultural infrastructure. Policies have not always been clear cut; protectionist and promotional solutions were sometimes applied alternately or even simultaneously.

Canada directed its first unambiguously protective cultural legislation against American magazines. In 1925, four U.S. magazines had larger circulations than the leading Canadian journal (then as now *Maclean's*); the *Saturday Evening Post* rubbed salt into the circulatory wounds of its Canadian competitors by accurately describing itself as "Canada's best-selling magazine." The subsequent campaign against U.S. magazines illustrates the typical alignment of commercial and cultural forces behind campaigns for cultural sovereignty. Publishing entrepreneurs seeking an advantage against their U.S. competitors combined with a nationalist intelligentsia who argued that American magazines were "a menace to Canadian ideals and to the moral development of the youth of this country." It was difficult to portray the *Saturday Evening Post* or *Ladies Home Journal* as immoral influences, so the target became "pulp" magazines imported from the United States, with titles like *Black Mask, Dime Detective,* and *Spicy Adventure,* "the off-scourings of the moral sewers of human life, . . . a putrid flood of undisguised filth." Aroused Canadians demanded that something be done "to dam this trash flowing over the border." The King Liberal government evaded demands for a magazine tariff in the 1920s by offering Canadian publishers a tax incentive, a "drawback" on the import duties they paid on special grades of papers. In 1930, R. B. Bennett's new Conservative government obliged the Magazine Publishers'

Association of Canada with a tariff that quickly had the desired effect: by the mid–1930s, Canadian circulation was up 65 percent and that of U.S. magazines down an equal amount.[21]

Unlike magazines, the newspapers Canadians read were owned and published in Canada, but after World War I Canadian dailies became much more like their American counterparts. Wire services reinforced homogeneity, using the new teletype machine to speed stories simultaneously to a network of subscribing newspapers, which reprinted them with little editing or rewriting. Canadian newspapers, whether English or French, drew virtually all of their international news from Associated Press and United Press International. Thus Canadians learned about the League of Nations through the eyes of U.S. correspondents in Geneva in stories that reflected America's attitude as an isolationist nonmember. Canadian front pages emulated U.S. dailies by using larger photos, bolder type, and banner headlines to report sports, crime, and the marital problems of movie stars. Editors padded the inside pages with columns on bridge, hobbies, auto repair, and personal advice distributed by U.S. syndicates. The most popular new feature was the American "comics," black-and-white strips on weekdays and a color section on Saturday—Canada was not yet ready for newspapers on the Christian Sabbath. Circulation of the *Toronto Star Weekly* doubled when it acquired *Bringing Up Father, Barney Google, Mutt and Jeff,* and five other U.S. strips in 1923. The audience for the comics was not restricted to children or to the semi-literate; Prime Minister Mackenzie King was said never to miss his favorite strip, *Tillie the Toiler*.[22]

American mass culture dominated the sports pages as well. As journalists hammered larger-than-life heroes out of Babe Ruth, Jack Dempsey, and Bobby Jones, America's sports heroes became Canada's. Baseball had been Canada's summer game since the sport's mid-nineteenth-century beginnings, and historian William Humber's research proves that "Canadians created the game as much as their American neighbours." By the 1920s, however, baseball had imprinted itself as "America's national pastime," and Canadian cultural nationalists mistakenly cited the ubiquity of the game in Canada as further evidence of "Americanization." Transborder leagues did attach many of the Canadian teams in minor professional baseball to a binational network based in the United States. In 1922, for example, the Brantford Red Sox, Hamilton Tigers, London Tecumsehs, and Kitchener Beavers made up half of the class "B" Michigan-Ontario League, while teams from Calgary, Edmonton, and Vancouver competed in the class "B" Western International League; the Toronto Maple Leafs played in the International League, one step below the majors. Yet every Canadian ball fan reserved the deepest love for a team in the American or National League. By the mid-twenties baseball's World Series had become Canada's greatest "national" sporting event, with crowds packed in front of newspaper offices to watch the games charted out on a scale-model diamond from a wire service description. During the 1920s, U.S. money also revolutionized Canadian hockey. In 1924, Boston millionaire Charles Adams bought the National Hockey League's first U.S. franchise, and before the next season began, bootlegger William V. "Big Bill" Dwyer bought the Hamilton Tigers and moved them into the new Madison Square Garden as the New York Americans. New York drew two hundred thousand customers to their seventeen home games—more than the combined attendance of any four cities of the Western Canada Hockey League. "How long will Canada be able to hold its teams?" asked a Toronto sportswriter. When the NHL awarded franchises to a Chicago financier, a New York coffee tycoon, and a Detroit syndicate that included a Ford and a Kresge among its members, hockey entrepreneurs in small Canadian cities sold stars like Eddie Shore and Dick Irvin to the U.S.-based teams before the players could "jump" themselves. Canada's winter game had been transformed into a continental commercial spectacle. Only four of the ten NHL teams were based in Canada, and the league's "Canadian" division was brought up to full strength by adding the New York Americans! In 1928, the New York Rangers became the first of the U.S. NHL teams to win the Stanley Cup, donated by former governor general Lord Stanley's trophy to honor "the leading hockey club in Canada."[23]

Government intervention to protect Canadian commercial sport lay half a century in the future. What became the most characteristic Canadian promotional response to the conundrum of cultural sovereignty was the approach adopted in broadcasting: the creation of publicly financed infrastructure. Radio broadcasting in the United States and Canada began almost simultaneously, but subsequent development of the medium in the United States was much more rapid. During the 1920s, the United States determined that radio was to be a private enterprise supported financially by the sale of advertising time, with the government's role limited to regulation by the Federal Radio Commission. By 1930, there were 612 U.S. stations, and two private networks had spread across the country, the National Broadcasting Company and the Columbia Broadcasting System. Canadians debated whether to follow the private commercial model of the United States or to make radio broadcasting a public noncommercial monopoly as was being done in Britain. By a U.S.-Canadian agreement reached in 1924, Canada obtained exclusive use of 6 frequencies and partial use of another 11 of the 95 then in operation. Canadian broadcasters grumbled that "86 percent of the impulse carrying power of the atmosphere" had been handed over to extol "the superior qualities of American soap, pills and jazz." The weaker signals of the small transmitters of Canadian stations were often drowned out by interference from more powerful U.S. stations. By 1929, most of Canada's 297,000 radios were tuned to American stations. Even the Mounties at northern RCMP detachments got their daily bulletins over KDKA Pittsburgh. More than reception influenced these choices. Canadian stations offered news, lectures, or recorded music, while the American network stations featured comedy, drama, and live variety. Canadian listeners quickly made clear that they preferred U.S. shows such as *Amos and Andy* to Canadian programs such as *Uncle Dick's Talks for Boys and Girls*. Commercial stations in Canada soon decided that the best way to compete with U.S. stations was to buy and rebroadcast U.S. shows. CFRB Toronto affiliated with CBS, CKGW Toronto joined the NBC network, and stations in other cities hurried to follow. By the end of the 1920s an estimated 80 percent of the programs Canadians listened to were American. As one writer protested, "Canada's radio consciousness" was "throwing us all the more under United States influence." [24]

The King Liberal government referred the broadcasting question to a royal commission chaired by a bank president, Sir John Aird. Aird and his fellow commissioners visited Europe and the United States and held public hearings before concluding that broadcasting in Canada should be a public monopoly with strictly limited commercial content. The Canadian Radio League, a lobby group for public broadcasting, use the slogan "Britannia rules the waves—shall Columbia rule the wavelengths?" and told Canadians that the choice was "the State or the United States!" The creation in 1932 of the Canadian Radio Broadcasting Commission, which became the Canadian Broadcasting Corporation (CBC) in 1936, marks the most visible difference between the cultural industries of Canada and the United States: Canada has a publicly owned and publicly financed national broadcasting system, and the United States does not. Significantly, however, the CBC was not given a monopoly; private broadcasting continued and flourished. As a mixed public and private enterprise, Canadian broadcasting borrowed from both the British and the U.S. answers to the radio question. U.S. programs did not disappear. Among the most popular shows on the new coast-to-coast public radio network were those that the CBC bought from NBC and CBS![25]

Canada found no cultural dam to hold back Hollywood. On weekends in interwar decades, over a million Canadians sat in the dark in front of the screen, and 98 percent of the movies they watched were products of the suddenly famous Los Angeles suburb. Canada's small-scale feature film industry succumbed rapidly to Hollywood competition after World War I. It died for economic rather than artistic reasons, for a host of talented Canadians contributed to Hollywood's golden age: director Mack Sennett, producers Louis B. Mayer and Jack Warner, and too many performers to be counted. Gladys Smith—better known as Mary Pickford, "America's Sweetheart"—learned her craft in Toronto; Norma Shearer of Westmount, Quebec, and Marie Dressler of Cobourg, Ontario, won the first two Academy Awards for best actress. The supreme irony was that Raymond Massey, Hollywood's best Abraham Lincoln, was Vincent Massey's younger brother! But U.S. films dominated the screens of the world, not simply those of Canada. U.S. moviemakers gained a head start between 1914 and 1917 and consolidated their position by vertically integrating production, distribution, and marketing during the 1920s. Giant Hollywood studios devoured Canada's independent producers not because they were Canadian but because they were independent. Within the American industry itself, the "Big Five"—Paramount, MGM, Warner Brothers, Fox, and RKO— produced 90 percent of all feature films by 1929. These major studios regarded Canada as part of their "domestic" box office, and they extended their distribution and marketing northward through Famous Players Canadian Corporation. Famous Players monopolized the giant "movie palaces" in prime downtown locations and forced independent theaters to "block book" their films if they were to have films to exhibit. The Canadian federal government used its toothless antimonopoly legislation—the Combines Investigation Act of 1923—to prepare a report on Famous Players, but a 1931 Ontario prosecution based on the evidence in the report was dismissed. The judge found Famous Players' practices to be ruthless, but not technically illegal.[26]

With no Canadian film industry to add a commercial voice, Canadian cultural nationalists met the U.S. movie menace on moral terrain. Each Canadian province censored motion pictures, watching out for films that demeaned clergymen or marriage and for "the revolver that every he-man seems to have on one hip." Censors also snipped "spread-eagle Americanism"—close-ups of the Stars and Stripes and movies in which the U.S. Army won World War I were particularly vulnerable to the scissors. Canadian elites worried that by holding authority figures up to ridicule, U.S. movies might do more to inspire social unrest "than all the Bolshevist agitators." They need not have been concerned. During the Depression of the 1930s, Hollywood's "dream factory" became one of the most important buttresses of the status quo in both countries. Canadian governments attempted to neutralize Hollywood by making their own movies. The Canadian Government Motion Picture Bureau (CGMPB) and provincial film agencies in British Columbia and Ontario were modest operations that made scenic documentaries that were virtuous but dull. When these pictures were screened, Canadian audiences headed to the lobby for popcorn; like moviegoers everywhere, they wanted entertainment, not education, and the cinematic experiments of Ontario and British Columbia ended in the 1930s. The CGMPB survived to make a more substantial contribution after it was restructured as the National Film Board in 1939.[27]

Americans found it difficult to take Canadian complaints about U.S. movies, magazines, and radio seriously. Historian Emily Rosenberg describes the ideology of Americans who dealt with foreign nations as "liberal-developmentalism": "the belief that other nations could and should replicate the American experience." To do this, foreigners had not only to welcome U.S. trade and investment but to accept "the free flow of information and culture." When Canada's Parliament first discussed restricting U.S. magazines, for example, the *New York Times* laughed at Canadian fears of "cultural extinction" and invoked the First Amendment's promise of freedom of the press. "We have learned better, . . . the Canadians, too, may learn." If Canada did ban U.S. magazines, the *Times* suggested "an agreeable form of reciprocity. As Canada bootlegs rum to us, we could bootleg literature to Canada." The U.S. government and the industries concerned took Canadian cultural policies more seriously. Earnings from cultural exports were significant, so much so that the U.S. Department of Commerce cooperated with cultural exporters such as the Motion Picture Producers and Distributors of America (MPPDA) to keep foreign markets open, part of the process historian Michael Hogan has called government-business "associationalism." The State Department instructed American consuls in Canada (and everywhere else the United States did business) to monitor cultural nationalism closely. Canada's cultural concerns were invariably interpreted as masks for economic protectionism—which they sometimes were—but Americans were seldom able to distinguish economic protectionism from genuine concerns about culture and nationality. The State Department and the MPPDA, for example, protested provincial movie censorship as a cultural trade barrier. By and large, however, Canada's timid cultural nationalism gave the United States little to worry about compared to that of Britain. Overt cultural protectionism usually drew an immediate response, but Canadian attempts to promote domestic mass culture (and domestic high culture, for that matter) were usually ignored because these attempts did not seriously threaten the profits of the U.S. exporters. The documentary niche the National Film Board chose represented no danger to Hollywood's domination of feature film production, nor did U.S. broadcasters fear the demonstration effect of Canadian public radio. Corporate America showed a great deal more hostility to Ontario Hydro, the government-owned electrical power utility, than it did to experiments in public film production or broadcasting.[28]

Did the continentalization of popular culture prove that Canada was being turned into a cultural as well as an economic colony of the United States? In serious music, art, drama, and dance, Britain remained, as it had always been, the arbiter of Canadian tastes. Even in terms of popular culture, in many respects Canada in the interwar period had a better sense of itself as a nation than it had ever had. To use sport as an example, Canadian football evolved under unique rules distinct from those used in the U.S. game, even though teams hired American "imports" to help them win the national championship, the Grey Cup. Every Canadian fan knew that Vancouver sprinter Percy Williams, "the World's Fastest Human," had spurned U.S. colleges to train in Canada for his double gold medal performance at the 1928 Olympics, and that the Edmonton Grads had won seventeen consecutive North American women's basketball championships against the best the United States could send onto the court. And despite all the hot air about Canadian-American kinship, Canadians clung to their sense of national moral superiority, buttressed with negative stereotypes of the United States. To Canadians, the U.S. political and judicial systems were corrupt, and American society was immoral, violent, and materialistic. English and French Canadians, women and men, children and adults, businessmen and trade unionists shared these stereotypes. The *Canadian Unionist*, the newspaper of the All-Canadian Congress of Labour, summed it up succinctly: the United States was a country "where murderers go unhanged . . . where prohibition is the rule and bootlegging has been the practice . . . where child labour laws will not hold water and where negroes may not vote." Viewed through eyes narrowed by such a priori reasoning, American mass culture did not inspire pledges of allegiance to the Stars and Stripes. Instead, concluded *Canada and Her*

Great Neighbor: A Sociological Survey of Opinions and Attitudes in Canada Concerning the United States, it provided further evidence of things Canadians thought they already knew. U.S. magazines, wire service news, radio programs, and movies left Canadian readers, listeners, and viewers "convinced of the depravity of Americans." As William Phillips, the first American minister to Canada, soon discovered, the "much-talked-of 'invisible border' was in fact a very real barrier." Exactly where Canada stood was difficult for the few Americans who gave it any thought to understand. Canada had become more autonomous from Great Britain and could be prickly about that autonomy. Yet the British Empire connection manifestly still mattered, and autonomy from Britain did not herald the absorption of the Dominion into the United States. As the short section on "Canadian Relations" in a text on U.S. foreign policy explained, "it is certain that if Canada ever achieves complete independence, it will not be for the purpose of joining the United States."[29]

The "Mingling" of the Canadian and U.S. Peoples

Many individual Canadians and Canadian families, however, continued to choose America. In the 1920s, the southward flow of Canadian migrants resumed at almost the levels of the 1880s. One of the justifications for actively seeking U.S. investment continued to be (as it would be later for Mexico) the need to create economic growth and to provide jobs for these migrants at home. "Import dollars and keep our children" was how Quebec's Premier Louis-Alexandre Taschereau put it; better "to import American dollars than to export Canadians to the United States." But the inflow of capital failed to check the outflow of people. The U.S. Immigration Act of 1921 imposed quotas on Europeans but exempted Canadians from restrictions, despite some congressional demands that they be included. By 1923, observers noted that "the tide is once more flowing freely," and U.S. immigration statistics record over a million arrivals from Canada between 1919 and 1930. Canadians increased from about 6 percent of total immigration into the

United States to more than 25 percent. These statistics exaggerate the number of permanent migrants—more sophisticated calculations show net migration from Canada to the United States at about 385,000—but even so this was 4.3 percent of the total Canadian population. In the 1930 U.S. Census, the 1.3 million Canadian-born were the third largest group of foreign-born, after only Germans and Italians.[30]

As before, the émigrés went south for work. *Canadian Forum* speculated that "there is not a man in Canada under fifty years of age who would not pack up and move to the States tomorrow if he got a good business offer." U.S. employers found Canadians to be "reliable" employees, which meant, wrote a sarcastic Canadian commentator, "that they are more afraid of losing their jobs than are native-born Americans." A survey for the Canadian magazine *Maclean's* reported that eight out of ten of the emigrants preferred Canada but chose the United States for "better opportunities." Before World War I, unskilled workers and farm families had made up most of the exodus from Canada; after 1920, highly skilled and well-educated workers accompanied them in greater numbers, such as band leader Guy Lombardo and his "Royal Canadians," university professor John Kenneth Galbraith, and bank robber Alvin Karpis—a future "Public Enemy Number One." Because American branch plants dominated the advanced sectors of the Canadian economy, industrial research was done in the home laboratories of the parent corporations; thus Canada lost a substantial percentage of the "trained brains" graduated each year from its universities. *Maclean's* discovered that between 1919 and 1926, 11 percent of University of Toronto graduates, 15 percent of University of Western Ontario graduates, and 36 percent of graduates from Nova Scotia's Acadia University had moved to the United States. In medicine and engineering the figures were substantially higher. Canada was losing, commented J. B. Brebner, "if not the cream, at least the top milk of her population." The best American graduate schools attracted some of the best young Canadian scholars, many of whom took academic appointments in the United States after they completed their doctorates. In 1927, six hundred Canadians taught in U.S. universities, twice as many as twenty years earlier. Although this was often cited as an example of "intellectual internationalism," writes historian Carl Berger, "it was emphatically a one-way street": very few American students or professors came to Canada.[31]

Despite their anguish about the out-migration of Canadians to the United States, however, Canadians were outraged in 1930 when Congress imposed on Canada the same immigration requirements as on migrants from outside the hemisphere. Accustomed to unregulated movement across the border, Canadians' racist sensitivities were offended when they had to "join Latvia and Japan on the quota list" if they wished to live and work in the United States. Entry to the United States from Canada now had to be made through a formal "port of entry" staffed with guards, customs officials, and immigration officers, all of whom had "the manners of longshoremen." Some 15,000 Ontarians who crossed daily to work in Detroit suddenly found themselves unemployed. The U.S. Department of Immigration began to unceremoniously deport those foreign-born who became public charges. Canadians were appalled by reports of naturalized Canadians being deported not to Canada but to their places of birth: in one case, U.S. authorities sent Vancouver journalist Herbert Upjohn from Los Angeles to Shanghai, "handcuffed to sixty Chinese." Canadians should have hailed the closing of the border as a demographic blessing: allowing for the fertility of these vanished Canadians, Canada would have had a population of 16 million in 1931, rather than the 10.4 million actually counted in the Dominion census. Instead, Canadians in 1930 lamented the lost opportunities in the United States. Most of them thought that the new immigration policies were temporary; no Canadian or American could have imagined that the Great Depression of the 1930s had permanently altered the once-easy population movement across the U.S.-Canadian border.[32]

The End of Prosperity

As a response to the deepening Depression, the same Congress that shut the border to Canadian migrants effectively closed it to Canadian potatoes, beef, butter, and poultry exports with the Smoot-Hawley Tariff Act of 1930, the highest duties in U.S. history. Prime Minister Mackenzie King quietly sent a series of emissaries to warn President Hoover of Smoot-Hawley's serious economic and diplomatic effects. The *Literary Digest* and *The Nation* made the same case to the American public: Canada was "the best customer of the U.S.A.," two-way trade was the highest between any two nations in the world, and Canada bought one-third more from the United States than it sold to that country. Why jeopardize this with a tariff war? The president offered the prime minister an exchange: he would exempt Canada from the new tariffs in return for a Canadian promise to cooperate in one of Hoover's pet projects, a St. Lawrence Seaway to open the Great Lakes to oceangoing ships. The seaway would lower transportation costs to and from the U.S. Midwest and keep farmers voting Republican. But Hoover doomed the deal by leaking the offer to the press. His clumsy revelation backed the prime minister into a corner. Trading a seaway for a tariff exemption would mean yielding to U.S. pressure before a binational audience, and the prime minister understood that it was time to cater to his country's psychic need to stand up to Uncle Sam. King rejected Hoover's proposal to link the seaway and trade issues and retaliated for Smoot-Hawley with countervailing tariff increases and additional levies on steel and on fruits and vegetables. Canada had fired the second shot in the North American theater of the international trade war that exacerbated the Great Depression.[33]

This counterattack did not save King's Liberals from defeat in the Canadian election of July 1930. As in 1911, the opposition Conservatives played the card of anti-U.S. chauvinism with consummate skill. "Tens of thousands of American workmen are living on Canadian money," Conservative leader R. B. Bennett told his audiences, promising still-higher "red-blooded" tariffs. A Conservative government would stand up to "Mr. Hoover's rum-chasers" and end the indignities caused by Prohibition enforcement. One Conservative candidate called Mackenzie King "the right-hand man of the American government" and urged voters to send him "back where he belongs—back to work in New York City for the Rockefeller foundation." Once in office, the new government's first actions were to pass a five-page list of tariff increases and to slam Canada's door against immigrants. The irony of Canadian anti-Americanism was never more obvious: these Conservative policies were mirror images of U.S. Republican protectionism and nativism.[34]

Prime Minister Bennett proposed to replace vanished trade with the United States with expanded trade within the British Empire. He had scant success, however, in his attempts to reach reciprocal tariff agreements with Britain and the other Dominions. A much-publicized Imperial Economic Conference in Ottawa in 1932 aroused U.S. fears of a British Empire trading bloc, but its practical results were few. The United States need never have worried that its economic influence on Canada would diminish: even as tariff warfare and the Depression cut the total volume of Canadian-U.S. trade in half in the early 1930s, the Canadian economy intertwined with the American. As *Forbes* magazine explained, a high Canadian tariff, even with British Empire preferences, was, "from the American angle . . . not so bad, after all." U.S. exporters could easily out-hustle "the slow-going Britisher" for the Canadian market. "If worst comes to worst . . . , all that United States industry, following hundreds of examples, would need to do, is to establish more branch factories in Canada, get in on the protection to Canadian industry and, incidentally, avail itself of the present or coming policies of preference to manufacturers of any part of the British Empire." Operating in Canada was simplicity itself: "No questions would be asked and no conditions would be imposed" upon American capital. Thus the Conservatives' tariff increases escalated the number of U.S. branch plants in Canada from 524 in 1929 to 816 in 1936. In that year, U.S. companies controlled a quarter of manufacturing in Canada, a third of the mining, and two-thirds of the petroleum industry.[35]

That this situation caused no alarm to Canada's Conservative government illustrates the limits of its anti-Americanism. As a State Department briefing paper explained to President Hoover before he received the prime minister in Washington in 1931: "for political reasons . . . Mr. Bennett frequently finds it advisable to criticize us despite the fact that he personally is friendly to this country." True to this analysis,

Bennett tried to keep his brief meeting with the president almost a secret, refusing the already traditional photographs on the White House lawn; President Hoover's terse press release thanked "Mr. Bennet" for his visit. Hoover's ignorance of and indifference to Canada contributed a dimension of difficulty to U.S.-Canadian relations, as did Bennett's abrasive personal manner, but long-standing circumstances, not personalities, were at the root of bilateral problems. Diplomatic appointments and state visits illustrate the striking asymmetry of national power. Although Bennett had denounced the opening of a Canadian mission in Washington in 1927 as "the end of our connection with the Empire," in 1931 he appointed his confidante and brother-in-law, William D. Herridge, to replace Vincent Massey as minister to the United States. The political hacks Hoover chose to succeed William Phillips were without discernible competence, an indication of how lightly the White House took the new legation in Ottawa. In 1927, Governor General Lord Willingdon had made an official visit to Washington as Canada's head of state, but Hoover never found time to accept Ottawa's reciprocal invitation. Offended that Hoover was preoccupied with Latin America and ignored Canada, the *Ottawa Citizen* advised the president to "look North. If the goodwill of South America is worth cultivating, surely the goodwill of Canada is worth keeping."[36]

There were, in fact, notable joint initiatives during Hoover's and Bennett's two-year overlap in office. In 1932, at Britain's request, Canada contributed its entire Pacific Fleet of two destroyers to help the United States to prop up the dictatorship in El Salvador against a revolution. And Hoover and Bennett agreed to build a St. Lawrence seaway. A treaty was amicably negotiated and duly signed in July 1932 by Canadian minister W. D. Herridge and American secretary of state Henry L. Stimson. Had the seaway been constructed as a vast anti-Depression public works project and opened with pomp and circumstance during King George VI's visit to North America in 1939, Hoover and Bennett might be hailed by historians as great architects of binational amity. The collapse of the project illustrates how U.S.-Canadian relations move beyond the control of individual presidents and prime ministers. The president had to satisfy the Senate, and in 1934 the Seaway

Treaty failed to get the necessary two-thirds majority. The power of the provinces within the Canadian federation constrained the prime minister. Bennett ignored Quebec's objections to the seaway but ran aground when Ontario repudiated its pledge to pay part of the Canadian share of construction costs. The seaway languished for another quarter-century, and the historical reputations of Herbert Hoover and R. B. Bennett languished along with it.[37]

New Deal America—No Deal Canada

Like the Americans who voted for him, Canadians didn't at first know what to make of Franklin Roosevelt. "We have little to expect from Roosevelt," editorialized the *Canadian Forum*, "we only knew we could expect nothing at all from Hoover." The month of the inauguration, March 1933, was the pit of the Great Depression, with one-third of the workforce out of work in both countries. The new president served Americans an alphabet soup of federal regulatory and welfare agencies: the National Recovery Administration, the Agricultural Adjustment Administration, the Tennessee Valley Authority, the Federal Emergency Relief Administration. Roosevelt's "New Deal" did not stimulate full recovery, but it redefined the role of the state by broadening the federal government's managerial role in the economy. Through the Works Progress Administration and the Social Security Act, the New Deal rooted the modern welfare state in America. In 1933, the United States and Canada lagged far behind Western Europe in government acceptance of responsibility for individual citizens; by 1940, the United States had begun to catch up.[38]

The New Deal dealt Canada a mixed hand. Securities regulations interfered with borrowing in U.S. money markets, and Canadian pulp and paper companies had to accept NRA production and pricing rules to maintain access to U.S. newsprint buyers. The Roosevelt experiment also aroused unprecedented interest among Canadians. The Liberal Party invited Raymond Moley and Averill Harriman from Roosevelt's "brains trust" to Ontario to explain "the Meaning of the N.R.A.," and

British Columbia's Liberal premier proposed a "little New Deal" to the people of his province. The New Deal's specific influence on Canadian public policy is difficult to measure; as Harriman told the Canadian Liberals, "the New Deal is a point of view, not a fully developed social or economic theory." Those Canadians who sighed, "Oh, for a Roosevelt!" were more envious of the president's jaunty activism than of any of his particular programs. W. D. Herridge, who regularly entertained New Dealers at the Canadian legation in Washington, urged his brother-in-law R. B. Bennett to emulate Roosevelt. Specific legislation did not matter: ordinary Americans did not understand the New Deal "any more than they understood the signs of the zodiac." In January 1935 the prime minister paid the president the sincerest of compliments, that of plagiarism. In a series of radio talks modeled on FDR's "fireside chats," Bennett announced his own New Deal to Canadians. Bennett's conversion was an eleventh-hour attempt to save his Depression-doomed government, but he had a larger objective in common with Roosevelt. Both leaders espoused government intervention to save capitalism in North America, and they explained themselves to disgruntled conservatives in identical language.[39]

Their electoral fates, however, could not have been more different. Americans reelected Franklin Roosevelt with the largest majority yet accorded a president; extrapolating for the differences of the parliamentary system, Canadians rejected Bennett equally massively. They returned to the prime ministership William Lyon Mackenzie King, who had condemned Bennett's New Deal as "Hitlerism, Fascism or Communism." In 1936, while Roosevelt's WPA reduced U.S. relief rolls with a massive public works program, King set up commissions to investigate the Depression rather than agencies to relieve it. In fairness to King, Canada's dilemma was a failure of finances as much as of imagination: the Dominion could not afford the expenditures the United States undertook. The most frequently compared programs of America's New Deal and Canada's "no deal" were those for unemployed single men. In the United States, such men could join the Civilian Conservation Corps and build parkways and campsites; in Canada, they were dispatched to remote relief camps run by the military to dig holes and fill them up again. "While American CCC youths earn a dollar a day and their keep," an article in *The Nation* pointed out, "Canadian camp workers are paid twenty cents a day, less deductions." These national differences could be seen in microcosm in the International Peace Garden that straddled the North Dakota–Manitoba boundary. The Peace Garden centered on a cairn that read, "We two nations pledge ourselves that as long as men shall live, we will not take up arms against one another." By 1938, the American side of the Peace Garden had bloomed because the CCC had built a dam and planted a real garden; the Canadian side remained untended prairie.[40]

North America's binational labor movement also flowered during the New Deal. On both sides of the border, workers had confronted capital at the end of World War I. It seemed, writes historian David Montgomery, "that a unified movement . . . might be in the offing," an international movement "very different from the American Federation of Labor." In the industrial history of both countries, 1919 was the most strike-torn year. Among the 3,600 strikes in the United States and the 336 strikes in Canada were general strikes in Seattle, Washington, and Winnipeg, Manitoba. But in both countries, employers and governments joined forces to repress the labor revolt. The defeat of the attempt to organize the steel industry set the tone for the 1920s, as bosses used traditional union-busting techniques, combined with the carrot of "welfare capitalism"—benefit programs designed to avert organization. Faced with antiunionism in various guises, neither the American Federation of Labor (AFL) nor its Canadian affiliate and counterpart, the Trades and Labour Congress (TLC) of Canada, found a way to organize the fastest-growing sector of the North American economy, the technologically advanced mass production industries such as steel and automobile manufacturing. Union membership dropped in both countries during the 1920s, from five million to three million in the United States, and from four hundred thousand to three hundred thousand in Canada; the number of industrial disputes reached forty-year lows. When the American Federation of Labor held its 1929 convention in Toronto, the *Toronto Globe* noted that "the day of the firebrand and the spellbinder is gone" and that "the strike is discredited, except as an absolutely last resort." The *Globe* praised the AFL and the TLC for their political nonpartisanship, the opposite of the British model of an independent Labour Party. AFL president William Green's speech to the convention, replete with references to "the imaginary boundary line [with] no standing armies," was as vapid as anything a gathering of Rotarians might have listened to. Although seven of every ten unionized workers in Canada belonged to AFL unions, convention speakers criticized independent Canadian unions. "There is no room for two Labor movements in North America," Green made clear.[41]

The explosive growth of industrial unions that started three years later took the AFL and business by surprise. The social movement for unions organized by industry was born on the shop floors of both countries, as workers sought dignity and decent lives in the midst of economic uncertainty. Working-class discontent alone, however, would not have produced the mass industrial insurgency; U.S. New Deal labor legislation helped to make the new unions possible. Section 7(a) of the National Industrial Recovery Act, revised and strengthened as the Wagner Act in 1935, outlawed the most effective antiunion techniques of employers and established the National Labor Relations Board to supervise union certification. As important as the legislation was the new legitimacy that such recognition gave the labor movement. "The president wants you to join the union," organizers told workers as they signed their union cards. Union ranks swelled with recruits from the mass production industries until the AFL was unable to contain the growth within its craft union ranks. A rift began during the 1935 AFL convention, which led to the departure of the industrial unions as the autonomous Congress of Industrial Organizations in 1938. Under President John L. Lewis of the United Mine Workers of America, the CIO charted new political and industrial directions. In 1936, CIO unions violated a sacred AFL principle by committing money and campaign workers to the Democratic Party to ensure Roosevelt's re-election. In 1937, the CIO's United Steel Workers won recognition from U.S. Steel, and its United Auto Workers (UAW) signed a contract with General Motors (GM) after a six-week "sit-down" strike at GM's plant in Flint, Michigan. The GM strike, says historian Sidney Fine, was "the

most significant American labor conflict in the twentieth century."
The CIO had transformed industrial relations in the United States, but
at the heavy price of a profound division within the American labor
movement.[42]

The CIO had an instant presence in Canada through the Canadian
locals of seven of the founding industrial unions that left the AFL. As
a result, this division was reproduced in the ranks of Canadian labor
when AFL president Green ordered the TLC to expel the CIO deviants.
Unfortunately for unorganized workers in Canada, the CIO's success
did not travel north as completely as did this schism. The CIO was too
organizationally overburdened to expand and more inclined to accept
Canadian autonomy than the AFL was. "Canada must develop its own
leaders if it is to have a sound labor movement," was how Sidney Hillman of the Amalgamated Clothing Workers put it. The CIO contributions to campaigns in Canada were a handful of organizers and the
near-magic power its name inspired in working people. As historian
Irving Abella demonstrates, "it was on the assembly lines of Oshawa
and Sarnia [Ontario], and not in the union offices of Washington and
Detroit, that industrial unionism in Canada was born." That, of course,
was also how the CIO worked in the United States, by helping local in-
surgents to build their own effective industrial unions. Canada's Flint
was Oshawa, where the UAW used conventional tactics rather than the
"sit-down" strike to win a contract from GM, and there were other vic-
tories in steel in Nova Scotia and in the garment trade in Montreal.[43]

But just as there was no Canadian New Deal, there was to be no
northern carbon copy of CIO success; the Canadian trade union renais-
sance was on a much smaller scale. Part of the problem was the U.S.
connection, which allowed Canadian businessmen and their political allies to use "the nationalist stick to beat the labour dog." The CIO
struck genuine terror into the hearts of middle-class Canada, shocked
by the massive violence of U.S. industrial disputes. Police and militia
regularly broke strikes in Canada, but deaths were rare; the eighteen
dead at Republic Steel in Chicago in May 1937 simply confirmed Canadians' impression of the brutality of American society. "This country . . .
should be grateful that it is not going through such experiences as the

United States," commented editorials. The CIO was also denounced as "communist," and editorial cartoons showed John L. Lewis as a comrade of Joseph Stalin. Communists were prominent among CIO organizers in both countries, but those in Canada were homegrown "Reds," not U.S. imports. The premiers of Quebec and Ontario, Maurice Duplessis and Mitchell Hepburn, both declared war on the CIO. Duplessis used special anti-radical legislation to disband the Montreal local of the United Steel Workers. Hepburn denounced the United Auto Workers as alien agitators and deployed provincial police against the Oshawa strikers. General Motors had better sense; corporate headquarters instructed the managers of its Canadian branch plant to sign a contract with the UAW virtually identical to that in force in Michigan. The Oshawa strike, wrote labor economist Norman Ware in 1937, "has brought the working people of Canada and the United States closer together." The disparity in CIO fortunes on each side of the border,

Canadian Membership in International Unions, 1911–1992

Year	Total Union Membership	Membership in International Unions	Percentage of Membership in International Unions
1911	133,132	119,415	89.7
1921	313,320	222,896	71.1
1931	310,544	188,219	60.6
1941	461,681	288,005	62.4
1951	1,028,521	725,613	70.5
1961	1,446,942	1,040,208	71.9
1971	2,210,554	1,371,109	62.0
1981	3,487,231	1,557,792	44.7
1992	4,089,000	1,253,000	30.6

Sources: Data for the years 1900–1990 are from David Arrowsmith, *Canada's Trade Unions: An Information Manual* (Kingston, Ont., 1992), 53–54; 1992, from Canada, Bureau of Labour Information, *Directory of Labour Organizations in Canada, 1992–93* (Ottawa, 1992), xiv.

however, underlines the importance of New Deal labor legislation in making trade unions an accepted part of American economic life. "The crucial difference between Canada and the United States in this period," writes historian Craig Heron, "was the role of the state." In 1940, the CIO had three million members in the United States and fewer than fifty thousand in Canada; the binational gap in overall "union density" reached a new high. Historian David Brody's words describe the situation perfectly: "the two movements came close to having a unitary institutional history, [but] with the Canadians generally marching a half step to the rear."[44]

By 1938, the United States was the more advanced welfare state, Canada the backward northern neighbor. America resounded with the vibrant working-class movement, a movement that Canadian workers and their leaders struggled to emulate. In the United States, the success of the New Deal mitigated demands for more radical change; in electoral politics, it incorporated most of the American left into an amorphous coalition behind Roosevelt and the Democratic Party. The bankruptcy of Canadian responses to the Depression had the opposite effect and helped to build the Co-operative Commonwealth Federation, a third party with a name borrowed from the American Populist moment that dedicated itself to social democratic solutions to the problems of industrial capitalism. These divergent directions would shape the evolution of the welfare states of Canada and the United States, but their effects lay in the future.[45]

5   World War to Cold War, 1939–1947

The United States and Canada moved suddenly to the embrace of alliance between 1938 and 1941. The world context of U.S.-Canadian relations changed fundamentally in the 1930s, as Japan, Fascist Italy, and Nazi Germany destroyed the capacity of the international community to control aggression. President Franklin Roosevelt and Prime Minister Mackenzie King thus laid the foundations of a formal U.S.-Canadian defense alliance in the late 1930s. By the time Canada joined Britain in war against Germany in September 1939, King could be assured of U.S. goodwill and cooperation, even though America remained neutral until the attack on Pearl Harbor in 1941. In the Ogdensburg agreement of August 1940, and the Hyde Park Declaration of April 1941, King and Roosevelt set in motion joint U.S.-Canadian preparations to defend North America.

Once the United States became a belligerent, however, Canada lost whatever limited utility its leaders imagined that it had as a link between the United States and Britain. For the duration of World War II, Canada and the United States made the difficult adjustments of actually working as partners in arms—and the smaller partner did most of the adjusting. Economic adjustments worked in Canada's favor, however. War built further economic integration, but it also strengthened Canada's economy relative to that of the United States. War also exposed the imbalance and the ambivalence of the bilateral relationship, and in 1945 Canada's ties to Britain still ran far deeper than those to the United States. Their wartime role also gave Canadians a sense that Canada could be a significant "middle power" nation with an independent international role to play in the new United Nations. Formal bilateral wartime institutions (the Permanent Joint Board on Defense was the single exception) lapsed with the surrender of Germany and

Japan in 1945, and postwar expectations were that some of the prewar distance would return to U.S.-Canadian relations. But almost before the shooting war against Fascism was behind them, the confrontation with the Soviet Union replaced it as the context for the U.S.-Canadian interaction. Even more abruptly than the world war, this cold war led to a new set of conflicted intimacies.

Foundations of Alliance

One very minor event of the Roosevelt New Deal took place in Toronto, where the American Optometric Association drafted its industry-wide NRA code in July 1934. The conventioneering optometrists were among the millions of U.S. tourists who discovered Canada during the decade. After 1920 the automobile allowed Americans of more modest means to have a northern vacation, and after 1930 the weak Canadian dollar (a U.S. dollar was worth $1.25 Canadian in 1932) made Canada more affordable still. In 1922, 95,000 U.S. cars entered Ontario; in 1932, there were 730,000. "The Dominion is such a glorious vacation country," the *Cleveland Plain Dealer* exulted that same summer. Overall, 8.9 million Americans came to Canada in 1933 in autos, while 417,132 Canadian cars entered the United States. Transborder tourism earned Canada an annual $130 million (CDN) surplus. "Most tourism between any two countries in the world" was added to "longest undefended border" and "largest volume of trade" on the list of North American "world firsts" of which every Canadian and virtually no American was aware. Canada's biggest Depression tourist attractions were the Dionne quintuplets, born in May 1934 in the northern Ontario hamlet of Callander. Three million visitors made the long trek north to gawk at the five chubby little girls in their fenced playground at "Quintland." The Americans among them returned to the United States to reinforce the prevailing cinematic image of Canada as a bucolic wilderness where Mounties played by Nelson Eddy crooned to passionate French-Canadian beauties played by Jeanette MacDonald, as in *Rose Marie* and *Indian Love Call*. *The Country Doctor*, Hollywood's version of the Dionnes' story, depicted the quints' parents as rustic simpletons, and the physician who delivered them as a "simple soul" who worked "for the pure joy of helping people." Little wonder that most Americans, wrote literary critic Edmund Wilson, thought of Canada as a "gigantic wildlife reserve situated conveniently next door." Canadians complained about American ignorance of their country— "for the love of Mike, are there nothing else in our Dominion but Indians, French-Canadian lumberjacks and North West Mounted Police?" Yet they also collaborated in building this innocent image, as the techniques the Ontario government used to market the Dionne quintuplets in the United States attested.[1]

U.S. ignorance nonetheless deeply offended Canadians, each of whom could relate a personal story of an encounter with an uninformed American. To promote better understanding of Canada's importance to the United States, Columbia University professor J. T. Shotwell persuaded the Carnegie Endowment for International Peace to sponsor four "Conferences on Canadian-American Affairs" and to publish a twenty-five-volume series on "The Relations of Canada and the United States" between 1936 and 1945. The scholars attracted to the newly invented field of "Canadian-American relations" were mostly Canadians or Canadian-born academics in U.S. universities; "the Americans who turned up," complained one of the former, "were second-string men." Yet for all this high-powered Canadian expertise on the United States, an investigation commissioned by the Carnegie Endowment found that "the amount of formal instruction which Canadians received about the United States was extraordinarily slight." Canadians learned almost nothing about the United States in school; everything, it seemed, came from popular culture or oral tradition. Canadian educators justified their neglect by arguing "that no more attention should be given to the United States than Americans give to Canada." Canadians knew what they thought of the United States, and saw no reason to learn anything that might change their minds! An analysis of seven Ontario newspapers from 1921 to 1934 found editorial comments on the United States to be overwhelmingly negative; yet the editorials "expressed no real fear" of the United States, save for their anxiety about U.S. trade unions. When 1,200 Canadian high school students were given a list of adjectives and asked which best characterized Americans, 973 chose "boastful," and only 54 chose "law-abiding." Yet 850 added "friendly."[2]

U.S.-Canadian relations warmed noticeably after Franklin Roosevelt entered the White House in 1933. Toward Latin America his "Good Neighbor Policy" replaced "Dollar Diplomacy" enforced by the "Big Stick." Although Canada was not a member of the Pan-American Union, and the United States was cool to its membership, it was obvious that Roosevelt and Secretary of State Cordell Hull intended the informal good neighborhood to extend north within the hemisphere as well as south. Franklin Roosevelt was the first—and is still the only—U.S. president to take more than a passing interest in Canada. Like much about FDR, that interest is difficult to explain. There was a sentimental connection through the Roosevelt summer home on Campobello Island in New Brunswick. But there was obviously more. The conspiratorially minded might argue that Canada permitted FDR to have an opening to the world that would not alarm the isolationists in Congress, a politically safe route to broader international goals through the seemingly innocuous bilateral relationship. Whatever the reasons for Roosevelt's interest, he became the first American president to be "genuinely popular in Canada," wrote a young historian named C. P. Stacey in 1936, in part because of "the simple fact that he has contrived to make Canadians feel that he is interested in and friendly to their country."[3]

Roosevelt's attention to good relations with Canada began almost with his inauguration. In quest of worldwide reciprocal tariff cuts, in April 1933 he welcomed Prime Minister R. B. Bennett to the White House for discussions. Roosevelt so impressed the prime minister that Bennett praised the president's "wide vision, unselfish courage, . . . steady courage, and sincerity" in a speech on the CBS national radio network. Congress gave Roosevelt discretionary power in the Reciprocal Trade Agreements Act in 1934. Cordell Hull and Mackenzie King signed the U.S.-Canadian trade agreement in November 1935, a month after Bennett's electoral defeat. In return for Canadian "most-favored-nation" treatment of American manufactured goods, which reduced tariffs on almost a thousand items, the United States admitted most

Canadian fish, forest, and farm products. After seventy-five years as an explosive issue, the harsh economic reality of the Great Depression brought a reciprocity agreement with scarcely a whimper of domestic protest in either country. Initiated by a Conservative government and concluded with its Liberal successor, the treaty exemplifies the underlying structural continuities and ambiguities of Canada's relationship with the United States.[4]

Japanese expansion into China, the Ethiopian adventures of Benito Mussolini's Italy, and Hitler's rise to power in Germany had made the world a much more dangerous place by the late 1930s. The defense question in U.S.-Canadian relations no longer meant protecting the United States from Britain or Canada from the United States, but protecting North America from a threat from Europe or Asia. Franklin Roosevelt injected defense into the bilateral dialogue in July 1936 when he made the state visit no previous president had scheduled. Speaking at the Citadel in Quebec, Roosevelt remembered the "brave French, brave British, and brave American colonists" who had fallen in battle there. Americans and Canadians were not "foreigners" to one another, and amid "the grave problems that face the world today" it was time to "tighten the close bonds which already unite our two peoples." Although the *New York Times* was careful to report that "political alliances were not considered," correspondent John MacCormac described the visit as "a mile post in the relations of Canada, the United States and Great Britain." Canadians were thrilled that the president had noticed them; in Montreal, crowds jammed the station, hoping to glimpse him through the window of his railway car. *Saturday Night*—a Canadian magazine that had recently howled for protection against U.S. competition—gushed approval: "President Roosevelt showed a just appreciation of the relationship between his country and ours. . . . There is a common quality of North Americanism which to a large extent overrides international boundaries."[5]

It was the second meeting for Roosevelt and King, and the beginning of a personal friendship between "Franklin and Mackenzie." The friendship was never as intimate as King liked to believe—he never screwed up his courage to tell Roosevelt that his few close friends called him "Rex"—but there was warmth that had never existed before between a president and a prime minister. King clung tenaciously to the dream of Ottawa's special role as a "linchpin" between Washington and London to build "an alliance of three great democratic groups in the interest of world peace." Lord Tweedsmuir, Canada's governor general from 1935 to 1940, also cultivated trilateral friendship. He helped orchestrate Roosevelt's initial visit in 1936 and addressed the graduating class at the Naval Academy at Annapolis and both houses of Congress in 1937. The "regrettable differences of opinion," he quipped, were in the past; now "the future of civilization [lay] in the hands of the English-speaking people." British newspapers praised the visit. "Canada is the natural interpreter of Great Britain and the United States to one another," was how the *Standard* put it; "Britons turn no jealous eye upon such cordial exchanges between the peoples of Canada and the United States." British diplomats and politicians doubted that Canada could make any real contribution, but U.S.-Canadian friendship could be a useful development in the Anglo-American alliance so long as it did not become so intimate that Canada was lost as a military resource to the Empire.[6]

In August 1938, with the newspapers full of news of German military strength, President Roosevelt raised the issue of North American defense after accepting an honorary degree at Queen's University in Kingston, Ontario. He updated the Monroe Doctrine to the new global situation: "The Dominion of Canada is part of the sisterhood of the British Empire," he told the special convocation assembled in the football stadium. "I give to you the assurance that the people of the United States will not stand idly by if domination of Canadian soil is threatened by any other Empire." King adumbrated the Canadian corollary in less memorable language: Canada understood its reciprocal responsibility to be sufficiently well armed that, "should the occasion ever arise, enemy forces should not be able to pursue their way, either by land, sea or air to the United States, across Canadian territory." President and prime minister had served public notice that Canada and the United States might become active allies, not simply passive friends. Few British Canadians disapproved, and the cautious enthusiasm in

Britain undercut their antagonism. In the United States, the hazy commitments to a benign neighbor were sufficiently vague that isolationist sentiment was not aroused. Why had an American president not said the same thing fifty years ago, Roosevelt wondered in a letter to Lord Tweedsmuir. The answer should have been obvious: a half-century earlier it would have been unthinkable for the United States to have made such a pledge or for Canada to have accepted it.[7]

To Roosevelt, the Canadian connection offered a politically safe way to use hemispheric security to send a warning that would perhaps "have some small effect in Berlin." To King, the exchange with the president signified that "we have at last got our defence programme in good shape. Good neighbors on one side; partners within the Empire on the other." But Canada had not done any strategic planning with Britain, let alone with the United States, and of course none could be contemplated between the United States and Britain. Likely enemies lay outside the hemisphere, and as the Canadian Department of External Affairs reminded King, Roosevelt had said exactly nothing about "military support for other democracies outside the Americas." Both King and Roosevelt applauded British appeasement of Germany. After Chamberlain's concession to Hitler at Munich, Roosevelt wrote to King that "We in the United States rejoice with you, and the world at large, that the outbreak of war was averted." Whatever the personal views of the president and the prime minister, however, domestic political constraints blocked more outspoken foreign policies. Each was watched carefully by isolationists in Congress and Parliament who were determined that their countries not intervene in a European conflict. A series of Neutrality Acts between 1935 and 1939 sponsored by Senator Gerald P. Nye forbade U.S. sales of armaments or loans to belligerent nations. "The United States are acting wisely in this regard," applauded Canadian anti-interventionist Member of Parliament Agnes Macphail. A month after Munich, an article in the *American Mercury* predicted that Canada would remain neutral if Britain went to war because its "spirit of Empire . . . would never stand the strain of war." Migration, trade and investment, and popular culture had made Canada "a part of the United States in all save the formal act of transfer." That formal transfer would occur when Britain entered a European war; French-speaking Quebec would withdraw from the federation, and "the remaining provinces will seek admission to the American Union."[8]

Yet although each country had outspoken isolationists, U.S. isolationism had a broad popular base and was legitimated by a long tradition of "no entangling alliances." Canadian isolationists never overcame the emotional bond that the English-Canadian majority felt with Britain. Mackenzie King confided to his diary in October 1938: "I do not like to be dependent on the U.S.; change of leaders there might lead to a vassalage so far as our Dominion was concerned. There [is] more real freedom in the B[ritish] C[ommonwealth] of Nations, and a richer inheritance. This I truly believe." In a major European war touched off by fascist aggression, wrote the prime minister, Canada's "self-evident national duty" was to fight at Britain's side.[9]

In May and June of 1939, the Royal Tour of King George VI and Queen Elizabeth put Canada's British connection on continent-wide display. Three million adoring Canadian subjects—almost a third of the population—greeted George and Elizabeth as they visited each of the nine provinces over four weeks. When the blue-and-gold-painted Royal Train turned south to take Their Majesties to the United States for a four-day interlude, Canadians watched carefully for signs of *lèse majesté*. There were few; American crowds were also enthusiastic—"the British take Washington again," proclaimed one headline—but George VI reminded them repeatedly that he was Canada's king as well as Britain's. To emphasize this, his first stop at the New York World's Fair was at the Canadian pavilion. "The King and Queen heaved a sigh of rather satisfied relief when their train crossed back into Canadian territory," according to the *Winnipeg Free Press;* another journal described Their Majesties' pleasure that the "tough-looking American police had been replaced by the scarlet-coated mounties."[10]

Neutral America, Belligerent Canada, 1939–1941

No law compelled Canada to join Britain in the war against Germany; the Statute of Westminster of 1931 gave each British Dominion the constitutional right to remain neutral. For English Canada, that right existed only in theory, and Canada's sentimental bond to Britain coincided with the country's national interests. Mackenzie King stage-managed the decision to placate French Canadians, so that when Parliament assembled, only 4 of the 252 MPs spoke for neutrality. The seven-day delay between the British and Canadian declarations allowed Canada to buy munitions and aircraft in the United States before Neutrality Laws required Roosevelt to add Canada's name to the prohibited list. The King government hoped to avoid a massive contribution of Canadian infantry for Europe, but Hitler unfortunately refused to cooperate with these best-laid plans. The "phoney war" of the winter of 1939–40 ended abruptly when the German Blitzkrieg swept over France in May 1940. A Canadian brigade was among the British troops evacuated from the continent without their weapons. When France asked Germany for an armistice on 17 June, Canada suddenly found itself promoted to Britain's most important ally! Nothing better illustrated the desperate military situation of the British Empire-Commonwealth.[11]

In historical retrospect, the U.S. entry into World War II has taken on an air of the inevitable. Roosevelt made his pro-Allied sympathies reasonably transparent. He persuaded Congress to bend the Neutrality Acts to allow "cash-and-carry" purchases; the Allies bought $50 million worth of munitions in the first seven months of war on this basis. Public opinion, measured by the new polls conducted by George Gallup, showed that 84 percent of Americans wanted an Allied victory, while only 2 percent cheered for the Axis; 14 percent had no opinion. One history of Canadian-U.S. relations goes so far as to conclude that "after the fall of France U.S. neutrality became an ever more transparent fiction," as if there had been an inexorable Roosevelt plan to lead America into war with Germany. In August 1940, the president traded fifty old American destroyers for leases on British bases in the Caribbean and in Newfoundland, the British colony that Canada coveted as a tenth province. In a fireside chat in December, Roosevelt proposed to make America the "arsenal of democracy," and in March 1941, he signed the Lend-Lease Bill, which allowed him to provide Britain with up to $7 billion in arms and supplies. In April, U.S. warships began to guard North Atlantic convoys against submarines, and in August, Roosevelt had his first face-to-face strategy session with British prime minister Winston Churchill.[12]

The difficulty with this neat chronology is that Roosevelt, Churchill, and Mackenzie King did not know what was ahead when France collapsed in June 1940. Whatever Roosevelt's personal convictions—which were not consistently interventionist—the president could not simply decide to join Britain at war. Non-interventionist sentiment persisted in Congress and in the country, personified in Charles Lindbergh, spokesman for the America First Committee backed by Sears-Roebuck millionaire Robert Woods. In search of his unprecedented third term as president in 1940, Roosevelt guaranteed he would "never send American boys to fight in any European war," and his Republican opponent Wendell Willkie made the same promise. As late as the autumn of 1941, only 41 percent of Americans were prepared without qualification to enter the war.[13]

This context of uncertainty explains the alacrity with which Mackenzie King and Roosevelt turned the mutual promises of 1938 into a military alliance. The Ogdensburg Agreement was announced on 18 August 1940—the second anniversary of Roosevelt's speech in Kingston. King traveled at Roosevelt's request to join the president in Ogdensburg, New York, where the president had gone to inspect the American First Army. Eight divisions of U.S. troops so near the border once would have terrified Canadians, but with Britain battling to avert German invasion, the ninety-four thousand soldiers became a reassuring presence. The press did not report that the First Army had no modern weapons, and that trucks armed with lengths of telephone pole played tanks in their maneuvers. King's defense predicament dwarfed Roosevelt's: virtually all of Canada's armed forces stood watch in Britain against the Axis. If Britain fell, the entire force would be lost, yet King and his generals would not consider bringing them home. Roosevelt proposed a partial answer to this dilemma—a Permanent Joint Board on Defense (PJBD) to plan "the defense of the north half of the western hemisphere." Details of defense cooperation were left for the PJBD to work out; it was to be a bilateral institution removed

from public view that would suggest action to still-sovereign governments, sort of a military version of the International Joint Commission.
Roosevelt pressed King about the possibility of American bases in
Canada, but the prime minister demurred by promising that "facilities" would be available when necessary.[14]

Through their summit diplomacy, the two leaders had reached an
informal executive agreement far more significant than any previous
U.S.-Canadian treaty, an agreement that was never debated in the U.S.
Senate or in Parliament. Although the president's sudden telephone
call left Mackenzie King no time to consult his cabinet, the PJBD reflected precisely the sort of arrangement Canadian strategic planners
had hoped to conclude with the United States. Not surprisingly, newspaper comment and public opinion in Canada were overwhelmingly
positive, even from the English-Canadian business community, the
bastion of anti-Americanism in the Dominion. U.S. minister in Ottawa Pierrepont Moffat reported that "the old fear that cooperation
with the United States would tend to weaken Canada's ties with Great
Britain has almost entirely disappeared. Instead, Canada believes that
such cooperation would tend to bring Britain and the United States
closer together." From a U.S. perspective, the board was a "prototype
of many subsequent organizations established . . . to increase the ef-
ficiency of their crusade against the enemies of civilization." Roosevelt
was the leader who ran the political risk by dealing with a belligerent,
but Canada was a benign belligerent that the president could safely
use to make a point; a June 1940 Gallup poll had found that 81 percent
of Americans would go to war to defend their northern neighbor. The
isolationist *Chicago Tribune* supported the PJBD as "common sense,"
and as "a contract of limited liabilities" that made it *less* likely "for this
nation to engage in any European military adventures." The Roosevelt
administration accordingly stressed the defensive nature of the relationship with Canada; Undersecretary of State Sumner Welles contended that the Canadian arrangement paralleled that with the other
American republics, simply providing a planning mechanism in the
event Canada were attacked by a non-American power. Yet the United
States had now given structure to Roosevelt's pledge not to "stand idly
by" if Canada were attacked.[15]

When Mackenzie King explained Ogdensburg to Parliament, he emphasized that the U.S. alliance allowed Canada to funnel men, women, and material to Britain, secure in the knowledge that the United States sheltered the hemisphere. His goal had been not just to protect Canada but "the defence of the British commonwealth of nations as a whole," and "the British government was kept duly informed of what was taking place." This was not strictly true. Churchill had known nothing of Ogdensburg in advance; on learning of it, he cabled King that history might judge him more harshly than public opinion in the event that "Mr. Hitler cannot invade us and his Air Force begins to blench under the strain." It was Churchill who judged too harshly. King's U.S. compact was the only course that military circumstance left open to Canada to support the British Commonwealth. The prime minister continued to revere the metaphor of Canada as North Atlantic "linchpin" between Britain and America, the exact term Churchill used to describe Canada as "the binder-together of the English-speaking peoples." In practical terms, however, this linchpin role was insignificant. King's single contribution was to act as conduit between Roosevelt and Churchill in distasteful discussions over the disposition of the Royal Navy should Hitler conquer Britain. In a broader sense, the linchpin notion was a useful propaganda artifice. Hollywood's *Sherlock Holmes and the Scarlet Claw* (1944) concludes with Holmes extolling to Dr. Watson Canada's value as a bridge across the North Atlantic. As historian David Reynolds has argued, however, the real basis of eventual British-American cooperation was not "latent cultural unity" but "similar geopolitical and ideological interests" fully acknowledged only during the crisis of 1940–41.[16]

The dollars-and-cents significance behind the high-sounding speeches about the U.S.-Canadian alliance came to the fore in March and April 1941. In peacetime, Canada had balanced its chronic trade deficit with the United States through a trade surplus with Britain and Western Europe. War upset this balance; it increased imports from the United States, ended sales to Europe, and turned sales to Britain into credit transactions financed by Canada. In 1940, Canada spent $744 million (CDN) in the United States and earned only $451 million (CDN). Canada refused to accept U.S. aid under lend-lease, but the act loomed momentous: by diverting British purchases to the United States, it produced a foreign exchange nightmare for Canada. This time Mackenzie King broached the subject with Roosevelt. After brief discussions at Hyde Park, on 20 April 1941 they announced an agreement to rationalize "mobilizing the resources of this continent." The United States would supply Canada with components for munitions bound for Britain as part of British lend-lease aid and, more important, would increase its purchasing in Canada to bring bilateral trade closer to a balance. Mackenzie King exaggerated what had happened at Hyde Park when he told the House of Commons that it was the foundation of a "new world order," but its departure from previous U.S.-Canadian economic experience could scarcely be exaggerated. This was no doubt why King repeated six times during the speech that his intent at Hyde Park had been "maximum aid to Britain." [17]

U.S. foreign policy historians ignore or brush past the agreements at Hyde Park and Ogdensburg, but they are conspicuous even in survey textbooks of Canadian history. Canadian nationalist historians excoriate Mackenzie King for selling out Canada's British birthright for Yankee pottage, and thus leading Canada down the American fork to "a continental system dominated by the United States." But Canada embarked on that road not because its leaders loved Britain less but because they loved the mother country more—sometimes more than prudent calculation of national interest might have dictated. It was a case, as J. L. Granatstein explains in his title, of *How Britain's Weakness Forced Canada into the Arms of the United States.* And what safer place could there have been in 1941 than in America's arms? [18]

Big and Little Brothers-in-Arms

"Yesterday, December 7, 1941—a date which will live in infamy— the United States of America was suddenly and deliberately attacked by naval and air forces of the Empire of Japan." Thus began Franklin Roosevelt's war message to Congress after Japan's surprise success against the U.S. Pacific Fleet at Pearl Harbor. The attack on Pearl Harbor focused U.S. public and official opinion on a single objective—the defeat of Japan. Pearl Harbor contributed, to use historian Robert Divine's phrase, to the "triumph of internationalism" in the United States. Within a week, Hitler thrust America directly into the British Commonwealth's war with Germany and Italy by his unnecessary and, in retrospect, illogical declaration of war against the United States. Without Hitler's misjudgment, the Roosevelt administration would have had to fight a Pacific war and to continue only to supply material to the war across the Atlantic. Instead, the German declaration evoked the eventual Anglo-American grand strategy: to fight a holding action in the Pacific on the premise that Japan could not stand alone, while concentrating Allied forces on Germany.[19]

The Combined Chiefs of Staff—the commanders of the three armed services of Britain and the United States meeting with Roosevelt and Churchill, or their special representatives—did Anglo-American strategic planning. The principal point of friction between the United States and Britain concerned the location and timing of a second front. With the Soviet Union bearing the brunt of the land war in 1941–42 on Germany's eastern front, Roosevelt and his advisers worried about a Soviet collapse or a withdrawal from the war. Thus convoys with American lend-lease supplies flowed into the Soviet Union when channels were open. British leaders believed, rightly, that Allied forces were unprepared for a cross channel push in 1942 or 1943. Instead, they urged an attack upon Germany's flanks and a massive strategic bombing campaign to undermine the German military-industrial machine. Thus, Britain and the United States agreed on the North African campaign to contain and destroy Germany's more isolated forces to clear the way for a coordinated invasion of southern Europe through Sicily and Italy in 1943, with a cross-channel invasion of Europe to come later.

On these decisions hinged the fates of a million Canadian servicepeople, and billions of Canadian dollars hinged upon them. Canada's contribution to British grand strategy before 1941 had been negligible, despite the Dominion's indispensability to British survival during U.S. neutrality. After Pearl Harbor, however, the Mackenzie King government's impact on Anglo-American grand strategy was nonexistent.

King complained to Churchill of Canada's exclusion from the Combined Chiefs, but his objections were not relayed to Washington. General Maurice Pope eventually became a semiofficial Canadian observer and was allowed access to censored documents; he attended exactly one of the Combined Chiefs' two hundred meetings. Mackenzie King did not participate in any meaningful way even in the two wartime meetings that took place in Quebec City in August 1943 and September 1944. Pressed by his advisers, King quietly requested, again through Churchill, admission to the sessions. Roosevelt rejected the idea instantly; if Canada took part, he argued, Brazil, Mexico, and a dozen smaller allies would demand a place. King never asked again. While Churchill and Roosevelt planned the Normandy landings of June 1944, King contented himself with a ceremonial photograph sitting between the two men who decided the future of Canada's combatants. Neither of them evidently felt any need for a Canadian "linchpin." As King later recalled privately, his role had been "not so much a participant in any of the discussions as a sort of genial host, whose task . . . was similar to that of the General Manager of the Chateau Frontenac [Hotel]."[20]

Canadian leaders quickly concluded that bilateral Canadian-U.S. wartime cooperation worked better than the trilateral variety. Two-thirds of the PJBD's work had been done in 1940–41, when Canada was at war and the United States at peace. Each country had five representatives: a cochair, an officer from its army, navy, and air force, and a delegate from the U.S. Department of State and the Canadian Department of External Affairs, who reached consensus on draft recommendations to the two governments. "The Canadians had to recognize American power; the Americans had to cater to Canadian sensitivities," wrote Hugh Keenleyside, one of the former. As a result the PJBD, was remarkably successful in working out proposals that were mutually satisfactory to Washington and Ottawa. Nine of the thirty-three recommendations dealt with the nettlesome problem of Newfoundland, which Canada and the United States competed to defend. Canadian board members quickly explained to their U.S. counterparts that there would be no permanent U.S. military bases in Canada; it was to be "a defense board, not a real-estate board," American chair Fiorello

LaGuardia remarked. There were two tough decisions. In Basic Plan No. 1, Canada reluctantly agreed to put its forces under U.S. "strategic direction" in the event of an attack on North America. Canada refused to concede this strategic subordination in plan ABC-22 for action against Axis troops by joint forces elsewhere on the globe. Although the U.S. military members of the PJBD hated the concept, such a counterattack was to be "effected by mutual cooperation." Thus the board allowed the very junior partner to retain a face-saving degree of its sovereignty. Fortunately for Canadian dignity, no crisis occurred to force the issue.[21]

The Canadian government pressed to expand bilateral ties beyond the PJBD in an effort to expand the Canadian role in strategic and industrial planning. U.S. generals and diplomats firmly resisted such suggestions, wary of creating a Canadian precedent that other nations in the Americas would insist upon. The Departments of War and the Navy politely but emphatically rejected a Canadian request in 1941 to establish a Canadian Joint Staff in Washington independent of representation within the British military mission. Secretaries Frank B. Knox and Henry L. Stimson contended that it was adequate to work through the Joint Board and for Canada to have representatives at conferences between U.S. officials and the British Joint Staff Mission on issues "in which Canadian interests are involved." The United States proposed a compromise in which Canada would station its military members of the PJBD in Washington, a compromise Canada rejected. American affronts to Canadian pride continued until July 1942, when the U.S. high command eventually acquiesced, and Major General Maurice Pope became chief of a Canadian Joint Staff in Washington. The protracted negotiations left an "undertone of acrimony" that historian Stanley Dziuban describes as "one of the least happy aspects of the U.S.-Canada World War II relationship."[22]

After the collapse of France, the United States took an increasingly assertive military posture to forestall any Axis troops from a foothold in the Western Hemisphere. Newfoundland was critical as a base for air and naval patrols against German submarines in the North Atlantic. Because Canada had tried since 1867 to make the British colony a Canadian province, the new military installations that the United States created in the destroyers-for-bases agreement generated political difficulties. The Canadian government insisted that its "special concern" with Newfoundland's fate be formally recognized in Anglo-American plans. The U.S. military presence, with its attendant nylon stockings and Hershey bars, cheered Newfoundlanders enough to intensify Canadian concerns about the colony's future. The Canadian garrison in Newfoundland seemed to be there as much to resist peaceful U.S. absorption as to repel Hitler's hordes. The Canadian troops accomplished their twin missions: in 1949, Newfoundlanders chose to join Canada in a bitterly fought referendum. The U.S. bases, however, remained.[23]

German conquest of Denmark and control over Vichy France posed a new security threat from Danish and French possessions in close proximity to vital Atlantic shipping lanes. The Roosevelt administration considered the Danish colony of Greenland to be part of the Western Hemisphere and integral to hemispheric defense. Britain pressed Canada to occupy Greenland, and Canadian defence minister J. L. Ralston made preparations to do so. U.S. assistant secretary of state Adolf Berle, furious at what he perceived as Canadian interference, accused Canada of "plain grand imperialism on a miniature scale." The United States feared that a Canadian occupation would provide Berlin with an excuse for offensive action against the island. The United States acted to avert either possibility. In April 1940, U.S. Navy ships began to patrol the Greenland coast, and the United States provided the government of Greenland with munitions. Mackenzie King, anxious that Canada not get out of step with the United States, reassured Roosevelt and cancelled Ralston's expedition. After this minor unpleasantness, the United States predominated; in April 1941, the Danish minister in Washington agreed to the construction of U.S. airbases in Greenland.[24]

Canada, the United States, and Britain had greater difficulty coordinating defensive questions and diplomacy toward Vichy France and the Free French movement under General Charles de Gaulle. The Vichy governments of Marshal Pétain and Pierre Laval clearly collaborated with Nazi Germany, but the United States wished to keep Vichy officially neutral to cancel the potential damage the French fleet could cause if used by Germany. Winston Churchill took a harder line toward Vichy. Canada's position was complicated by its large French-Catholic minority; Marshal Pétain's promise to restore traditional Catholic values in a rejuvenated France won the Vichy regime sympathy among some French-Canadian Roman Catholics. Mackenzie King worried that Vichy would declare war on Canada and exacerbate King's political problems in a Quebec already alienated from the war effort by the imposition of military conscription. By early 1942, Canada was the only Dominion that retained diplomatic relations with the Vichy regime. At issue were the Vichy-controlled French islands of St. Pierre and Miquelon off the Newfoundland coast, which posed potential security problems. The Roosevelt administration and the King government both preferred, however, to maintain the status quo of French overseas possessions in the Western Hemisphere.[25]

In December 1941, General de Gaulle created a crisis in Anglo-American–Canadian relations when he dispatched Free French Forces to capture the tiny islands. Vice-Admiral Emile-Henri Muselier carried out the invasion with British-supplied ships that sailed from Halifax, Nova Scotia, under Canadian military noses—to U.S. fury and Canadian embarrassment. De Gaulle's precipitous action crystallized the conflicting trilateral approaches. De Gaulle's intervention dismayed Mackenzie King, but British acquiescence made clear that they preferred the Free French Forces in control of St. Pierre and Miquelon rather than Canadian authorities; the Americans were determined not to compromise their Vichy policy. British ambassador in Washington Lord Halifax urged that nothing be done about the occupation but agreed that Hull should discuss a possible agreement among King, Churchill, and the Vichy in which Churchill would request that de Gaulle withdraw his forces. But Churchill enraged Hull with a speech in Ottawa defending de Gaulle and criticizing Vichy. From Hull's perspective, de Gaulle's invasion threatened the Allied goal to keep Vichy neutral; from Churchill's vantage point, Free French Forces would be important to the Allies' North African campaign and in the reconquest of Europe. Churchill prevailed, and Hull, as was often the case, had to swallow his pride. Yet this was a victory for the Free French and

Churchill, not for Canadian policy, as some authors contend. In the spring of 1942, Canada recalled its ambassador from Vichy for consultation but stopped short of breaking relations. By the fall, an agreement with Admiral Darlan cleared the way for the Allied invasion of North Africa, and both Canada and the United States were able to distance themselves from Vichy.[26]

Such diplomatic wrangles were a diversion from the main task of winning the war against the Axis. Both the German submarine threat on the North Atlantic and the Japanese peril in the Pacific required active Canadian-U.S. military cooperation. Two years of battle before Pearl Harbor gave the Royal Canadian Navy (RCN) seniority as battle-hardened veterans. There had been inevitable resentment when, in September 1941, even before Pearl Harbor, RCN ships operating outside Canadian coastal waters were placed under the command of the neutral Americans. That situation was reversed in May 1943; for the remainder of the war the Royal Canadian Navy commanded the Northwest Atlantic forces, including U.S. vessels. Throughout the war the RCN protected not only Canadian coastal and transatlantic shipping but also transports leaving and entering Boston and New York harbors. As Stetson Conn and Byron Fairchild observe in their history of hemispheric defense, "the whole framework of cooperation, naval as well as military," rested as much on Canada as on the United States and Britain.[27]

In the North Pacific, the principal Canadian-U.S. joint action was to respond to the Japanese occupation of the Aleutian Islands of Attu and Kiska in June 1942. For the next two years, Canadian naval vessels, air force squadrons, and almost five thousand infantry were stationed in the area. Canadian forces participated in this sector, however, because of the persistence of Canadian senior officers rather than from any real bilateral spirit of sharing the military burden. John Hickerson of the State Department, the U.S. secretary of the PJBD, urged that Canadian infantry join the Aleutian operations, and the head of Canada's Pacific Command, Major General George Pearkes, was keen to do so. In May 1943, Major General Pope requested a Canadian role through U.S. chief of staff George Marshall. But senior U.S. Navy officers resisted; Admiral Ernest King argued that Canadian involvement would simply "complicate" logistical problems and serve no useful military purpose. Nor were Mackenzie King and his cabinet eager that Canada help to liberate the Aleutians. The Canadian Army had suffered massive casualties in the defense of Hong Kong in December 1941 and in the futile assault on the French port of Dieppe in August 1942. Those soldiers had all been volunteers. Most of the Canadians assigned to the Aleutians were conscripts drafted to fight only in North America; their deaths would have come with a high political price. Thus, the 15,000 U.S. troops who fought the Japanese on Attu in May 1943 did so with only 8 Canadian "observers" among them. Five hundred and forty nine GIs died and 1,148 were wounded; only 23 of the 3,000 Japanese soldiers lived to be taken prisoner. All of the Canadian observers survived unharmed, much to Prime Minister King's relief. In August 1943, after protracted bilateral negotiations, a Canadian brigade combined with the Americans in a joint assault on Kiska, only to find that the Japanese had evacuated the island. Not only were Canadian troops denied a military victory, but they suffered the additional indignity of an overzealous U.S. customs officer who levied duty on their equipment as they moved into Alaska.[28]

Canada's First Division landed in the invasion of Sicily in July 1943, yet General Dwight D. Eisenhower refused to permit any reference to the Canadian presence in what was billed as an "Allied" or an "Anglo-American" campaign. Eisenhower had sound military reasons for his refusal. German intelligence listened to the radio, so that announcing the presence of the Canadian army would supply the enemy with details about troop deployments. But King took the question of recognition so seriously that he telephoned the White House during dinner to arrange for Lester Pearson of the Canadian Mission to see the president. Pearson won a promise that the Canadian involvement would be given due public acknowledgment, once the landings were underway. Such were the demeaning appeals required of a small country that was, as Pearson put it, "uncomfortably squeezed in between" the United States and the United Kingdom. It was all very far from the role of Anglo-American "linchpin" that King had envisioned for Canada in 1940.[29]

After Pearl Harbor, Mackenzie King's personal rapport with Franklin Roosevelt won no special concessions, for leading the United States to war left the president precious little time to worry about relations with Canada. King's call to the White House about the Italian invasion, for example, was handled by aide Harry Hopkins. Still, the Roosevelt-King pairing was unique in the U.S.-Canadian relationship. They overlapped in office for a decade, from King's return to power in October 1935 until Roosevelt's death in April 1945. The president and the prime minister met for "summit diplomacy" on eighteen occasions, twelve of them after Canada went to war in 1939. Nationalist historians of Canada argue that King eroded the British connection and turned Canada into an American dependency. Blinded by "the President's easy charm," suggests Donald Creighton, King failed to look out for Canada's interests at these meetings. But the restructuring of the U.S.-Canadian relationship was more the product of historical circumstance than it was of strengths or deficiencies in Roosevelt's or King's personal character. Like every president and every prime minister, the two personified the fearful asymmetry between the United States and Canada. King's options, like those of every other Canadian prime minister, were severely constrained by this asymmetry. King struggled constantly to maintain Canada's freedom of action, and it is difficult to imagine another Canadian leader who could have been significantly more successful. Although he never in public acknowledged problems in the U.S.-Canadian relationship, in private King was never naive about U.S. power. He was constantly preoccupied with guarding Canada's sovereignty. He knew, however, that "if the Americans felt security required it [they] would take peaceful possession of part of Canada." All he could do was to try to keep that from happening.[30]

North American Arsenals for Democracy

The United States granted Canada a voice in Allied wartime economic councils, although that voice was never as loud as Canadian leaders believed it should have been. Relative national contributions to Allied munitions production illustrate Canada's frustration but also explain Anglo-American unwillingness to share power. From Washington's perspective, Canada's 5 percent of Allied munitions production was much smaller than Britain's 33 percent or the United States' 61 percent; thus Canada had to be excluded from the economic planning boards to justify the exclusion of other small Allied countries. From Ottawa's angle, Canada supplied five times as much war material as did all of those smaller Allies combined, as well as vast quantities of food and essential commodities. Canadian remonstrations never won representation on the Munitions Assignments Board, but by November 1942 its protests brought a place on the Combined Production and Resources Board. Canada was at first excluded from the Combined Food Board, despite huge Canadian exports of meat and grain. In this case, the Canadian approach was to maneuver representatives onto seven of the ten Food Board sub-agencies while negotiating for full membership, which came at last in November 1943.[31]

No American-British-Canadian collaboration had the long-term impact of the production of nuclear weapons. In June 1942, at British insistence, the Combined Chiefs added Canada as a minor third party in a scientific project code-named "Tube Alloys"; three months later, "Tube Alloys" became the top secret Manhattan Project to develop an atomic weapon. At Quebec City in August 1943, Roosevelt and Churchill established a Combined Policy Committee of three Americans, two Britons, and the Canadian minister of munitions and supply, C. D. Howe, to supervise the program. Atomic consultation, like most wartime cooperation, was imperfect. Howe was not invited to a Combined Policy Committee meeting until the spring of 1944. But although Howe and Mackenzie King had no part in the decision to drop the atomic bomb, the Canadian leaders were within the small circle who knew what was to happen to the Japanese city of Hiroshima on 6 August 1945.[32]

Atomic weapons development underlined several features of the Anglo-Canadian-American relationship. The first was growing U.S. scientific and technological supremacy, illustrated by the speed with which American scientists pulled ahead of British researchers once the Manhattan Project was initiated. A second was that the United States sometimes depended on imported Canadian resources: Canada was invited to Manhattan because it was one of two major world sources of uranium. A third feature was that the U.S. government often took Canadian compliance for granted; Washington did not bother to check with Ottawa when it contracted with Consolidated Mining and Smelting in British Columbia to construct a heavy water plant. Yet despite the occasional indignities it endured, Canada derived indisputable benefits from charter membership in the atomic club. Wartime nuclear collaboration constructed the heavy water pile for the production of plutonium at Chalk River, Ontario, and provided Canadian scientists, in historian Donald Avery's words, "a chance to play in the scientific big leagues." These facilities and this knowledge helped to make Canada a world power in the peaceful applications of atomic energy in the postwar years and allowed Canada's somewhat hypocritical boast that it was the only country with the capacity to build nuclear weapons that chose not to do so.[33]

Less significant in the long term than nuclear cooperation, but more controversial at the time, was the construction of such U.S. military-industrial facilities as the Canol oil project at Norman Wells, Northwest Territories. Initiated in 1942 to supply oil products along the route of the projected Alaska highway and for Alaska-based military aircraft, the project involved the expansion of production at Imperial Oil's Norman Wells facility, the construction of a pipeline to Whitehorse in the Yukon, and the construction of a refinery at Whitehorse to produce aviation gasoline. Under the terms of the U.S.-Canadian agreement, the pipeline and refinery would be the property of the U.S. government and would be operated under U.S. authority, but at the end of the war, the Canadian government would be given the first option to purchase the facilities. Canol was highly contentious in U.S. political and military circles because its expense and use of scarce resources in wartime seemed to bear little relationship to the actual military benefit of the project. Canol nonetheless provides an excellent example of a U.S.-Canadian bilateral military-industrial project in wartime, as well as an indication of the keen American interest in longer-term oil development prospects for strategic use in the Canadian Northwest.[34]

A fifteen-hundred-mile highway through that Northwest to link Alaska to the rest of the United States became the dream of West Coast politicians in both countries during the Depression. British Columbia premier T. D. Pattullo actually journeyed to Washington in an attempt to promote the project, but Ottawa's fears of lost sovereignty forestalled serious discussion. War against Japan brought U.S. military pressure to build the road, but as with Canol and U.S. bases, Canadian nervousness remained. In February 1942, Canada reluctantly agreed to the PJBD's recommendation that construction begin. The United States built the road with American labor and bore the entire expense of $148 million (U.S.). "Money didn't mean a fucking thing to them Americans, . . . you never saw such waste," recalled a Canadian truck driver. The highway opened by the end of 1943 and carried thirty million tons of supplies and equipment to U.S. forces in Alaska in 1944. Its military importance declined rapidly thereafter, as the war of attrition against Japan moved to its atomic climax. Certainly construction of the highway undermined Canadian sovereignty in the region—northerners claimed that the U.S. Army answered the telephone with the phrase "American Army of Occupation"—but as with so many other aspects of the U.S.-Canadian wartime relationship, the Canadian government had little option. At war's end, Canada paid the United States for its work (as it did for all U.S. installations in Canada) and ceremonially took control of the highway. Both countries ignored the sovereignty of the Native peoples who hunted, fished, and trapped the lands the road traversed. For these First Nations, the Alaska Highway remained a permanent physical and psychological scar across the landscape.[35]

In most respects Canada fared well in its wartime economic relations with the United States. The Hyde Park Declaration of April 1941 immediately relieved Canada's balance of payments problem. The further arrangement that "each country should provide the other with defence articles which it is best able to produce" meant a substantial increase in U.S. military purchases from Canada. Economic competition was partially set aside to serve the greater cause of Allied victory. Wartime economic expansion brought both economies to full employment and created more manufacturing orders than could go around.

There was sudden and unprecedented cooperation in previously competitive areas such as agricultural exports: the United States admitted Canadian oats and barley in order to allow U.S. corn farmers to divert acreage to oilseeds that in turn were exported to Canada. Total bilateral trade was nearly $4 billion (U.S.) between 1941 and 1945, moving closer to balance each year until Canada for the first time ran a trade surplus with the United States in 1945. Canada was therefore able to avoid what desperation compelled Britain to do: sell overseas assets to meet its payments to the United States, or transfer title to territory in return for material assistance, as in the destroyers-for-bases deal of 1940. As historian Robert Bothwell puts it, Canada became the "exception to the general rule of mendicancy that obtained in the wartime alliance"; alone among U.S. allies, it paid its own way in money as well as in blood.[36]

On 1 January 1944, the two missions established in 1927 officially became embassies, and the "ministers" were elevated to ambassadorial rank. This redesignation was symbolic; the real wartime transformation was the profusion of bilateral lines of communication beyond traditional diplomacy, the contacts political scientists would later call "trans-governmental bureaucratic relations." Bureaucrats related transnationally on the five economic agencies set up to implement Hyde Park: the Materials Coordinating Committee, the Joint Economic Committees, the Joint War Production Committee, the Joint Agricultural Committee, and the Joint War Aid Committee. In addition, each of the profusion of federal bureaus that sprang up in both national capitals to regulate the wartime economies dealt directly with its analogue. Even Canadian cabinet ministers used extradiplomatic avenues to press policy issues upon influential Americans. Minister of Munitions and Supply C. D. Howe prepared the ground for Canadian membership on the Combined Production and Resources Board during a 1942 fishing trip with Donald Nelson, chair of the United States War Production Board.[37]

Such contacts misled some historians to interpret the war years as the first stage of an inexorable amalgamation of Canada into a U.S.-dominated continental economy. But as historian R. Warren James concludes, "any tendency to subservience was fiercely resisted by Canadian officials," and the flurry of wartime cooperation created the appearance of a greater degree of industrial integration than in fact took place. The Hyde Park Declaration did not mean, as *Time* magazine would later claim, that "in effect, Canada had become an economic 49th state." The five joint economic agencies had impressive titles, but only the Joint War Production Committee and the Materials Coordinating Committee actually did anything. The Joint Economic Committees, which had been supposed to plan for the postwar period, produced nothing of any consequence and were disbanded in March 1944. There was no general free trade area, and national tariffs remained in force except on specific defense items. Canada's trade surpluses between 1942 and 1945 were not because of Hyde Park, but because there was a strong demand for Canadian munitions and natural resources. Nor was Hyde Park's goal "that production programs should be coordinated" entirely achieved. Much of Canada's war production continued to be built to British, not American, designs and specifications. During World War II, Canada achieved massive industrial growth without heavy U.S. direct investment. Public investment made up for its absence, some of it into Crown corporations (the Canadian term for government-owned enter prises) and some into private industry—including American branch plants for ALCOA, Ford, and General Electric. There were almost no nationalizations: the purchase of a uranium mine at Great Bear Lake to create Eldorado Nuclear was an exception. During World War I, Canada's industrial production had been confined to artillery shells; in World War II, Canada's factories contributed tanks, vehicles, aircraft, naval frigates, and ocean freighters. In his comparative study of the economic effects of World War II, Alan Millward lists Canada as one of two countries for which wartime economic stimulation produced "a permanently effective acceleration of the development process."[38]

The frothy rhetoric of cooperation and the easy informality of trans-border contacts gave Americans an exaggerated notion of the degree to which barriers between the United States and Canada had disappeared. U.S. assistant secretary of state Adolf Berle described in his diary an afternoon talk with Hugh Keenleyside, assistant undersecretary in the Canadian Department of External Affairs. Keenleyside, Berle wrote, had told him that "this is now one continent and one economy; that we shall have to be integrated as to finance, trade routes, and pretty much everything else; and in this I so thoroughly agree with him that it is refreshing. We talked long and happily about it— though much lies in the realm of dreams." Keenleyside understood this "dream" very differently: "For war purposes we were prepared to go as far as would be beneficial for our joint effort to defeat the worst threat ever faced by Western civilization." Postwar "industrial cooperation" was not a blueprint for continental integration, but "the exact opposite"; through "shared production schemes" Canadian industries would receive "a guaranteed percentage of the American market" and thus would enhance Canadian economic integrity, not diminish it. Hyde Park was an informal agreement, without the force of a treaty; although officials from both countries repeatedly spoke of continuing the Hyde Park "spirit" into the postwar years, actual cooperation temporarily declined. Wartime agencies, except the Permanent Joint Board on Defense, were dismantled, wartime bureaucrats returned to their business careers, and Canadian political anxiety about dependency on the United States reawakened and intensified.[39]

Strangers beneath the Skin

Effusive declarations about shared democratic values obscured the societal differences that persisted between the two countries. The way in which each country dealt with ethnic diversity furnishes a wartime window onto these contrasts. In the United States, World War II accelerated the cultural assimilation of the French-Catholic "little Canadas" of New England, which 1930s immigration restrictions had begun. As historian Gary Gerstle has shown, wartime propaganda and military service invited once-despised "Canucks" to a new identity as working-class Americans. "The younger generation is turning away from tradition and finds the American way more interesting than the life of their fathers," lamented Jacques Ducharme in 1943; "there is no future in the maintenance of survival." Franklin Roosevelt felt no such sadness. "The French-Canadian elements . . . are at last becoming a part of the American melting pot," he exulted to Mackenzie King, "and most of them are speaking English in their homes." The president proposed "some sort of planning . . . by which we can hasten the objective of assimilating the New England and Canada's French Canadians into the whole of our respective bodies politic." King had no such objective and did not reply; French Canadians were 30 percent of Canada's population. Maintaining the delicate harmony between French and English had been the principal task of his long political career, and the wartime debate over conscription had heightened French-Canadian alienation. The president's suggestion and the prime minister's silence illustrate the difference between a bicultural Canada and an America that imagined that it could have one hegemonic culture; that Roosevelt offered such advice shows that even the president who knew Canada best had a fundamental gap in his understanding.[40]

The metaphors of "melting pot" and "mosaic" are often used to depict the two countries' differences with regard to cultural pluralism. The United States is the assimilative "melting pot" that recasts ethnic minorities into uniform English-speaking Americans; Canada is the "mosaic" that encourages the cultural survival of diverse ethnic groups. This melting pot/mosaic metaphor may perhaps accurately describe a historically greater degree of ethnic diversity in Canada, but there is no evidence that this diversity resulted from a greater Canadian appreciation of, or tolerance for, cultural minorities. As historian Allan Smith argues, "circumstances have imposed the pluralist idea" upon Canada, and many English-speaking Canadians "have bitterly resented those circumstances." War removed some of the restraints on this resentment. As during World War I, English Canada imposed military conscription upon French Canada. U.S. and Canadian wartime policies toward naturalized citizens of German and Italian origin were almost indistinguishable, and in both countries, the white majorities reacted with near-identical racism to the perceived security threat posed by the Japanese minorities of the Pacific Coast states and British Columbia. Even before Pearl Harbor, the Permanent Joint Board on Defense had advocated that "policies of a similar character" be devised to deal with "elements in the population of Japanese racial origin" in the event of war with Japan. Although there is little evidence of a coordinated plan, 125,000 Japanese and Japanese Americans and 22,000 Japanese and Japanese Canadians were simultaneously relocated to internment camps away from the coast. Roosevelt's Executive Order 9066 of 19 February 1942 preceded Canada's Privy Council Order 1486 by only five days: in both countries the internees were herded behind barbed wire and deprived of their liberty and their property.[41]

According to historian Roger Daniels, however, after the orders were issued, the Canadian government treated the internees with greater severity. In the United States, the War Relocation Authority tried to "rehabilitate" all "loyal" Japanese Americans into mainstream society as rapidly as possible. Internment camps offered English-language schools and even college extension courses. Thousands of American-born Japanese were allowed to volunteer for military service in Europe, and thousands more were released from internment camps on the condition that they remain off the Pacific Coast. In 1944, the U.S. Supreme Court ruled that this restriction on their mobility was unconstitutional, and large numbers of Japanese Americans returned to California. Canada's B.C. Security Commission made no attempt to reintegrate Japanese Canadians; its camps were simply holding pens. The Canadian armed forces rejected Japanese-Canadian volunteers, and releases from custody came more slowly and carried more restrictions. Canadian courts rejected Japanese-Canadian legal appeals, and the ban on returning to the Pacific Coast continued in force until 1949. The most dramatic measure of these U.S.-Canadian differences, however, were the identical numbers who chose to be voluntarily repatriated to Japan, four thousand from each country, or five times as many proportionately from Canada as from the United States. Daniels attributes the differing treatment of the Japanese-American and Japanese-Canadian minorities not to different attitudes on the part of politicians and publics, which he describes as "almost interchangeable"; it was "the American constitution, with its tradition of judicial review which was largely responsible." Thus the American impulse to assimilate individuals rather than to acknowledge social groups worked to the advantage of Japanese Americans.[42]

Canada seemed so familiar to the U.S. service people stationed there, and yet it was different. Bob Hope, Tallulah Bankhead, and Shirley Temple came north to entertain them and made appearances to help sell Canadian victory bonds. Hollywood's contribution to cultural unity was the movie *Captains of the Clouds,* in which Canada's air ace "Billy" Bishop pinned RCAF pilot's wings on James Cagney. Young toughs in Toronto sported "zoot suits," although the suits touched off no riots like those in New York and Los Angeles. But war severed many peacetime cultural connections. The rationing of gasoline, oil, and tires shrank transborder tourism, and travel and immigration restrictions disrupted binational baseball leagues. The *Sporting News* reported that Canadian teams had gone back to the game's "dead-ball" era because the King government's War Exchange Conservation Act banned new Rawlings baseballs as "non-essential" imports. Import substitution created indigenous Canadian replacements. American feature films were joined on Canadian movie screens by the "Canada Carries On" documentaries from Canada's National Film Board, and more radio dials turned to the CBC to hear Canadian war news and war soap operas. American periodicals became harder to find because "pulp magazines" were prominent on the list of restricted imports.[43]

To the despair of Canadian children and those adults who secretly devoured them, comic books were also restricted. Unlike Britain and Australia, English Canada had developed no indigenous comic strips but instead imported them from the United States. Canadian comic artists who sought their fortunes on the funny pages migrated south, among them Harold Foster, who drew *Prince Valiant,* and Joe Shuster, creator of *Superman,* the quintessential crusader for "Truth, Justice and the American Way." Canadian youngsters absorbed *The Batman, Captain Marvel,* and *Walt Disney's Comics and Stories* as avidly as their counterparts in the United States. The U.S.-Canadian trade agreement of 1935 had removed the tariff, although newsstands raised the ten-cent cover price to twelve or fifteen cents. There are no accurate statistics of comic book circulation in Canada, but between 1937 and 1940, the value of magazines imported into Canada from the United States increased from $2.25 to $6.5 million (CDN). In the winter of 1940–41, Canadian kids found that their favorite comic titles had suddenly vanished from the racks in Canadian pharmacies, tobacco stores, and bus depots.

Shutting out U.S. comic books quickly spurred a domestic Canadian comic industry. *"Wow" Comics #1* reached the newsstands in the summer of 1941, and by 1945 four companies were printing comic books for a national market. Because of wartime shortages, the pages were in black and white; only the covers were colored. Between the covers of these "Canadian whites," kids discovered a miniature replica of the familiar American comic panorama: detectives, superheroes, cowboys, secret agents. Some of the characters were transparent "swipes" from the United States. "Captain Wonder," a Canadian boy who doubled as a costumed crime fighter, was a carbon copy of "Captain Marvel," complete with an ancient mystic and lightning flashes to effect the transformation. But despite such obvious imitations of American material, the Canadian comic books were distinctively Canadian. As patriotic propaganda for the war effort, they outdid the efforts of the government's Wartime Information Board. In every issue, a gallant Canadian serviceman (and in one case a servicewoman) such as "The Sea Fury" or "The Invisible Commando" crushed a crude stereotype of a German or a "Jap." "Johnny Canuck," "Canada's answer to Nazi oppression," was drawn by Toronto artist Leo Bachle to "typify the Canadian character." Johnny had no superheroic powers; when he "sent Hitler's generals reeling through the air with a single blow," he used the same human muscles as any other "fine fighting Canuck." His female counterpart was "Nelvana of the Northern Lights," a superheroine in a miniskirt who defended the sovereignty of the Canadian North from the evil "Kablunets." Canada's British connection was a recurring theme. Three comic book war heroes—"Spanner Preston," "Ace Barton," and "Pilot Officer Jimmie Clarkson: The Sign of Freedom"— were Canadians flying in the Royal Air Force. In a strange inversion of the U.S. exclusion of Canada from wartime strategy, readers of these comic books would never have known that the United States was one of Canada's allies.[44]

Below the surface of cooperation, after six years of war, lurked Canadian indignation at U.S. self-satisfaction at having "saved the world for democracy." Canadian leaders heartily resented their marginalization within the Allied strategic command, although none publicly complained about it. Ordinary peoples' complaints were also for private Canadian consumption. The memories of *Six War Years* collected by oral historian Barry Broadfoot are replete with bitter anti-Americanisms. A Canadian contractor insisted that the ten-month drama of the Alaska Highway was "balderdash, hoopla . . . generated by public relations types in the American Army." The "real" highway had been built only after the war by Canadians. A construction worker on the project remembered that "there was fighting and knifings and murders, . . . and white soldiers kicking black soldiers off the sidewalks." "We didn't like the Americans," a Canadian soldier commented about his U.S. comrades. "I was always amazed at how many of these fellows showed up drunk, half-drunk or with a hangover," remembered an RCAF officer. "We never wanted the Yanks around us, their air support," claimed a Normandy veteran; "they'd bomb anything that moved, Canadians, British, their own, . . . anything that moved." But although Canadians' stereotypes of the United States remained unaltered, their image of themselves was profoundly reshaped by justifiable national pride in their wartime accomplishments. In addition to its economic and military contributions to victory, during the war years Canada laid the foundations of the welfare state that had been created in the United States during the Great Depression. National unemployment insurance was implemented in 1941, a Canadian version of the Wagner Act in 1943, and universal family allowances (government grants to parents of children under eighteen) in 1944. Canadians evinced no desire to protect these gains with isolation within North America; almost 80 percent of them wanted their country to be active in postwar preservation of world peace. In World War II, concludes historian J. L. Granatstein, Canada leapt psychologically from "semi-autonomy" to "genuine nationhood."[45]

The United States emerged from four years of war as the most powerful country on the globe. On those infrequent occasions when Americans thought about Canada, they were more uncertain than ever what to make of it. Any understanding of Canada as the third most important military and industrial power in what came to be called the "Free World" discorded sharply with the bucolic northern Canadian wilderness depicted in such movies as *Springtime in the Rockies* and in hit songs such as Glenn Miller's "Under Blue Canadian Skies." Was Canada a country or a British colony? "The American," wrote Harvard history professor Crane Brinton in 1945, has "a hard time understanding the fact that, though he sees the face of George VI on Canadian postage stamps, . . . Canada is an independent nation." Even in the minds of U.S. leaders, wrote Lester Pearson privately from Washington, Canada was "suspended . . . somewhat uneasily . . . between the position of British colony and American dependency."[46]

A New World Order Frozen by Cold War, 1945–1947

The United States and its allies turned their attention to the shape of the postwar order well before the end of hostilities in Europe and the Pacific. With Britain and the Soviet Union, it dominated the transitional process, and its preoccupations tended to determine the context within which lesser nation-states such as Canada would function in the post-1945 years. The political and economic institutions of the postwar order grew from several major international conferences between 1943 and mid-1945. In Quebec in July 1943, Roosevelt and Churchill thought briefly about a future organization that would succeed the discredited League of Nations. At Moscow in October 1943, Cordell Hull, Anthony Eden, and V. M. Molotov continued on that theme. That autumn in Washington a more broadly based group of countries established UNRRA, the United Nations Relief and Recovery Administration. In July 1944, more than forty countries met at Bretton Woods, New Hampshire, to establish an International Monetary Fund and a World Bank to stabilize the postwar economic order. Meeting at Dumbarton Oaks, near Washington, from August through October 1944, representatives of the United States, Britain, the Soviet Union, and China talked of a

United Nations; the next spring some fifty countries met in San Francisco to adopt the UN Charter.

Where Canada would fit into this postwar international system was not of great concern to anyone but Canadians. U.S. officials found the contribution of Norman Robertson, Canadian undersecretary of state for external affairs, highly constructive, and noted but did not implement his comments about protecting the rights of middle powers. Canada played an important role in the creation of UNESCO, the United Nations Economic and Social Council, and became a charter member of that council. Canadians in the UN Secretariat also made important contributions. John Humphrey of the Human Rights Division joined Eleanor Roosevelt to draft the UN's Universal Declaration of Human Rights, an achievement he described as a major accomplishment of Canadian-U.S. cooperation. Americans and Canadians shared a strong new commitment to a stable world order and the economic restructuring and collective security that were essential to maintain it. They also came to share a growing disquiet over a perceived threat from "Russia," as the Soviet Union was universally described on both sides of the border. Increasing bipolarism between the Soviet Union and the United States, anxiety about communism, the economic reconstruction of Europe, and concern over nuclear weapons were the context for the U.S.-Canadian relationship during the transition from war to early cold war.[47]

Canada was no more than a vocal bystander in great power debates. Canada did not participate at Quebec, Moscow, or Dumbarton Oaks, except as a diplomatic whisper in the British ear. Nor did Canada have an impact on shaping the terms of the peace settlement. Canadian troops came home rapidly after victory in Europe because Canada was not one of the occupying powers and went unrepresented on the Allied Control Commission. Mackenzie King strongly favored a world rather than regional international organization for the postwar era, fearing that regionalism would result in continued dominance of international debate by a small number of powers; emphasis on regional security might enable the United States to slide back into prewar isolationism. But Canada played an active role at a May 1943 conference to discuss food and agricultural questions. Lester Pearson ably represented Canada, and he became chairman of both the interim commission and the formal organization created at San Francisco in 1945 as the UN Food and Agriculture Organization.[48]

Well before the United States forced Japanese surrender with two atomic bombs, it was evident that East-West tensions would follow the war. No one, however, could have anticipated the length, severity, and near insanity that came to characterize the cold war. Sources of conflict were diverse: Soviet anxiety for military security on its western borders, the question of war debts and reparations, the contribution of the Soviet Union to the war in the Pacific, the control of atomic weapons, Communist parties in Western Europe, Soviet espionage activities throughout the West. U.S. and Soviet mutual suspicion also derived from the deep U.S. legacy of anti-radicalism, and from Soviet memories of the unsuccessful 1919 Anglo-American intervention (which included Canadian troops) in the Bolshevik Revolution. These differences emerged at Yalta in February 1945, prior to Roosevelt's death, at the UN-founding meetings in San Francisco, and at Potsdam in July–August 1945. By that time the more acerbic Harry Truman was president and Clement Attlee the British prime minister; Mackenzie King, alone among the wartime leaders of the North Atlantic triangle, remained in power in Canada.

Although Canada preferred negotiation and accommodation to confrontation, Canadian and U.S. officials shared fundamental assumptions about the Soviet Union as a threat to the West and acted accordingly. English- and French-Canadian newspapers lauded Truman's Navy Day speech in New York in October 1945, which defined U.S. goals as a peaceful international open world order but announced that America would refuse to recognize any government "imposed on any nation by the force of any foreign power." Canadian undersecretary for external affairs Lester Pearson's understanding of the Soviet Union resonated with that of George Kennan of the U.S. State Department, later published under the pseudonym "X" in a *Foreign Affairs* article that circulated within the Canadian External Affairs Department. Pearson, who had returned as Canada's ambassador in Washington, seems to have imbibed the growing anti-Soviet sentiment. He wrote

King: "My own view . . . is that without some fundamental change in the Soviet state system and in the policies and views of its leaders, the U.S.S.R. is bound to come into open conflict with western democracy. This, of course, does not mean that war is inevitable, because changes and collapse do take place. But without them . . . the end must be conflict. The Russian leaders themselves insist on this." Pearson was less strident than Kennan, who argued that "we have here a force committed fanatically to the belief that with US there can be no permanent *modus vivendi*." Stalin had declared in February 1946 that international accommodation was impossible while capitalism and imperialism still guided Western policies. His words rang in the ears of Western leaders who counseled Truman to escalate his "get tough with the Russians" policy.[49]

Revelations of Soviet espionage in Canada fed such anxieties. In September 1945, Igor Gouzenko, a cipher clerk at the Soviet embassy in Ottawa, defected with details about a spy network that extended through Canada to the United States. His spymaster was Colonel Nikolai Zabotin, the military attaché. Zabotin had enlisted Canadians, as well as British scientists who had come to Canada for wartime atomic research. Canada, Britain, and the United States agreed to keep Gouzenko's revelations secret in order to catch the spies without rupturing relations with the USSR. Someone leaked: on 4 February 1946, journalist Drew Pearson spread the story to the millions of Americans who tuned in to his national radio show. FBI director J. Edgar Hoover, afraid that the Canadians would fumble an opportunity to demonstrate the menace of the tiny Communist parties of Canada and the United States, seems the likely source of Pearson's exclusive. In a message to Congress in March 1947, President Truman enunciated what would later be called the Truman Doctrine: "It must be the policy of the United States," Truman intoned, "to support free peoples who are resisting subjugation by armed minorities or by outside pressures." He asked for $400 million to confront what he assured Congress was Communist-inspired insurgency in Greece and threatened Soviet aggression in Turkey.[50]

Although U.S. officials still sometimes viewed Canada as a colonial fragment of the British Empire, the Truman State Department considered Canada "of the first order" because of the magnitude of the economic relationship combined with the reality of North American geography. But although Mackenzie King and his ministers shared Truman's concern about communism, in five meetings with Truman between 1945 and 1947, the prime minister resisted a more concrete military alliance. The Truman administration pressed for definitive steps to improve continental defense: weather stations, training facilities, and bases in the Canadian Arctic, and Canadian adoption of U.S. weapons and training in lieu of British. The best that Truman could wrest from King was a vague "Joint Statement for Defense Collaboration" issued in February 1947. The Joint Statement proposed "to increase the familiarity of each country's defense establishment with that of the other" by exchanging observers and the "encouragement" of standardization of arms and equipment. Compared to the fulsome language of Ogdensburg and Hyde Park, the document was cautious and noncommittal. "Permanent" and "quickly" had been replaced with "limited" and "gradual," and the last sentence was an escape clause: "either country may at any time discontinue collaboration."[51]

In this transitional period, when the cold war had yet to freeze solid, Canada sought acceptance for the role of a "middle power" ("small power" did not fit Canada's new self-image) in the Great Power shaping of world events. Canada did not want to provoke the Soviet Union, because conflict between the United States and the Soviet Union would inevitably involve Canada. As C. P. Stacey suggests, however, that objective remained illusory in the uncertain aftermath of World War II. "A so-called 'middle power' might make a loud noise . . . or take the line of quiet diplomacy . . . ; it came in the end to the same thing, and that was very little." World War II had altered the world balance of power, but Canada's foreign policy was still guided by the need to maintain familial relations with Great Britain and neighborly relations with the United States. The Soviet Union complicated both relationships.[52]

6 Canada in the New American Empire, 1948–1960

The modern U.S.-Canadian relationship dates from the intensified cold war that began in 1948. Britain's military and economic weakness, made painfully obvious in 1946–47, created new dilemmas for the other two sides of the "North Atlantic Triangle." Canada lost its historic British counterweight to the United States, and the United States was forced into Britain's old imperial role. With dizzying rapidity, the American-led struggle against the Communist specter brought a degree of intimacy between Canada and the United States that the war against Germany had never demanded. Both countries became charter members of the multilateral North Atlantic Treaty Organization (NATO) in 1949, and a year later, Canada followed the United States into a shooting war in Korea. Soviet nuclear bombs and long-range bombers made Canada indispensable to continental defense against transpolar air attack and prompted a peacetime U.S. presence in the Canadian Arctic and the bilateral North American Air Defense Agreement (NORAD) in 1957. A series of Defense Production Sharing Agreements seemed the logical corollary to military merger, and America's cold war quest for raw materials security further encouraged economic integration. Unlike earlier periods, U.S. direct investment in Canada and bilateral trade increased simultaneously. The U.S. domestic cold war "Red scare" echoed across the border in attempts to purge alleged Communists from the civil service, politics, the arts, and the labor movement. New cultural tidal waves of television and rock music rolled north as well. During the 1950s, Canada became an integral part of the new American Empire—a more integral part, grumbled nationalists—than it had been of the old British Empire. The main motif in U.S.-Canadian cold war relations was U.S. pressure for cooperation and conformity and an understated Canadian counter-effort for an independent voice. This contest was an unequal one. By 1960, some Canadians came to feel that they had lost it.

The United States, Canada, and the Origins of the Cold War

The only certainty about the origins of the cold war is that historians will continue to debate them passionately. Historic geopolitical rivalries, prewar ideological conflicts, and strains within the wartime alliance with the Soviet Union perhaps made East-West tension inevitable. Post-1945 contingencies, however, gave momentum to the cycle of measure and countermeasure that launched the cold war in earnest in 1948. The Truman Doctrine, write historians Lawrence Aronsen and Martin Kitchen, "let loose the genie of anti-communism and it was never possible, nor even deemed desirable, to get it back into the bottle." Thomas G. Paterson has shown how coercive U.S. programs for European economic reconstruction contributed further to ill will, and Gar Alperovitz has shown how the U.S. monopoly of atomic weapons fueled Soviet suspicion of U.S. intentions. Twenty million Soviet casualties in the "Great War against Fascism" left Soviet leadership determined to secure their borders against invasion by creating puppet regimes in Eastern Europe; a Communist coup backed by Soviet military force unseated the coalition government of Czechoslovakia in February 1948. In June, the Soviet Union closed the land corridor through Soviet-occupied Germany to Berlin. The West answered with a yearlong airlift of essential supplies until the Soviets lifted the blockade. After his narrow electoral victory over Republican Thomas Dewey in 1948, President Truman made "meeting the Communist threat" the centerpiece of his program, even if it required the occasional deliberate exaggeration of that threat. His 1949 inaugural address described the North Atlantic Alliance and the Marshall Plan as the foundations of U.S. foreign policy, and Truman won swift congressional approval of the Mutual Defense Assistance Act, which provided billions of U.S. dollars for the military buildup of the "free world." As if on some perverse cue, the Soviet Union detonated its first atomic weapon that same year, and China "fell" to communism when Mao Zedong's Red Army drove the discredited Chinese government of Jiang Jieshi into exile on Taiwan.[1]

In Washington, a powerful bureaucracy with a vested interest in demonizing the Soviet Union swiftly emerged. The National Security Act of 1947 created the unified organizational structure with which the United States fought the cold war: the integrated Department of Defense, the Central Intelligence Agency, and the National Security Council. The official assertion of U.S. strategic thought was NSC-68 (National Security Document 68) submitted to the president in April 1950. With the demise of Japan and Germany, the decline of the British and French empires, and the emergence of the Soviet Union and United States as the main "aspirants to hegemony," the historical international system had become a world of polarized powers. The Soviet Union, "animated by a new fanatic religious faith, antithetical to our own," sought "to impose its absolute authority over the rest of the world" through military conquest and subversion "by infiltration and intimidation." NSC-68 outlined the U.S. response to this Soviet threat: to "contain" the Soviet Union and to reject isolation and "develop a healthy international community" within the inter-American system and a rehabilitated Western Europe. To carry out this program, the United States needed overall military superiority alone and in concert with "other like-minded nations."[2]

Canada was inevitably among these "other like-minded nations." The ideology of NSC-68 became the keystone in the cold war arch that bridged the forty-ninth parallel, and its strategic and political assumptions became the context of U.S.-Canadian relations. Washington worried about the strength of Canadian commitment to the cold war crusade. Canada's leaders talked anticommunism, but their lack of action troubled the State Department. "The menace to freedom has never been greater or more insidious," Mackenzie King told the graduating class at William and Mary University in May 1948; "freedom is threatened not only by military force but by an organized conspiracy to establish a tyranny over the human mind." A month later, however, King's cabinet unanimously refused to send Royal Canadian Air Force planes or crews to Germany for the Berlin airlift. Combined with the persistent unwillingness to accept an expanded U.S. military presence in Canada, to the United States this suggested a lack of real resolve on Canada's part. Very few American officials understood the logic that underlay Canada's caution. Following bilateral defense discussions in Ottawa in 1946, George Kennan, head of the Policy Planning Staff in the State Department and one of the architects of containment, argued that Canadian leaders had to be convinced that the United States took Canada into its confidence on defense issues. But U.S. concerns about the degree of Canadian commitment continued. A State Department memo in early 1951 expressed displeasure about the level of the Canadian commitment: "In our estimate, Canada can do even more to fulfill its commitments under the North Atlantic Treaty and the U.N., and to meet its share in our hemispheric defence arrangements."[3]

Americans confused the Canadian quest for a policy distinct from, and more cautious than, that of the United States with a lack of policy. Canada stayed out of the Berlin airlift, for example, because it was not a member of the Allied Control Commission for the occupation of Germany. "The Russians" might make Canadian planes "the actual occasion for an incident which led to war." Moreover, wrote Defence Minister Brooke Claxton, Canada had "no say whatever in determining the policy"; the RCAF would "in fact have no status in the matter except as the subsidiary or paid help of the United Kingdom or of the United States." In retrospect, U.S. concerns about Canada's cold war reliability seem groundless. Canada regularly voted with the American bloc at the United Nations, and despite occasional deviations on specific issues, such as Communist China, Canadian governments never embarked on dramatically different foreign policy courses from those of the United States. Militarily, the Canadian shift in the 1950s from a defense strategy based on Britain to one tied to the United States was clear and rapid. Canadian governments, Liberal or Conservative, were always sensitive to the threat to Canadian sovereignty inherent in the expansion of their military relationship with the United States during the Truman and Eisenhower presidencies. Yet despite their caution, American radar networks soon spanned Canada's North, and Canada's military forces were consolidated under U.S. command through NATO and NORAD and armed with standardized American weapons. This strategic merger was so complete that in 1960 a Canadian colonel could observe ironically that "Canadians are obliged to accept a larger measure of dictation on defense matters from Washington than they were ever willing to take from London."[4]

Canada was drawn into the cold war dynamic of U.S. foreign policy for complex reasons, one of which was genuine dread of Soviet expansionism. Historian Denis Smith frames Canada's acquiescence to U.S. leadership within what he calls "the politics of fear." Canadian policymakers were desperately anxious that the United States step forward in defense of Western Europe and North America—"discharge her international responsibilities" was Lester Pearson's phrase. They were more afraid that the United States would reject the military and economic burdens of this role than they were of the problems that a "Pax Americana" would cause for Canada. But the Canadian Department of External Affairs' image of the Soviet Union was not identical to that of the U.S. State Department. Canadian officials agreed that "a fundamental cleavage inevitably exists" between East and West, but some argued that "it is a mistake to cast all the blame for the present tension on the Soviets." Canada's history predisposed Canadians to the conclusion that "both the Soviet Union and the United States are expanding powers." As Lester Pearson explained, communism alone was not the problem, but its "crusading and subversive power" had been "harnessed by a cold-blooded, calculating . . . Slav empire." Hume Wrong, Canadian ambassador to the United States, deplored "the blinding unbalanced fear and hatred of Russia and Communism prevalent in [the United States that] unfortunately seems to have penetrated the State Department."[5]

But this more nuanced explanation of Soviet behavior did not yield an alternative policy. And if Canadian anticommunism was kinder, gentler, and less histrionic than the U.S. variant, it was equally uncompromising. King and the prime ministers who followed him, Louis St. Laurent (1948–57) and John Diefenbaker (1957–63), were unyielding anti-Communists, as were their ministers of external affairs, St. Laurent, Lester Pearson, Sidney Smith, and Howard Green. None

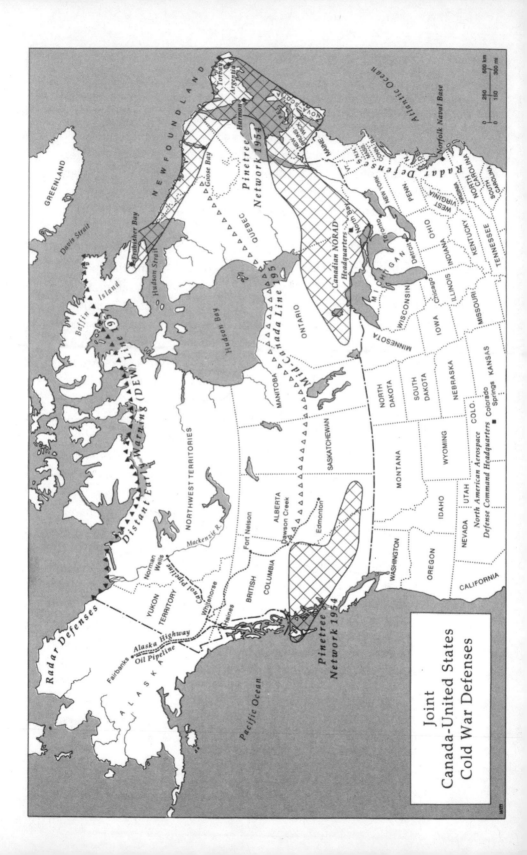

Joint
Canada-United States
Cold War Defenses

of these men questioned U.S. containment strategy; they quibbled only about tactics. They agreed with "the policy of firmness and containing the Soviet Union" but worried lest it "be pushed too hard and too fast." They had no doubt where Canada stood in a showdown between the United States and the Soviet Union. Canada might reject sending planes for the Berlin airlift, but as Mackenzie King confided to his diary, a real "fight against Communism" would be a very different matter: "it was quite certain that if war broke out . . . Canada would wish to come in instantly. . . . [T]here could be no two views on that score."[6]

In continental defense, Canadian leaders followed the U.S. lead out of fiscal reality as well as ideology. In the new world of bipolarism and long-range bombers, Canada had become a buffer state between the United States and the Soviet Union. If Canadians would not or could not defend themselves, the United States would perforce step in to do it for them. Minister of Defense Brooke Claxton told Prime Minister Mackenzie King in early 1947 that although Canada should strive to accomplish as much on its own as was possible, limited economic resources and common sense dictated cooperation with U.S. defense objectives and operations. Four years later, Claxton put it more bluntly: "it may be very difficult indeed for the Canadian Government to reject any major defence proposal which the United States Government presents with conviction as essential to the defence of North America." The conditions also impelled Canada into junior membership in America's cold war club. As a capitalist nation, dependent on international trade, the benefits were obvious. Defense cooperation with the United States was much cheaper than unilateralism. Canada could perhaps have stretched its capacity to the limit to create on its own the military infrastructure that would have made U.S. bases on Canadian soil and a cooperative system of air defense unnecessary. But Canadians did not have the political will to spend their money this way. Canada had been a colony protected in part by a parent country for most of the 350 years that Europeans had lived there; it did not require too extensive a rationalization to enjoy from the United States the security they had formerly accepted from France and Britain. Security did not come without an ultimate cost, however, as Canadians had twice learned in world wars and would learn again in Korea.[7]

Proud to March at America's Side

Canada and the United States were "present at the creation" in 1949 of the first major regional security alliance, the North Atlantic Treaty Organization. NATO emerged from the recognition, after the Soviet-directed coup in Czechoslovakia in 1948, that the United Nations could not fulfill a collective security role. The initiative came from Europe, where Britain, France, and the Benelux countries had united in the Brussels Pact, and from Canada, where diplomat Escott Reid had been putting words in the mouth of External Affairs Minister Louis St. Laurent about the need "for the free nations of the world to form their own closer association for collective self-defense." The first stage was secret "security conversations" among the United States, Britain, and Canada, and in the summer of 1948, U.S. undersecretary of state Robert Lovett met in Washington with the ambassadors of Canada and the Brussels Pact countries. Talks broadened to produce the North Atlantic Charter, in which twelve countries (the United States, Canada, Britain, France, the Benelux nations, Denmark, Iceland, Italy, Portugal, and Norway) pledged "that an armed attack against one or more of them in Europe or North America shall be considered an attack against them all."[8]

NATO meant something very different to Canada than it did to the United States. For America, it was a dramatic departure from the tradition of "no entangling alliances," which had been an article of faith and practice since George Washington's Farewell Address. The idea of permanently stationing the U.S. Army on European soil would have been unthinkable before the cold war, but Michigan senator Arthur Vandenberg, a Republican with impeccable isolationist credentials, provided critical congressional support to the NATO treaty because he believed that it would deter Soviet aggression so that U.S. troops might be kept out of Europe. Truman and his new secretary of state Dean Acheson had no such illusion: they perceived NATO as integral to the policy of containment already in operation, the military counterpart of the Marshall Plan for the economic reconstruction of Europe. Canadian emotional and military ties to Europe were deeper, but Canada entered NATO neither lightly nor as a decision made in Washington. To the contrary, the treaty offered the prospect of a multilateral counterpoise to U.S. influence. As Lester Pearson suggested, Canada sought in NATO safety in numbers precisely to avoid "seduction" by its southern neighbor. Escott Reid, a diplomat who worked closely with Pearson, explained that Canada had to "avoid being left alone with the United States . . . because of the great disparity in power between the two countries." NATO, along with the United Nations and the British Commonwealth, offered an opportunity "to redress the balance in North America." Canada also wanted NATO to be more than "an old-fashioned military alliance." St. Laurent spoke of "an overwhelming preponderance of *moral* force" as well as economic and military power. Article II of the charter, inserted at Canada's request, called on the signatories to "contribute toward the further development of peaceful and friendly international relations by strengthening their free institutions, by bringing about a better understanding of the principles on which those institutions are founded, and by promoting conditions of stability and well-being."[9]

After hints from Dean Acheson, Canada nominated U.S. general Dwight D. Eisenhower to be NATO's first Supreme Allied Commander, Europe (SACEUR). The "future of western civilization," said the new SACEUR, depended on NATO's success. But any hope that the alliance might enhance that civilization rather than simply permit it to survive died quickly, as the US cold war agenda swamped other voices, and NATO's military dimension overshadowed its other objectives. Secretary of State Acheson thought Canadians incurably inclined toward moralizing in foreign policy and utterly naive about international power politics. Although the NATO charter specifically gave each member nation the right to determine "as it deems necessary" its own military contribution, the United States pressed Canada to station troops in Europe, and in 1951, the St. Laurent government complied. Canada also followed the United States in an unprecedented rearmament. Although Canadian defense expenditures never reached levels proportional to those of the United States, between 1948 and 1953 they leapt from 6.8 to 43 percent of Canada's budget, and from 1.3 to 7.5 percent of the gross national product (GNP). Yet the conventional nonnuclear forces—the only forces Canada maintained—were overshadowed in NATO strategy by the nuclear weapons the United States would use in "massive retaliation" against Soviet attack. By 1955, NATO had so little concern for the ideals of "free institutions" that, at U.S. insistence, Canada shared NATO membership with a rearmed Germany and with such "democracies" as Greece and Turkey.[10]

World events, of course, catalyzed NATO's shift to a purely military emphasis: the creation of the Warsaw Pact, the USSR's mirror-image of NATO; the Soviet detonation of a "nuclear explosion" (President Truman's announcement avoided the words "atomic bomb"); and, most dramatically, the Korean War. "NATO owes the fact that it has built up its strength to the communist aggression in Korea," Brooke Claxton later remembered; "Korea came along and saved us" was Dean Acheson's more trenchant description. A former Japanese colony, the Korean peninsula had been partitioned between the USSR and the United States along the thirty-eighth parallel in 1945. Canada was injected into Korean affairs in 1948 when the UN General Assembly elected Canada to its commission to supervise the partition. The King government had been at first unwilling to serve, but the United States, Canada's nominator, pressed the matter. After a direct appeal from President Truman to Prime Minister King, Canada reluctantly consented. The commission was a failure, and the UN's planned reunification never took place. Instead, a communist People's Republic of Korea formed in the North and an unstable quasi democracy in the South. In June 1950, 110,000 North Korean soldiers with Soviet weapons swept across the thirty-eighth parallel to drive the weaker South Korean forces before them toward Seoul and the sea. Although no one in Washington had any illusions about South Korean president Syngman Rhee's dedication to democracy in Korea, the Truman administration was shocked by the attack and reversed its previous inclination to treat South Korea as outside the American strategic perimeter in the Pacific. To the surprise of the world, Canada included, the United States decided on military intervention at once. Dean Acheson immediately brought the issue before the UN Security Council, which (in the absence of the Soviet Union) condemned the North Korean invasion and authorized the use of force to repel it. Within five days, U.S. munitions flowed to the South Korean army, U.S. jets struck at the North Korean advance, the U.S. Seventh Fleet interposed between Mainland China and Taiwan, and General Douglas MacArthur embarked American troops for Korea from bases in Japan.[11]

There was no formal congressional declaration of war. Korea was described as a UN "police action," even if it was an essentially U.S. conflict. Had the early fighting progressed well for South Korean and U.S. troops, the multilateral dimension of the war might never have developed; but the U.S. forces fared badly, and the Truman administration soon appealed in general for UN assistance and specifically for Canadian forces. For Canada, the UN imprimatur and the U.S. anti-Communist mission left no doubt, despite memories of the domestic crises caused by two world wars and apprehension that Korea would broaden into a wider conflict involving China and the Soviet Union. Canada was also limited by the forces available to it, for its rearmament program remained in its early stages. The Canadian contribution, made gradually throughout 1950, eventually totaled 25,000 troops, three Royal Canadian Navy destroyers, and an RCAF transport squadron. Their symbolic significance meant more to the United States than their military import: 821,000 American GIs served in Korea. But the Canadians fought well—the second Battalion of Princess Patricia's Canadian Light Infantry won a U.S. Presidential Unit Citation for their stand at Kapyong in April 1951. Canadian troops remained in Korea until 1957, four years after an armistice ended the futile conflict where it began—with a polarized Korea divided at the thirty eighth parallel. Throughout these years, Ottawa heard a constant refrain from Washington that Canada was not carrying its share of the cold war military burden. In Korea, unlike the two world wars, morbid calculus supported the U.S. argument: 34,000 dead Americans were proportionately more than the 406 Canadians who never recrossed the Pacific.

Canadian leaders feared throughout that the Korean conflict was the wrong war at the wrong time, and that the USSR had drawn UN forces into a costly, unwinnable quagmire that would allow Soviet gains in other sectors of the globe. Canada repeatedly urged the United States to seek a negotiated settlement, but always did so quietly and confidentially. Many Canadian policymakers had private reservations about the resolution that authorized UN forces to attack across the thirty-eighth parallel, but Minister of External Affairs Lester Pearson voted in favor of it in the UN General Assembly. As General MacArthur's advance rolled northward, Pearson entreated the United States to respect its assurances to Canada that "when the United Nations forces were approaching the Chinese border, the United States would follow a very prudent and unprovocative course of action . . . so that the Government in Beijing would have no excuse for committing their forces in North Korea." The Canadian cabinet shared President Truman's fury when MacArthur crossed the Yalu River, triggering massive Chinese intervention. On 2 April 1951, in a speech in Toronto, Pearson described MacArthur's behavior as "a threat to the unity of the free world," and the Canadian government was delighted when the president finally ordered General Omar Bradley to "fire the son of a bitch" two days later, although there is no evidence of a direct connection between the Canadian protest and Truman's decision. Even after General Matthew Ridgeway replaced MacArthur, however, Canadian officials worried "that there was hardly a substratum of truth" in reports from the U.S. high command. After a visit to Korea, Defence Minister Brooke Claxton "came to have less and less confidence" in the U.S. Army's claim that they "had killed and wounded so many Chinamen for each hour or bomb." Concern over what they felt was U.S. irresponsibility in Korea colored later Canadian attitudes to U.S. escalation of the nuclear debate and to further adventures in Asia.[12]

But their concern did not scare Canadians out of the cold war. They feared the arrogance and overconfidence of U.S. power but simultaneously fell victim to a peculiarly Canadian form of hubris, bred of two centuries of feeling morally superior to the United States. Canadian leaders rationalized the necessity of their satellite status in the new American empire into a virtue. Because Canada had a "special relationship" with the United States (no one observed aloud that Britain and Australia also claimed "special relationships" with America), Canada had a unique ability to shape U.S. policy behind the scenes. If Canada seldom criticized U.S. international initiatives in public, no matter how strongly it opposed them, that did not mean that Canada was an American client-state. To the contrary: through "quiet diplomacy" conducted in confidence, Ottawa was using its "special relationship" to restrain Washington from even more dangerous decisions. In the Korean example, Canadians credited their influence with constraining the United States from full-scale war with China and from that greatest of horrors, dropping the atomic bomb. That this myth was completely impossible to prove—or disprove—only added to its attraction. In the words of an academic apologist, political scientist Peyton Lyon: "Even when Washington persists in policies that many Canadians consider misguided, it remains entirely possible that the Americans would have pursued these policies with greater vigor, or launched other misguided policies, without Canadian representation." The more difficult the international crisis, the more important Canada's quiet, constraining voice became. With nuclear weapons and long-range bombers to deliver them, the Americans might blow up the world at any minute.[13]

This same military technology made Canada's North critical to American cold war defense strategy. U.S. officials anticipated that any strike against the United States would come by air over the North Pole; hence the first line of strategic defense had to be a cooperative one in the Canadian Arctic. Although Canadian military planners were skeptical of the importance and imminence of any direct attack on North America, that was the conclusion of the Joint Military Cooperation subcommittee of the Permanent Joint Board on Defense in 1946. Korea and the Soviet nuclear bomb gave the situation greater urgency and made the establishment of a largely U.S. defense system on Canadian territory a major element of the bilateral relationship. The three air defense radar systems that went up in Canada between 1950 and 1957 illustrate how rapidly changing U.S. perceptions of defense requirements could arouse Canadian political sensitivity, and how that sensitivity could in turn frustrate the United States. Each radar network was constructed at American insistence, and each raised questions of financing and control. After protracted negotiations, the Pinetree Network, which ran just north of the Canadian population centers along the U.S. border, became a joint enterprise. Press releases delicately skirted the fact that the United States paid two-thirds of its cost. When U.S. air defense strategists insisted upon another line farther north,

Canada used its own "McGill Fence" radar technology and paid for, staffed, and named this Mid-Canada Line on its own. But when the National Security Council (NSC-139 and NSC-159/4) concluded that the threat of a Soviet nuclear attack necessitated a Distant Early Warning (DEW) Line across the Arctic, Canada conceded U.S. financing and operation. The DEW line highlighted Canada's dilemma: although the U.S. cold war strategy was unvarying, the details of U.S. tactics were subject to change without consultation and with little advance notice. It was impossible for Canada, even if it chose to do so, to make itself secure enough to eliminate the Pentagon's pressure for American bases, troops, and equipment on Canadian soil.

The Canadian position on continental defense was consistent: defense cooperation with the United States was desirable and inevitable, but the United States should be granted no long-term rights of occupation to defense sites. Facilities should be joint enterprises under Canadian command whenever possible, and the presence of American troops on Canadian soil should be avoided when feasible and phased out quickly when it was not. These objectives were easier to set than to achieve—there were fifteen thousand U.S. servicepeople stationed in Canada by the mid-1950s. Canada's goal shifted to retaining as much control over this U.S. presence as it could. U.S. troops were governed by the Visiting Forces Act, passed by Parliament in 1947. The act granted U.S. commanders the right to enforce military discipline upon their troops while on Canadian soil. Any violations of Canadian law, however, came under the jurisdiction of Canadian courts. Matters were complicated when Newfoundland joined the confederation in 1949, and Canada became the landlord for the U.S. leases signed by the British that still had ninety years to run. These bases might have been in North Carolina rather than Newfoundland. The Internal Revenue Service collected taxes, the U.S. Post Office delivered the mail, and U.S. law governed even Canadian civilian employees, who were forbidden to join labor unions and were not covered by workmen's compensation or Canadian unemployment insurance. On more than one occasion, U.S. Military Police had stood off Newfoundland policemen at gunpoint. "We can only imagine," confided a Canadian cabinet minister, "what the attitude of the United States would be if the position were reversed." In November 1949, *Maclean's* magazine revealed the "national shame" that "the Yanks rule a part of Canada." To the chagrin of the Canadian government, however, the United States was unmoved by Canada's discomfiture. To renegotiate leases with Canada would set a dangerous precedent for U.S. bases in other countries. Washington refused to alter the Newfoundland leases without a quid pro quo—a base for the Strategic Air Command at Goose Bay, Labrador. In 1952, after hard-nosed bargaining carried out through the PJBD, the legal status of the Newfoundland bases changed to reflect the Visiting Forces Act, and U.S. B-29 bombers were in readiness in Labrador for an atomic offensive against the Soviet Union. This was the only long-term lease the United States bullied Canada to grant, however; Goose Bay reminded Canadian leaders, writes historian David J. Bercuson, of "the need to protect Canada's sovereignty not only from Soviet attack, but from American encroachment as well." [14]

When U.S. officials thought about it, Canadian sensitivity irritated them as much U.S. insensitivity infuriated Canadians. American ambassador to Canada Stanley Woodward complained on his retirement in 1953 that Canadian nationalism complicated defense cooperation, and when President Dwight Eisenhower visited Ottawa that November to meet with Prime Minister St. Laurent, the defense of North America against nuclear attack overshadowed the rest of their agenda. Air defense integration had been the subject of extensive discussions of the Permanent Joint Board on Defense, and at PJBD recommendation Canada had conceded the right of U.S. interceptor flights over Canada. The eventual solution to air defense cooperation was to merge it in NORAD, the North American Air Defense Command. NORAD came into being because the Royal Canadian and U.S. air forces wanted it. The Royal Canadian and U.S. armies and navies, each steeped in hoary tradition, retained a degree of aloofness from each other despite NATO and the integration of their weapons. But the RCAF and the USAF, the youngest services, moved to easy familiarity. Under their new "system of integrated operational control," NORAD's American commander in chief and his Canadian deputy would coordinate "mutual self-defense" of "the Canada–United States region." NORAD evolved slowly because triservice rivalry meant that the United States had no single system of its own until the mid-1950s; "integration of the Canadian and American air defense systems," writes historian Joseph T. Jockel, "brought Canada into what had been a purely American state of confusion." As a result, official Canadian approval on 24 July 1957 came from the new Conservative government of John Diefenbaker. Subsequent events revealed that Diefenbaker and his cabinet had only the vaguest idea how much of Canada's national sovereignty they had signed away.[15]

Integrating Affluence

Junior membership in America's cold war club also proved indispensable to Canadian economic self-interest. Canada was a capitalist country—a "free enterprise" country in the new rhetoric of anticommunism—and more dependent on international trade than the United States. Just as Britain's military weakness ordained a Canadian-U.S. defense alliance, Britain's financial problems dictated closer Canadian economic ties to the United States. Before 1939, Canada had sold more to Britain and Europe than it bought from them, a trade surplus that allowed Canadians to buy more from the United States than they sold there. Peace did not restore this happy situation; instead, Western Europe's postwar economic plight reduced purchases of Canadian grain, fish, and lumber at the same time as Canadian demand soared for consumer goods from U.S. factories. It was a currency problem rather than a trade imbalance; Canada's transatlantic customers could not pay for what they bought in U.S. dollars, nor could their currencies be converted into U.S. dollars. As a result, the years 1946 and 1947 turned into a reenactment of the economic crisis of 1940–41: Canada faced a massive shortage of U.S. dollars to cover its debts in the United States. In November 1947, the Canadian government imposed emergency controls on imports and outflows of currency and unhappily considered further constraints. These restrictions to trade displeased the U.S. government, but it obligingly ignored the fact that Canada had contravened the 1938 U.S.-Canadian trade agreement and loaned Canada $300 million (U.S.) to help meet the emergency. Alternative longer-term solutions, however, were obviously necessary. Canada had hoped for increased multilateral trade as a way out of its dilemma, and its representatives accordingly had worked hard for the General Agreement on Tariffs and Trade (GATT) signed in Geneva that same November. But Europe remained too economically weak to offer any real answers; more plausible resolutions to Canada's problems lay in Washington.[16]

Canada's first request was to be sheltered beneath the wing of the U.S. European Recovery Program announced by Secretary of State George Marshall in June 1947. Canada did not request aid from the Marshall Plan, but if European recipients were allowed to spend their Marshall Plan money on Canadian exports, Canada's shortfall of U.S. dollars would be greatly reduced. Canada appealed for justice rather than charity. Its dollar crisis had been caused in large part by two billion dollars (CDN) loaned to Western Europe in 1946 and 1947. As C. D. Howe pointed out, Canada had spent "more per capita to assist European recovery" than had the United States. The Truman administration conceded Canada's principle, and in return, Canadians did their best to aid administration attempts to sell the Marshall Plan to Congress and the American public. In his speech to Congress, the president specifically cited Canadian generosity to Europe as a justification for the Marshall Plan, and as a reason why it "should not be restricted to purchases within the United States." This "off-shore purchasing" was singled out by congressional critics such as Ohio Republican senator Robert Taft, and Canadian diplomats, politicians, and businessmen waited anxiously while the legislation dragged through Congress. In April 1948, the plan and the provision for purchases from Canada were finally approved. "We should give Canada a lot of credit for this," Truman's assistant secretary of state Willard Thorp later commented; "Canada is forgotten; nobody remembers that Canada had anything to do with the Marshall Plan [yet] Canada made a substantial contribution." Canada was not forgotten financially, however. Historian J. L. Granatstein estimates that during the first two years of its operation, the Marshall Plan put $1.155 billion (U.S.) into Canadian coffers.[17]

Canada's second goal was to bring its trade with the United States closer to a balance. After cautious probing, Canadian emissaries made a startling proposition in October 1947 for "a comprehensive agreement involving, wherever possible, the complete elimination of [customs] duties." As the State Department account of the undisclosed meeting explained it, "they feel that Canada must either integrate her economy more closely with that of the United States or be forced into discriminatively restrictive policies involving greater self sufficiency . . . with corresponding danger of friction with the United States, if not economic warfare." Not even the fact that discussions were underway was disclosed to the press, and the secret negotiations moved swiftly. State Department trade officials felt that a sector-by-sector trade agreement would die in Congress, and they countered with a broader offer of "substantially free trade between the two countries" in which "each [country] would retain its separate tariff vis-à-vis third countries." This assuaged Canadian anxiety about their historic relationship with Great Britain, so that by March 1948 all but the details had been roughed in. Apart from quotas on agricultural products, which were essential to domestic politics in both countries, the draft agreement abolished all tariffs between them. A State Department memo described it as "a unique opportunity of . . . knitting the two countries together—an objective of United States foreign policy since the founding of the Republic." [18]

The 1948 U.S.-Canadian free trade agreement never reached either legislature. Congressional opposition would perhaps have doomed the agreement; in the Canadian Parliament, the huge Liberal majority would eventually have forced it through, but only after a rancorous debate. Mackenzie King's initial enthusiasm for free trade wore through as he weighed the likely political side effects. He thought back to the Liberal Party's 1911 electoral disaster over reciprocity; this new and more far-reaching agreement "would be twisted into a final endeavor to bring about economic union with the United States, which would mean annexation and separation from Britain." On further reflection, he wondered if this might not be perilously close to the truth. The "long objective of the Americans," he wrote in his diary, "was to control this continent [and] to get Canada under their aegis. If I was an American, I would have the same view specially considering Russia's position."

King abruptly decided to break off discussions, and free trade evaporated from the binational agenda for another forty-six years.[19]

Despite this, the volume of Canadian-U.S. trade, already the largest two-way commodity trade in the world, became larger still. Canada's imports from the United States reached about 70 percent of total imports during World War II and remained there after the war. The dramatic postwar change was the increase in the percentage of total Canadian exports now destined for U.S. markets. Between 1946 and 1951, Canadian exports to the United States more than doubled in real terms (from $888 million CDN to $2,298 million CDN). The United States absorbed 38 percent of Canada's total exports in 1946 and 59 percent in 1951. Canadian exports to Britain stagnated (from $598 million CDN to $631 million CDN) and declined in proportional terms from 26 percent of total Canadian exports in 1946 to only 16 percent in 1951. This precipitous decline of Anglo-Canadian trade was not a Canadian decision, or a "sell-out" of Britain, as some Canadian nationalists murmured. Despite millions in Canadian aid, Britain simply could not afford to buy very much from Canada, leaving its former colony, in historian Bruce Muirhead's words, "no choice other than to exploit the one reliable market it did have, the United States." The United States thus achieved one of the historic goals of its Canadian policy—"knitting the two countries together" and detaching Canada from a British Empire preferential trading system without any comprehensive free trade agreement.[20]

American demand for Canadian resources fueled a resource boom of greater dimensions than that of the 1920s. In the 1920s, raw materials had been shipped south to manufacture consumer products; in the 1950s, U.S. consumer demand was augmented by the military needs of America's new global defense posture. Canada was a nearby and reassuringly stable foreign supplier in a turbulent world; as a Department of Defense research report explained to President Eisenhower, critical resources produced in Canada were "almost as good emergency insurance as resource production in [the] continental United States." The best example of trade directly linked to military demand was the hundredfold increase in the value of U.S. uranium imports from Canada between 1948 and 1959, but the value of imports of aluminum, copper, lead, nickel, zinc, and iron ore had surpassed their World War II peaks by 1950, doubled by 1955, and increased again by half by 1960. Much of their production was controlled by U.S. mining multinationals: lead and zinc, for example, came from American Smelting and Refining and from American Metal Corporation.[21]

Among the most profitable commodities the United States sent north was popular culture, for which Canada continued to be the most important single external market. Canadians bought 40 percent of all the U.S. books and 80 percent of all the U.S. magazines sold abroad; they were the second largest absolute (after Britain) and by far the largest per capita consumers of U.S. movies. Two new technologies spurred mass cultural exports after 1945: vinyl 33 and 45 rpm records, which brought rock 'n' roll to a vast teenage audience, and television, in which the United States gained continental and world programming leadership as it had with cinema and radio. As before, there were large percentage profits in Canada for U.S. cultural industries; once a cultural product has been produced, language and geography made the marginal cost of exporting it to Canada minimal, and Canadians bought pop culture at prices that were "slightly higher in Canada." Unlike the 1920s, after 1945 Canadian governments made no use of protectionism to achieve cultural sovereignty. After Canada's intelligentsia vented its dismay about the menace of American mass culture through the Royal Commission on National Development in the Arts, Letters and Sciences (the Massey Commission) in 1951, Canada followed the commission's recommendation of state promotion of high culture and the continued support of the public infrastructure such as the Canadian Broadcasting Corporation (CBC) and the National Film Board (NFB). This cultural promotion, as before, was never a serious threat to the U.S. firms exporting cultural products. NFB documentaries would not reduce Canadian consumption of Hollywood's feature films. Canada's new public television service, far from a being a threat, actually bought programs from U.S. networks: *I Love Lucy* and *I Was a Communist for the FBI* came to Canadian screens via the CBC![22]

On the two occasions on which Canada pondered restricting sales of American culture, U.S. entertainment exporters did not need Washington's help to neutralize Canadian cultural sovereignty policies that threatened their interests. Beginning in 1943, U.S. magazines skirted Canada's periodicals tariff by printing "Canadian editions" in Canada with minimally different editorial content and advertising aimed directly at Canadian consumers. *Time* used its wholly owned Canadian subsidiary to dissuade the St. Laurent and Diefenbaker governments from tax changes that would have made this ruse uneconomic. In 1947, faced with controls on Canadian distribution because of the currency crisis and with the possibility that the NFB would begin feature film production, the Motion Picture Association of America sold the Canadian government on the "Canadian Co-operation Program." This transparent flimflam promised to display Canada to the world through the work of Hollywood studios. Producers were to be "encouraged" to use Canadian locations whenever appropriate, Canadian news in the newsreels was to be increased, and scriptwriters promised that Canada would be mentioned as frequently as possible in the dialog of features made in Hollywood! The wonder is not that the plan achieved no results, for Hollywood did not intend it to, but that this bizarre scheme took in such an otherwise hard-headed Canadian as cabinet minister C. D. Howe.[23]

Hollywood's recourse to this deceit demonstrated that economic relations would never be trouble free. From the Canadian perspective, two historic problems continued: how to ensure continued access to their American market during outbreaks of congressional protectionism and how to deal with byzantine U.S. customs procedures. During the early 1950s, for example, the U.S. Tariff Commission and Congress toyed with protection against a variety of Canadian agricultural products, against fish fillets, and against lead, zinc, and oil. The Eisenhower administration addressed potential friction points promptly and continued the long-standing preference to work quietly and informally through special bilateral institutions rather than engage in open diplomatic wrangling. Within a year of taking office, Eisenhower had cooperated with the St. Laurent government to establish a cabinet-level Joint U.S.-Canada Committee on Trade and Economic Affairs. As the State Department explained, such institutions afforded an opportunity not only to resolve existing problems but also to anticipate and head off emerging issues.[24]

Economic questions received broader consideration by a commission chaired by Clarence B. Randall, head of the U.S. Council on Foreign Economic Policy. Personally involved in iron ore development in Canada and undaunted by the failure of free trade in 1948, Randall persistently advocated the economic integration of the two countries. His committee's 1954 report touched on all of the critical postwar economic issues: foreign aid and economic assistance, foreign investment, agriculture and raw materials, trade policy, labor standards, and currency convertibility. In spite of disagreement from Congress with the report's proposal for aggressive trade liberalization, Eisenhower recommended and Congress approved an extension of the Trade Agreements Act, which cut tariffs on specific items up to 15 percent, simplified customs procedures for imports, and provided income tax incentives to encourage U.S. private foreign investment.[25]

Not that American capital needed much encouragement to invest in Canada. The foundations of a U.S. branch plant economy had been laid there much earlier by, among other things, Canada's "national policy" of protective tariffs. Until 1940, the tariff had created a crude inverse relationship between trade and foreign investment: higher Canadian tariffs reduced U.S. exports but increased U.S. investment in Canada; lower Canadian tariffs increased exports and reduced U.S. investment. In the melodramatic words of historian Stephen Scheinberg, Canada "could only choose the gravedigger, to be buried by American exports or by American branch plants." During the 1950s, however, both trade and the U.S. economic presence in Canada expanded rapidly at the same time. The State Department calculated that U.S. direct foreign investment in Canada grew from $3.58 billion (U.S.) in 1950 to $8.33 billion by the end of 1957, an increase more significant than that of U.S. direct foreign investment in Latin America over the same period. The bulk of that investment was in manufacturing ($3.51 billion) followed by oil ($2.15 billion) and by mining and smelting ($1 billion). Canadian estimates set the value of total American investment, direct and portfolio, at $16.72 billion at the end of 1960. This represented 75 percent of all foreign investment in Canada, as compared to 60 percent in 1939. British investment had fallen from 36 to 15 percent over this same period.[26]

Defense production was a fundamental element of economic integration: as it became truly continental in scope during the 1950s, parts of the Canadian economy became northern extensions of what President Eisenhower would later call "the military-industrial complex." The Statement of Principles of Economic Cooperation, signed in October 1951, was the first of a series of industrial defense accords that brought U.S. capital and technology to Canada on a far larger scale than had the Hyde Park Declaration during World War II. The United States interpreted its Buy-American Act so as to permit military purchases in Canada. Not only official Washington but also the U.S. Chamber of Commerce recommended the "highest practicable degree of standardization and coordination in the production of military equipment and in defense planning." A series of Defense Production Sharing Agreements, the first in 1958, extended this arrangement and permanently exempted Canada from the Buy-American Act. By 1960, eight of Canada's fifteen most important defense contractors were subsidiaries of American corporations, among them Pratt & Whitney, Westinghouse, General Motors, and General Electric. General Dynamics named its aircraft subsidiary in suburban Montreal "Canadair," but the interceptors it turned out were U.S. F-86 Sabre Jets.[27]

"No other nation as highly industrialized as Canada has such a large proportion of industry controlled by non-resident concerns," two political economists reported to a gathering of Canadian academics in 1956. Observing this fact was much easier than accounting for it. Economist Peter Kresl argues that lack of opposition to foreign ownership was caused by a labor movement dominated by U.S.-based unions. Certainly the 1950s marked the apex of this tendency: more than a million Canadian workers, 72 percent of organized workers in Canada, belonged to unions headquartered in the United States. Although union density—membership as a percentage of the nonfarm labor force—crept toward U.S. levels, the Canadian working class seemed destined to continue to march a half-step behind its U.S. counterpart. A year after the American Federation of Labor and the Congress of Industrial

Organizations reunited in 1955 as the AFL-CIO, in Canada the Trades and Labour Congress and the Canadian Congress of Labour suddenly found each other. The only outspoken left-wing critic of U.S. investment in Canada was Tim Buck, leader of the Communist Party. Canadian Communists had been spared some of the harassment heaped on their U.S. comrades by the House Committee on Un-American Activities, but Communist advice was no more likely to be listened to in Canada than in the United States.[28]

Mainstream analyses of the significance of the high level of U.S. direct investment remained a decade in the future. When these analyses came, they pointed out potential problems: U.S. firms might make decisions not in Canada's best interest; they would be subject to extraterritorial U.S. laws; they would do all their research and development in the United States; they would concentrate primary extraction in Canada and manufacturing in the United States. In the 1950s, however, most Canadians remained complacent about the extent of U.S. ownership of their economy. In the continental prosperity of the 1950s, Canada's postwar economic problems seemed long in the past. For seven years of the decade, the Canadian dollar, with Queen Elizabeth's portrait on it, was actually worth several cents more than the U.S. bill that after 1957 was emblazoned with the phrase "IN GOD WE TRUST."

At the State Department, Clarence Randall continued to press for U.S.-Canadian free trade. Randall understood the political impediments that had checked free trade in the past but insisted that circumstances had altered; with Europe moving toward a common market that could include Britain, North American economic integration might prove essential. The advantages of free trade with Canada would outweigh the disadvantages to some sectors of the U.S. economy, and these would be mitigated if integration with Canada were phased in over a twelve- to fifteen-year period. In 1957, Randall persuaded the State Department to conduct a study of economic integration between the two countries. But Secretary of State John Foster Dulles put an abrupt damper on Randall's prescient enthusiasm. It would be "inappropriate now for the United States to propose an economic integration," Dulles warned Randall in July 1957. Canadians were "rightly proud of their national independence and are eager to control their own destiny. . . . There might be Canadian concern that the economic integration of both countries would in effect subject Canada to preponderant United States economic influence. Therefore, . . . any initiative [for free trade] should come from Canada." Better to deal with areas of friction as they arose, such as Canadian concern over the "voluntary" import restrictions President Eisenhower imposed on oil, or the PL-480 program, which dumped U.S. agricultural surpluses on international markets, to the anguished protests of Canadian farmers. Washington also rebuked Canada for its trade with "Red" China (as the People's Republic of China was universally known in the period), specifically as it involved sales by U.S. subsidiaries in Canada. This last was an ominous portent for the 1960s and Canadian commerce with Castro's Cuba, but in the 1950s, quiet diplomacy on both sides kept it out of the headlines.[29]

Canada Falls Out of Step, 1958–1960

By the time President Eisenhower made his second official visit to Ottawa in July 1958, Secretary of State Dulles had warned him that the Conservative government of John Diefenbaker was "strongly nationalistic" and inclined more to Britain than to the United States. NORAD had further institutionalized defense cooperation, but Eisenhower requested assurance from Diefenbaker that the high level of cooperation that had characterized the Liberal years—for the Liberals had held power in Canada continuously since 1935—would continue under the Tories. A fundamental question soured U.S.-Canadian defense relations during Diefenbaker's prime ministership: whether there should be nuclear weapons in Canada and who should control them. During his first two years in office, Diefenbaker took clear steps toward acceptance of Canada's nuclear role. Perhaps no one anticipated how strong the political backlash would be on this issue when it reached public debate in 1959 and 1960. What triggered the debate was a series of decisions related to the strategic defense of Europe and North America and Canada's military role in that defense. In late 1957, NATO, confronted with the reality of significantly superior numbers of Warsaw Pact ground forces, decided to rely on nuclear weapons. The Canadian role as part of a strike force in the event of war required that its American-designed CF-104 Starfighters carry nuclear warheads. The Canadian forces, however, did not order nuclear warheads for the missiles carried by the CF-104s.[30]

The issue of nuclear weapons became more volatile when Prime Minister John Diefenbaker announced to Parliament in February 1959 that his government had "reluctantly" decided that, for reasons of strategic necessity and to fulfill Canadian obligations under NORAD, nuclear weapons would have to be based in Canada. His government negotiated with the United States over the placement of nuclear weapons at two U.S. Air Force bases in Newfoundland. The U.S. Atomic Energy Act stipulated that American nuclear weapons abroad had to be under control of American forces; to circumvent this restriction there were discussions of a "two key" or joint control program, in which the use of the weapons would have to be approved by both countries. At the same time, the Diefenbaker government canceled its contract with the A. V. Roe Company to manufacture a "Canadian" interceptor, the CF-105 Avro Arrow. Diefenbaker's decision about the Arrow project reflected an unhappy realization that Canada could not afford to build military aircraft without the hope of foreign sales, and that none of Canada's allies—certainly not the United States—was going to buy the Arrow. The Arrow cancellation was a major blow to the aircraft industry in Canada and to the expectations with which Canada had greeted the postwar era; it cost Ontario, Canada's largest province, almost twenty-five thousand jobs. In its place, the government substituted U.S. Voodoo interceptor jets; renaming the RCAF Voodoos the "CF-101" did nothing to stem a nationalist backlash. The new interceptor was to be armed with Genie air-to-air missiles and supplemented in the air defense system by American Bomarc ground-to-air missiles. Both the Genies and the Bomarcs compounded Diefenbaker's nuclear dilemma, for they required nuclear warheads to be effective. Even with their nuclear tips, however, neither the Genie nor the Bomarc missile would be any use against the ICBMs—Inter-Continental Ballistic Missiles—that now supplemented the Soviet Union's force of manned bombers.[31]

The ICBMs were a constant reminder that there was still a cold war, and Diefenbaker remained personally strongly committed to it. His distaste for the burgeoning nonaligned movement more than matched that of the Eisenhower administration. In 1958, in the UN Security Council, Canada had supported the president's invasion of Lebanon, the first test of the "Eisenhower Doctrine." Two months later, in a speech to the UN General Assembly, Diefenbaker denounced the Soviet Union and its leader Nikita Khrushchev and expressed concern about Fidel Castro's tilt toward the Soviet Union and the dangers of a Communist foothold in the Western Hemisphere. Yet in meetings in Montebello, Quebec, in July 1960, U.S. officials had been stunned by the fervor of Canadian criticism of U.S. policies in Cuba. But arms sales to Canada were still on target, and Diefenbaker had expressed personal appreciation to Eisenhower for ensuring that the U.S. defense budget in 1960 included a $244 million allocation for Bomarc-B missiles. The Canadian prime minister sent mixed and confusing signals.[32]

Diefenbaker's apparent confusion stemmed from a public backlash and a lack of consensus within his government and civil service about Canada's accepting nuclear weapons. Within the government, Minister of External Affairs Howard Green led the opposition, abetted by Undersecretary Norman Robertson, who had been Canadian ambassador in Washington in 1957–58. This opposition led to a lengthy debate over these apparent decisions and ultimately to the refusal of the Diefenbaker government to implement the North American defense decisions to which he had agreed—albeit without sufficient thought. Although the U.S. State Department perceived a clear deterioration in relations with Canada, Diefenbaker continued to maintain that the two countries shared the "same ideals and objectives." He and members of his government, however, suddenly became much more interested than the Eisenhower administration in talks to discontinue nuclear weapons testing and eventual nuclear disarmament. Christian Herter, who had become U.S. secretary of state on Dulles's death in 1959, believed it important to persuade Diefenbaker to ensure continued strong and united U.S.-Canadian defenses. He and President Eisenhower worked without success to avert Canada's cancellation of a planned joint air defense exercise euphoniously alliterated as "Sky Shield." It seemed very distant from Louis St. Laurent's declaration in 1953 that "Canada has been proud to march at the side of the United States, and to recognize the leadership this great country is providing for the free and independent nations."[33]

What had happened to cloud the sunny feelings of that day only a year earlier when President Eisenhower and Prime Minister Diefenbaker had opened the St. Lawrence Seaway together? In fact, nothing represents the bilateral relationship during the cold war better than that seaway. In 1951, Canada, determined to have the long-sought link between the Atlantic and the Great Lakes, threatened to construct it unilaterally. The Eisenhower administration favored the venture for commercial reasons, but its economic logic had never been enough to convince Congress. After the seaway had languished in political impossibility since the 1930s, the administration suddenly resurrected it as indispensable infrastructure for American national security. The two hundred miles of channels and locks would move strategic raw materials, most notably iron ore from Labrador and northern Quebec, into the industrial heartland of the United States. In 1954, President Eisenhower played this cold war card to trump the congressional shills for competing railroad and Atlantic port interests, and the project sailed ahead. The president and Queen Elizabeth II opened the seaway in June 1959 with a glittering ceremony at St. Lambert, Quebec. The *Montreal Star* reported "scattered, hesitant applause" for Eisenhower's single halting sentence in French and hearty cheers for the Queen's fluency. "We like you, but we all fell in love with the Queen, Ike," boomed a voice during a quiet moment. Nothing could better capture Canada's different attitudes to its new and its old imperial allies. The Royal Yacht *Britannia* cruised up the seaway so that Queen Elizabeth could repeat the ceremony with Vice President Richard Nixon at Massena, New York. The seaway, the vice president told the crowd sweating beneath a blazing sun, was "a symbol of a united past and a hopeful sign for the future." Then, just as the Massena High School Band hit the final note of "The Star Spangled Banner," its bass drummer fainted dead away. Was this portent meant for Nixon, for the U.S.-Canadian relationship, or for both?[34]

7   The Moose That Roared, 1961–1968

The cinematic surprise of 1959 was the British comedy *The Mouse That Roared*. In the movie, a tiny European kingdom named the Grand Duchy of Fenwick, governed by Peter Sellers in three roles, attacks the United States. It must have seemed to the U.S. government at that time as if Canada had borrowed the Grand Duchy's tactics. From Washington's perspective a sudden and perplexing pattern of confrontation supplanted fifteen years of Canadian accommodation to U.S. wishes. Prime Minister John Diefenbaker and his Conservative colleagues were, alas, much less amusing company for Americans than Peter Sellers. The Canadian "moose" roared about nuclear weapons, about relations with Cuba and China, and about U.S. foreign investment; even long-dormant cultural nationalism reverberated. Unlike the movie, the showdown did not end when Canadian voters rolled the credits on the Diefenbaker government in 1963 and replaced them with Lester Pearson's Liberals, or when bullets in Dallas recast Vice President Lyndon Johnson in the part of President John F. Kennedy. Instead, a U.S. war in Southeast Asia was added to the script of Canadian-U.S. problems, which loomed larger than the individual actors in Ottawa and Washington. On the movie screen, incredibly, the Grand Duchy of Fenwick accomplished its strategic objective of winning American aid, and Fenwickers and Americans lived happily ever after. But Canada and the United States had to cope with each other in the real world, not on the screen.

Kennedy, Diefenbaker, and the Cold War

In the 1960 presidential campaign, John F. Kennedy upstaged the leading cold warrior of his generation. The shopworn pieties of Republican Richard Nixon contrasted poorly with the new politics of the young Democratic senator from Massachusetts. The Republicans, Kennedy charged, had allowed the Soviet Union to seize nuclear missile superiority and yet had failed to maintain adequate conventional armed forces. Kennedy painted the now-traditional picture of East-West relations as a struggle between two conflicting ideologies: "Freedom under God versus ruthless godless tyranny." But the new and improved cold war he sold the electorate in four television debates promised that the "Communist tide" could be not just halted but rolled back: "I ran for the presidency because I do not want it said that . . . the years when our generation held political power . . . were the years when America began to slip [and when] the balance of power began to turn against the United States and the cause of freedom." [1]

Historians dispute the balance between the individual and the broad impersonal force in shaping history. The causes of the increasing strain on the U.S.-Canadian relationship in the early 1960s are a case in point: how much can be attributed to the reciprocal antipathy that developed between John F. Kennedy and John G. Diefenbaker? It has become a Canadian cliché to contrast the confident, cosmopolitan, Harvard graduate who was president with the insecure, teetotaling, small-town Saskatchewan lawyer who was prime minister. Matinee idol Cliff Robertson portrayed Kennedy the war hero in the movie *PT 109;* a film about Diefenbaker's career (such an unlikely production is difficult to imagine) would have featured an unknown character actor. From their first meeting, the two men held each other in hearty contempt. Despite his Germanic surname, Diefenbaker was a sentimental British-Canadian nationalist; he believed that the new president had inherited a "hatred" for Britain from his father, "anti-British buccaneer" Joseph P. Kennedy. Diefenbaker's strident Soviet-bashing at first glance seemed common ground with Kennedy, but Diefenbaker was content to have the cold war remain a rhetorical conflict. He would have much preferred Richard Nixon in the White House. During his June 1960 visit to Washington to discuss the U-2 crisis, Diefenbaker had advised the Republicans to cancel the television debates because "there was no advertising value in it for Nixon." Diefenbaker's inexperience in international affairs, a weakness of which Liberal Opposition leader Lester Pearson often reminded him, made him hesitant and indecisive. Kennedy displayed the same machismo in both his international and his interpersonal relations.[2]

But a policy as well as a personality gulf separated Kennedy and Diefenbaker. The Kennedy administration's altered understanding of the bipolar balance of power was far more decisive in shaping U.S. foreign policy—and thus the U.S.-Canadian relationship—than their personalities. The abrupt transition in that relationship in the early 1960s is understandable only from this perspective. In the thirty-five months Kennedy held office before his assassination in Dallas, he demonstrated that his gut appeal to American nationalism, pride, and anticommunism was more than campaign bombast. The administration believed that the Soviet Union and its satellites had become more aggressive. Communism could thus no longer simply be contained: it had to be confronted everywhere and rooted out where possible. Weapons and space were the only programs to receive significant budget increases: Kennedy tripled the power of the U.S. nuclear arsenal and expanded and re-equipped conventional forces to prepare for a "flexible response" across the globe. Kennedy centralized the foreign policymaking process in the White House, the National Security Council (NSC), and the Pentagon, with a corresponding shift of power away from the State Department. This trend toward the "imperial presidency" had been underway since the late 1930s, but it was intensified by both the style of the Kennedy administration and the crises that engulfed it in the early 1960s. These institutional shifts enhanced the authority of Robert McNamara at the Department of Defense and of McGeorge Bundy and his successor Walt W. Rostow at the NSC; they diminished the influence of Dean Rusk and the State Department, which had been traditionally knowledgeable about, and more sensitive toward, Canadian concerns. The structural changes were, of course, made without any thought to Canada, but as happened with more frequency, such changes influenced the course and nature of U.S.-Canadian relations.

The first two meetings between Kennedy and Diefenbaker, in Washington in February and in Ottawa in May 1961, revealed the Kennedy administration's worldview and where Canada fit into it. Most of the foreign policy issues that the two governments would face surfaced during those initial discussions: bilateral defense, nuclear weapons, Berlin, Fidel Castro in Cuba, insurgencies in Southeast Asia, and North American aid to what had come to be called the "Third World"—less-developed nations aligned behind neither the United States nor the Soviet Union. Some Canadians, most notably Minister of External Affairs Howard Green, had criticized the United States as excessively hostile to the USSR, blind to opportunities to negotiate with the Communist bloc, and too quick to label social and political unrest in the Third World as Communist inspired. In its intelligence estimate "Trends in Canadian Foreign Policy," the CIA suggested that Diefenbaker's Conservative government might take Canada in a divergent direction. Canada had entered a new phase of increased "sensitivity" to American influence in its cultural, economic, and military affairs. The CIA anticipated that Canada would continue to seek a more independent foreign policy, pressing for disarmament, arms control and a nuclear test ban, and an end to the U.S. blackball of Communist Chinese membership in the United Nations. Canada would maintain its basic commitments to NATO and NORAD, the CIA predicted, but the Conservatives would exploit the latent anti-American sentiments among the Canadian public for electoral advantage. A Liberal return to power in Ottawa might soften the Canadian resistance to the storage of nuclear weapons on Canadian soil.[3]

Kennedy and his senior advisers saw the Diefenbaker government, Howard Green in particular, as willfully oblivious to the threat posed by Nikita Khrushchev's expansionist Soviet regime. Khrushchev, they lectured the Canadians, had been emboldened by the success of the Soviet orbital space flights, by Communist gains in Laos, and by Castro's success in Cuba. Between the first and second U.S.-Canadian meetings, the spectacular failure at the Bay of Pigs of a U.S.-backed invasion of Cuba presumably emboldened Khrushchev still further. The wily Russian, Kennedy and Rusk warned Diefenbaker and Green, would entertain disarmament discussions for propaganda purposes while he stepped up pressure around the vulnerable periphery of the "free world": guerrilla war in Southeast Asia, destabilization efforts in Iran, and continued manipulation of East Germany to force the West's hand on Berlin. The Canadians did not seem to listen. Diefenbaker's aide from the Department of External Affairs, Basil Robinson, suggests that the prime minister had formed an "irrational prejudice" against Kennedy and Dean Rusk before they arrived in Ottawa for their second meeting in May 1961. Kennedy, preoccupied with his scheduled June summit with Khrushchev in Vienna, was patronizing and dismissive of Canadian concerns. The Bay of Pigs disaster in April 1961 should have taught the president caution. Instead, Kennedy blamed the fiasco on the State Department and resolved never again to let this irresolute foreign policy bureaucracy embarrass him. "The message of Cuba, of Laos, of the rising din of Communist voices in Asia and Latin America," Kennedy told an assembly of newspaper editors, was that "the complacent, the self-indulgent, the soft societies are about to be swept away with the debris of history." The United States, "in concert with all the free nations of this hemisphere," had to take a more realistic look at the Communist menace.[4]

Kennedy expected Canadians to take a "realistic look" at Cuba, where the administration did not want them to accommodate Castro. Diefenbaker and Kennedy were more of one mind on Cuba than any other item on their agenda. The prime minister supported the American-backed filibuster into the Bay of Pigs and condemned Cuba as a "bridgehead of international communism" in the hemisphere, an anti-Castro posture at odds with that recommended by his own Department of External Affairs. Howard Green opposed any further U.S. intervention in Cuba, fearing complications throughout Latin America. The Kennedy administration rebuffed as "unhelpful" Green's suggestion that Canada mediate between the United States and Cuba; instead, it asked Canada to help by joining the U.S. economic boycott.

After securing a large reserve of his favorite Havana cigars, Kennedy had cut off Cuba from U.S. markets with the Trading with the Enemy Act. As they had in regard to China, Canadian leaders refused U.S. requests to cut off trade relations with Cuba. Again, however, the Canadian government could not always stop U.S. extraterritorial trade laws, specifically the Foreign Assets control regulations, from discouraging Canadian subsidiaries of U.S. parent companies from doing business with Cuba. Over the next twenty years, paradoxically, Canadian trade representatives in Havana proved valuable to the United States, for they informally gathered intelligence useful to the CIA. They had no direct part, however, in fantastic CIA covert operations to remove Castro by lacing his cigars with LSD or by blowing him up with explosive clamshells while he swam in the Caribbean.[5]

Kennedy also pressed Canada to expand its aid to Latin America to parallel his Alliance for Progress program and to join the Organization of American States (OAS). This departure from longstanding U.S. opposition to Canadian membership was directly linked to the cold war and to Cuba: the president hoped that Canada would assist U.S. attempts to rally hemispheric solidarity against Castro. Formerly restricting membership to "republics," the OAS charter had been amended at U.S. insistence to read "states" so that a constitutional monarchy such as Canada could be eligible. President Eisenhower had discussed participation confidentially with Diefenbaker, but Kennedy delivered his invitation to become partners "against the encroachment of international communism in this hemisphere" in a speech to the Canadian Parliament. The prime minister had been seriously considering the idea, but the president's public appeal left him no room for maneuver: if he agreed, Diefenbaker would be seen to have surrendered to U.S. coercion. The most that Canada would concede was to send an observer to the meetings of the OAS Economic and Social Council.[6]

Southeast Asia posed further problems for the bilateral relationship. To Canada, which had firsthand experience, Vietnam seemed like a hotter and less hospitable Korea. When the French colonial regime in Vietnam had fallen in 1954, the Geneva Accords had divided that unhappy country at the seventeenth parallel. Ho Chi Minh's Communist-nationalist coalition controlled the north, with what increasingly emerged as a U.S. client state under Ngo Dinh Diem in control to the south. The Geneva Accords, to which the United States was not a signatory, established a three-member International Commission for Supervision and Control (ICSC) for Vietnam whose task was to establish the division at the seventeenth parallel, supervise a cease-fire, and oversee elections in 1956 that would lead to eventual reunification. Without prodding from the United States, Canada joined the ICSC as the "Western" representative on the commission to balance Soviet bloc Poland and nonaligned India. The elections never took place, and the Canadian ICSC representatives became at best apologists for and at worst accomplices to an expanding U.S. presence in South Vietnam. The Diefenbaker government had strong reservations about Kennedy's increases in U.S. military involvement in the region. Even the military advisers the president sent were a possible violation of the 1954 Geneva agreements. The Kennedy administration saw the Canadian reservations as further evidence that the Canadians seriously underestimated the Soviet threat. Vice President Lyndon Johnson minced no words after his fact-finding mission to Indo-China: the "battle against Communism must be joined in Southeast Asia with strength and determination to achieve success."[7]

Kennedy hoped to make further progress on an agreement for the storage of U.S. nuclear weapons at U.S.-leased military bases in Newfoundland. The United States was willing to accept an agreement for U.S. custody and joint control, the system used at bases in Great Britain, in return for definitive Canadian agreement to at last arm its air defense missiles with nuclear warheads. Canada needed the warheads not simply to fulfill its agreed-upon obligations to NORAD and NATO but also to allow the weapons to function at all. Diefenbaker, along with his minister of defense, Douglas Harkness, personally favored this course but still refused to act. To the prime minister, Canada's nuclear role was a domestic political problem more than an issue in Canadian-U.S. defense relations. He was sensitive to public complaints about Canada's defense partnership with America, the most articulate and influential of which was a book by James M. Minifie, CBC correspondent in Washington. First published in February 1960, *Peacemaker or Powdermonkey* went through five printings in its first year and remained in print throughout the decade. Minifie argued that Canada's vision of NATO as the foundation of a "North Atlantic Civilization" had been "betrayed and prostituted," and that Article 2 of the NATO charter had "become the deadest letter in the diplomatic cemetery." NORAD, he pointed out, did not protect Canadians from Soviet attack; instead, it guarded the bombers of the U.S. Strategic Air Command, the instrument of "massive retaliation," a policy in which Canada had no say. Minifie's alliterative title stated his solution: Canada had to stop acting as America's "powdermonkey" in NATO and NORAD and assert itself as a world "peacemaker" through the United Nations. Within the cabinet, several ministers, with Green being the most outspoken, remained adamantly opposed to a nuclear role for Canada as long as there was any hope of an international disarmament agreement. Diefenbaker hoped that if he stalled long enough, the problem would go away. Kennedy knew that it would not. The president planned no serious progress toward disarmament in Vienna and wanted to enhance defense capability in a forward area along the route of a Soviet air attack on the United States.[8]

Neither U.S. nor Canadian officials were pleased with the nonresults of the bilateral Kennedy-Diefenbaker encounters. Two sessions of summit diplomacy had yielded no meeting of minds on nuclear weapons, Latin America, or Southeast Asia. To the Kennedy administration, Canada's foot-dragging on storage and acquisition of nuclear warheads was an obvious dereliction of its duty to NATO and NORAD. Howard Green's prattle about disarmament, East-West negotiations, and Communist China's place in the world community all undermined U.S. cold war strategy. These policy differences were exacerbated when, after the second meeting, Kennedy carelessly left behind a memo written by NSC adviser Walt Rostow. In "What We Want from Ottawa Trip," Rostow spoke of the need "to push the Canadians" toward a series of U.S. positions in Latin America and Asia. After he discovered the memo in his wastebasket, an infuriated Diefenbaker complained to U.S. ambassador Livingston Merchant that good neighbors did not "push" each other into anything. Kennedy privately dismissed Diefenbaker as "a prick," but to Washington, the prime minister's petulance confirmed that a once-dependable cold war ally was now a question mark. Had Canada become one of the "soft" nations destined for the "debris of history?"[9]

Berlin, Cuba, and the Nuclear Weapons Debate

Kennedy had warned Diefenbaker to expect a "Berlin crisis" before the end of 1961, and after his unsatisfactory discussions of German re-unification with Khrushchev in June, the president decided that Berlin would be the "great testing ground of Western courage and will." To demonstrate his courage, Kennedy increased the defense budget, mobilized military reservists, and began a major program of fallout shelter construction. Khrushchev responded to this saber rattling with barbed wire, land mines, machine gun emplacements, and finally a cement barrier to block the flow of refugees from East to West Berlin. The Berlin Wall stood for the next thirty years as the concrete symbol of the cold war and of Kennedy's overreaction. The Berlin crisis sharpened the urgency of U.S.-Canadian defense discussions. Diefenbaker continued to perplex the United States: he announced that "Canada stood firmly beside its NATO allies" and imitated Kennedy's bomb shelter program with the "Diefenbunker," and yet he continued to refuse nuclear weapons. Washington's bewilderment was an accurate reflection of what was going on in Ottawa, where the antinuclear Department of External Affairs vied with the pro-warhead Department of National Defence. Diefenbaker seemed to have sided with the latter, until a White House leak of Kennedy-Diefenbaker correspondence again made it seem that he was bending to American pressure. When bullying miscarried, Kennedy tried flowers and candy: the United States agreed to purchase Canadian-built F-104Gs for European NATO allies through the U.S. Military Assistance program, a $200 million deal for the Canadian aircraft industry. But the prime minister remained coy, and Canada's nuclear virginity continued intact.[10]

The Berlin situation was compounded by the Soviet military buildup in Cuba during the summer of 1962. Then, on 16 October, United States U-2 reconnaissance flights photographed medium-range ballistic missile sites under construction along the north coast of the island. The subsequent Soviet-U.S. confrontation, remembered as the Cuban missile crisis, brought nuclear catastrophe closer than at any moment during the cold war. Kennedy at once formed an ad hoc executive committee to plan and implement his administration's response. The strongest voices on the committee included Defense Secretary McNamara, National Security Adviser McGeorge Bundy, Kennedy's brother Robert, and Joint Chiefs of Staff chairman General Maxwell Taylor; Secretary of State Dean Rusk was conspicuously silent. Rusk's invisibility reflected the State Department's limited impact on the decisions, and that in itself foretold problems for Canada. In a television address on 22 October, Kennedy announced a U.S. naval blockade to prevent nuclear warheads from reaching Cuba and called upon Khrushchev to remove the missiles. U.S. warships scoured the Caribbean, turning back Soviet naval vessels and boarding one freighter. On 28 October Khrushchev agreed to remove the missiles in return for an American pledge not to invade the island.[11]

The biggest questions of the Cuban missile crisis—why use an ultimatum rather than negotiations? were the missiles in Cuba a real threat to the United States or only to the president's prestige?—are largely irrelevant to the impact of the crisis on relations with Canada. What mattered to America's allies were Kennedy's choice of a unilateral response and his thoughtless (there is no evidence of malice) disregard for their opinions. As America's partner in NORAD as well as in NATO, Canada had a double claim to consultation. Instead, the Canadian ambassador in Washington, Charles Ritchie, remained unsummoned to the State Department until literally the eleventh hour. Diefenbaker, Howard Green, and Douglas Harkness saw the photographic evidence and received a perfunctory briefing in Ottawa from former U.S. ambassador to Canada Livingston Merchant only after the president's television address had already been scripted and scheduled. Millions of U.S. viewers (and Canadians, for the CBC carried the address) would know as much two hours later. Kennedy followed up Merchant's synopsis with a message promising that he would try to keep the prime minister informed. As Diefenbaker wrote years later, he "knew the difference between consultation [and] the presentation of something which is, or which is about to become, a *fait accompli*." Britain had no role in shaping American policy, but its ambassador to the United States, David Ormsby-Gore, was a Kennedy friend, and British prime minister Harold Macmillan received personal telephone calls from the president early in the crisis. Some "special relationships" were more special than others. The United States ignored Canada, its closest ally, during what it believed to be the gravest crisis of the cold war. The situation, however urgent, allowed more time for consultation than there would have been in the event of imminent nuclear attack, but there is no evidence that Kennedy ever considered consultation. His only communication with Diefenbaker before the last-minute Livingston Merchant mission to Ottawa was a letter of 19 October excoriating Canada for supporting a UN resolution calling for a moratorium on nuclear testing. This was, the president claimed, "tantamount to Canada's abandoning the Western position." Canadian policies were tilting in the wrong direction, and the "action intellectuals" who ran Washington had no time to listen to dissenting voices.[12]

Other US allies were infuriated by Kennedy's unilateralism—France's Charles de Gaulle empathized with Diefenbaker—but all remained silent until well after the confrontation ended. Canada was the lone ally to delay instant compliance with U.S. defense requests. The United States asked Canadian forces to move, in the grotesque acronymic language of the military, from DEFCON (Defense Condition) 5 to DEFCON 3 (DEFCON 0 was nuclear holocaust). Although he had left Livingston Merchant with the impression that he was "on side," Diefenbaker neither refused this request nor cooperated with it—he simply did nothing. His indecision made little difference to Western readiness to repel Soviet attack: Minister of Defense Harkness quietly ordered the Canadian Chiefs of Staff into readiness, and Canada's NORAD forces that were integrated with the USAF had already automatically moved to DEFCON 3. The chief of naval staff on his own initiative ordered Canada's Atlantic fleet to sea. Two days later, Diefenbaker authorized the Canadian armed forces to join their U.S. counterparts in DEFCON 2. Although Diefenbaker hoped for a multilateral negotiated settlement of the crisis that would be less provocative of the USSR, he was never openly critical of the United States. After Kennedy's address, Diefenbaker proposed that a UN commission visit Cuba to determine the "facts." This was interpreted in Washington as disbelief in U.S. evidence, but Diefenbaker described the evidence he had seen as "ample" and argued that the Soviet Union had "reached out across the Atlantic to challenge the right of free men to live in peace in this hemisphere." [13]

Like Kennedy's brinkmanship, Diefenbaker's indecision is easier to explain than to defend. As did the American public, Canadians gave the president's Caribbean cowboy drama the highest ratings; when Diefenbaker's two days of delay were disclosed, almost 80 percent of Canadians disapproved in a Gallup poll. In retrospect, it is interesting that the prime minister's assessment of Kennedy now comes closer to the historical consensus. Diefenbaker feared that Kennedy was too determined to erase the embarrassment of the Bay of Pigs and the rumors that he had been routed by Khrushchev at Vienna and on Berlin. Kennedy, he wrote, "was perfectly capable of taking the world to the brink of thermonuclear destruction to prove himself the man for our times, a courageous champion of Western democracy." Yet Diefenbaker himself was too preoccupied with image, too determined to demonstrate that Canada was not "a satellite state at the beck and call of an imperial master." [14]

The Cuban missile crisis snapped U.S. patience on the unresolved issue of nuclear weapons for Canada. The U.S. campaign to convince the Diefenbaker government to accept warheads for its missiles had been handicapped by multipartisan resistance to nuclear arms in the Canadian Parliament. The New Democratic Party (NDP), social democratic successor to the Co-operative Commonwealth Federation (CCF), and the Liberal Party were, if anything, more opposed to nuclear weapons than the governing Conservatives. Although Diefenbaker's mail ran two to one against nuclear arms, opinion polls showed a majority in favor. Canada's antinuclear posturing had a strong element of hypocrisy in it—Canada was, said critics, a "nuclear dope peddler" who had earned millions selling to the United States the uranium it used to build its nuclear arsenal. The Cuban missile crisis had demonstrated the utter impracticality of Diefenbaker's notion of storing critical nuclear components in the United States until the actual need to fire the missiles occurred. However much debate there was about the effectiveness of a nuclear-tipped Bomarc, Genie, or Honest John missile for its intended military purpose, no one could deny that Canada had agreed to acquire the weapons for its NORAD and NATO forces. On 3 January 1963, U.S. general Lauris Norstad, NATO's supreme commander, said as much at a press conference in Ottawa. A week later the Liberal Party "rethought" its position on nuclear weapons—"flip-flop" was the word the other parties used.

The Kennedy administration could now escalate its pressure on Diefenbaker. Defense Secretary Robert McNamara ended further negotiations with Canada. The prime minister still refused to budge and instead announced that Kennedy had assured him that in the future NATO would increase conventional forces and rely less upon its nuclear deterrent. On 30 January, a bombshell press release dropped from the highest levels of the State Department and the NSC. George Ball and McGeorge Bundy flatly affirmed that Canada's weaponry was valueless without nuclear warheads, asserted that the Diefenbaker government had no practical alternate solutions for North American defense, and charged that Diefenbaker had distorted the nature of recent secret defense discussions with President Kennedy. The prime minister of Canada, in other words, was a liar. In a press conference the following day, Dean Rusk unapologetically reinforced the U.S. position. All of the evidence suggests that the Kennedy administration hoped to help Pearson and the Liberals topple Diefenbaker's Conservative government, but the president himself was allegedly furious at Ball and Bundy for using the blunt instrument of a press release rather than a diplomatic note. Kennedy supposedly feared that such an overt public rebuke from Washington would instead solidify Diefenbaker's position and hinder U.S. efforts to destabilize his government.[15]

Ball and Bundy were vindicated by the reaction from Canada. Canadian ambassador Charles Ritchie was recalled as a diplomatic protest (the first time this had happened in the bilateral relationship), but State Department reports showed that after an anticipated sudden flurry of nationalistic outrage at the U.S. incursion into Canadian affairs, both the newspaper editorials and the "man on the street" accepted the U.S. argument. Canadian political cartoonists pilloried Diefenbaker rather than the United States, and the *Globe and Mail* and the *Toronto Telegram*, ordinarily pro-Conservative, supported the acquisition of nuclear weapons and criticized the Diefenbaker government for failing to honor its obligation. Canadian opinion swung quickly and decisively against Diefenbaker. Within a week, his minister and his associate minister of defense, Douglas Harkness and Pierre Sévigny, resigned from the cabinet to protest the prime minister's unwillingness to accept the warheads. Parliamentary governments can survive their allotted five years only as long as they command a legislative majority: the Kennedy administration thus got near-instant gratification. Less than a week after the State Department press release, Lester Pearson's no confidence motion deflated the Diefenbaker government and forced a national election in Canada.[16]

American ambassador Walton Butterworth reported that Diefenbaker seemed "a man determined to take his party as well as himself into political oblivion," but the election on 8 April did not turn out exactly as planned by Pearson or, presumably, by the Kennedy administration. In addition to the defense debacle, Diefenbaker had given Canadians many reasons to vote against his Conservatives: he had handled the economy with equal incompetence. Once the campaign started, however, Diefenbaker adeptly exploited his difficulties with Washington to obscure his dismal domestic record. The Conservatives revived their anti-American campaigns of 1891, 1911, and 1930. One Conservative minister accused the United States of treating Canada like "a Guatemala or something" (which drew a protest from the Guatemalan ambassador) and warned, "don't push us around, chum." Diefenbaker argued that refusing nuclear weapons showed courage, not cowardice: "Canada was in both [world] wars a long time before some other nations were." What the U.S. embassy characterized as "outrageous histrionics" seemed to work—hecklers shouted "Yankee lover" at some of Pearson's rallies. Diefenbaker's 1963 campaign embodied the eerie Canadian ambivalence about the United States. Anti-Americanism was his ever-present text, yet he compared his role as "underdog" to that of President Harry Truman in 1948. Just like Truman, he told whistle stop audiences, "Everybody's against me but the people." Enough voters were with Diefenbaker that the Liberal Party won only a plurality rather than a majority in Parliament. Lester Pearson's minority government would have to depend on the support of other parties to govern and would be vulnerable to sudden parliamentary defeat just as the Conservatives had been. The warmth of President Kennedy's congratulatory telegram to new prime minister Pearson was nonetheless striking.[17]

Southeast Asia and North America

The day after his government took office, Prime Minister Pearson announced that Canada would acquire nuclear weapons for its forces. By August the two countries had reached agreement on the delivery of nuclear warheads to the Canadian forces, and by October there was agreement on the storage of nuclear weapons by the U.S. forces at American bases in Canada. A five-year dispute had been resolved in favor of the U.S. position. "The welshing and double-dealing which characterized our relations with our partners" had ended, wrote Canadian columnist Pierre Berton; "anti-Americanism is finished as a political issue." This, of course, was nonsense, which is why journalistic profundities become such fun for historians. Liberal minister of external affairs Paul Martin later recalled that he and Pearson had chosen nuclear weapons for Canada with a "heavy heart."[18]

And their colleague Walter Gordon, minister of finance, was already at work on a budget that would become a bilateral economic incident. Between 1955 and 1957, Gordon had chaired a Royal Commission to consider "Canada's Economic Prospects." The investigation revealed an alarming (to Gordon) degree of U.S. control of Canadian manufacturing, mining, and petroleum extraction. The Diefenbaker government had buried the Gordon report—a sign that there were limits to Diefenbaker's dislike of the United States. Gordon now made the report's conclusions the basis for proposed tax legislation that discriminated against corporate and individual foreign investors, including a 30 percent "take-over tax" on shares in Canadian corporations sold to nonresidents. Wall Street exploded, as did its echoes in Montreal and Toronto, Bay and St. James streets. After formal U.S. protest, the take-over tax was withdrawn and the other changes modified. Far from restricting U.S. foreign investment, Gordon found himself shortly thereafter in Washington begging successfully that Canada be exempted from Kennedy's proposed restrictions on foreign borrowing in the United States. When National City Bank of New York attempted to purchase the Mercantile Bank of Canada, however, Gordon accomplished one economic nationalist goal through legislation forbidding foreign control of Canadian chartered banks.[19]

But Diefenbaker was gone, and Gordon at worst a minor irritant. With Lester Pearson in charge up north, Americans could readjust to their habitual image of Canada (if they had one) as "the great-out-of-doors where some millions of squatters have unaccountably settled, a museum of old-fashioned qualities miraculously frozen in ice." Canada was a nice, nearby respite from the stress of American life, perfectly captured in the lyrics of Andy Williams's hit "Canadian Sunset": "a weekend in Canada, a change of scene." After his return from one of many such weekends, Dean Acheson wrote to a friend that things were "all very relaxed as Canada usually is." The retired secretary of state joked that Gordon's "boner on the Budget" had been "as stupid a performance as the Bay of Pigs." Canadians, he concluded, were "as Walt [Butterworth] said, a tribal society, naive, terribly serious about the wrong things and not at all aware of their real problems. . . . Their best move would be to ask us to take them over; and our best move would be to say, no."[20]

But the most corrosive public issue within the United States in the 1960s soon brought painful division to the U.S.-Canadian relationship as well. On the deepening and tragic involvement of the United States in Vietnam, Canada proved a most ambivalent ally. In September 1963, two months before his assassination, Kennedy starkly defined American policy: "We want the war to be won, the Communists to be contained, and the Americans to go home." Kennedy had increased military aid to the South Vietnamese and twice increased U.S. forces. The Americans killed in action during the Kennedy presidency died as "advisers," but there were sixteen thousand such advisers serving in Vietnam by the time of JFK's death. Canada's attitudes and behavior with regard to U.S. policy in Southeast Asia remained contradictory. The Pearson government sympathized with U.S. anti-Communist aims, but Canadian leaders were skeptical whether Vietnam represented an unambiguous case of external communist aggression. As a putative middle power, Canada preferred strong international organizations and negotiated settlements; Canada's limited direct involvement in Vietnam was consistently premised on a belief in the value of negotiation and de-escalation of military conflict. From the Canadian perspective, it was critical that the war not escalate to involve China and the Soviet Union in a wider war in which Canadians would have to participate. Canadian diplomats ran messages between the United States and North Vietnam, a secret revealed when Rand Corporation analyst Daniel Ellsberg turned the *Pentagon Papers* over to the *New York Times* in 1972. Canadians grew publicly critical of U.S. military tactics and took in more than 50,000 American "draft dodgers" or "war-resisters"—the term one chose made an immediate political statement. The differences over Vietnam that alienated Prime Minister Pearson and President Johnson underline the greater importance of political structure and national interest than of personality in foreign relations. U.S. leaders had been strongly supportive of "Mike" Pearson for years; although he never for a moment sacrificed his conception of Canada's interests, no international figure of his generation had been as good a friend toward the United States. Yet within two years newspaper cartoons would show Lyndon Johnson berating the Canadian leader for his intrusive statements about the U.S. war in Vietnam.[21]

Like U.S. domestic opposition to the Vietnam War, U.S.-Canadian division over Southeast Asia emerged slowly. When Pearson met with Kennedy at Hyannis Port, Massachusetts, in 1963, he empathized with the president's dilemma of how to extricate the United States from Vietnam but offered little advice save caution. Kennedy did not live long enough to make the fatal mistakes on Vietnam that would have blighted his career; his legacy to Lyndon Johnson was not an easy one. Lyndon Johnson continued what he believed had been Kennedy's policies and kept Kennedy's team virtually intact: Kennedy became one of America's most revered presidents, and in Canada he is remembered in the names of streets and schools across the country. Lyndon Johnson is among those presidents most detested. It is difficult for anyone under sixty years of age to recall that Johnson was not always uncelebrated in either country: his Great Society program and his civil rights legislation caught imaginations on both sides of the U.S.-Canadian border. In January 1964 Pearson met the new president in Washington to put the finishing touches to a Columbia River Treaty and an international park at Franklin D. Roosevelt's Canadian summer island of Campobello. The two leaders amicably explored world issues ranging from China and Southeast Asia to Cuba and the Congo, and inched closer to an agreement to rationalize North American automobile production. "We have no problems that cannot be solved," enthused Johnson, "no future that cannot be shared." Pearson was less effusive. "The days of easy and automatic relations," he warned, "are over . . . I know that in the future we are going to have problems and difficulties." The prime minister described the binational connection in the male discourse characteristic of the era; it was like a man's relationship with his wife: "At times it is difficult to live with her. At all times it is impossible to live without her."[22]

The two leaders next met in September 1964 in Great Falls, Montana, as Johnson flew to Vancouver and Seattle to look at the Columbia River development—significantly, it was his first trip outside the United States as president. Pearson again spoke of neighborly ties and the mutual desire to keep the fence between them in good repair. Johnson caught on in Vancouver: he suggested that cooperation such as the Columbia River project was possible because "we respect our differences." That was exactly what the "Agreement Governing Trade in Automotive Products," the Autopact, did—guarantee respect for national differences. "Canadian" cars were American cars made behind a protective tariff in Windsor, Oakville, or Oshawa, Ontario, by wholly owned Canadian subsidiaries of U.S. auto manufacturers Chrysler, Ford, or General Motors. Workers in the industry belonged to a single international union, the United Automobile Workers (*les Travailleurs unis de l'automobile* in Quebec). Although the agreement was touted as a sectoral step toward free trade, it was, in fact, an experiment in managed trade such as those hoped for by Canadian planners immediately after World War II. Autopact carved up the North American market so that each country manufactured something close to the same percentage of total automobile production that it consumed. Parts and accessories could be shipped either way free of duty. The deal from the outset favored the smaller Canadian automobile industry; historian Bruce Muirhead points out that "the Auto Pact almost single-handedly fixed Canada's visible balance of trade deficit." The question becomes why the United States agreed to it. The answers are intricate: the big three automakers liked it because it permitted plants to specialize and eliminated small production runs; parts manufacturers were pleased that it stopped Canada from subsidizing their Canadian competitors, the State Department pretended it was a step toward ultimate free trade. Lyndon Johnson professed not to like it and later accused Canada of "screwing" the United States. He supported it, however, because Lyndon Johnson paid his political debts; the president owed Lester Pearson for sending Canadian soldiers to Cyprus as a UN Peace Force to keep Greece and Turkey from tearing up NATO with their blood feud over the island. Democratic senator Vance Hartke of Indiana, an opponent of the automobile agreement, later charged that there had been "a direct trade-off": in return for Autopact, Canadians had promised to "come and involve themselves in the war in Vietnam."[23]

If so, it was an implicit promise quickly broken. By the time Johnson and Pearson signed the Autopact at the president's Texas ranch in January, the cruel cycle of U.S. escalation in Vietnam had been set in motion. The political and military situation had deteriorated, the South Vietnamese army had proven ineffective, and the United States had increased the number of advisers and had begun to drop American commando saboteurs into the North. In the spring of 1964, Secretary of State Dean Rusk requested and received the services of Blair Seaborn, the Canadian member on the International Control Commission, to make contact with North Vietnamese leaders. Seaborn, explained Rusk to the U.S. ambassador in Saigon, Henry Cabot Lodge, was to find out "what is on Ho Chi Minh's mind" and to "get across to Ho and his colleagues the full measure of U.S. determination to see this thing through." Ultimately Seaborn made five visits to Hanoi, three in 1964 and two in 1965. The message Seaborn delivered in June 1964 warned that although the United States had no desire to overthrow the Democratic Republic of Vietnam, it regarded the Vietcong guerrillas in South Vietnam as under DRV control and would use the military means necessary to confine the DRV north of the seventeenth parallel set in the 1954 Geneva Accords. The North Vietnamese response that Seaborn brought back was ominous: its action south of the parallel would cease when the United States withdrew and when a neutral government in line with the National Liberation Front program was in power in Saigon. "It would be unwise at this stage," Seaborn advised the State Department, for the United States to expect to bring the North Vietnamese to heel by military or economic means. If anyone in Washington heard this advice, no one heeded it. In August 1964, reported attacks by North Vietnamese torpedo boats on U.S. destroyers propelled the Gulf of Tonkin Resolution through Congress. The resolution gave President Johnson carte blanche "to take all necessary measures to repel any armed attack" through executive action.[24]

Canadians "breathed a concerted sigh of relief" at Lyndon Johnson's landslide electoral victory over conservative Republican Barry Goldwater that November. "Johnson . . . hides one of the most finely trained minds in American public life beneath a Texan veneer," commented the *Winnipeg Free Press*; affairs in Southeast Asia would be sorted out by a responsible president. In March 1965, "responsible" Lyndon Johnson launched Operation Rolling Thunder—punitive bombing attacks against North Vietnam. Johnson seemed to leave the door ajar for negotiation; the alleged purpose of the bombing was to bring the North Vietnamese to the table, and the State Department continued to seek

Seaborn's services as a go-between. This was the backdrop against which Pearson accepted Temple University's World Peace Award in Philadelphia in April. His speech was sympathetic to the United States. He described the war in Vietnam as among those "spurious 'wars of national liberation' which are really wars of Communist domination"; U.S. "motives were honorable; neither mean nor imperialistic. Its sacrifices have been great." Bombing, alas, had not produced "the desired political response from Hanoi." Almost hesitantly, Pearson suggested that "a suspension of air strikes against North Vietnam *at the right time*"—the words were underlined in his speech—might allow Hanoi to save face and begin negotiations. The proposal was the quintessence of Canadian cold war advice to the United States. Pearson had, however, challenged the foundation of U.S. policy through a decade of war under Johnson and Richard Nixon—that Hanoi would never negotiate in good faith unless the United States made it pay a heavy military price.[25]

The speech stung Johnson. The president felt that his Vietnam policy was a moderate course between "hawks" such as General Curtis LeMay, who demanded "all out war," and the antiwar movement gaining momentum in Congress and on campuses. Chairman of the Senate Foreign Relations Committee J. William Fulbright and his colleague senator Wayne Morse were consistent critics, and the first university teach-in took place at the University of Michigan only a month before Pearson's speech at Temple. President Johnson had been working hard to "domesticate" this dissent, and now that "oh so clever Canadian" Pearson had come "into [our] own backyard and [told] us how to run the war." Pearson had deliberately failed to clear his remarks with Bundy or Rusk, knowing in advance that they would disapprove. "You pissed on my rug!" the president bellowed the next day at Camp David, grabbing the prime minister by the shirtfront. "All those details," writes journalist Richard Gwyn, "have passed into Canadian folklore, enshrining the memory of Johnsonian coarseness and Pearsonian bravery." Pearson's bravery in this instance is apocryphal. After Johnson's tongue-lashing, the prime minister told the press that Canadians "would want to continue supporting the United States effort to bring peace to the people of Vietnam." Even when safe in Canada, he thanked the president for "speaking to me so frankly" and pronounced Johnson's "exposition of the American case for planned and limited air retaliation . . . reassuring and impressive." Johnson biographer Robert Dallek writes that "Pearson's support encouraged Johnson to pursue the policy he described." But Pearson also warned Johnson that Canadian public opinion was turning against U.S. policy in Southeast Asia, and that "a minority Government, cannot merely brush off these criticisms . . . Canada is . . . anxious that its leaders do not appear to be merely echoes of the United States." In his diary, Pearson noted that Johnson was being absorbed by Vietnam, and worried that the president might prove to be unequal to the challenge.[26]

Pearson's Temple speech was not the cause of Johnson's decision later that year to stop the bombing temporarily. Yet the president wanted to keep the prime minister onside. Before the United States resumed air attacks in 1966, he assured Pearson that it was only because Hanoi had showed no willingness to talk, and that only military targets would be attacked. Pearson was not persuaded. Like Senator J. William Fulbright, he had little confidence in a military victory and less in the viability of a South Vietnamese state. Because Pearson feared a general Asian war, the Canadian government attempted a diplomatic contribution independent of Washington. Minister of External Affairs Paul Martin selected retired diplomat Chester Ronning, Canada's senior China expert, to sound out Hanoi about peace. Born in China, Ronning had contacts no American diplomat could match: he knew both Ho Chi Minh and China's Zhou Enlai personally. To the U.S. State Department, this diminished rather than augmented his credentials, as did Ronning's outspoken advocacy of China's admission to the United Nations. Although the Canadian Department of External Affairs did not know it, the United States already had a secret line of direct contact with Hanoi; the use of Ronning was superfluous from the U.S. perspective. Dean Rusk was especially displeased by Martin's decision to send Ronning to meet with officials in Saigon (including American ambassador in Saigon Henry Cabot Lodge) as well as in Hanoi. Canada's even-handedness implied that there might be wrongs on both sides. The Canadian government was excited when North Vietnamese prime minister Pham Van Dong hinted to Ronning that Hanoi would negotiate if the U.S. bombing ceased. But Washington was unimpressed and refused to believe North Vietnam could be sincere. Nor did a second Ronning mission in June 1966 produce any results; the North Vietnamese told him bluntly that Canada's pressure for a peace offensive was pointless at a time when the United States was stepping up its attacks. The State Department described both Ronning missions as "negative." Its own use of Blair Seaborn as a conduit for belligerent messages to Hanoi was one thing, but independent Canadian attempts to be diplomatically helpful were quite another. In Vietnam as in Cuba, Canada had yet to find a course of action that did not involve prudent consideration of U.S. objectives and regular consultation with Washington officials.[27]

Responding to both political pressure and also to personal conviction, the Pearson government took a more critical line against the war. In May 1966, Pearson called for a cease-fire and a phased withdrawal by both North Vietnam and the "forces of other governments." Over the next year, Paul Martin traveled to Tokyo, Warsaw, and Moscow in a fruitless effort to promote peace negotiations. To his frustration, the Poles and the Soviets imagined that Canada had Johnson's ear; they asked repeatedly why Canada had not used its influence in Washington to end the fighting. In April 1967 in California, Pearson again suggested a bombing halt, and his government began to nag the Johnson administration about a negotiated settlement. It took no action, however, to reduce the flow of Vietnam-bound war material produced in Canada under the Defense Production Sharing Agreements. Between 1959 and 1970, the U.S. Department of Defense contracted $2.65 billion (CDN) worth of military equipment in Canada. Napalm, the petroleum-based explosive that symbolized Vietnam's obscenity to the U.S. antiwar movement, was manufactured in a plant in Quebec; the men of the Special Forces, who epitomized the American martial spirit to the war's champions, wore Green Berets knitted in Ontario. There could be no more ironic illustration of the complexity of the Canadian-U.S. relationship.[28]

Public protest against Lyndon Johnson's war mounted rapidly in Canada in 1967 and 1968, as it did in the United States. There are petitions against the war in the Johnson papers from Canadian individuals, groups, and schools. "Can you rest easily being a part of the brutal machine that America has unleashed . . . in South-East Asia?" a college classmate in Toronto wrote to Johnson's press secretary Bill Moyers. This protest rooted itself in traditional Canadian images of U.S. corruption and violence. Like everything else in Canada, however, the Canadian antiwar movement was tinged by cultural proximity to the United States. Chants of "Hey, Hey, LBJ—How many kids did you kill today?" reverberated at McGill and the University of Manitoba, just as they did at Columbia and the University of Michigan. In May 1967, when the president made an unannounced whirlwind tour of "Expo '67," Montreal's World's Fair, the couple who shouted "Johnson, assassin" during his speech were hustled out. The man who countered "All the way with LBJ" was allowed to remain. As in the United States, by no means all Canadians opposed the war in Vietnam, as the estimated 2,500 to 3,000 Canadians who served in the U.S. military during the war bore testimony.[29]

Johnson helicoptered to the prime minister's summer home at Harrington Lake, Quebec, to listen to yet another Canadian proposal "for breaking the Vietnam deadlock." Crafted by Minister of External Affairs Paul Martin, the plan called for both sides to cease active hostilities and retreat to create a demilitarized zone; the provisions of the 1954 Geneva Accords would apply while a negotiated settlement was worked out in "Big Four" talks among the United States, the Soviet Union, Britain, and France. Johnson and Rusk were polite enough to return to their helicopter without puncturing Pearson and Martin's attempt to revive Canada's dream of being a "linchpin" among the great powers. The *New York Times* dismissed the plan in one sentence. The Johnson administration is "giving careful consideration to halting the bombing," Pearson reported to Parliament. "If so, that's news to Washington," commented the *Washington Post*. The next day a "State Department spokesman" announced that the United States had "doubts about [the plan] because it would place the prestige of the President dangerously on the line" if he accepted these terms and North Vietnam rejected them. "Unless [the peace proposal] proves to have some effect," editorialized the *Toronto Globe and Mail,* "Mr. Pearson's much-touted 'quiet diplomacy' will appear even more ineffective than it does at present." Absolutely nothing came of the plan, of course. For Canadians, the "special relationship" with Washington would soon have less credibility than stories of the Rocky Mountain Sasquatch.[30]

As much as they may have disagreed on Vietnam and whatever their personal assessments of one another, Pearson and Johnson kept the lines of communication open. Pearson's assessment of Johnson's Vietnam dilemma was as astute as any other at the time. Pearson wondered, wrongly, if Johnson really had control over the U.S. military, or if he had decided to let the military have its way in Vietnam in the (mistaken) belief that this would permit his domestic program to win in the United States. When in March 1968 Johnson announced both a cessation of bombing of North Vietnam and his own decision not to seek reelection, Pearson wrote the president, warmly endorsing his decision on the bombing.[31]

In the Johnson-Pearson 1960s, U.S.-Canadian relations returned to the equilibrium that had characterized the years before Kennedy and Diefenbaker. The Liberal government had managed for the moment to diffuse Canadian nationalist complaints about the U.S. economic presence in Canada. Vietnam, on the other hand, not only occasioned friction both between the United States and Canada but also generated domestic dissent against the established orders in both countries. Intergovernmental differences over the Vietnam War before 1968 should not be exaggerated, however. There were strong and legitimate voices in both countries who saw the American policy as militaristic and imperialistic, and who blamed the Johnson administration for this. But the Pearson government shared the ideological assumptions of its southern neighbor, and the differences between the two were more tactical than fundamental and stemmed essentially from the different interests of a middle power such as Canada and a major world actor on the world stage such as the United States. Given the differing levels of power involvement in the world, there would always be a distinction in the national interests of the two countries. Given that power reality, in any conflict, American policy would always prevail.[32]

The Warfare State and the Welfare State

On the surface the 1960s were the decade of North American, even of worldwide, cultural convergence. For Canada, "convergence" meant moving toward an American norm; it went without saying that Canada was not going to assimilate the United States. To nervous Canadian cultural elites, ominous evidence of convergence was everywhere. Broadcasting was most foreboding because of its influence upon the young. Beyond the fact that the 70 percent of Canadians who lived close to the border could pick up American broadcasts over the air, most "Canadian" entertainment broadcasting was of U.S. origin. On AM radio, English-Canadian teenagers listened to Elvis and the Everly Brothers, and French Canadians to Quebec singers covering direct translations of American rock. After the "British invasion" in 1964, Canadian kids watched their Commonwealth cousins, the Beatles, on the *Ed Sullivan Show*, telecast every Sunday evening by the Canadian Broadcasting Corporation just before *Bonanza*. The state-owned CBC vied with the private CTV to see which network would pay more to purchase the rebroadcasting rights to these and other popular U.S. programs: when the CTV bought up baseball's World Series, the CBC countered with NFL football. Even Canada's "anti-imperialist youth," whose goal was "national self-determination and independence from the American Empire," borrowed their style and their strategies from the civil rights and antiwar demonstrations they watched on television.[33]

Canada mirrored the United States, but as Alice found out, a mirror can do strange things to images. Viewed from forty years distance, the 1960s stand out as the decade of greatest Canadian domestic divergence from the United States. It was between 1960 and 1970 that three of the characteristics that today most distinguish the two countries were set in place: the launching of the New Democratic Party, a social-democratic political party of the labor movement and the left that challenged the Liberals and the Conservatives; the development of a more extensive Canadian welfare state, complete with a national medical insurance plan; and the official national legislative recognition of Canada's bicultural English-French nature. The last of these phenomena has everything to do with Canadians' definition of themselves as being different from Americans, but a detailed discussion of the Official Languages Act of 1969 is not apropos in a book on U.S.-Canadian relations. The former two occurrences, however, were interrelated and are of great relevance to that relationship. How did it come about that post-1960 Canada developed a viable labor-left band within the legitimate political spectrum and a comprehensive welfare state at precisely the moment that both of these hopes died in America? William H. Chafe summarizes the literature on the United States effectively: "the Vietnam war assuredly destroyed Lyndon Johnson's dream of a united America committed to a 'Great Society.'" The hot war in Asia completed the work of the cold war in fragmenting the U.S. left: the AFL-CIO stood staunchly behind President Johnson, while others "who began as true believers in liberal reform became skeptics instead, alienated from their society and committed to revolutionizing its central values and structures." In Canada, these same people enlisted as New Democrats or remained in the strong left wing within the Liberal Party. Nudged from inside and out, the Liberal government of Lester Pearson between 1963 and 1968 gave Canada universal pension and national health systems—the Canada Pension Plan and Medicare. The latter came from the example of the New Democratic provincial government of one of the prairie provinces; the relevant chapter in Granatstein's *Canada 1957–1967* is entitled "Medicare: Saskatchewan Moves the Nation." [34]

Historians of each country have written about the strange death of liberal America and the curious creation of social-democratic Canada in splendid isolation, as if these things occurred on different planets. Seymour Martin Lipset's *Continental Divide: The Values and Institutions of Canada and the United States* (1990) attributes the differences primarily to the ideological foundations laid by the American Revolution, which assigned to the United States an "American Whig Ideology," with its "emphases on individual success and equality of opportunity, rather than of results," and to Canada a "Canadian Tory Identity," with its "greater emphases on the state and communitarianism." In Lipset's words, "The United States, set in a classically liberal-Whig mold,

stands out among developed countries in the relative lack of involvement of its governments in fields such as . . . welfare, health care, and
urban amenities." "Tory Canada," on the other hand, Lipset argues,
has throughout its history had both a more active national state and
a more vibrant political left than has the United States. Readers who
have reached this chapter of *Ambivalent Allies* will know that this conclusion is inconsistent with the histories of the two countries: until the
1950s, Canada was America's backward neighbor in both regards. Historian Robert Bothwell's conclusion that "Lipset's contrast of a classically Liberal U.S. society with a . . . Tory Canadian counterpart is . . .
somewhat overdrawn" is a gentle way of suggesting that Lipset's argument is incorrect.[35]

A more convincing explanation for U.S.-Canadian differences in
these regards is the huge contingency of the cold war and the massive emotional and fiscal resources the United States expended to fight
it. U.S. liberals expended their reforming energy defending New Deal
liberalism from McCarthyite smears but were unable to hold back the
right-of-center consensus that created what historian Stephen J. Whitfield calls *The Culture of the Cold War*. By the 1960s, a "military-industrial
complex" had fastened its grip so tightly on the United States that its
antidemocratic implications came to disturb President Eisenhower.[36]

Canada fought the cold war, too, complete with a Red scare, a northern Joe McCarthy (George Drew, Diefenbaker's predecessor as leader
of the Conservative Party), and branch plants of General Dynamics.
But the Canadian experience of these things was different from that
of the United States. Canadians went to Reds-under-the-bed movies such as *My Son John*, watched television programs such as *I Was a
Communist for the FBI*, or read comic books such as *Walt Disney's Uncle
Scrooge*, in which Scrooge defeated Asian insurgencies led by cartoon
Communists named "Wahn Beeg Rhat" or "Hassan Ben Jaild." But
they had been inundated in American pop culture for half a century,
long enough to learn to pass it through their national perceptual fil-
ters. Many things about cold war America repelled them. They were
annoyed to learn that the U.S. Immigration Service had thousands of
Canadian names among the 250,000 on its inventory of aliens to be de-

nied entry to the United States because of radical political connections, and they exploded when Herbert Norman, Canada's ambassador to Egypt, took his own life after the U.S. House Un-American Activities Committee revealed his youthful Communist indiscretions. And just as Canada of the 1960s lacked such amenities as M&Ms, Hershey Bars, and Fritos Corn Chips, it did not have a full-scale American-style "military-industrial complex." Its military was proportionately smaller and had less status and influence. Because of Canada's subordinate roles in planning the world wars and the Korean War, there were no Canadian Douglas MacArthurs. There were no Canadian "Dr. Strangeloves" either, or at least none in Canada, because there were no "Think Tanks" like the Rand Corporation to nurture them. Canada's national security bureaucracy was small, and without the U.S. separation of powers between the legislature and the executive to hide behind, it was constrained by legislative supervision. Most important, defense industries were smaller, both in absolute terms and relative to the overall economy. Canada enjoyed a lucrative trade in component parts for U.S. weapons, but after the cancellation of the AVRO Arrow interceptor, its defense industries were a profitable sideline but never the engine of the country's manufacturing economy. Tourists from both countries saw what this meant when they visited Seattle, Washington, and Vancouver, British Columbia, only 148 miles apart. A defense-based economy gave Seattle a completely different urban geography and made the two cities "distant neighbors." The percentage of the Canadian national budget devoted to defense declined steadily after 1955, and the share of GNP spent on the military fell even faster. In the United States, the opposite occurred. By the end of the 1960s, the United States was spending 59 percent of its national budget, and almost 10 percent of its GNP, on defense, as compared to Canada's 18 percent of its budget and 2.45 percent of GNP. Canada, safe (if nervous) under the U.S. nuclear umbrella, bought a social security state instead of a national security state. The United States battled the Communist threat around the globe and in the process built a warfare state instead of a welfare state.[37]

8   The Ambivalent Ally, 1968–1984

Pierre Elliott Trudeau was prime minister of Canada longer than any other save Sir John A. Macdonald and William Lyon Mackenzie King. With Trudeau as its leader, the Liberal Party held power in Ottawa for fifteen years, broken only by the brief Conservative interregnum of Joe Clark in 1979–80. The parliamentary system permits longer political careers; after Franklin Roosevelt successfully defied the two-term tradition, a constitutional amendment limited U.S. presidents to eight years in office. Trudeau served opposite five presidents: Lyndon Johnson, Richard Nixon, Gerald Ford, Jimmy Carter, and Ronald Reagan. None of them liked him very much except Carter. The relative stability in leadership on the Canadian side from the late 1960s through the early 1980s contrasted sharply with the instability on the U.S. side and made the bilateral relationship more uncertain. Canadians discovered that it was much less fulfilling to be America's junior partner than it had been to be Britain's, and that the "bonds of sentiment and loyalty" were missing on both sides. Partnership with America offered the material benefits of selling armaments and automobiles to the United States; it brought the spiritual poverty of continued complicity in the U.S. war in Vietnam. A strident new Canadian nationalism demanded that Trudeau's government act to stop the "Americanization" of Canada by controlling U.S. investment and blocking American popular culture. When Trudeau retired and Ronald Reagan was elected to a second term in 1984, the "special relationship" had become something only for historians to ponder.[1]

Distinct Societies

At no time in the twentieth century did Canada and the United States diverge so sharply as when America was "coming apart at home" over race and Vietnam. Canadians, of course, had always con-sidered their country fundamentally different from the United States, but events of the late 1960s and early 1970s buttressed their national narcissism about small North American differences and their long-standing conviction of moral superiority. U.S. social critics offered con-firmation. "Society in the United States is close to disintegration," a Michigan trade unionist told an Ontario audience in February 1968, "because of its failure to deal with the problems of poverty and urban life." Events of the next few months bore him out, as violence swept the United States in the wake of the murder of Martin Luther King Jr. The Washington correspondents for Canadian newspapers reported in de-tail both the rioting and looting by "gangs of Negro youths . . . within a few blocks of the White House" and the brutal treatment meted out to them if "policemen wearing riot helmets equipped with plastic vi-sors, waving rifles, shotguns and pistols" arrived to stop them. Cana-dian editors poured out their preconceptions: "The American people claim to be the most democratic in the world," wrote Montreal's *Le Devoir*, "but this great military and economic power is a sick nation [that] tolerates systematic injustice, hatred, [and] poverty." The United States "has never reached that state of civilization in which its people were prepared to commit their security to the rule of law," observed the *Toronto Globe and Mail*. Canadian editors tendered lofty condescen-sion. "The writing has been on the wall for many years," the *Winnipeg Free Press* offered; "Congress must not procrastinate any longer either on civil rights or . . . strict controls on the sale of firearms." The only chance for Americans to escape "the smoldering hell they have built with racial prejudice," contributed the *Globe and Mail*, was to "spend billions . . . and end the Vietnam war to make the spending possible." "America has, since its beginnings, been characterized by a unique tradition of violence," wrote journalist Claude Ryan after an assassin claimed Robert Kennedy two months later. "We thought this tradition was over. The events of recent years have proved unfortunately that is not the case." The Canadian rock group The Guess Who howled its critique of the Republic: "I don't need your war machine, I don't need your ghetto scene—American woman, stay away from me."[2]

Some Americans felt the same way. The Guess Who's song reached number one on the U.S. pop charts, and for the first time since the early nineteenth century, Americans migrating to Canada outnumbered Canadians moving to the United States. Since the end of World War II, prosperity in Canada had combined with U.S. immigration controls to reduce the net migration of Canadians to the United States. Even so, between 1946 and 1957, 293,000 Canadians had emigrated south while only 78,000 Americans moved to Canada. Professionals who could qualify for a U.S. "Green Card," however, formed a higher proportion of the people Canada lost. For example, throughout the 1950s this "brain drain" siphoned off the equivalent of about 20 percent of Canada's engineering graduates each year. In the 1960s, the Vietnam War and U.S. urban violence helped Canada hold its own people and absorb some its neighbor's. Young single Canadian males who moved to the United States were liable to the draft after one year's residence, which no doubt helped many choose Halifax over Houston. Between 50,000 and 125,000 (estimates vary that widely) U.S. men of that same generation chose Canada as well. These war resisters (or "draft dodgers") accounted for a considerable part of Canada's net migration advantage of 250,000 entering to 150,000 leaving over the period from 1965 to 1975. Half of Canadians, however, wished that the war resisters would stay home, according to a 1968 poll; this percentage was perhaps more a negative comment about the United States than a statement of support for the Vietnam War. America's problems made Canadians feel better about their country. Even those disinclined to anti-American nationalism, such as historian Michael Bliss, observed in 1970 that Canada "is a more attractive country vis-à-vis the United States than it has ever been."[3]

Apart from their differences of opinion over wartime expatriates, Canadians liked the fact that Americans were taking favorable notice of them. The six million U.S. visitors in Canada's centennial year of 1967 found that Canada had clean, safe cities with skyscrapers, and that not all Canadians were lumberjacks or trappers who wore stocking caps and checked jackets. Montreal's World Fair—"Expo 67"—drew a host of admiring U.S. comment. Extolling "the good new buildings" and "the shining new subway," the *New York Times* concluded that Americans could "learn about other things than fairs from this Canadian jewel city." Two years later, Montreal landed a major league baseball team, appropriately named the "Expos." That decision showed how little Americans understood about Canada: the barons of baseball would have been far more shrewd to award the first foreign franchise to Toronto, Canada's financial capital and coming metropole; Montreal was about to be convulsed by *québécois* ethnic nationalism in search of an independent Quebec. Canada dealt with the Quebec independence movement with both carrot and stick. An Official Languages Act in 1969 made French and English equal in national institutions; and in October 1970 massive military repression crushed the cells of the Front de liberation du Québec (the Quebec Liberation Front), which had carried out two political kidnappings. During this "October Crisis," the Canadian government suspended the civil liberties of twenty-one million Canadians to catch a handful of terrorists—without significant domestic protest. The contrast between Canadian and American approaches to dissent was instructive: Canadians, expatriate U.S. intellectual Edgar Z. Friedenberg noted, were remarkable for their "deference to authority." [4]

By 1970, the stirrings of Canadian nationalism exploited by John Diefenbaker and encouraged by Walter Gordon became an anti-American whirlwind that could shake even somnolent academic seminars on U.S.-Canadian relations. At Columbia University in November 1970, a former Canadian cold warrior recanted at gale force. Professor James Eayrs of the University of Toronto eloquently summarized the case of Canada's new nationalists. NATO, NORAD, and the PJBD might endure, but "the spirit of Ogdensburg has long since evaporated" and "the identity of basic aims shattered." The United States had betrayed Canada's trust, wearing anticommunism as "a protean disguise . . . behind which American oilmen as well as American airmen could go about their stealthy business." Canada had become nothing more than "a continental chore-boy for the Strategic Air Command," a place for SAC pilots to "practice their bomb runs." Eayrs posited that "the main strategic threat to Canada comes not from our north but from our south," from "a new generation of American imperialists." Canada's duty, he concluded, was to break off its U.S. alliance in order to provide moral support to "the millions of Americans trying to compel a change of policy" in Vietnam, to say "goodbye to good neighborhood in the interests of us all. Otherwise a future president of the United States— perhaps some young opponent of the [Vietnam] war now in Canada or jail—will say to a future prime minister of the neighbor still unknown: 'Where were you when we needed you?'" Twenty Canadian journalists rushed to file their stories; the one U.S. journalist who covered the seminar appears to have missed Eayrs's speech.[5]

Sleeping with an Elephant

Pierre Elliott Trudeau had no patience with such nationalist passion. The Liberal Party chose him to replace Lester Pearson because he promised an answer to the Quebec question, and in June 1968 the electorate gave him a majority government—155 of the 263 seats in the House of Commons—for that same reason. The new prime minister was not about to give in to Canadian nationalism any more than he was to the québécois variant. Trudeau questioned all of the foreign policy myths of post-1945 Canada: "Quiet Diplomacy," the "helpful fixer" role, the "linchpin" function, the "special relationship." Nothing was sacred. Former Canadian ambassador to Washington Charles Ritchie, reassigned to London, found "the climate in Ottawa very anti-NATO" and heard "a great deal of talk of neutrality for Canada based on the Swedish model." Even "the 'British connection' seems to be receding out of view. Only the crown remains." Trudeau eviscerated the Canadian Department of External Affairs much as John F. Kennedy had done to the U.S. State Department a decade earlier. In quest of an imperial prime ministership, he concentrated authority in the prime minister's office and relied on his special adviser Ivan Head rather than experienced diplomats. The resulting "denigration of External Affairs" (to use political scientist Kim Nossal's term) undermined the department that had handled the bilateral relationship. Trudeau subjected every aspect of

Canada's external policy to review. The result was a six-pack of book-lets issued jointly as *A Foreign Policy for Canadians* in 1970, which pro-posed that Canada refocus its trade and international ties beyond North America toward Europe, Asia, and Latin America. Those Canadians who read the series of light discussion papers—not a very demand-ing intellectual task, historian J. L. Granatstein has commented—were struck by the "curious absence" of a paper on Canadian-U.S. relations. The feeble response was that *all* the papers, to some degree, were about Canadian-U.S. relations! "Seventy percent of Canada's foreign policy is predetermined by the Canadian-U.S. relationship," Trudeau had once commented. Canada's goal, he argued, "should be to maximize free-dom of movement with regard to the remaining thirty percent."[6]

Lame-duck Lyndon Johnson was spared a meeting with Pierre Trudeau. Instead, new Republican president Richard Nixon welcomed him to Washington in March 1969, continuing the invented tradition that the first foreign leader greeted at the White House would be the Canadian prime minister. The two men managed their profound dis-like for each other remarkably well. The Watergate tapes revealed that Nixon's private term for Trudeau was "that asshole"; what Trudeau called Nixon remains hidden from the historian: it would have been no more complimentary, but surely would have been expressed more elegantly. Otherwise, president and prime minister spoke frankly from the first: Trudeau opened two unpleasant defense subjects. In Europe, Canada would halve its NATO contingent to five thousand (he did not tell the president that his cabinet had at first considered leaving NATO altogether); in North America, Canada objected to the new Safeguard Anti-Ballistic Missiles being sowed in the fields of North Dakota and Montana. A missile system to destroy missiles, Trudeau argued, would escalate an East-West arms race and postpone Canada's goal of nuclear disarmament. And Canada intended to recognize formally the People's Republic of China.

Nixon's nonreactions surprised the prime minister. The president understood the need for NATO reductions—he wanted American troops back in the United States as well. The Safeguard system would go ahead, with Canada getting regular reports of "plans and developments in the ABM field," in the hope that Canadians would come to appreciate its strategic necessity. On China, Nixon had already accepted the advice of his national security adviser Henry Kissinger (Nixon brought Secretary of State William Rogers out only for ceremonial display) that recognition was inevitable and desirable. Kissinger's business contacts on the Trilateral Commission had favored recognition since 1963, but the Vietnam War and the Cultural Revolution had impeded it. Canadian recognition might smooth the way for a U.S. opening to Beijing; in any event, what Canada did was of no great consequence. Nixon pressed one issue of his own—the U.S. plan for a continental oil policy. That already existed, Trudeau responded disingenuously. Western Canada provided parts of the United States with oil and natural gas; Eastern Canada imported an equal amount pumped by U.S. companies in Venezuela. It was after this visit that Trudeau made his famous—to Canadians, that is—remark that "Living next to you is in some ways like sleeping with an elephant; no matter how friendly and even-tempered is the beast, one is affected by every twitch and grunt."[7]

Although he made no secret of his distaste for America's Asian war, Trudeau never nagged Nixon to make peace, as Pearson and Paul Martin had done with Johnson. He understood that no Canadian should harbor illusions that friendly counsel from Canada would bend Nixon on the war. In quest of international stature in his undeclared campaign for the Republican nomination, Nixon had made a major speech to Toronto's Empire Club (the name derived from the British "Empire" but was nonetheless apt) in which he affirmed his faith in the "domino theory" and bluntly stated that "the future of Canada as well as the United States is tied to the creation of a free and prosperous empire in Asia." Trudeau understood that Americans themselves would have to confront their president. The U.S. antiwar movement had intensified since Pearson's address at Temple University in 1965. There was now an articulate congressional opposition, and antiwar protest turned to the active resistance graphically displayed in the streets of Chicago during the 1968 Democratic national convention. Grassroots connections between Canadian and U.S. opponents of the war proliferated as a sort of Underground Railroad (the comparison was made often) led draft evaders north. There were Canadians among the protestors in Chicago, and on Canadian university campuses students denounced Canadian complicity in providing arms to the United States. Trudeau gave them little satisfaction. His protests were symbols, such as his speech to a delegation of Mennonites in Winnipeg that Canada should be "a refuge from militarism" for draft resisters. This pleased no one— ultra-left antiwar pickets that same day passed out leaflets reading "Death to Trudeau."[8]

As part of his policy of "Vietnamization," President Nixon reduced American ground forces from half a million to fewer than one hundred thousand, but stepped up the U.S. air offensive in search of "peace with honor." With Henry Kissinger assuring them that this goal was "at hand," American voters gave Richard Nixon resounding reelection over the "acid, amnesty and abortion" Democrat George McGovern in November 1972. Trudeau was less fortunate: a week earlier, Canadian voters had reduced his government to a minority. It was time, he was persuaded, to speak out on Vietnam: the new Parliament resolved against the war in January 1973, infuriating the Nixon administration and relegating Canadian diplomats in Washington to the "shit list" with such neutral countries as Sweden. Canada came off the list some weeks later when it agreed to be America's designate on a new international commission to supervise a proposed ceasefire. For four months Canada kept a staff of 290 in Vietnam who did important work supervising exchanges of prisoners of war. But the commission, described as a "masquerade" and a "charade," had no success in its larger assignment of supervising the ceasefire: North Vietnam was not about to stop fighting on the eve of victory. The Canadians came home in frustration on 31 July 1973; the last American troops followed shortly thereafter. Without its U.S. strings, the puppet government in Saigon collapsed in twenty months.[9]

In Ottawa, the fate of Trudeau's minority government dangled on the parliamentary votes of the nationalist New Democratic Party. The long-awaited position paper on Canadian-American relations had been issued just before the election, provoked by a change in U.S. economic policy that is the subject of the next section. *Canadian-American Relations: Options for the Future* made clear that "the United States is Canada's closest friend and will remain so," but the paper proposed that Canada reduce its dependence on the United States. Minister of External Affairs Mitchell Sharp (in Trudeau's cabinets, the position was a revolving door) gave the policy a name: the "Third Option." This option repackaged the long Canadian search for counterbalances to the United States. Pearson and St. Laurent had tried multilateral international organizations such as the United Nations and NATO; Diefenbaker had offered the chimera of a revitalized British connection; now Trudeau and his ministers of external affairs offered the world. There were no discernable results; nor was the United States particularly discomfited by the attempt. As NSC adviser Brent Scowcroft told two historians years later, Washington simply thought, "there go the Canadians again." American economic realities, not Canadian foreign policy illusions, brought about the bilateral conflicts of the Nixon-Trudeau years.[10]

Canadian Economic Nationalism

Canadian economic nationalism predated Pierre Trudeau—in truth, the prime minister thought it a nuisance and a distraction from the things he really cared about. Until the mid-1950s, Canadian economic nationalism took the form of protective tariffs against imported U.S. manufactured goods; thereafter, although protection remained important, economic nationalists fulminated against U.S. foreign investment. There was an enchanting illogic in this: it was the protective tariff that had brought U.S. direct investment to Canada in the first place. The reaction that began against U.S. direct investment in the late 1950s built to a nationalist crescendo in the "Waffle movement" of 1969, so-called because its members demanded that the New Democratic Party "waffle" to the left, away from the political center. Young "Wafflers" (one of the authors of this book among them) wore two campaign buttons. One bore the label of a popular ginger ale overprinted with the phrase

"Nixon Drinks Canada Dry;" the second called for "An Independent Socialist Canada." Not many Canadians agreed with the Waffle's prescription, but by 1972, two-thirds of them accepted its diagnosis of the disease.[11]

Historians point to the irony that nationalist reaction occurred when the *proportion* of foreign ownership in Canada was at an historic low. There had been, however, an immense absolute increase in U.S. direct investment during the postwar resource boom; in earlier periods foreign investment had been more diverse in its origins, and a substantial proportion was British portfolio investment, which English Canadians did not regard as "foreign." The 1960s shattered the fantasy that foreign investment was a phase through which Canada would pass, as the United States once had. The nationalists had two good arguments against direct foreign investment: branch plants manufactured for the Canadian domestic market and not for export, and they did little "R&D"—research and development—in Canada. This meant fewer high-skill jobs for the demographic waves of the baby boom that entered Canada's labor market in the 1970s and 1980s. The nationalist revulsion against U.S. foreign investment was also indivisible from the more general anti-Americanism and, like it, was born of confidence rather than despair. During the 1960s, as Canadians grew richer selling automobiles and armaments to Americans, their median income moved to U.S. levels for the first time in the country's history.[12]

The Liberal government at first fell back on the venerable Canadian method of investigating intractable problems. In 1968, Walter Gordon had prodded the Pearson government to set up a task force headed by University of Toronto economist Mel Watkins to investigate foreign ownership in the Canadian economy and to suggest ways to encourage Canadian ownership. The resulting report reflected Gordon's contention that Canadians had to choose either colonial status vis-à-vis the United States or economic independence. Such views were not welcome within the Liberal Party in 1967. Gordon's successor as finance minister, Mitchell Sharp, buried both Gordon's ideas and the Watkins report. The only nationalist economic institution created in the 1960s was the Canadian National Energy Board, designed to establish more

national direction over exploration, development, and the export marketing of petroleum and natural gas. In 1970, the House of Commons
Standing Committee on External Relations commissioned economist
Ian Wahn to write a second report on foreign investment; he recommended a target of 51 percent Canadian ownership for Canadian industry. Minister of National Revenue Herb Gray prepared a third
analysis of the deleterious impact of foreign investment on Canada for
cabinet discussion in early 1971.[13]

Richard Nixon's "New Economic Policy" did more than any of these
reports to demonstrate to Canadians the dangers of dependence and
to inspire economic nationalism and the Third Option. The world,
Canada included, had gained economic ground on the United States in
the 1960s, as America confirmed the long-term impossibility of a "guns
and butter" economic strategy. By 1970, the United States faced major
balance-of-payments difficulties and the paradox of rising unemployment, economic stagnation, and high inflation. In August 1971, the
president announced an increase in the dollar value of gold and the
suspension of the gold convertibility of the dollar, thus effectively de-
valuing the U.S. dollar. Nixon served notice to all trading partners that
the United States would improve its trade balance through a 10 percent
surtax on all imports. The U.S.-Canada Autopact had shifted the balance of trade in the industry by $800 million in Canada's favor: only
rapid action by the State Department kept Secretary of the Treasury
John Connally from including Autopact's cancellation in the president's speech. These actions were taken without significant (in the case
of Canada, without any) international consultation within the world
economic order established at Bretton Woods and in the GATT (General Agreement on Trade and Tariffs). Congress seemed even more
protectionist than the administration, so that, for Canada, confrontation appeared unavoidable. "Economic power will be the key to other
kinds of power in . . . the last third of this century," Richard Nixon
told an audience in Kansas City. The "elephant" had rolled over on the
"mouse."[14]

Canadian finance minister Edgar Benson and minister of external
affairs Mitchell Sharp, neither one a nationalist, believed that the "spe-

cial relationship" had died. But a pilgrimage to Washington by Trudeau in December 1971 and Nixon's official visit to Canada in April 1972 offered some damage control. Trudeau's personal intellectual respect for Henry Kissinger helped to moderate the prime minister's reaction to the policies of the Nixon administration. Kissinger's pragmatic influence on the White House and the high degree of White House control over foreign policy in the Nixon administration aided reconciliation. Canada cajoled from the Americans an understanding that the import surtax would not be applied to Canada (the tax was short-lived in any event) and that Canada would not be penalized if the now-floating Canadian dollar began to sink, thus improving the position of Canadian exports in the United States.[15]

Such developments, and the Trudeau government's minority position in Parliament, gave advocates of a nationalistic economic policy new political influence. The Canada Development Corporation (CDC), a government-initiated holding company that mobilized Canadian investment capital to "buy Canada back" from foreign investors, came into being that same year. This Crown corporation exemplified exactly the type of "discriminatory" economic policy that troubled Washington. Over the next decade, the CDC made substantial investments in mining, chemical, and pharmaceutical companies operating in Canada, even though the Canadian government eventually divested itself of its majority holding in the corporation. The Third Option of enhancing trade with Asia and Europe also gained impetus. The Nixon administration at first barely noticed the creation in 1974 of the Foreign Investment Review Agency (FIRA) to "screen" foreign acquisitions of Canadian corporations to determine if they were "in the national interest." The CDC and FIRA exemplified economic nationalism's capitalist dimension, premised on the notion that, given a jump start by government, Canadian entrepreneurs could retake the economy through the private sector. Economic nationalism's socialist dimension came to the fore when Canadian nationalism fused with the energy crisis generated by the 1973 Arab-OPEC oil embargo to create Petro-Canada, a national oil company. Although Petro-Canada never had the monopoly position that the Mexican government gave PEMEX, this Crown corporation launched the Canadian government into the petroleum industry—a sector about two-thirds U.S.-controlled.[16]

Canada's more nationalistic energy policies probed a sensitive nerve in the United States. Every American administration since World War I had been committed to national oil security, because U.S. dependence on foreign oil kept increasing. By 1970, the U.S. armed forces obtained 40 percent of their supplies from foreign sources. Between 1960 and 1975, total U.S. energy consumption doubled, with the use of oil and natural gas growing fastest; imports multiplied from 23 to 39 percent of this demand. Canada's contribution grew significantly: U.S. oil imports from Canada more than tripled to 18.7 percent in 1967, the year that imports from Canada exceeded those from the Middle East. This growth took place despite U.S. import barriers to Canadian oil that in 1968 kept wells in Alberta shut down for want of access to the American market. The Nixon administration believed that U.S. national oil security could be achieved if the northern Canadian tar sands were developed and pipeline facilities expanded for delivery of crude oil. The Nixon administration also knew that American national oil security depended on the availability of oil to its allies—Japan and Western Europe. Canada was more reliable than any other foreign supplier because of its political stability, its existing economic interdependence with the United States, and the relative invulnerability of means of transport. Canadian imports should thus be treated as part of domestic U.S. production. The Pentagon was especially anxious about the post-1980s, when it was anticipated (wrongly, as it turned out) that production in the Western Hemisphere would decline. The Arab-OPEC oil embargo in 1973–74 pushed Washington to act. Nixon's National Energy Policy of April 1973 included a continuing search for secure world supplies, an end to import controls, and the establishment of a National Energy Office. The crisis assigned Canada an expanded importance in American thought as an oil producer in the 1970s: a Senate investigation of the geopolitics of energy concluded that in spite of the major political obstacles involved, "an energy effort in Canada" seemed to be "an obvious priority."[17]

But Canada had its own energy problems of which Washington was oblivious. During the Arab-OPEC embargo Canadian oil exports to the United States increased substantially, but Canadian imports from Saudi Arabia increased by a greater percentage. In the Canadian election of July 1974, Trudeau regained his parliamentary majority and was no longer dependent on the nationalist NDP; Canada's desire to assure its own energy self-sufficiency, not simple anti-Americanism, inspired Canada to consider an embargo on oil exports to the United States. A U.S. Senate Foreign Relations subcommittee urged the importance of "persuad[ing] the Canadian Government to delay implementation of its announced objective of curtailing exports to the United States"; Canada relented on an embargo but over U.S. objections imposed a tax increase on oil exports and increased export prices for natural gas. The dramatic increase of $14.4 billion in U.S. expenditures on oil imports during the first eleven months of 1974 underlined U.S. vulnerability. If a Third World country had challenged U.S. plans, American policymakers would have been neither surprised nor unduly alarmed; when Canada seemed, from the U.S. perspective, to move in a similar direction, surprise and disapproval was immediate. Yet Canadian economic nationalism escaped the worst of U.S. wrath because the Nixon administration was enfeebled by the crisis brought on by its political corruption. A bungled burglary of Democratic Party headquarters during the 1972 presidential campaign—Watergate—left Richard Nixon little time to be angry with Canada. When he resigned in August 1974, one step ahead of impeachment, new president Gerald Ford and Secretary of State Henry Kissinger immediately established the Strategic Petroleum Reserve to store crude oil for emergency use.[18]

Closing the "Candy Store"

Canada's most successful novel of 1973 was a political thriller by retired Major General Richard Rohmer. In *Ultimatum*, a Canadian government refuses U.S. demands to surrender vast quantities of natural gas; after a heroic resistance, Canada is militarily overwhelmed and annexed to the United States. The astonishing thing about *Ultimatum*'s success was not that a novel with a preposterous plot, cardboard characters, and wooden dialogue could top the best-seller list—in those respects, Rohmer's book was no worse than any of Tom Clancy's or Robert Ludlum's books; what was surprising was that a *Canadian* rather than an American novel could lead Canada's best-seller list. Sixty percent of the books sold in Canada that year were U.S. books, and only 25 percent were Canadian. Most of the latter were textbooks, cook books, and how-to books: less than 1 percent of the mass-market fiction sold in Canada had been written there. Lobbyists for Canada's other cultural industries—magazines, film, television, recorded music—could cite similar figures. If the United States determined 70 percent of Canada's foreign policy, how much more completely did America set Canada's cultural agenda? Cultural exports were critical to a U.S. economy with balance-of-payments difficulties: by the 1970s, popular culture had become America's second largest export income-earner after agriculture. Canada's three-quarters English-speaking population and its geographic proximity made it the cheapest foreign market for U.S. popular cultural industries to produce for and to deliver to, and profit margins were accordingly very high. As a *Time* executive told a reporter in 1975, "they don't call Canada the candy store for nothing."[19]

Canada's concern about cultural "Americanization," as always, had two faces. One was the sincere concern of an alarmed nationalist intelligentsia that had grown larger as the baby boomers poured into colleges and universities. The other face was the economic self-interest of cultural entrepreneurs who wanted to produce movies, record music, own sports franchises, publish magazines and books, and earn a living at it. All demanded, and some received, the support of Canada's government. Government policy also had two sides, one promotional and the other protectionist. These two techniques were not exclusive and could be applied simultaneously. Canada's magazine publishers, for example, could receive special postal privileges and tariff protection at the same time. But in the new Canadian nationalism of the 1960s and 1970s, the balance swung in favor of protection. As before, the U.S. government ignored promotion but retaliated swiftly against protection, usually at the behest of a U.S. cultural industry that had cried foul at Canadian government interference with access to its "candy store."[20]

The attempt of Canadian magazine publishers to eliminate the competition of the "Canadian editions" of *Time* and *Reader's Digest* was a well-picked bone of bilateral contention. By the 1970s, the controversy had spun around the Canadian-U.S. cultural sovereignty cycle—agitation, investigation, legislation, retaliation, and Canadian capitulation—three times over two decades. Canadian magazines would protest, with justice, that *Time* and *Reader's Digest* had an unfair advantage. Then a government investigation would conclude that the Canadian publishers had a solid case: given the vast sales of the two magazines in the United States, the unit cost of the editorial content was tiny. By adding a few pages—exactly four, in *Time*'s case—they were allowed the same tax treatment as entirely Canadian magazines. The Canadian government would draft legislation to end this privilege, *Time* and *Reader's Digest* would complain to Washington, the United States would threaten countermeasures, and the Canadian government would shrug its shoulders. But the issue refused to go away, and in 1975 the Trudeau government's Bill C-58 gave the two "Canadian editions" a choice: to "Canadianize" with 75 percent Canadian content or to join the dozens of U.S. periodicals that circulated freely in Canada without tax exemptions for their advertisers. *Reader's Digest* chose to stay and become a model cultural corporate citizen; after it became obvious that the Ford administration could not save it, *Time* published its last "Canadian edition" in March 1976.[21]

The Broadcasting Act of 1968 was another attempt by the Trudeau government to "safeguard, enrich and strengthen the cultural, political, social and economic framework of Canada." Although every radio and television station had to be Canadian-owned to receive a broadcasting license, Canada's mixed public and private radio and television system was itself the principal purveyor of American recorded music and programming to Canadian audiences: like *Time* magazine, broadcasters found it cheaper, and thus more profitable, to purchase what they transmitted in the United States rather than to incur the costs of producing it themselves. By buying and retransmitting U.S. programs, said nationalist critics, private TV broadcasters in Canada turned their broadcasting licenses into "licenses to print money." The public televi-

sion network, the CBC, did this not in the name of profits but in order
to compete for viewers with the private networks and with U.S. stations close to the border. Ratings showed that, given a choice, Canadians preferred U.S. entertainment programs to their Canadian counterparts. The Broadcasting Act of 1968 created a new federal regulatory
body, the Canadian Radio and Television Commission (CRTC), to enforce "Canadian content" rules that required that all stations, public
and private, offer "programming . . . of a high standard, using predominantly Canadian creative and other resources and predominantly
Canadian in content and character." The CRTC had teeth: it could deny
license renewal to violators of its "CanCon" rules. On AM and FM radio, 30 percent of the songs played had to meet criteria for "Canadian-
ness" that were sometimes confusing: Mick Jagger recorded in Toronto
could be "Canadian," and Neil Young recorded in New York "foreign."
For television, the CRTC insisted on 60 percent Canadian content, with
50 percent in the "prime time" evening hours. "Canadian content,"
however, was loosely defined: both the Super Bowl and the World Series were considered to be of sufficiently wide interest in Canada to
qualify.

Thus, although the CRTC's CanCon rules denied airtime to U.S. programs and recordings, they did not do enough damage for Washington to take serious notice. The expansion of cable TV, however, led to a
flagrant use of "cultural sovereignty" to pick U.S. pockets and to line
those of Canadian broadcasters. Canadian cable companies simply
stole the signals of U.S. stations and retransmitted them to Canadians
who paid them for this stolen property. To compound this theft, a section of Bill c-58 required Canadian cable operators to "strip" the ABC,
CBS, or NBC broadcast of a program and "simulcast" the Canadian
rebroadcast in its place. Canadian viewers could watch *Dallas* or *Mork
and Mindy*, but their "cultural sovereignty" to watch Canadian rather
than U.S. commercials was carefully guarded. Because Bill c-58 had
also laid *Time* to rest, it became the most controversial cultural irritant
in U.S.-Canadian relations.

The Trudeau government's promotional policy for Canadian feature films, on the other hand, rang no alarm bells in Hollywood and

brought no diplomatic notes from Washington. The Canadian Film Development Corporation (later Telefilm) subsidized producers of Canadian feature films, and the federal government granted generous tax credits to induce parallel private investment. As with popular music, a liberal set of rules defined a "Canadian" feature film. In 1979, $160 million (CDN) of public money was spent to produce sixty-seven "certified Canadian features," ten times as many as a decade earlier. Cultural nationalists called it the "Second Golden Age" of Canadian film, overlooking the fact that there had not been a first one. For their money, Canada's taxpayers got poor imitations of Hollywood, movies made, wrote film critic Martin Knelman, "in the shadow of the American eagle, or of the MGM lion, or of Mickey Mouse." To guarantee sales in the United States, the filmmakers imported U.S. stars, selected stories that would appeal to U.S. audiences, and disguised Canadian locations as Anywhere USA. Some of the movies were Hollywood projects that producers found a way to "Canadianize" to earn tax breaks and subsidies. The best picture nominees for the 1979 Genie Awards (Canada's attempt at a northern Oscar) were instructive. *The Changeling* was a haunted-house thriller starring special effects and George C. Scott. *Meatballs* was fun at summer camp with Bill Murray; the camp was supposed to be in the United States, not in Ontario, where it was actually filmed. Reviewers described *Jack London's Klondike Fever*, which starred Rod Steiger as London, as "a pathetic piece of bad historical fiction"; it was embarrassingly like the movies Hollywood had made about Canada in the 1930s and 1940s, except that in 1979 Canadian taxpayers paid for it themselves. Only one feature actually starred a Canadian actor: Christopher Plummer played Sherlock Holmes in *Murder by Decree*, filmed in London with an international cast. The final film made the other four look like *Casablanca*. *Yesterday* was a tearjerker about an American hockey player at Montreal's McGill University during the Vietnam War era and his *québécoise* girlfriend. The English-Canadian McGill students were beer-swilling racist boors, the professors stuffy old Englishmen, and the French Canadians hot-headed, bomb-throwing radicals. Rather than building a Canadian popular culture, wrote a critic, such movies confirmed that Canada was a "land of mediocrity, habitat of sycophants to a cut-rate U.S. dream." Holly-wood had no reason to protest to Washington about the CFDC: the U.S. film community simply went to Canada and stuck its snout in the public trough.[22]

Did these attempts to assert "cultural sovereignty" change anything? The death of *Time* allowed the Canadian news magazine *Maclean's* to absorb its readers. For television, the CRTC strictly enforced content regulations, so that the quantity of Canadian television production showed an impressive increase. Canadian news and public affairs programs and children's shows won praise from American commentators. The most obvious broadcasting failure was English-Canadian television drama, which was almost nonexistent. In 1978, 91 percent of the news watched by English-speaking Canadians was domestic, but 89 percent of their TV entertainment was American. Even French Canadians watched U.S. entertainment shows, sometimes dubbed into French, for 60 percent of their TV viewing. For Canadian music, the CanCon regulations for air play combined with an old-fashioned protective tariff on imported tapes and LP records to launch a domestic industry and the individual careers of dozens of Canadian singers: Anne Murray, Bryan Adams, k.d. lang. Some critics sniffed haughtily, however, about "filling the airwaves with undistinguished rock-and-roll—acceptable as long as it is played by a band from Sudbury or Winnipeg, but not if it comes from Des Moines." Feature films remained Canada's vast wasteland; critics lampooned the "reel estate boom" of the late 1970s created by CFDC dollars. The cultural sovereignists replied truculently to all charges: "Sure, it's junk, but at least it's *our* junk." To argue that these policies had established "cultural sovereignty" required a leap of faith that not even they could make. But the fact that the ultimate goal remained elusive did not persuade the Trudeau government to eliminate the policies. An academic observer noted in 1976 "indications that U.S. tolerance levels are not as high as they were a few years ago." This put the problem in the mildest terms possible; in the 1980s and 1990s, these "irritants" became festering sores to the members of Congress who spoke for the U.S. cultural exporters afflicted by them.[23]

"Donkeys Are Much More Companionable Beasts"

The limited results produced by the warm personal relationship between Jimmy Carter and Pierre Trudeau illustrate how dramatically the possibilities of summit diplomacy had shrunk during the four decades since Franklin Roosevelt and Mackenzie King had reshaped North America. No president ever worked harder than Jimmy Carter to understand the issues in U.S.-Canadian relations. During the now-traditional first visit from the Canadian prime minister, Carter showed his expertise with an analogy to Trudeau's 1969 aphorism about the U.S. elephant and the Canadian mouse. The elephant symbolized the Republicans, he noted, but now "the donkeys are here, and donkeys are much more companionable beasts." Carter demonstrated this by choosing Kenneth Curtis, a former governor of Maine with a firsthand understanding of Canada, as his ambassador in Ottawa. Edmund Muskie, later Carter's secretary of state, was from the same border state. But U.S.-Canadian relations had moved beyond the influence of individual presidents and prime ministers and their appointees. Although no pivotal new problems developed between 1977 and 1980, Carter and Trudeau were unable to translate personal goodwill into bilateral bliss. U.S.-Canadian relations did not become significantly worse, but neither did they become significantly better. It was a case, wrote Lawrence Martin, Washington correspondent for the *Toronto Globe and Mail*, of "shattered expectations."[24]

Martin was too harsh. There were achievements, such as Carter's 1976 amnesty for American draft resisters, most of them in Canada, a decision that was popular in both countries. But each leader faced domestic obstacles that impeded answers to binational questions. Trudeau's problems were posed by the provinces. The Conservative government in Alberta vehemently opposed Trudeau's national energy policy, and in Quebec a Parti Québécois government under René Lévesque dedicated to Quebec independence was elected in November 1976, only a week after U.S. voters chose Carter. Carter's difficulties came from Congress, caused by the post-Watergate weakness in the presidency and Carter's own outsider status in Washington. As an example, when diplomats drafted the East Coast Fisheries Resources Treaty and a treaty to resolve the maritime boundary in the Gulf of Maine in 1979, the president lacked the legislative influence to push them through the Senate. Carter complained in considerable frustration in November 1980 to Senator Frank Church, a fellow Democrat and chairman of the Senate Foreign Relations Committee: "The agreements are very much in the national interest of the United States . . . the agreements followed two years of hard bargaining and are fair to both sides. . . . Close cooperation with Canada is vital to the national security of the United States." Church refused to budge.[25]

America's massive domestic energy demand also limited Carter's policy on U.S.-Canadian energy issues. He never doubted that the "acid rain" that Canada complained about came in part from U.S. coal-fired generating plants, but the larger goal of U.S. energy self-sufficiency led him to support a plan to convert oil-fired plants to coal. Because of increasing U.S. dependence on imported energy, the president promised to work closely with Canada and Mexico to develop complementary North American energy policies. The 1977 U.S.-Canadian pipeline treaty showed how difficult domestic considerations could make such cooperation, despite good presidential and prime ministerial intentions. In January 1977, Carter had written to Trudeau about energy imports from Canada as a way to offset U.S. reliance on imported oil. But as an aide wrote to National Security Adviser Zbigniew Brzezinski, the treaty was a technical agreement: "The Canadians feel strongly . . . that the treaty should not be elevated to the Carter/Trudeau level." Were it to become the subject of summit diplomacy, he added, "This could suggest that a decision had been made on the trans-Canadian route, as opposed to transport by sea from Alaska. No such decision has been made, and the issue is potentially sensitive to both countries."[26]

Carter administration officials prepared carefully for the official visit by Trudeau to Washington in February 1977 and took pains not to offend Canadian "sensitivities." An insightful memo identified a number of "sore points to be avoided": any suggestion that Canada and the U.S. were alike, and any implication that U.S. and Canadian approaches toward the rest of the world were identical. "Bear in mind," the memo suggested, "that Canadian policy toward China and Cuba has evolved more rapidly than ours." "Don't suggest," it continued, "that U.S. problems can be dealt with through development of a US-Canadian 'continental policy,' e.g. in energy." "Don't refer to a 'special relationship' between the US and Canada." And finally, the memo cautioned Carter not to "offer comments on the merits of Quebec separatism." Carter's briefing notes emphasized Trudeau's intelligence, his multilingualism, his international expertise, and his love for vigorous outdoor sports such as skiing, scuba diving, and canoeing. But Carter's staff understood Trudeau's desire to assert Canadian identity, to reduce Canada's economic dependence on the United States, and to strengthen linkages with Europe and Japan. The State Department suggested that at the official White House dinner the president express the appreciation of the American people to the prime minister for "providing us with extra natural gas, fuel oil, and electric power this winter."[27]

Trudeau spent three hours with Carter and addressed a joint session of Congress. Carter's and Trudeau's mutual respect contrasted starkly with Trudeau's and Nixon's reciprocal contempt. The two leaders clearly had a meeting of minds and engaged effectively on a personal level. Both men were warm, engaging, and intelligent as well as committed to a positive bilateral relationship. In a handwritten note to Trudeau and his wife Margaret following their visit, Carter emphasized how much he and Rosalynn had enjoyed their company and looked forward to seeing them often in the future. He signed his letter "Your friend Jimmy" and thanked Trudeau for sharing his extensive experience with a "new President." "I feel," he added, "that our countries are being drawn ever closer together."[28]

Although an interpersonal success, the visit yielded few concrete policies. The global agenda included the forthcoming international summit, NATO and North American defense, strategic arms limitation, and policy toward South Africa, Cuba, Jamaica, and the Caribbean. But by mutual agreement Carter and Trudeau did not raise the Middle East or China. Some bilateral issues were also declared off-limits: countervailing duties, draft resisters in Canada, and Canadian tax law c-58, which prohibited tax deductions for advertising in U.S. magazines addressed to Canadian audiences. Canadian officials requested discussion of St. Lawrence Seaway tolls, but U.S. Transportation Secretary Brock Adams objected that to concede Canada's right to assess tolls at the Welland Canal would "make all U.S. traffic between Great Lakes ports and the high seas subject to unilateral Canadian pricing practices." [29]

America's massive domestic energy demand put U.S.-Canadian energy issues at the top of the binational agenda. The U.S. Department of Energy insisted that Carter make clear to Trudeau the importance of transporting Alaskan natural gas to the lower forty-eight states. Secretary of Energy James Schlesinger pointed to the sharp decline in crude oil exports to the United States from western Canada, dropping from 1.3 million barrels a day in 1973 to only 315,000 by early 1977. Unless Canada agreed to continue supplying crude oil to refiners in the northern United States, he warned, those states faced major shortages. The United States had to collaborate with Canada, Schlesinger explained to Carter, because "in the short term it is clear that Canada holds almost all the energy cards." The United States could not, he concluded, neglect Canadian input as it had in 1973 when the Trans-Alaskan Oil Pipeline proposal had been approved. Schlesinger urged the president to support the construction of a pipeline that would link Kitimat in northern British Columbia with the interprovincial pipeline in Edmonton, Alberta, thus making it possible to move Alaska crude to the U.S. Midwest. [30]

Schlesinger traveled to Ottawa for meetings on energy issues in December 1978, and in early 1979, Vice President Walter Mondale met with Canadian ambassador to the United States Peter Towe to discuss a range of bilateral issues, including the maritime boundary and fishery negotiations, the Alaska pipeline, and developments in the energy sector. The National Security Council was concerned by what it viewed as Canadian unilateral procurement decisions: two Canadian steel firms were awarded the pipe contracts, much to the chagrin of the U.S. steel industry, which viewed the bidding process as "rigged" and urged retaliation. U.S. officials were also disappointed that Canada evaded a clear commitment to issue coordinated policy statements in support of prebuilding the southern leg of the Alaska Gas Pipeline to carry exports of Alberta natural gas. They responded positively, however, to Canadian willingness to consider a Canadian location for a Strategic Petroleum Reserve and to Canadian cooperation in conducting a joint study of opportunities for increased electricity exchanges.[31]

The Carter administration also hoped to encourage Canada, then still not a member of the Organization of American States (OAS), to play a more active role in the inter-American system. Before Vice President Mondale's visit to Ottawa, both Secretary of State Vance and National Security Adviser Brzezinski had discussed this issue with President Carter, who agreed that the administration should encourage Canadian interest in nonproliferation, human rights, and peacekeeping and should try to obtain Canadian agreement to provide technical and academic assistance in the Caribbean and Latin America. Like other Carter initiatives, however, the attempt to woo Canada to membership in the OAS bore no fruit; Canada remained outside the organization for another decade.[32]

Trudeau, President Carter, and Rosalynn Carter met again in March 1979 in New York for a private lunch without advisers present. This was their first meeting since 1978 when both leaders had attended the Bonn Economic Summit. The wide-ranging conversation suggested their knowledge of world affairs, their intellectual curiosity, and their mutual respect. They reviewed global issues: the situation in Iran, Southeast Asia, and the Middle East. Carter praised Trudeau's strong commitment to international peace, acknowledged the prime minister's contribution to nuclear arms limitation and control, and thanked him for Canada's support of the U.S. position on SALT II. Turning to North America, president and prime minister spoke of energy, fisheries, maritime boundaries, and the Autopact. Trudeau conveyed concern that Canada was not receiving an equitable share of investment or of research and development expenditures.[33]

The informal summit conversation took place at a delicate time in Canadian politics, with a national Canadian election scheduled and an impending referendum on Quebec independence. Carter told the press that he sincerely hoped that Canada would remain united. His statement confirmed the consistent policy of his administration, one of the few Carter policies that subsequent U.S. administrations followed. Carter had given Trudeau a U.S. platform to make the case for Canadian unity during their first meeting in February 1977. Quebec's Parti Québécois premier René Lévesque did his best to reassure Wall Street that an independent Quebec would welcome U.S. capital and Washington that an independent Quebec would join NATO and NORAD. But despite these assurances, no Carter administration official ever gave Quebec independence even the slightest encouragement, and the U.S. State Department kept "an eagle eye" on the Quebec independence movement. It is impossible to know what role this position played in the resounding defeat of the Parti Québécois referendum on the question in May 1980, but there can be no doubt that U.S. coolness to an independent Quebec contributed to the voters' choice of a unified Canada.[34]

Positive as their relationship was, Carter and Trudeau shared office as heads of government for only a little more than two years. In May 1979, the Progressive Conservative Party defeated Trudeau's Liberals in a general election. Before the election, the CIA had assessed its implications for the United States. If the election resulted in a Liberal minority government, the CIA concluded, the Liberals would have to rely on the parliamentary support of the "leftist NDP," who would demand limits on foreign investment, increased development of Canadian resources by Canadians, the cancellation of the natural gas export deal, and the renegotiation of the 1965 Autopact. The CIA report pointed out that Trudeau's platform called for an increase to 50 percent in Canadian ownership of petroleum industry assets. During his campaign, Trudeau had also "scored" the agreement to sell additional natural gas to the United States when winter fuel shortages were possible in Canada. Trudeau promised Canadian voters that he would not do so without guarantees that the Alaska pipeline would be built and "without fully exploring the possibility of future replacement of exports with Alaska gas." But despite these concerns about the Trudeau reelection that did not happen, the CIA did not believe that Joe Clark's minority

Conservative government would change much in U.S.-Canadian relations. The main concern in official Washington was possible political instability in Canada, and there was some hand-wringing about a minority government led by a young and inexperienced prime minister without significant support in Quebec. The State Department briefing paper prepared for Brzezinski concluded, "We will have to take this into account in dealing with Canada over the next several years." After his first official meeting with the new prime minister, however, U.S. ambassador Thomas Enders left with the impression that Clark was in a better position than the Liberals had been to negotiate with Alberta on energy issues, and that he was anxious to assist President Carter on energy, as long as the United States imposed no mandatory controls on prices and production.[35]

Like Trudeau, however, Jimmy Carter also took a political beating. The Soviet invasion of Afghanistan and the overthrow of the shah of Iran in 1979 virtually guaranteed his electoral defeat by Republican Ronald Reagan in November 1980. The Iranian revolution thrust Canada briefly into U.S. headlines. On 4 November 1979, armed supporters of the Iranian fundamentalist leader Ayatollah Khomeini seized the US embassy in Teheran—the visible symbol of the shah's link to the West. Sixty-six American hostages remained in their hands until 20 January 1981, just after Ronald Reagan's inauguration. Canada's ambassador to Iran, Kenneth Taylor, and his staff engineered the escape of five U.S. diplomats who had evaded capture in the onslaught on the embassy. It was the brightest moment in Conservative prime minister Joe Clark's ten-month minority government. Minister of External Affairs Flora MacDonald agreed to provide false Canadian documents to the Americans and arranged to evacuate the Canadian embassy. Disguised as Canadians (eh!), the five Americans left Teheran with the last of the Canadian diplomats in January 1980. The public response in Ottawa and Washington was predictably ebullient. The daring rescue came too late to save Carter from political defeat, but it made Canadian ambassador Kenneth Taylor a hero and brought him the post of consul general in New York City. U.S.-Canadian relations enjoyed a rare moment of euphoria. President Carter personally wrote to tell Taylor "how deeply grateful all Americans are for the assistance you rendered our people in Tehran. We shall always remember . . . that you were ready to help us in a moment of real need."[36]

Tweaking the Eagle's Beak

The escalation of bilateral conflict between 1968 and 1980 had been gradual and low-key; after Trudeau's reelection in February 1980 and Ronald Reagan's inauguration, that escalation became more rapid and more public. Reagan's conservatism and his commitment to restore American prestige in the world made a clash likely; Canada made it certain by taking a stronger position on energy controls. In October 1980, Trudeau's finance minister Allan MacEachen made the National Energy Policy (NEP) part of his budget. World oil prices had sharply increased in the course of the 1970s, and Canadian producers hoped to reap the windfall, but the NEP established a price differential between domestic and international sales and between "old" and "new" oil. For old oil, sources developed before 1973, prices could not exceed 75 percent of world levels. Only the price for new oil, or for oil produced by expensive innovative technologies, would be allowed to rise to world levels. The NEP also included export controls, production taxes, and a petroleum incentives program, which subsidized oil and gas exploration and development by Canadian firms. To encourage frontier development, the NEP established a royalty system that favored the operations of Canadian firms in frontier regions and restricted licenses for frontier projects to firms with a minimum of 50 percent Canadian equity. The NEP coincided with the objectives of the Foreign Investment Review Agency (FIRA), the Canada Development Corporation, and Petro-Canada: to increase the level of Canadian ownership in the oil and gas industry. The target (which would surely have seemed modest to an American had the shoe been on the other foot) was 50 percent by 1990. To that end, in 1981 and 1982, Petro-Canada purchased the Canadian subsidiaries of several foreign-owned firms, including Petrofina Canada and BP Canada.[37]

The NEP drew fire from Alberta, the principal oil-producing province, from the American firms that operated in Canada, and from the Reagan administration. It touched off a crisis in U.S.-Canadian relations that demonstrated the difficulty that Washington often has in distinguishing between specific bilateral problems with Canada and the broader open-door objectives of U.S. foreign policy. What especially troubled the U.S. Congress and sectors of the U.S. business community was that the NEP coincided with hostile takeover attempts by Canadian firms against U.S. companies, such as Seagram's pursuit of Conoco. It was in that context that the House of Representatives Committee on Government Operations discussed the establishment of an American equivalent to FIRA.[38]

Immediately after the budget address, Carter's ambassador Kenneth Curtis had expressed his concern to new minister of external affairs Mark MacGuigan—the fifth to hold that position in a Trudeau cabinet. In March 1981, the Reagan Department of State, directed by ham-fisted Alexander Haig, formally protested the NEP and implied that retaliation might follow against Canadian investments in the United States. Cooler heads withdrew the implication, but the context was not favorable for Reagan's visit to Ottawa that month. The president pointedly stressed that U.S. economic policy was to deregulate the private sector, not to increase state intervention. Responding to a journalist's question about Canada's new energy policy, Reagan touched on the real issue from Washington's perspective—energy security. "The proper goal for us must be energy independence in the United States," said the president, "not that we would take advantage of either of our neighbors there with regard to energy supplies," he added carefully. Comments from the Reagan administration and the American oil industry soon became less circumspect. Myer Rashish, undersecretary of state for economic affairs, described the NEP as "discriminatory . . . favoring domestic investment." He emphasized that the national security implications of restrictions on U.S. private foreign investment in energy posed the problem. In September 1981, Robert Hormats, assistant secretary of state for economic and business affairs, told the Economic Policy Council of the United Nations Association that the United States would combat other countries' attempts to interfere with foreign investment. On Canada, he was blunt: "I am frankly surprised that a major developed country, provider, and host for so much international investment would adopt such nationalistic and short-sighted policies, . . . Such policies, if unchallenged, are likely to encourage other countries to adopt . . . similar measures."[39]

Canadian officials denounced the Rashish speech—somewhat unfairly, given that Rashish had persuaded Haig to withdraw his original threat of retaliation—but the Reagan administration stood by his remarks. The *Toronto Globe and Mail* interpreted the Hormats speech on its front page as "sweeping public condemnation of Canadian-ownership programs." Lawrence Eagleburger, assistant secretary of state for economic affairs, criticized such Canadian reactions as "unconstructive"; the United States did not challenge the NEP goal of "Canadianization," but rather the means used to achieve it. Eagleburger tried to sensitize U.S. business to Canadian perceptions of U.S. domination. From the perspective of the Reagan administration, however, Canada had adopted the mentality and policies of the Third World. The very real differences between Trudeau and Reagan over relations with the Soviet Union and with the Third World and the Canadian tolerance for nonalignment encouraged such beliefs.[40]

Under pressure from newly appointed U.S. ambassador to Canada Paul Robinson, U.S. trade representative William Brock, and Treasury Secretary Donald Regan, the Trudeau government backpedaled on those parts of the NEP that most distressed the Reagan administration. But although Robinson maintained that the United States would be nonconfrontational in its response to the NEP, the administration challenged the NEP before a GATT panel. In his fall 1981 budget speech, finance minister MacEachen promised that the Canadianization provisions of the NEP would not be applied to other sectors of the economy and that FIRA would not be strengthened. Instead, FIRA procedures and criteria were relaxed: only firms with more than two hundred employees would be subject to a full FIRA review if they were to be acquired by foreign investors. Yet after a year of the Reagan presidency, economic and foreign policy disagreements had plunged the

U.S.-Canadian relationship to its lowest point since the Diefenbaker-Kennedy years. A sinister likeness of Pierre Trudeau graced the 25 June 1982 cover of William F. Buckley Jr.'s *National Review,* one of the few magazines President Reagan had been known to read. George Schultz replaced the abrasive Alexander Haig as U.S. secretary of state in July 1982 and drew on his business connections with the Alberta oil industry to ease binational tension; what Schultz heard about the NEP from Alberta oilmen would scarcely have inclined him favorably toward Trudeau and his government![41]

Other issues loomed small next to U.S. concern for energy security. U.S. policy toward Latin America lurched from crisis to crisis, but Canada remained peripheral to the inter-American system. A nationalist Mexico kept its back turned to North America until after 1984. Thus Canada had only tenuous access to the region. Canada's Latin American policy diverged from that of the United States only in the Canadian opposition to the U.S. use of military force. The Canadian government remained as anxious as the U.S. government professed to be to promote political democratization, open-market economies for trade and investment, and regional stability. For example, the Socialist government of Salvador Allende in Chile (1970–73) received little support from Canada when faced with U.S. destabilization. During the military coup that killed Allende, the Canadian embassy sheltered Chileans seeking refuge. The official Canadian understanding of the coup, however, paralleled the U.S. version: that Allende had lost control of his government, threatening a more radical initiative from the extreme left. With the cold war still in full stride, and Cuba a player on the Soviet team in regional politics, Canada remained more loyal to its cold war commitments in Latin America than elsewhere.[42]

Canadian interest in Latin America increased when the Central American crisis escalated after 1980. Some Canadian voices—like some American voices—raged against the U.S.-supported Contras' attempt to depose the Sandinista government of Nicaragua and objected to the failure of the United States to restrain the Salvadoran army and its military-linked death squads. But as on Vietnam a decade earlier, in his official statements Trudeau walked the tightrope between anticommunism and condemnation of U.S. policy. In 1980, following the murder of Archbishop Oscar Romero and the rape and murder of four U.S. missionaries, the Trudeau government supported a UN resolution condemning human rights violations by the Salvadoran government and called for an end to U.S. military aid. Canada later sponsored a UN resolution condemning human rights abuses in the U.S. client-state of Guatemala. Secretary of State for External Affairs Allan MacEachen urged his U.S counterpart George Schultz to seek nonmilitary solutions in Central America. In April 1983, Trudeau criticized U.S. policy and distanced Canada from the U.S. approach. There is no evidence, however, that Canadian criticism had the slightest moderating effect on the Reagan administration's Latin American policy.[43]

Canada was not forewarned of the U.S. decision to invade Grenada in October 1983. The invasion of a tiny Caribbean island with barely a hundred thousand people symbolized for many Canadians the Reagan administration's foreign policy extremism and its amplification of the cold war. Grenada's Marxist government had friendly relations with Cuba, and Cuban advisers had constructed an airstrip, which the Reagan administration claimed was designed to be used by Cuban and Soviet aircraft. (British engineers on the project flatly rejected the claim.) The airstrip and the alleged danger to a thousand U.S. students on the island from factional conflict were offered as justifications for the invasion. Whatever the truth of U.S. claims, Canada's U.N. ambassador Gérard Pelletier condemned the United States in the UN General Assembly on grounds that an invasion was neither a "legitimate exercise of the right of self-defence" nor consistent with the principle of the prohibition of the use of force in international relations.[44]

Canada kept up its cold war military commitments on paper, but Trudeau subjected Canada's Department of National Defense to the same "denigration" that he meted out to the Department of External Affairs. In reality, wrote a journalist in a play on the lyrics of Canada's national anthem, it was the "True North *not* strong and free." The Trudeau government renewed NORAD, now renamed the North American *Aerospace* Defense Command. It retained its NATO membership despite reductions in personnel and equipment to its armed forces; Canada's per capita expenditures for NATO were the lowest of any member of the alliance. But despite domestic pressure not to do so, the Trudeau government allowed the United States to test its new cruise missile in Canada—the Canadian North made a good surrogate for Siberia, and providing a test range for U.S. missiles was a much cheaper way to show defense solidarity than actually buying weapons.[45]

Trudeau had observed that Canadian spending on defense could not win America's ear to alter the cold war agenda; his final foreign policy endeavor was therefore something completely different—his "peace initiative" in 1983 and 1984. The Reagan administration had from the outset taken a hard line against the Soviet Union, the "Evil Empire." The Strategic Defense Initiative (SDI)—"Star Wars"—was designed as much to beggar the USSR, should the Soviets attempt to emulate it, as it was to improve U.S. defenses. Most independent scientists regarded the project with derision, but the SDI held out the opportunity, if it worked, of making Soviet heavy ICBMs obsolete and favoring the more flexible U.S. arsenal of land-, air-, and sea-based missiles. It also threatened to undermine the framework of nuclear deterrence. The Soviet destruction of Korea Airlines Flight 007 triggered massive world reaction, in Canada as well as the United States, and Trudeau worried that East-West relations would continue to deteriorate.[46]

Trudeau's peace initiative was neither precipitous nor unplanned. The prime minister believed in nuclear nonproliferation, had spoken eloquently on arms reduction at the 1978 UN special session on disarmament, and had courted others who shared his concerns. Against the advice of senior members of the Canadian foreign and defense policy establishment, Trudeau established a formal government working group to produce a policy initiative. On 27 October 1983, Trudeau delivered an address titled "Strategies for Peace and Security in the Nuclear Age." Trudeau concluded that there was "acrimony" in East-West relations, that there was fault on both sides, and that a "vision of a world transformed" was absent. Few could have questioned the need for improved communication between Washington and Moscow. Trudeau was not soft on the Soviets: he asked the Soviet Union to reform itself and to "modify its own objectives towards the West." His sincerity did not soften Washington's hard line, however. Lawrence Eagleburger summarized the State Department's view of Trudeau: the prime minister seemed like "a leftist high on pot." As Canadian ambassador Allan Gotlieb observed, the Reagan administration bitterly resented Trudeau's "habit" of giving "moral equivalence" to the United States and the USSR. Without strong support from Washington, the peace initiative was meaningless; Washington was not merely unreceptive but was dismissive. The Soviet Union and China were no more encouraging. Only such countries as the German Democratic Republic and Romania offered support; were these Canada's real international peers? From the perspective of Reagan's Washington, Trudeau had received a lesson in realpolitik. The most damning assessment came from former Canadian ambassador to Moscow Robert Ford, who stated the obvious: the Canadian government lacked the power to effect change in either East or West.[47]

The failed peace initiative was humiliating proof of Canada's international irrelevance. For whatever reason, Trudeau's Third Option had gone from tragedy to farce. Economically, Canada was tied as tightly to the United States as ever, but its never-easy relationship with its southern neighbor had become more difficult. In historian John English's words, Trudeau had "enjoyed tweaking the eagle's beak"; he had also learned how difficult it was for Canada to move beyond range of the eagle's talons.[48]

9   Republicans and Tories, 1984–1993

After 1984, with Republicans Ronald Reagan and George H. W. Bush in the White House, and Prime Minister Brian Mulroney's majority Conservative government in power in Ottawa, U.S.-Canadian relations shifted toward significantly greater ideological affinity that paved the way to accommodation on once-divisive issues. The international context for the relationship during the decade began with an escalation of the cold war and ended with the toppling of the Berlin Wall and the collapse of the Soviet Union. Two developments symbolized the transformation in North America: Canada and the United States transcended the political barriers that had long defeated efforts to conclude a free trade agreement in 1987, and the Mulroney government made Canada a member of Organization of American States in 1989, although it did not sign the now obsolete cold war Rio Treaty. Military cooperation expanded after George H. W. Bush succeeded Reagan, as the Mulroney government endorsed the Bush administration's invasion of Panama in December 1989, and Canada became America's enthusiastic junior partner in the U.S.-led Gulf War against Iraq in 1991. The 1993 North American Free Trade Agreement among Canada, the United States, and Mexico created a North American free market that would have been unthinkable in the Canadian political environment a decade earlier.

The United States and Canada in a Changing Global Context

The tensions over the Trudeau government's National Energy Policy and Canadian screening of foreign investment had eased by the time that Pierre Trudeau left office in 1984. His replacement, Liberal finance minister John Turner, held the prime ministership for only weeks before Mulroney's Tories drove the Liberals from power in Ottawa. Mulroney's arrival and Reagan's second mandate marked a more general international trend toward the more conservative, probusiness policies labeled "neoliberalism" by scholars and "conservative" in popular discourse. Even Mexican president Miguel de la Madrid was drawn toward neoliberal economic policies in the new North American environment. This new conservatism depicted its dedication to market economics as nonideological, at the same time that it intensified the rhetoric of the cold war. This incongruity was heightened by Mikhail Gorbachev's ascendance in the Soviet Union, which brought détente, internal economic reform, and eventually the demise of the Soviet system.[1]

Ronald Reagan entered office in 1981 and pledged to restore U.S. international prestige after what he described as years of humiliation for the United States: the defeat in a "noble cause" in Vietnam; the embarrassment of the Iranian hostage taking; the Soviet invasion of Afghanistan; another oil embargo; the fear of economic decline; and the perception that communism had won a new foothold in the hemisphere with the Sandinista ouster of the Somoza government in Nicaragua, all in 1979. The Reagan administration pledged itself to a Hollywood-style world struggle with the Soviet Union, the "evil empire" in the president's idiom. Reagan ludicrously called the anti-Sandinista mercenaries in Nicaragua "freedom fighters" and praised Oliver North, the National Security Council member who ran the scandalous Iran-Contra operation, as a national hero. The president articulated what came to be known as the Reagan Doctrine: a promise to support anti-Communist movements anywhere in the world that resisted Soviet and Soviet-surrogate forces. Reagan boosted the military budget and expanded U.S. forces abroad at the same time that his administration reduced foreign aid. George Ball, undersecretary of state in the Kennedy and Johnson administrations, suggested that Reagan's message to the poorer countries of the world could be characterized "by a cartoon of the Thomas Nast genre showing a bloated millionaire descending from his limousine to tell a group of ragged urchins: 'Why don't you do as I did, utilize the free market and you'll all be rich.' "[2]

The sense of American decline did not originate with Reagan, however: it brought him to office. President Carter had warned Americans in 1979 against "a crisis of confidence . . . that strikes at the very heart and soul and spirit of national will." The Reagan Republicans exploited this fear that the United States would yield world leadership to Japan and the European community. U.S. debt had mushroomed; the American share of world trade seemed threatened, and the United States appeared to have lost international leadership in technological innovation. The economic and political world order established under U.S. hegemony at the end of World War II was in disarray, but the United States could no longer dictate the outcome of international deliberations. American-authored global solutions gave way to trading blocs and regional organizations. The Uruguay Round of GATT negotiations fragmented repeatedly as Europe and Japan rejected the U.S. insistence on an end to agricultural and other production subsidies.[3]

The Reagan administration defined its international agenda for the 1980s as "principled realism." That foreign policy agenda altered little when former vice president George Bush succeeded Reagan in 1989. Indeed, it is important to recognize the continuity between the Reagan-Bush era and the long-standing goals of U.S. foreign policy. *National Security Strategy of the United States,* a White House document released in 1990, stated those goals forthrightly: the safety of the nation and its "way of life"; the creation of an "international environment of peace, freedom and progress"; the admission that "the flourishing of democracy in America did not require a completely democratic world," coupled with the conviction that "it could not long survive in a largely totalitarian one"; a commitment to the "prosperity of the free market system" and an "open international economic system." This list was entirely consistent with the worldview of Woodrow Wilson, Herbert Hoover, or Franklin Roosevelt.[4]

Brian Mulroney's Conservative government was much more comfortable within this context than its predecessors had been. The Trudeau Liberals had appeared to threaten the foundation of U.S. foreign policy—an open door world. Foreign investment review and a national energy policy challenged American corporations'—and thus America's—access to raw materials, sources of energy, and markets at a time of crisis. Days after the Tory victory in September 1984, Prime Minister–elect Mulroney announced in New York that "good relations, super relations with the United States, will be the cornerstone of our foreign policy." As proof, the Conservatives promised that the National Energy Policy would be scrapped, and that the Foreign Investment Review Agency would become "Investment Canada": a government agency to encourage foreign investors. Canada, said its new chairman of the board, was "open for business again."[5]

The two conservative governments shared an ideological compatibility that bridged the forty-ninth parallel. The Reagan administration took a decidedly harder line on the USSR and its alleged surrogates than had Carter. U.S. policy toward Canada did not change in the course of the 1980s, but Canadian policy shifted to reflect this and other U.S. goals. The improvement in U.S.-Canadian relations after 1984 derived from the ideological orientation of the Tory government, not from the imposition of U.S. official views on a hesitant Ottawa. Both Republicans and Tories accepted the older assumptions of the cold war, although "middle power" Canada continued to prefer multilateral solutions to international problems. Both spoke of arms control. Both professed a commitment to balanced budgets and to trade liberalization, privatization, and deregulation. Both pursued the final three goals with considerably more zeal than they pursued fiscal prudence. Policy compatibility extended to president and prime minister: Reagan and Mulroney liked one another personally. Reagan was one of the few presidents who actively sought a closer relationship with Canada, and who consistently made improved trilateral North American relations and liberalized trade a priority of his administration.

Greater affinity did not mean, however, that the governments of either country were monolithic. The Reagan administration divided over the Central American crisis, with the State Department under George Schultz seeking with limited success to restrain the White House, the National Security Council, and the Pentagon. Congress also sought to restrain the Reagan administration's support for counterinsurgency in Nicaragua and El Salvador, and during the time that Joe Clark served as Mulroney's secretary of state for external affairs (1984–91), he made efforts to push the United States toward negotiated, international settlements in Central America rather than the military solution favored by the Reagan White House. Clark thus sought to work, for instance, with the Contadora Group of Latin American countries, which for several years sought a mediating role in the Central American context.[6]

Mulroney and Clark were not close, however, and there is little doubt that Clark was more inclined to seek alternative policy directions on relations with the United States than was the prime minister. Mulroney made a brief visit to Washington in September 1984 and welcomed the reelected president to Canada at Quebec City in March 1985. The so-called Shamrock Summit, which spanned St. Patrick's Day, recaptured an amity missing since the 1950s. Mulroney joined the president in a corny rendition of "When Irish Eyes Are Smiling," "a public display of sucking up to Reagan" that, a nationalist historian of Canada suggests, "may have been the single most demeaning moment in the entire political history of Canada's relations with the United States." Their agenda recalled the 1950s, as Mulroney and Reagan signed an agreement to spend $1.5 billion (U.S.) on an expansion of the northern air defense system, costs to be shared on a 60/40 United States/Canada basis. Both affirmed their commitment to the Defense Development and Production Sharing Agreements that had been part of cold war military-industrial integration, and agreed to further reduce trade barriers on defense products. The darkest storm cloud on the bilateral horizon, the sensitive environmental question of acid rain pollution, was deferred until "further study" by "special envoys" from each country. The "new partnership" promulgated at the Quebec City summit was a conscious dismissal of the conflicts of the previous two decades.[7]

The following year, meeting in Washington, Reagan and Mulroney renewed the NORAD agreement for another five years. NORAD renewal, once routine, suddenly became a contentious issue in Canada. The acronym now stood for the North American *Aerospace* Defense Command, and renewal would involve Canada in the Reagan administration's Strategic Defense Initiative—the plan to station antiballistic missile laser weapons in space, known popularly as "Star Wars." Prominent members of the U.S. scientific and defense establishment argued that SDI would destabilize Soviet-American relations, undermine efforts to conclude a meaningful reduction in nuclear armaments, and lead the Soviet Union to further weapons buildup. The proposed space weapons violated U.S. obligations under the Strategic Arms Limitation Treaty (SALT) of 1972 and seemed to contradict President Reagan's announced intention to pursue Strategic Arms Reduction Talks (START) with the Soviets. In this charged political atmosphere, a consensus on SDI in the Canadian Parliament was impossible. A joint Canadian Senate–House of Commons committee report supported the need for the United States to undertake basic research on SDI technology but expressed serious reservations about its implications for Soviet-American relations. The decision was a very Canadian compromise between the "hawks" who shared the Reagan perspective and the members of Parliament who regarded the president's approach as provocative and irresponsible. The best Mulroney could provide Reagan was a telephone call to encourage him to press on with research without Canadian participation and a promise that Parliament would not overtly prohibit the involvement of Canadian companies in SDI.[8]

The prime minister's telephone call to the White House was evidence that the channels of communication were more visibly open between the two countries than they had been since the difficult years of the Diefenbaker-Kennedy relationship, with the exception of the brief Carter-Trudeau meeting of minds. One of the features of the new relationship was the greater frequency of high-level meetings. Mulroney and Reagan pledged to meet annually to review outstanding issues. Reagan's secretaries of state and Mulroney's ministers of external affairs met even more frequently; George Schultz and Joe Clark conferred six times in 1985. The improved relationship also owed a good deal to the energy and diplomatic skills of Allan Gotlieb, Canadian ambassador to Washington from 1981 to 1989. Gotlieb's most original contribution was to court Congress; he understood that nothing could be accomplished on trade policy or environmental controls without active congressional support, and that a hostile and protectionist Congress could do infinite damage to Canadian interests. Tories and Republicans worked so well together that by January 1986, Ronald Reagan could boast in his weekly radio address that he had achieved his promised "renewed spirit of friendship and cooperation with Mexico and Canada," and that the "most productive period in Canadian-American friendship" was at hand.[9]

Environmental Impasse

For Canadians unhappy with the "new partnership" between their country and Reagan's America, "Star Wars" made the defense issue appear extraterrestrial and made concern about foreign investment seem outmoded. Pollution affected people's lives every day, so that environmental issues aroused the most widespread Canadian concern. By the early 1980s, a chapter with such a title as "Binational Responsibilities for a Shared Environment" had become de rigueur in the edited collections published on Canadian-American relations. One such chapter explained the new interest: "opinion surveys . . . indicate a growing disposition, especially among the well-informed and educated, increasingly to accept elements of the ecological perspective." The most disputatious environmental issue was that of airborne sulfur dioxide and nitrous oxides from automobiles, heavy industry, and coal-fired generating plants in the U.S. Midwest, pollutants that fell on the northeastern states and the Canadian provinces with each rain shower, poisoning lakes and forests, eroding buildings, damaging human health. "The subject of acid rain engaged passions like no other," Ambassador Allan Gotlieb remembers of his eight years in Washington. But the Reagan administration had already circled the wagons against the environmentalist attack and denied that a problem existed. In 1983, two Canadian National Film Board documentaries on acid rain were declared "foreign propaganda" by the U.S. Information Agency.[10]

At their Shamrock Summit Reagan and Mulroney had appointed Drew Lewis, former U.S. secretary of transportation, and William

Davis, former Ontario premier, to study acid rain—an inexpensive sop to Canadian and New England concerns. A year later, the prime minister met the president with the envoys' conclusion in hand: "acid rain imperils the environment in both countries." A jaunty Reagan promised action, and a jubilant Mulroney showed off Canada's new influence in Washington, announcing that acid rain had become "a front-burner issue." "After Mulroney left Washington," the *Washington Post* quipped twenty months later, "the burner was turned off." The Reagan administration was unwilling to enforce the legislation that had been in place since the Nixon administration—the Clean Air Act of 1971— let alone to take the initiative against transboundary air pollution. Administration spokespersons blamed congressional opposition from industrial and coal-producing states, notably Ohio, Michigan, and West Virginia, which had a vested economic interest in blocking action. One outspoken Ohio representative, Charles Lukens, demanded the expulsion of Ambassador Gotlieb because the Canadian ambassador had challenged a vitriolic Lukens speech blaming acid rain on Ontario. Canada did not, Gotlieb admitted, "have clean hands," but Canadian governments were attempting to resolve the problem, while the United States had actually moved backward. Canada paid former White House staffer Michael Deaver a six-figure salary to lobby for new legislation, again without result. Vice president George Bush journeyed to Ottawa to absorb parliamentary criticism, but the visit was a public relations gesture, rather than a sign of action in Washington. As Gotlieb concluded, the acid rain experience demonstrated that Canada was like any other foreign country: its diplomats could accomplish little unless the U.S. administration was prepared to take a firm, positive stand.[11]

The Conservatives changed tactics. "You are a major part of our problem," Prime Minister Mulroney told the Americas Society in New York in March 1988, warning the United States to stop "polluting your neighbor's property with destructive wastes." The *Toronto Globe and Mail*'s correspondent observed cynically that "Mr. Mulroney's rebuke, a tacit admission that Canada can make no headway with the Reagan Administration, nevertheless serves to trumpet the Canadian cause to voters back home." The urge to stand up to Uncle Sam often grips Canadian governments in election years, and the prime minister's political theater answered nationalist nervousness that Canada had conceded too much to the United States. Mulroney refused suggestions that his government make an acid rain treaty a quid pro quo for agreement on another issue that the Reagan administration cared about—free trade or the SDI—lest the United States propose similar "linkages" of its own. In the absence of a U.S.-Canadian treaty, the Ontario government took unilateral measures to reduce sulfur dioxide emissions from the province's industries by 66 percent by the mid-1990s. Mulroney and George H. W. Bush ("the environmental President") promised in a 1991 accord to enforce their own countries' existing air quality laws—hardly a bold step toward "binational responsibility for a shared environment." Five years later, despite reductions in sulfur dioxide emissions on both sides of the border, acid rain remained at issue. In September 1996, the Canadian cochair of the International Joint Commission resigned to protest U.S. failure to invoke the Clean Air Act against increased pollution from midwestern power plants.[12]

The lack of answers to the environmental dilemma of the Great Lakes, the world's largest source of "fresh" water, was equally disheartening. Anxiety about the lakes was almost a century old, but Lake Erie had to be pronounced "biologically dead" before the Nixon and Trudeau governments could conclude the Great Lakes Water Quality Agreement in 1972. The agreement was renewed by Carter and Trudeau in 1978, with the added pledge that "zero discharge" of toxins would be permitted. But as with the acid rain accord, each country was to act in parallel, subject to its own laws rather than to a treaty binding under international law. Parallel domestic laws had not only to be enacted but also to be enforced, and the binational Great Lakes Water Quality Board (GLWQB) that supervised the agreement observed virtually no progress in this regard. Each year's report revealed new pollutants and expanded problem areas within the "Not So Great Lakes" system, and environmental lobby groups accused both governments of "only paying lip service to [their] cleanup promises." In 1989, even this lip service stopped. The U.S. cochair of the GLWQB described zero discharge of toxins as "unrealistic," and his Canadian counterpart suggested that because the rate of deterioration of the Lakes had slowed, "the light at the end of the tunnel" was in sight. "That light . . . may be a radioactive lamprey [eel] or a hunk of phosphorescent material," wrote a disillusioned editorialist; "we enter the nineties with the depressing prospect of confronting monsters more numerous than those we set out to vanquish."[13]

Another Carter initiative met a fate similar to the Great Lakes Water Quality Agreement at the hands of the Reagan administration. In 1979, a Carter-Trudeau East Coast Fisheries Agreement that contained potentially effective provisions for managing fish stocks passed Parliament easily but failed in the U.S. Senate. Despite the president's personal plea that delay "would be detrimental to the conservation of the fishery resources," the New England fishing lobby prevailed, and its senators defeated the treaty and its resource management proposals. Ronald Reagan made no attempt to revive it, and Canada petulantly dispatched destroyer escorts and even a submarine to drive New Englanders from the scallop beds of George's Bank. At a time when their governments professed to be uniquely attuned to one another, the United States and Canada were unable to work out a mutual response to the problem of managing the fish resources of the Atlantic Coast. As on other critical environmental issues, the "new partnership" between the United States and Canada yielded a meager result. The suspicion lingered that perhaps, given the broader agenda of the Republicans and Tories, no more was intended.[14]

The Free Trade Debate

No bilateral issue of the twentieth century evoked in Canadians such strong personal and political emotions as the debate over free trade with the United States. The handful of Americans who paid any attention to Canadian affairs were bemused by the passions that the Canada-U.S. Free Trade Agreement (FTA) aroused in the "Great White North." The initiative came from Canada, which had talked about free trade as early as 1983. The objective of the Canadian government and the businesspeople who exported to the U.S. market was not so much to expand trade as to maintain security of access to their U.S. markets. Congress was inclined toward protectionism, and an Omnibus Trade Act loomed in Washington, recalling the days of the Fordney-McCumber and Smoot-Hawley tariffs.[15]

The first suggestions for free trade came from studies by such Canadian think tanks as the C. D. Howe Institute; then important national magazines and newspapers, such as *Maclean's* and the *Toronto Globe and Mail*, cautiously supported the idea. The Canadian Chamber of Commerce and the Canadian Federation of Independent Business came aboard as major lobbyists in favor of an accord. Free trade acquired bipartisan respectability in Canada when the Royal Commission on the Canadian economy, chaired by former Liberal finance minister Donald Macdonald, concluded that an agreement with the United States would injure only a small number of the industries that his commission had studied. Free trade was the best long-term policy for Canada's economic future, said Macdonald; all that was necessary to achieve it was for Canadians to take "a leap of faith."[16]

Brian Mulroney was a late convert to this new religion. Campaigning for the Conservative leadership in 1983, he had told reporters that Canada "could not survive with a policy of unfettered free trade." At the Shamrock Summit, however, Mulroney and Reagan agreed quietly (it was not mentioned in the official statement) to examine reducing trade barriers. In the summer of 1985, a joint statement of both houses of the Canadian Parliament recommended that Canada explore free trade with the United States and introduced the phrase "comprehensive trade agreement" into the discussion. Ronald Reagan strongly and warmly endorsed the Mulroney government's free trade feelers, quite in contrast to the disinterest that the president expressed toward bilateral environmental problems. The severe U.S. trade deficit with Canada explained Reagan's alacrity: $7.3 billion in 1981, $13.1 billion in 1982, $14.3 billion in 1983, and $23.3 billion in 1986.

In May 1986, Ottawa and Washington announced "wide-ranging talks" between Simon Reisman on the Canadian side and Peter Murphy on the American. For sixteen months, news of their negotiations filled Canadian newspapers and appeared every now and then in the business pages of the *New York Times* and the *Washington Post.* Just hours from the deadline at which the talks would have broken off in failure, Reisman and Murphy reached a draft agreement. On Monday, 5 October 1987, U.S.-Canadian relations made U.S. front pages for the first time since the Iran hostage escape. The agreement was much too complex for small U.S. dailies to summarize easily; most of them simply reprinted "U.S., Canada to Try Free Trade" from the *New York Times.* The tiny *Durham (North Carolina) Morning Herald* looked deeper into the draft agreement, however. "CANADA TO HAVE ACCESS TO ALASKAN OIL" the *Herald* warned readers who, like the headline writer, were oblivious to the fact that Canada exported millions of barrels of oil to the United States annually.[17]

Neither the United States nor Canada regarded the detailed free trade agreement in 1988 as a complete success. It eliminated over a ten-year period tariffs in commodity trade in industry and agriculture; liberalized Canadian controls on foreign investment; provided national treatment for U.S. firms operating in Canada; and provided limited bilateral access to government procurement contracts in each country. Most important to Canada was the establishment of bilateral dispute settlement panels to circumvent the political vagaries of U.S. trade laws. Cultural industries proved especially contentious: the first paragraph of article 2005 exempted Canada's cultural industries from the FTA, but the second paragraph reserved the U.S. right to retaliate against Canadian cultural protectionism. Canadian concern that Canada's social programs might be defined as unfair trade subsidies remained unresolved, as exactly what constituted an "unfair subsidy" under the terms of the FTA was left undefined.[18]

The Reagan administration's understanding of the agreement was evident in its *Statement of Administrative Action* that accompanied the presentation of the agreement for Senate approval. The administration anticipated few modifications in U.S. law to implement the FTA; significantly, the administration promised to pursue further liberalization of Canadian investment controls, to extend the agreement to energy and cultural industries, and to eliminate technology transfer requirements and other performance requirements not barred by the FTA. For the steel industry, the administration assured Congress that nothing in the FTA precluded reaching agreement with Canada to reduce Canadian steel exports. In the area of government procurement, although the agreement liberalized competition, there were major exceptions on the American side. The Defense Appropriations Act and the Berry Amendment were left unchanged; these require the Department of Defense to purchase solely from U.S. suppliers all textiles, clothing, shoes, food, stainless steel flatware, certain specialty metals, buses, ships, and components. As well, chapter 13 of the FTA did not alter the 50 percent differential in favor of domestic U.S. suppliers for all procurement of hand tools.[19]

The Canadian energy industry was as anxious to consolidate and expand its market access to the United States as the U.S. government and energy industry were determined to ensure guaranteed access to Canadian resources. The main impediments to U.S. investment and trade had been Canadian government controls such as FIRA and the National Energy Program. Thus, the FTA stipulated that Canada could not establish a higher price for its energy exports than the domestic price, and in the event of Canadian desire to conserve resources and reduce exports, Canadian suppliers were required to maintain exports to the United States at a level that was proportionate to "Canadian total export shipments of that commodity in relation to total Canadian supply." Canada had insisted that the FTA leave the basic conditions of the automobile industry untouched, so that U.S.-Canadian trade continued to be governed by the Autopact of 1965, despite continuing criticism from the "Rust Belt" of northern deindustrializing states, whose governors and congressional delegations believed that the Autopact had worked only to the advantage of Canadian auto producers. Not all Canadian industries were "winners," of course. Textile producers and the garment industry, traditionally highly protected, feared FTA provisions that stipulated that textiles and apparel would not be considered products of either Canada or the United States unless they underwent a double transformation in either or both countries. A garment had to be produced in Canada or the United States from fabric produced in either country.[20]

Canadian business was thus not monolithic in its endorsement of the FTA. Support in Canada for the FTA came, naturally enough, from industries that were already well established in U.S. markets and feared their loss through congressional protectionism, such as the oil and natural gas industries. Textiles and the garment industry, boot and shoe manufacturers, the furniture industry, wine and liquor producers, brewers, and farmers all had serious reservations about their capacity to compete with American producers. Commercial bankers disliked the specific provisions that opened banking in Canada to U.S. competition, although in general they supported a bilateral agreement. In spite of this sectored business opposition, provincial Liberal governments in Quebec and Ontario, home to more than half of Canada's population, endorsed the Free Trade Agreement with the United States, the former enthusiastically and the latter grudgingly. The New Democratic Party opposed the FTA; the Ontario NDP promised to ignore it if they were elected, although following their provincial victory in 1990 this promise went unfulfilled.

"Free trade was one of the most significant policy issues in the life of the Canadian nation," write Bruce Doern and Brian Tomlin, "and Canadians had to look deep into their national soul to decide where they would stand." Most did such soul-searching: a survey in February 1988 found that 90 percent of Canadians had an opinion on the five-month-old FTA then before Parliament and Congress. No issue better illustrates the disproportionate relative importance of the U.S.-Canadian relationship to the publics of each country: only 39 percent of Americans interviewed were aware of the agreement. There were two visions of Canada's relationship with the United States involved in the debate as well as two divergent visions of the nature of Canadian society, one nationalist, and one continentalist; one market-driven, and the other based on the conviction that what had made Canada distinct from (and superior to) American society was the role of the state in shaping a more harmonious, egalitarian society in which there was a more equitable distribution of social services. Critics of the agreement felt that far more had been lost in the autumn of 1988 than simply tariff and nontariff barriers to trade with the United States. They cited the considerable evidence that a profound restructuring of Canadian society was among the goals of free trade advocates, and that Canada's more generous social programs would be scaled back to create a "level playing field" for economic activity in the two countries. Toronto multimillionaire Conrad Black expressed precisely the perspective on the FTA that terrified opponents of Canadian-American economic integration. The Canadian "quest for an identity independent of the Americans," Black contended disapprovingly, was the source of all of Canada's problems. "[It] has given us a prime rate five points above that of the United States; top tax rates almost 20 points higher; a sharply higher price index; a growing and proportionately much larger public sector deficit despite the American defence burden; and only seventy percent of the U.S. standard of living. We are wedded to a redistribution of money between regions and individuals which makes excessive taxation and public sector insolvency almost inevitable."[21]

As the debate developed, the polarization between Canadian proponents and antagonists of free trade with the United States intensified. Proponents contended that new global realities dictated that Canada had to make a major break with the "National Policy" mentality of the nineteenth century; without free trade and international economic competitiveness the Canadian economy would stagnate, they argued. Free trade advocates portrayed their opponents as wild-eyed radicals, nationalist-isolationists out of touch with the "real world," graybearded relics from the long-defunct "Waffle" wing of the NDP. The American market was too important to the Canadian economy, they maintained, to risk its loss to congressional protectionism. The antagonists of the FTA were, in fact, more diverse, and their arguments more subtle. On one hand were those who argued that Canada's longterm interests would be better served by expanding Canada's trade with the rest of the world, rather than by hitching the Canadian economic wagon to the United States. This restated Canada's hope for multilateral alternatives, last expressed in Trudeau's "Third Option." The traditional concern remained that the FTA would diminish economic sovereignty, leaving power in the hands of U.S.-based corporate head offices. The most ubiquitous denunciations of the free trade deal focused on the potential dangers to Canadian identity posed by still-greater economic integration with the United States. In the 1980s, this argument had a dimension not present in 1891 or 1911: the fear that the FTA was part of a conservative corporate agenda to "harmonize" Canada and the United States by undermining Canada's more generous social programs, from national medical care to unemployment insurance. *Montreal Gazette* political cartoonist "Aislin" depicted the free trade agreement as a salivating Uncle Sam, bib tucked securely under his chin, about to indulge in the culinary delight of roast Canadian beaver.[22]

At the FTA signing ceremony in the White House Rose Garden on 28 September 1988, President Reagan remarked that the open Canadian-U.S. border had become a "symbol for the future" and was no longer an "invisible barrier of economic suspicion and fear." In Canada, however, the issue was far from resolved: emotions and rhetoric mounted to a crescendo in the Canadian national election that November. The opposition Liberal and New Democratic parties made rejection of the FTA, and suspicion and fear of the United States, the focus of their electoral campaigns. The victory of the Tories decided the fate of the agreement. The Mulroney Conservatives earned only 43 percent of the popular vote, but the distortions inherent in a multiparty parliamentary system gave them 60 percent of the seats in the House of Commons. Their opponents of free trade with the United States claimed a moral victory, but the election committed Canada to the accord.[23]

Domestic Politics and Bilateral Relations

The "new partnership" so happily pronounced by Reagan and Mulroney in 1985 began to unravel in the economic recession of the early 1990s, just as it had in hard times in the past. After the Gulf War euphoria had faded, the United States returned to its economic and social realities, and Americans increasingly found the Bush administration's performance wanting. Even before the American people chose Democrats Bill Clinton and Al Gore to lead them in November 1992, President George H. W. Bush had been forced to get tough with Canada on trade policy. Harassed from the right in the primaries by "America Firster" Patrick Buchanan, an erstwhile continentalist who dreamed of adding English Canada to the union, the Bush administration refused to accept the Canadian preference for binding arbitration through the GATT of several outstanding trade disputes and vigorously investigated a series of Canadian exporters for alleged dumping or other unfair trading practices. Despite Prime Minister Mulroney's "vaunted friendship with Mr. Bush," noted a Canadian journalist, the president "has not exerted any detectible pressure to block recent U.S. trade complaints about steel and beer." It was, he concluded, "a useful reminder of an eternal truth: foreign allies are nice, but re-election is vital. The choice between friendship and survival is an easy one." Bush did not, of course, survive.[24]

Turbulent Canadian domestic politics contributed a new dimension to renewed bilateral tension. Canada resumed its perennial debate about national unity following the failure of the Meech Lake Constitutional Accord in June 1991. The unsettled waters of the Canadian federation received further disturbance in the rise in western Canada of the Reform Party, led by Albertan Preston Manning, son of the very popular former Social Credit premier of the province. Some saw Manning as a Canadian equivalent of Ross Perot, unsuccessful third-party candidate for the presidency in 1992. The resemblance was superficial. Manning frequently drew his historical analogies from U.S. examples, but the only valid similarity was that both men capitalized on widespread alienation and frustration with government and mainstream political parties, and on hostility to elites in Ottawa and Washington.[25] In Quebec, resurgent nationalism manifested itself in increased support for the provincial Parti Québécois and for a new federal party called the Bloc Québécois, both dedicated to an independent Quebec nation-state. Significantly, both the *québécois* nationalists and the Reform Party professed enthusiastic friendship toward the United States and were highly supportive of the free trade agreement and of closer economic ties to America. A constitutional agreement that would satisfy Quebec, Alberta, the other eight provinces, and the Canadian national government continued to be elusive. In October 1992, Canadians decisively rejected one such proposal in a national referendum.

The referendum defeat prompted Brian Mulroney's resignation, his popularity at a historic low for a Canadian prime minister. The *New York Times* praised Mulroney as "a good friend to the U.S., a close ally on global issues and a strong partner in demolishing trade barriers." Canadian editorialists censured him for precisely those same things: "Mulroney's bosses too often seemed to be Presidents Reagan and Bush," offered the Sherbrooke, Quebec, *Record*. "He seemed to cozy up much closer to U.S. leaders than most Canadians want." One particularly cruel editorial cartoon showed President Clinton offering the former prime minister a job on the White House kitchen staff. If the specter of a fragmented Canada on their northern border unsettled Americans, however, they gave few visible signs. U.S. humorist Calvin Trillin suggested that Canadians resolve their constitutional crisis by forbidding all discussion of it, requiring that "the tougher saloons in Toronto display signs that say 'No spitting, fighting or constitution talk.'" On the eve of the constitutional referendum that threatened to "tear the upper half of the continent apart, . . . creating serious potential problems for U.S.-Canadian relations," a Knight-Ridder correspondent reported that "the soul-rending Canadian vote [was] hardly noticed" in the United States. The defeat of the Mulroney proposal was widely reported. But once it became clear that even if Canada were indeed to break up, it would be at a maddeningly slow Canadian pace, journalists remembered the newsroom maxim that "No one cares about Canadian politics."[26]

The event of 1992 that most revealed the enduring ambivalence of the U.S.-Canadian relationship was neither the defeat of George Bush nor the departure of Brian Mulroney, but the victory of the Toronto Blue Jays in baseball's World Series—a triumph repeated a year later. When major league baseball expanded to Montreal in 1969 and Toronto in 1977, the most crotchety among Canada's cultural nationalists mistakenly decried the Expos and the Blue Jays as further evidence of their country's "Americanization." As baseball historian William Humber has pointed out, however, the game's nineteenth-century origins were as much Canadian as they were American. Canadian baseball fans remained delightfully untroubled by the supposed U.S. cultural Trojan Horse in their midst. Although the Blue Jay team that confronted the Atlanta Braves nominally represented the "American" League, the twenty-five United States–born and Latin American–born players on their roster were understood to represent Canada as surely as twenty-five Canadians could have done. "All Canadians are taking this seriously," reported a U.S. correspondent; "up there, it's them against Uncle Sam." At ceremonies before the first game in Atlanta, a confused Marine color guard flew the Canadian maple leaf flag upside down, and an equally confused country singer butchered the tune and lyrics to "O Canada": Canadians had televised confirmation of their national angst about American ignorance and arrogance. They savored the outpouring of American apologies, President George H. W. Bush's among them, as "the greatest mass acknowledgement of Canada's existence by Americans since former Ambassador Ken Taylor helped spring the [Iran] hostages." And when the series came to Toronto, there was no counter demonstration, no booing of the "Star Spangled Banner." Canadians forgave their neighbor, further proof of their own moral superiority, and the Jays' six-game triumph was doubly sweet on that account.[27]

Incorporating Mexico

Ronald Reagan's dream of a North American economic area dwarfed the nightmares of Canadian opponents of free trade. The president envisioned including not only Canada but also Mexico and the Caribbean; his Caribbean Basin Initiative was followed by the Bush administration's Enterprise for the Americas Initiative. The signatures seemed barely dry on the bilateral Canadian-U.S. agreement before

Canada joined the United States and Mexico in negotiations for the completion of a trilateral North American free trade agreement. The Republican free enterprise agenda for hemispheric trade and economic development, although vaunted as a new departure, in some ways echoed the development ideology and tactics of the Eisenhower administration in the 1950s.

The North American Free Trade Agreement (NAFTA) initiative came from Mexico, encouraged by Reagan administration overtures. The new Mexican government of Carlos Salinas de Gortari took power in 1989, anxious to expand and protect Mexican markets in the United States and elsewhere, to attract foreign investment to Mexico, and to resolve some of the political, social, and diplomatic problems in Mexican-American relations. Whatever the Mulroney government might have preferred, it decided in the fall of 1990 that it had no real choice: although Mexican economic and political ties to Canada were minimal, preservation of the perceived gains of the Canadian-U.S. bilateral accord required that Canada enter the trilateral negotiations.[28]

In late August 1992, George Bush, Brian Mulroney, and Carlos Salinas announced the conclusion of NAFTA, subject to ratification by the legislatures of each country.[29] Support for this trilateral North American agreement within Canada was less vigorous than it had been for the Canada-U.S. FTA two years earlier, but opposition forces were correspondingly less apocalyptic in their resistance. Had the Canada-U.S. FTA been seen as an unqualified success, some of the opposition to NAFTA might have been mitigated; but there was a widespread perception in business and academic circles as well as among the general public that the loss of several hundred thousand Canadian industrial jobs during the recession that began in 1990 could be attributed to the impact of the FTA. From the point of view of Canadian exporters, the FTA had proved to be no panacea in resolving cross-border trade disputes. Harassment of Canadian exporters of softwood lumber, Honda automobiles, steel, and beer by U.S. protectionist lobbies and their allies in Congress, the International Trade Commission, and the Department of Commerce soured many Canadian producers.[30]

NAFTA furthered the objectives of the Reagan and Bush administrations, in spite of the facts that Mexico had initiated the negotiations and that Canada had voluntarily joined them. The NAFTA agreement provided for the elimination of tariff barriers to trade among the three countries over a period of ten to fifteen years. It substantially liberalized investment regulations in Mexico in such as areas as the pharmaceutical and oil and natural gas service industries and provided for gradual liberalization of tariffs in the agricultural sector. Mexico held the line against U.S. pressure to open its oil and gas industry to direct investment in exploration and development. Canada sought to protect its agricultural marketing boards and once again successfully exempted cultural industries from the agreement. Canada lost its battle to retain more liberal access for its textile and apparel industry to non–North American yarns: NAFTA stipulated that the fibers from which yarn derived also had to be from North America. In the auto sector, Autopact was once again spared by the agreement, although a change in rules of origin made it more difficult for non–North American manufacturers to enter the North American market from Canada. All three governments placed considerable importance on NAFTA provisions for a wider coverage of cross-border trade in services, including transportation, professional services, management, accounting, engineering, and legal services in Mexico. Both Canada and the United States believed that opportunities for their telecommunications firms were substantial.[91]

Business groups in Canada, the United States, and Mexico coordinated their lobbying efforts trilaterally to secure legislative passage of NAFTA. Opposition came from the Canadian Labour Congress (CLC) and the Quebec-based Confederation of National Trade Unions, in the United States from the AFL-CIO, and from several independent union federations in Mexico. But unlike the business supporters of NAFTA, its trade unionist opponents were unable to coordinate a transnational alliance. The official Mexican trade union movement, linked to the ruling Institutional Revolutionary Party (PRI), supported free trade. The division among autoworkers—the Canadian Auto Workers in 1985 had separated from their American parent the UAW—illustrated the limitations upon a concerted response to NAFTA by the Canadian and

U.S. labor movements. Both the CLC and the AFL-CIO contended that free trade with Mexico would undermine wages and increase unemployment as jobs moved south to take advantage of low-wage Mexican labor. Organized labor argued that NAFTA would accelerate the trend toward industrial restructuring, corporate takeovers, large-scale plant closures, and a shift of capital to Mexican *maquiladoras* (in bond border factories). In an effort to assuage organized labor in each country, negotiators added a side agreement to NAFTA to maintain existing labor standards, primarily in Canada and the United States.[32]

Environmental groups also added their critique to a trilateral free trade agreement, before and following the conclusion of the accord in August 1992. The legal counsel for the Canadian Environmental Law Association contended before the Canadian Parliamentary Committee on External Affairs and International Trade that when principles of deregulated trade are negotiated by institutions that have no mandate or experience and little real interest in environmental issues, "the results of such agreements are often disastrous insofar as they enshrine economic principles that are at odds with the objectives of environmental protection and resource conservation." NAFTA paid lip service to the concerns of environmentalists in both the general provision that no country could lower its environmental standards in order to attract investment, and in another "side accord" that created a trilateral Commission for Environmental Cooperation.[33]

In Mexico, with the power of the PRI behind him and a compliant media on his side, President Salinas won ratification for NAFTA without difficulty. The Canadian parliamentary system similarly assured an easy passage in Ottawa, as Mulroney's Conservative majority in the House of Commons steamrollered the Liberal and NDP opposition. In the more complex world of U.S. politics, NAFTA faced the stiffest test: winning congressional approval required Democrat Bill Clinton to put his young presidency on the line and to rely heavily on Republican support. The U.S. opponents of NAFTA were strange bedfellows: organized and unorganized labor, environmentalists, consumer groups, the protectionist left, and the populist right of Texas billionaire Ross Perot variously denounced the agreement as a big business plot to exploit cheap Mexican labor and lax Mexican environmental standards. Americans would hear, Perot warned, a "giant sucking sound" as their jobs drained south to Mexico. Yet the agreement gained support from archconservative broadcaster Rush Limbaugh, corporate icon Lee Iacocca, and liberal Democratic New Jersey senator Bill Bradley. On 17 November 1993, NAFTA passed the U.S. House of Representatives, 235 to 200. The bipartisan nature of the narrow NAFTA majority in the House underlined the complexity of the issue; 132 Republicans and 102 Democrats voted in favor, while 43 Republicans and 156 Democrats voted against. The Senate majority came more easily three days later, 61 to 38: the United States, Canada, and Mexico had formally agreed to embark on their trilateral experiment in North American economic integration on 1 January 1994.

10 A North American Trajectory? 1994–2000

The conclusion of the North American Free Trade Agreement seemed at last to answer definitively the century-old questions that had tormented Canadians about their country's relationship to the United States. Whether for better, as NAFTA's Canadian supporters maintained, or for worse, as its critics insisted, the three countries had taken a major step toward the economic integration of North America, and the continental economy was not about to go away. The official relationship between Canada and the United States was "comfortable and unruffled," concluded two professors who examined it; "the big bilateral issues have been dealt with, and the current big issues are not bilateral ones." In the last decade of the twentieth century, and in the twenty-first century, the U.S.-Canadian relationship had to be worked out not only in a trilateral North America, which included Mexico, but also in hemispheric and global contexts.

Yet the Canadian ambivalence born of North American asymmetry lived on. In October 1993, the Liberal opposition electorally obliterated Brian Mulroney's hapless successor as prime minister, Kim Campbell, and reduced the Conservative party to two parliamentary seats. Prime Minister Jean Chrétien and his Liberal government quietly adopted Mulroney's North American agenda but abandoned Mulroney's effusive enthusiasm for Canada's southern neighbor. Chrétien and his ministers understood that too much praise from the United States sometimes played badly at home.[1]

North American Economic Integration

Chrétien's comments on the Canadian-U.S. relationship were designed to distance himself from Mulroney, who had presented himself
as a close personal friend of Presidents Ronald Reagan and George H. W.
Bush. "Business is business and friendship is friendship," Chrétien announced, "and the two cannot be confused." There would be no more
presidential–prime ministerial vocal duets at summits, the new prime
minister made clear; "besides, I am not a good singer," he joked to reporters. The difference between the rhetorical and the real Chrétien
soon became apparent in his approach to NAFTA, however. On the
campaign trail he had promised to tear up the agreement if it were
not substantially renegotiated, but once Chrétien was elected, NAFTA
suddenly looked like a better deal for Canada. Chrétien, observed a
journalist, approached NAFTA exactly as Mackenzie King would have:
"Abrogation if necessary, but not necessarily abrogation." A savvy politician himself, President Bill Clinton understood Chrétien's domestic dilemmas. A year earlier, Clinton himself had faced the questions
of how to support NAFTA without alienating the Democratic Party's
trade union voters and how to differentiate his position on NAFTA
from that of his Republican opponent, George H. W. Bush. Clinton
therefore stood silent beside Chrétien and Mexican president Carlos
Salinas for Canadian television cameras when the three met met for
Seattle in November 1993. Clinton smiled generously when Chrétien
announced that they had agreed on "improvements" to NAFTA with
regard to dispute settlement and exports of Canadian energy and water. U.S. trade representative Mickey Kantor bluntly said that no real
changes to NAFTA had been made, and some Canadian newspapers
dismissed the "improvements" as "a face-saving measure, and a lame
one at that." But minor changes and the Clinton photo-op allowed
Chrétien to claim that he stood up to the Americans and enabled him
to proclaim NAFTA effective on 1 January 1994.[2]

Once in force, NAFTA sold itself. Expressed as a percentage of Canada's GDP, exports to the United States almost doubled, to 35 percent,
between 1990 and 2000. Canada's Department of Foreign Affairs and

International Trade (DFAIT) reported in 2001 that Canada's merchandise trade with the United States had increased 80 percent in value in the first five years of NAFTA and had more than doubled with Mexico in the same period. Canadian exports to the United States and Mexico in that period increased 80 and 65 percent, respectively. Both U.S. and Mexican investment in Canada also increased in those years, by 63 percent for the United States and 300 percent (from a much smaller base) for Mexico. NAFTA could not claim all the credit for the increases. The weak Canadian dollar, which fell below seventy cents U.S. in 1997, contributed to the export boom. NAFTA's dispute resolution mechanism, despite criticism, made the U.S.-Canadian trade environment less quarrelsome; by 1998 more than fifty disputes had been resolved under the rules-based procedures established by NAFTA.[3]

Nevertheless, some disputes continued to resist solution. Most persistent was the export of Canadian softwood lumber to the United States, a dispute two decades old. The Canadian share of the U.S. lumber market doubled between 1975 and 1984, from 17 percent to almost 35 percent. U.S. lumber producers alleged that the stumpage fees—the tax on each harvested tree levied by provincial governments—were below market value and, thus, constituted an illegal subsidy to Canadian producers. The United States initiated countervailing duties in 1982, 1986, and 1991. In each instance, the U.S. Department of Commerce found that the Canadian practice did not justify the countervailing duties, but American trade law and sympathetic senators from lumber states made it easy for U.S. lumber producers to continue to harass their Canadian competitors. In the 1996 Softwood Lumber Agreement, Canada agreed to impose export restraints in return for U.S. agreement to stop actions against Canadian softwood lumber imports. When that agreement expired in 2001, however, U.S. lumber producers successfully renewed their attack; they won duties that Canadian exporters described as "catastrophic." The softwood lumber dispute demonstrated that despite presidential speeches about the U.S. commitment to free trade, U.S. domestic politics would trump these principles. Canadian governments contended with considerable justice that under NAFTA the exports should be duty free. The U.S. answer, expressed by lumber producers and their political patrons, was blunt: Canadian provincial governments should abandon their stumpage system and follow the U.S. system of selling timber rights at auction.[4]

U.S. cultural industries took this same attitude to Canadian cultural policy: that there would be no trade disputes over cultural exports if Canada would only agree to do things as they were done in the United States. American policymakers and cultural industry interests dismissed Canadian complaints of U.S. cultural domination and did not understand, much less sympathize with, Canadian policies to achieve cultural sovereignty. Cultural trade with Canada is important to the United States for its economic value: Canadians remain the most important single group of foreign consumers of American popular culture, importing more than four billion dollars of cultural commodities annually, four times the value of U.S. cultural imports from Canada. In television broadcasting, for example, the Canadian television viewer's love affair with U.S. programs intensified during the 1990s. By 2000, in addition to CBS, NBC, ABC, and Fox, Canadian cable systems carried twenty-two U.S. specialty channels. Nielsen reported that Canadian viewers spent 36 percent of their television time watching these channels, as compared to 7.4 percent watching the Canadian Broadcasting Corporation (CBC), the national publicly supported network. Most humiliating, in 2000 the U.S. shows *Who Wants to Be a Millionaire, ER,* and *Ally McBeal* all rated among of Hockey Night in Canada.[5]

Given similar U.S. dominance of virtually every popular cultural genre in Canada, many Canadians asked why the United States could not simply tolerate Canada's modest assertions of cultural nationalism. The U.S. response was that any cultural concessions it might make to Canada would be expected by other U.S. trading partners. NAFTA gave Canada the right to protect its cultural industries, although it provided the United States the right to demand compensation for any injury those policies caused to U.S. producers. In their first years in office, however, the Chrétien Liberals showed no sign that cultural industries mattered to them. The Canadian cabinet approved mergers in publishing and in film distribution in which Canadian enterprises were swallowed by the U.S. entertainment conglomerate Viacom. Canadian cultural nationalists searched for appropriate denunciations for the Liberals: "Cowards? Hypocrites? Or Canadian puppets on American strings?" [6]

Stung by such criticism, the Chrétien government made a sudden nationalist advance on two cultural fronts in January 1995. The Canadian Radio-television and Telecommunications Commission ruled, as Canadian law required it to, that Nashville-based Country Music Television be removed from Canadian cable systems in favor of the New Country Network, a Canadian competitor. Heritage Minister Michel Dupuy cited the cultural exemption in NAFTA as the basis of Canada's right to protect its cultural industries. U.S. trade representative Mickey Kantor replied with threats of retaliation, also as permitted by NAFTA. A trade war over television regulation was resolved by a merger, as Country Music Television absorbed the New Country Network. A journalist described the situation in the vernacular of the country music genre: "the hurtin' is over and the lovin' has started between the country music broadcasters." [7]

The second Canadian assertion of cultural sovereignty targeted *Sports Illustrated*. *SI*'s corporate parent Time Warner had discovered a technological loophole in Canada's ban on the importation of split-run editions of foreign magazines; *SI* did not send copies across the border but simply beamed its U.S. edition to a Toronto printing plant by satellite, added a couple of Canadian stories, and became a "Canadian" magazine in which Canadian advertisers were permitted tax deductions for their advertising costs. To the cheers of Canadian magazine publishers, Ottawa slapped on an 80 percent excise tax. To Canada's fury, the U.S. trade representative sidestepped NAFTA and instead launched a broader complaint to the World Trade Organization about Canadian magazine policy. In June 1997, the WTO upheld the U.S. complaint, condemning Canada's postal subsidies to domestic magazines as well as the excise tax on split-run editions. Canada blustered with Bill c-55, which lifted the ban against split-run magazines but imposed heavy fines if they accepted Canadian advertising. Not surprisingly, U.S. trade representative Charlene Barshefsky dismissed the new policy as "the same old story" and warned of U.S. retaliation. The issue was deemed serious enough that President Clinton telephoned Prime Minister Chrétien urging compromise. On 27 May 1999, a trade war was averted with what was in effect a managed trade agreement similar to that in softwood lumber. Canada permitted foreign-owned magazines exported to Canada to carry a modest amount of Canadian advertising: 12 percent, gradually increasing to 18 percent. Canada also agreed to end restrictions on foreign ownership of magazines.

Sheila Copps, the cabinet minister responsible for cultural policy, put on a brave face and announced the agreement as a victory, but Canadian cultural nationalists were unimpressed. They pointed out that the NAFTA cultural exemption applied only if Canada was prepared to endure the U.S. retaliation NAFTA also permitted. What would happen, they asked, if U.S. cultural industries "extend their attack to other cultural sectors?" The split-run magazine case, more than any other, demonstrated that determined U.S. opposition could indeed constrain Canada's cultural protectionist policies. But the Chrétien government also made no use of cultural promotion, to which the U.S. government traditionally offered no serious objection. Instead, the Chrétien government steadily withdrew support for those institutions that promoted Canadian culture: the CBC, the National Film Board, and Telefilm. The parliamentary grant to the CBC, for example, shrank by a third between 1993 and 2000. Such actions suggested that Canada was moving toward making Isoliation, ILS style, a cultural path is being a apparent convergence of U.S. and Canadian governments' understandings of "culture." Critics of this alleged convergence perceived it as a greater peril to Canada's cultural sovereignty than any threatened U.S. retaliation to specific Canadian policies of cultural protection.[8]

Canadians would have liked to sell more of their culture to Americans, but most of them recoiled at sending another resource south to the United States: fresh water. Roger Grimes, premier of economically depressed Newfoundland, shocked the country when he announced in 2001 that his province would consider bulk water exports; negative public reaction persuaded him to abandon the idea. Asked about the possibility that the United States would use NAFTA to demand exports of water, Prime Minister Jean Chrétien joked that the only water that

Canada would export would be in bottles with straws. But in the summer of 2001, the *Toronto Globe and Mail* challenged Chrétien's assertion. "As global warming heats up the land," reporter Eric Reguly argued, "aquifers vanish and population and the GDP rise, water demand will eventually outpace local or regional supply in some parts of the United States, increasing water values to the point that water import projects may become appealing." Canada, he warned, was already a defendant in a $10.5 billion NAFTA case filed by a California company that had been initially granted and then denied access to British Columbia water. The issue remained volatile even if poorly understood into the new century.[9]

A North American Environment

Canadian consternation about water exports illustrated how increased public concern about environmental quality intersected with the longstanding Canadian anxiety that Americans might defile or devour Canada's natural resources. Concern for the environment is not unique to Canada; survey research on the values held by Canadians, Americans, and Mexicans found more convergence on environmental protection than on any other issue. On many environmental questions, the acrimonious debates take place not among the three countries of North America, but within the societies of Canada, the United States, and Mexico. Environmentalists in all three countries feared that NAFTA as originally conceived would force environmental standards downward; in 1992–93, more than twenty Mexican, Canadian, and U.S. environmental nongovernmental organizations worked together to demand the North American Agreement on Environmental Cooperation, the so-called environmental "side-accord," which in turn built critical public support for NAFTA's passage.[10]

The new trilateralism, however, should not obscure the continued relevance of past bilateral Canadian-U.S. environmental accords. These accords continue to provide the framework for resolving U.S.-Canadian disputes over water and air pollution and to offer examples of workable models that might be applied more broadly across North America. The International Joint Commission, created by the Boundary Waters Treaty of 1909, continues its significant role as the "official nagger" about environmental problems. The IJC serves specifically as the "watchdog" for the Great Lakes" under the provisions of the Great Lakes Water Quality Agreement (1972/1978); its reports publicize progress, or the lack of it, in ridding the lakes of chemical effluvia. The IJC has pointed out to the public in both countries the failures of the U.S. Environmental Protection Agency and Environment Canada to respond to Great Lakes pollution; that success was presumably the reason why the U.S.-Canada Air Quality Agreement (1991) deliberately confined the IJC to a minor role in enforcing the air pollution agreement.[11]

As they have for two centuries, ocean fisheries created bitter U.S.-Canadian contention. U.S. fishery policy was laissez-faire and decentralized, while Canada relied on centralized government regulation. "Both approaches," concluded policy analysts, "have resulted in serious overfishing." The precipitous decline of the fish stocks only added heat to the struggle over the remaining fish. The 1985 U.S.-Canada Pacific Salmon Treaty disintegrated in 1997, when fishers disagreed on quotas and regulations. The Canadian and U.S. positions in the salmon war that broke out that August exactly reversed those in the Pacific sealing dispute of a century earlier. Canadian fishers accused Alaska fishers of wantonly overfishing their treaty quotas; U.S. fishers countered that the Canadian environmental argument concealed a commercial objective. To publicize their case, three hundred Canadian fishing boats blockaded the Alaska-Seattle ferry *Malaspina* at its berth in Prince Rupert, British Columbia; the Canadian fishers also desecrated the American flag, as their ancestors had done one hundred years before during the sealing war.[12]

The Clinton administration and the Chrétien government sought compromise, but Canadian and U.S. federalism complicated attempts by Washington and Ottawa to calm the situation. Governor Tony Knowles of Alaska and premier Glen Clark of British Columbia had no reason to make things easy for their distant national governments;

Clark went so far as to threaten to shut down a U.S. Navy torpedo range in his province if U.S. fishers refused to come to terms. The need to stand up to the United States dominated Canadian discourse on the dispute. A cartoon cover of *Maclean's* magazine showed the British Columbia premier fighting Uncle Sam for fish, and another in the *Globe and Mail* depicted a hungry grizzly labeled "Alaska" devouring a beaver as an hors d'oeuvre before a salmon dinner. As it had with acid rain, agreement came through the appointment of two distinguished commissioners to investigate. Political resolution was reached when their report led to a 1999 agreement on new quotas and a government-endowed Salmon Endowment Fund to support research and enhance salmon habitat. Environmental resolution has not yet come, however, and the binational Pacific Salmon fishery remains in grave danger.[13]

NAFTA offers no mechanism to deal with environmental differences. The North American Agreement on Environmental Cooperation says that each country can be found only in violation of its own laws. What gives the side accord some force, however, is that the NAAEC permits nongovernmental environmental groups in any of the three countries to make complaints to the Montreal-based Commission for Environmental Cooperation. Thus originated a front-page *New York Times* story in March 1998 headlined "Canada No Safe Haven for Birds or Bears." Environmental groups in Mexico and the United States, cheered on by their Canadian counterparts, had complained about Canada's lack of national regulations to protect endangered species. Canada's federal structure explained the absence; environmental regulations could not be applied to a province—British Columbia was singled out in the *Times* story—without its consent.[14] This embarrassing blow to Canada's self-image as a country of pristine natural beauty produced the result desired by the nongovernmental organizations (NGOs). In April 2000, Environment Minister David Anderson brought endangered species legislation before Canada's House of Commons; the academic relations officer of Canada's Washington embassy made certain that every Canadian Studies teacher in the United States knew that Canada had removed the blot from its environmental record. While organizations of private citizens had long worked across the U.S.-Canadian border to preserve wildlife—whooping cranes, wild ducks, and wolves—governments came on board only after these "non-governmental continental subsystems" had paved the way for legislation. Environmental protection is perhaps only the first of many causes in the new North America that will stimulate significant nongovernmental cooperation among Mexicans, Canadians, and Americans.[15]

North American Cultural Convergence?

Did this "new North America" mean that old national identities and the three nation-states that they buttressed were on the road to extinction, merged into a common North Americanism? Three social scientists who conducted survey research on the values of North Americans concluded in 1996 that "many of the cultural differences that have long divided Mexico, Canada, and the United States seem to be eroding," and observed "a gradual but persuasive decline in nationalism." But despite loudly proclaimed fears that migration would "Mexicanize" the United States, there seemed little evidence that U.S. nationalism was in decline. Mexican cultural nationalists were also concerned about the "cultural denationalization" that might accompany economic integration.[16]

It was Canadian nationalists, however, whose anguish about national identity was most palpable. For Canada, the NAFTA 1990s were a decade of diminishing national self-esteem. Canada faced a crisis of national political integration; in an October 1995 referendum, Quebec voters rejected "sovereignty" (however ill-defined, it was universally assumed to mean independent nation-statehood for the French-speaking province) by only a few thousand votes. Economic difficulties were highlighted by the bankruptcy of the T. Eaton Company, a national department store chain of iconic status; the sale of its assets to U.S.-owned Sears made the company's collapse doubly painful. Canadian beer drinkers suddenly thirsted for Budweiser and Coors Light, in defiance of the Canadian dictum that American beer was no better than piss. Canadian ice hockey lost entire teams to U.S. cities. The Quebec Nordiques decamped for Denver, and the Winnipeg Jets moved to Phoenix, while the remaining Canadian National Hockey League franchises struggled to survive. On the diamond, the once-mighty Toronto Blue Jays struggled, and the Montreal Expos became baseball's synonym for futility; Larry Walker, Canada's slugging outfield superstar, abandoned Montreal to win batting championships in Colorado.[17]

Walker was but one of tens of thousands of Canadians who took their talents south to earn more money. The traditional pattern of Canadian out-migration to the United States had reasserted itself in the 1980s, when 160,000 Canadians received "Green Cards" to become "resident aliens" in America. The number of Canadians who moved to the United States in other visa categories increased from 53,000 in 1980 to 77,000 in 1989, as the U.S.-Canada Free Trade Agreement eased the process. NAFTA made southward migration easier still; Statistics Canada estimates that four of every ten of these people are actually permanent migrants. This migration is on a much more modest scale than in earlier decades, however, both in terms of the total number of Canadian migrants and the proportion of the Canadian population they represent. In 1900, 1.2 million Canadians lived in the United States; the U.S. Census of 1990 counted only 744,830 from a Canadian population that was six times larger.[18]

Despite the evidence that emigration to the United States was low by historical standards, it became a national issue in Canada in the mid-1990s. Critics such as the *Globe and Mail* argued that "it is not so much the quantity as the quality" of the emigrants that mattered; the migration was a "brain drain" of Canada's best and brightest engineers, physicians, scientists, and entrepreneurs. The U.S. Immigration and Naturalization Service agrees that most Canadian immigrants are "well-trained professional workers." Canada responded to net out-migration to the United States as it always has: by recruiting migrants elsewhere in the world to take the places of the departing Canadians. Total annual immigration to Canada increased toward a target of about 250,000 immigrants a year, almost twice as many immigrants per capita as the United States accepts.[19]

Greater acceptance of immigrants continued to be one of the

Canadian-U.S. contrasts that Canadians used to define themselves in contradiction to Americans. From its beginnings as the parts of British North America that rejected America's revolution and remained loyal to the Crown, Canada's national identity always hinged on this contrast with the United States. Canadians have never stopped pointing to what they argue are significant differences between Canada and the United States: the official constitutional enshrinement of both French-English biculturalism and multiculturalism; a more generous welfare state that includes a national health care delivery system; the existence of an electorally viable social democratic party and a more effective labor movement; more generous government recognition of Native peoples; livable cities in which citizens experience much lower levels of urban violence; and effective gun laws and a murder rate a tenth of that in the United States.

Social science research and the events of the 1990s sustained some of these Canadian contentions and revised others. The strength of the sovereignty movement in Quebec questioned the vitality of biculturalism. Two sociologists found "differences of tone in ethnic and race relations in the two countries" but concluded that "the cultural differences between the two countries have not produced less pressure toward conformity in Canada." One public policy analyst found that social programs "provided significant support for a broader range of the population in Canada than in the United States," and another concluded that "the likely pattern of future development of social assistance policy in the U.S. and Canada is one of continuing distinctiveness." Canada's universal health care system "inspires pride" in Canadians, reported the *New York Times*, and "topped the list of reasons" that Canadians "rate their quality of life" higher than that of Americans. The NDP, Canada's social democratic party, governed Saskatchewan and Manitoba but was crushed at Ontario polls in 1995 and almost obliterated in British Columbia in 2001; trade union density in Canada continues to be more than twice that of the United States. The 2000–2001 report of the International Work Group for Indigenous Affairs praised Canada for breaking "new ground" with the creation of the majority Inuit northern territory of Nunavut and for working to settle land claims, while "Native peoples in the United States continue to battle for greater self determination." Two urban geographers found striking differences between Canadian and American cities, which they argue "reveal salient differences between Canada and the United States." Canada's already restrictive gun ownership laws became still more restrictive during the 1990s, and its murder rate remains about one-tenth of that in the United States.[20]

Does the external evidence that Canadians have become "Americanized"—tastes in popular culture or trends in teenage dress—mean that within their safe cities Canadians are in the process of becoming Americans? Mexican scholar Jorge Bustamente has studied the national consciousness of Mexicans who live closest to the U.S. border. Bustamente found that those Mexicans who seemed outwardly to be the most Americanized (*"agringado"*) displayed the highest levels of Mexican "cultural identity" when interviewed. Those who lived near the border, he concluded, might appear to be Americanized, but instead proximity to the border worked "to reinforce the us/them distinctions of ethnicity and identity." His conclusions perhaps have relevance to Canada, where almost 90 percent of the population lives within a 100-mile (160 kilometers to Canadians) drive of United States. The boldest assertion that Canadians were not becoming Americans came in two books from polling expert Michael Adams. In *Sex in the Snow: Canadian Social Values at the End of the Millennium,* published in 1997, and again six years later in *Fire and Ice: The United States, Canada, and the Myth of Converging Values,* Adams vigorously refuted "the myth of converging values" between the United States and Canada. Adams drew on a massive data base of 14,413 interviews to conclude that "at the most basic level of our values . . . Canadians and Americans are markedly different, and are becoming more so." [21]

In *Yankee Go Home?*—his thoughtful study of "anti-Americanism in Canadian life"—distinguished Canadian historian J. L. Granatstein concluded that in 1996 "Canadian anti-Americanism seemed as dead as the dodo." Yet anecdotal evidence suggested that anti-Americanism flourished in Canada, and that it continued to nourish a Canadian national identity; as they had for two centuries, Canadians continued to use Americans as the "other" against which they defined their "imagined community." Molson Breweries successfully promoted its "Canadian" lager beer with television commercials in which an actor shouted "I AM CANADIAN!" before delivering a string of homilies based on Canadian-U.S. differences: "I believe in diversity not in assimilation," "I speak English and French, not American," and "I have a prime minister, not a president," and concluding that "Canada is the best part of North America." Dubbed "Joe Canada," the actor became a folk hero, ranting live at fairs and exhibitions across the country before crowds wearing "I AM CANADIAN!" T-shirts that reproduced his slogans.[22]

The "Joe Canada" rant included the phrase "I don't live in an igloo or eat blubber, or own a dogsled," an illustration of the perverse pride that Canadians continue to take in U.S. unfamiliarity with their country; Comedian Rick Mercer turned U.S. ignorance into the CBC's "Talking to Americans," a segment of the highest-rated Canadian TV comedy program ever produced, *This Hour Has 22 Minutes*. Mercer visited the United States in the guise of a CBC news reporter to conduct "man on the street" interviews with Americans about bogus Canadian issues. Mercer found a Harvard professor who agreed that Saskatchewan should end its cruel seal hunt, oblivious to the province's plains location, and Columbia students who protested Canada's tradition of abandoning senior citizens to perish on northern ice flows. Mercer's greatest coup was tricking Republican presidential candidate George W. Bush into referring to Prime Minister Jean Chrétien as "Jean *Poutine*"; "poutine" is a Canadian snack food made of french fries topped with cheese curd and gravy.[23]

North American Security in Dangerous World

At the end of the 1990s, however, Americans abruptly began to pay attention to their long-ignored border with Canada. The U.S. Border Patrol had concentrated physical and human resources—nine out of ten of its officers—on the U.S.-Mexican border. As a result, reported the *Seattle Times* in October 1999 in a story that gained national attention, the northern boundary that all had imagined secure had become "a border out of patrol." This "leaky border is getting leakier," the *Times* warned, with "foreigners sneaking in, criminals sneaking out, terrorists, [and] drug couriers." The *Times* documented the relative ease with which illegal immigrants from third countries, usually in Asia, entered the United States across the long and lightly guarded U.S.-Canadian border. The boundary between Washington and British Columbia had also become the entry point for "B.C. Bud," a potent form of hydroponically grown marijuana that sold in California for between $600 and $900 a pound. The Royal Canadian Mounted Police estimated the total value of the 1999 B.C. crop at $6.5 billion. Many of the B.C. pot farmers, the RCMP were quick to point out, were Americans who moved to Canada to escape more severe legal penalties for plying their trade in the United States. The U.S. Drug Enforcement Agency placed the Washington–British Columbia border in the same category as the southwest U.S. border, and the Canadian government watched anxiously to see if Canada had joined Mexico on the annual U.S. blacklist of countries that the State Department believes are "soft on drugs."[24]

The *Seattle Times* had included "terrorists" among the potential perils that could enter the United States via Canada. Less than two months after "A Border out of Patrol" appeared, an alert U.S. customs officer at Port Angeles, Washington, noticed an unusually nervous visitor from Canada drive off the ferry from Victoria, British Columbia. Small wonder Ahmed Ressam dripped with perspiration despite the December chill; the automobile of this Algerian with a fake Canadian passport contained enough bomb-making material to obliterate the Port Angeles waterfront. Ressam was the third terrorist to be apprehended at the border with explosives, pointed out Texas Republican Representative Lamar Smith, an advocate of more restrictive border controls both north and south. Ressam's arrest was further evidence that Canada was "a sieve leaking terrorists. How many near misses can we tolerate?" Smith asked rhetorically. There had been more than 200 million legal border crossings in 1999, but suddenly transborder security problems threatened to outweigh transborder economic opportunities. The legislation to plug the holes in the Canadian sieve had already been passed but not put into operation. Section 110 of the 1996 U.S. Immigration Reform Act provided U.S. immigration officials enhanced powers to crack down on individuals they believed to be illegal. Vigorous lobbying by Canadians, and their U.S. trading partners, continued to keep Section 110 from being fully applied to Canada, but it remained an ominous indication of the potential damage that apprehension about U.S. security could inflict on the largest trading relationship that has ever existed in world history.[25]

Canada has consistently denied the U.S. assertion that Communist Cuba remains a threat to North American security; Canadian refusal to echo U.S. policy toward Cuba has been a bilateral irritant since the missile crisis of 1962. Canadians are not "genetically predisposed" to support Fidel Castro, as one lower-level U.S. official complained, but Canada's actions made it obvious, as two journalists put it, that "the Liberals wear Canada's relationship with Cuba as the badge of their independence in foreign policy." Canada's policy since 1959 has been consistent: that "constructive engagement" is the most effective way of persuading Castro to move toward greater democracy. More than 200,000 Canadians vacation in Cuba each year, and Canada provides nearly one-sixth of Cuba's annual direct foreign investment in such major sectors as tourism, mining, and oil development. The 1996 Helms-Burton law sharpened the Canadian-U.S. policy divisions. Although its Senate sponsor was North Carolina conservative Republican Jesse Helms, President Clinton signed the bill promptly, his eye on the Cuban-American vote. Helms-Burton empowered U.S. citizens, including naturalized Cuban Americans, to bring suit in U.S. courts against foreign nationals who "trafficked" in Cuban property confiscated during the revolution, and barred from the United States any foreign national found in violation. Clinton deferred Title III of the act, which provides for litigation in U.S. courts against foreign nationals, but the State Department informed one of the Canadian mining firms active in Cuba, Sherritt International, that its senior executives and their spouses and children would be banned from entering the United States as long as the company remained in violation of the law.[26]

This U.S. assertion of extraterritorial sovereignty incensed the Canadian government and public, and Jesse Helms spent several months as a favorite target of indignant Canadian editorial cartoons. Helms-Burton goaded the Canadian government into an even more proactive policy toward Cuba. Foreign Minister Lloyd Axworthy, who enjoyed tweaking the eagle's beak as much as any Trudeau-era minister, made an official visit to Cuba in 1997; Prime Minister Chrétien followed in 1998. Canada's efforts infuriated the U.S. State Department without perceptible impact on Castro. Constructive engagement moved the Castro regime neither toward democracy nor toward a liberalization of its treatment of dissent. Cuba rebuffed the Canadian plea to release Cuban dissidents who had been jailed for meeting with Chrétien during his 1998 official visit.

Canada's ambivalence toward the United States in defense and security issues has intensified with the uncertainties of the post–cold war years. Between 1960 and 1990, Canada was officially a stalwart U.S. ally in NATO and in NORAD, but at the same time resisted nuclear weapons and allowed its military to decline beneath the strength necessary to meet its commitments to those alliances. The post–cold war multilateral defense environment seemed tailor-made for Canada's preferred role as international peacekeeper, as NATO's original purpose of collective security against a Soviet threat to Western Europe became increasingly obsolete. Instead, NATO found a new role in response to crises in the Balkans, where both U.S. and Canadian military forces were engaged. The United States has been vocal in its concern about the potential threat posed by so-called rogue states and by international terrorism but has been imprecise in its definitions of what contribution it expects of its Canadian ally in these new contexts.[27]

The Liberal government of Jean Chrétien sent back mixed messages to Washington. Chrétien came to office without international experience and delegated—relegated might be a better word—the direction of foreign policy to the Department of Foreign Affairs and International Trade and to his foreign ministers, André Ouellette (1993–96), Lloyd Axworthy (1996–2000), and John Manley (2000–2003), with the prime minister playing a ceremonial cheerleading role. Bilateral security relations with the United States became strained under Axworthy, whose attempts to promote a "human security" agenda in international affairs were not well received in Washington. Axworthy's crusade for a world ban on antipersonnel land mines culminated in the multilateral Land Mines Treaty signed in Ottawa in 1997 by more than one hundred countries; the United States, however, was notably not among the signatories. The Clinton administration had no quarrel with Axworthy's argument about the civilian carnage caused by land mines, but the Pentagon convinced Clinton that security in the demilitarized zone between North and South Korea would be compromised by a general ban. It was ironic and unfortunate that the United States should have been one of the dissenters from the treaty, since American Jody Williams, a leader of the International Campaign to Ban Landmines, shared in the Nobel Peace Prize. Criticism from the *New York Times*, which urged the administration to "give top priority to the Canadian approach," rubbed salt into Clinton's land-mine wounds.[28]

John Hamre, U.S. deputy secretary of defense, dismissed Axworthy's human security agenda as a meaningless slogan. Pointing to Canada's minimal defense budget, which ranked 133 out of 185 UN countries when expressed in terms of percentage GDP, Hamre countered bluntly that the only things that really mattered in defense and security were "boots on the ground." Defense analyst Joel Sokolsky has suggested, however, that "what the Americans did not like about the Axworthy doctrine was not its 'human security' agenda; it was that the Canadian foreign minister had presumed to set that agenda for the international community." Prime Minister Chrétien's appointment of John Manley at the end of 2000 to replace Axworthy as foreign minister appeared to signal his government's determination to assure the United States of the Canadian desire for close and positive cooperation on security issues. No one, however, anticipated how profoundly the U.S. presidential election in November of that year would transform America's international relationships, both globally and within North America.[29]

11 Playing by New American Rules, 2001–2007

The presidential election of 7 November 2000 was not decided until 12 December, when a 5-4 decision by the U.S. Supreme Court awarded Florida's electoral votes to Republican George W. Bush, former governor of Texas. Democratic candidate Al Gore, Clinton's vice president, won 543,816 more popular votes than Bush, but Bush's four-vote majority in the Electoral College sent him to the White House. The November election had also given Republicans control over both houses of Congress. Sustained by this legislative majority, the new president boldly announced that in the post–cold war environment the United States would no longer be bound by the rules-based international system established in the half-century after 1945; instead, the United States would act unilaterally if his administration deemed it appropriate. Bush had already made clear his determination to profoundly reshape U.S. relationships with the world by 11 September 2001, when terrorists crashed two hijacked airliners into the twin towers of New York City's World Trade Center and a third into the Pentagon. Instantly labeled "9/11" by journalists, the terrorist attacks catapulted the Bush administration into a "Global War on Terror" marked by a U.S. obsession with domestic security, a military intervention in Afghanistan by a broad U.S.-led international force, and in 2003 an invasion of Iraq by a smaller U.S.-led coalition. Adept exploitation of the electorate's fear and patriotism also led "war President" Bush to a second term in 2004. During his first seven years in office, George W. Bush served opposite three Canadian prime ministers: Liberal Jean Chrétien until 11 December 2003; Liberal Paul Martin from 12 December 2003 until 6 February 2006; and Conservative Stephen Harper thereafter. The Chrétien-Bush relationship ranks among the least successful in the long U.S.-Canadian relationship. Martin and Harper each took office pledged to restore harmony between the two countries. But both prime ministers underestimated how resolutely George W. Bush would insist that U.S.-Canadian relations function according to the new Washington rules.

A Superpower Never Has to Say It's Sorry

The U.S.-Canadian relationship was, of course, peripheral to George W. Bush's larger international project, but the three years of the Bush presidency that overlapped with Jean Chrétien's prime ministership were especially rocky ones. The Canadian ambassador to the United States, Raymond Chrétien (the prime minister's nephew), had undiplomatically implied during the 2000 U.S. election that the Canadian government preferred a Democratic victory, and Canadians in general appeared to agree. A senior U.S. diplomat at the U.S. embassy in Ottawa later wrote that "it appears as if Prime Minister Chrétien and the Liberal government have never gotten past the fact that 'President Gore' does not reside in 1600 Pennsylvania Avenue." Personality differences divided the freshman president, elected without a popular majority, from the veteran prime minister who had won his third consecutive parliamentary majority in December 2000. But personality differences to only a minor degree explained intensified U.S.-Canadian tensions; instead, new U.S. policy directions provide the best explanation.[1]

George W. Bush did not invent American unilateralism. As Kim Richard Nossal reminds us, it "is deeply rooted in American political culture," and the visceral appeal of unilateralism resonates not only in the executive and legislative branches of government but also within the electorate. The Bush administration, however, quickly proclaimed its unilateralist creed with a belligerence reminiscent of James Knox Polk. It dismissed international agreements as disparate as the Kyoto accord on international warming, the biological weapons convention, and the UN agreement on small-arms trafficking. On 31 July 2001, *New York Times* columnist Thomas Friedman wrote, "The Bush team thinks that being the world's only superpower means never having to say you're sorry"; the United States, he suggested, was acting like "a new rogue nation . . . unconstrained by treaties or multilateral agreements." That same day in the *Toronto Globe and Mail*, Jeffrey Simpson echoed Friedman: "What we have in Washington now," he concluded, "are not only military hawks but diplomatic unilateralists who reflect a mixture of Republican muscularity, American triumphalism and deep-seated U.S. exceptionalism." U.S. allies were "cowed into silence since they understand that nothing they can say will dissuade the Americans."[2]

Bush's decision to revive Ronald Reagan's "Star Wars" delusion, renamed the National Missile Defense (NMD) system, prompted immediate Canadian anxiety. NORAD made it an unwilling NMD partner; Canada hosted early-warning radars that could be used in a ground-based missile defense system. The Chrétien government did its best to remain noncommittal on Canadian participation in NMD, a stance that reflected genuine division and uncertainty in the Canadian cabinet. The strongest objections came from outgoing foreign minister Lloyd Axworthy, but Defence Minister Art Eggleton assured U.S. defense secretary Donald Rumsfeld that Canada remained "open-minded on the NMD issue." The United States needed neither Canadian territory, air space, water, nor the Canadian military to implement a form of NMD, although Canadian nonparticipation would cast doubt on the future of NORAD. Vice Admiral Herbert Browne, deputy commander of U.S. Space Command, let Canadians know that there would be a cost if Canada remained outside. If U.S. satellites detected a rogue missile heading for Ottawa, the United States "would have absolutely no obligation to protect that city—unless Canada was an NMD partner." Eggleton described Browne's comments as "blackmail," although the State Department denied that they constituted official U.S. policy.[3]

The terrorist attacks on New York and Washington, carried out by men trained by al-Qaeda (Arabic for "the base"), tempered U.S. unilateralism and also built an unprecedented Canadian sense of solidarity with the United States. Canada provided critical support in the tense hours that followed; hundreds of U.S. and U.S.-bound airliners with some 30,000 passengers were diverted to Canadian airports. The stranded passengers were fed, sheltered, and welcomed everywhere while they waited for air traffic to resume. In Ottawa, hundreds of Canadians attached small tributes to the iron railings around the U.S. embassy: flowers, flags, notes, candles, and a birch bark scroll with "God Bless America." A crowd estimated at 100,000 gathered on Parliament Hill, and thousands more did the same in smaller ceremonies across the country. The *Toronto Star* received more than 2,600 letters from its readers offering condolences to the United States. After a visit to his home and native land, expatriate Canadian Robert MacNeil told his U.S. television audience that the "distance" that Canada maintained from the United States as "a psychological mechanism for asserting its own identity" had "narrowed down to maybe half a degree of separation."[4]

When President Bush asked U.S. allies to join an international coalition to fight a "global war against terrorism," many Canadians worried that their country might not be doing enough to assist the United States. British Prime Minister Tony Blair seemed to bring the right level of supportive rhetoric and military commitment, and in an internationally televised speech to Congress President Bush told the American people and the world that the United States "has no truer friend than Britain." Canadians took mild offense that the speech thanked almost every country on the globe *except* Canada for its support. U.S. secretary of state Colin Powell handled damage control: "Canada was one of the first on the scene, with all kinds of help for us," Powell told a press conference after a meeting with Canadian foreign minister John Manley. "We will be forever grateful." Prime Minister Chrétien's decision not to make a personal pilgrimage to "ground zero" in New York City drew angry calls on radio phone-in shows. Charges that Canadian security failures had contributed to the terrorist attacks fed Canadian fears that their country's response was inadequate. "The United States clearly views Chrétien as the sleepy night watchman on America's northern frontier," wrote two policy analysts, and a *Globe and Mail* editorial suggested that the Canadian government had been "asleep at the switch." Hastily conducted opinion polls showed that more than 70 percent of Canadians thought that Canada "should join the United States and also declare war on terrorism."[5]

The Bush administration made it immediately clear that although it would seek coalitions if they were possible, it would take unilateral military action if they were not. It moved quickly in the fall of 2001 to take military action to overthrow the Taliban government in Afghanistan for harboring al-Qaeda. Although under the NATO banner, the intervention was initially essentially a U.S. action, with the support of Britain, Canada, Australia, Germany, Denmark, and Norway. When the Chrétien government committed two thousand Canadian military personnel to the assault, only ten NDP MPs opposed military action. "This is not an American fight; it is ours," approved the *Globe and Mail*. Defence Minister Eggleton repeatedly assured Canadians (and any Americans who were listening) that Canada was "a full partner in the war on terrorism." In October 2001, Canada deployed a naval task force to the Persian Gulf and, in February the next year, sent a battle group from the Princess Patricia's Canadian Light Infantry to Afghanistan's Kandahar province to join the U.S.-led international force in what the Bush administration named "Operation Enduring Freedom." It was a military commitment that continued six years later.[6]

Afghanistan was only one aspect of an increasingly aggressive Bush administration foreign and domestic antiterrorism policy. At the end of October 2001, President Bush signed the USA Patriot Act, approved in the House of Representatives by a vote of 357 to 66 and in the Senate 98 to 1 (Democratic senator Russ Feingold cast the sole dissenting vote). The Patriot Act had sweeping implications for U.S. immigration, banking laws, money-laundering laws, and civil liberties. Many of its provisions had implications for Canada, in particular Title IV, "Protecting the Border." A subsequent "9/11 Commission" to investigate the September 2001 terrorist attacks reported that little had been done to improve security on the Canadian border despite concerns expressed during the Clinton administration; nor had the U.S. Border Patrol developed a northern border strategy. The case of Ahmed Ressam, the would-be terrorist bomber arrested at the border between Washington State and British Columbia in 1999, now took on new significance. Ressam had illegally immigrated to Canada in 1994 from Algeria and had subsequently trained as a terrorist in Afghanistan. Ressam evidently had had little difficulty obtaining false Canadian passports. The 9/11

Commission concluded: "We must be able to monitor and respond to entrances between our ports of entry, working with Canada and Mexico as much as possible." In July 2002, Congress created the Department of Homeland Security to integrate twenty federal agencies to eliminate duplication and overcome lack of coordination, in order to reduce the threat of subsequent terrorist attacks and minimize the impact of attacks that might occur. Within two years the Bush administration was spending as much on homeland security as Russia and China did on defense.[7]

Afghanistan was not the only country that the Bush administration accused of harboring terrorists. In his January 2002 State of the Union address, President Bush linked Iraq, Iran, and North Korea in an "Axis of Evil," as states that refused to operate within the values of the international system. (Canadian-born neoconservative White House speechwriter David Frum proudly took credit for the phrase and was summarily dismissed for his effrontery; the idea had been expressed by National Security Adviser Condoleezza Rice in 2000 before Bush took office.) The president renounced the cold war policies of containment and deterrence that had guided the United States for a half-century and in their place proclaimed what quickly came to be called the "Bush doctrine." The United States would henceforward reserve the right to take unilateral preemptive military action. The Bush administration codified its new Washington rules in September 2002 in *The National Security Strategy of the United States of America*. The document began with a cover letter over George W. Bush's signature that pledged his administration to "defending our nation against its enemies" and stated bluntly that the United States would "not hesitate to act alone, if necessary, to exercise our right of self-defense by acting preemptively." The document mentioned Canada specifically three times. (Mexico appeared only twice in the document, which perhaps cheered those Canadians who worried that Mexico overshadowed Canada in North America as perceived by a president from Texas.) Canada appeared in a list with Mexico, Brazil, Chile, and Colombia, as a U.S. partner in promoting "a truly democratic hemisphere" through the Organization of American States and the Defense Ministerial of the

Americas. Of greater significance for the U.S.-Canadian relationship, Canada was the only country to be named explicitly among "the family of transatlantic democracies" that the United States hoped to enlist, through NATO, into a coalition "of states able and willing to promote a balance of power that favors freedom." The Chrétien government no doubt took note of the subsequent phrase that "we must . . . ensure that the military forces of NATO nations have appropriate contributions to make in coalition warfare."[8]

The new national security document and President Bush's cover statement made clear that defense of the homeland could not stop at U.S. borders; the United States would take preemptive action against terrorists and the states that sponsored them before they could "unleash" their threat. In black and white terms, the president intoned apocalyptically that "Every nation, in every region, now has a decision to make. Either you are with us or you are with the terrorists." This manifest unwillingness to admit alternative views and approaches created inevitable tensions with the international community, including close U.S. allies such as Canada. As part of its defense of the homeland, in April 2002 the Bush administration had announced the establishment of the U.S. Northern Command (USNORTHCOM) to unify the defense of North America; on 1 October the USNORTHCOM became operational. Uncertain how to respond to this initiative, Canada accredited a senior military officer to serve as a liaison to USNORTHCOM. Canadian nationalists, led by former foreign minister Lloyd Axworthy, denounced USNORTHCOM as the military equivalent of continental free trade, the "stealth integration" of the Canadian and U.S. armed forces that "could threaten Canadian jurisdiction over the Arctic or limit Canada's ability to get involved in peacekeeping duties," and that would cause Canada to "lose its freedom to act independently on international issues."[9]

These Canadian nationalist critics could not have been wider of the mark. When a U.S.-led force invaded Iraq on 20 March 2003, Canada did not join Britain and Australia among "the coalition of the willing." The Chrétien government had plenty of time to ponder participation, because the invasion surprised no one. In a graduation address at the

U.S. Military Academy at West Point in June 2002, President Bush had warned that the United States would take preemptive action against "unbalanced dictators with weapons of mass destruction." Over the next nine months, the president and members of his administration left no doubt that the first "unbalanced dictator" to be targeted would be Iraq's Saddam Hussein, and they worked assiduously to persuade the world that he did indeed possess "weapons of mass destruction." In February 2003, for example, Central Intelligence Agency Director George Tenet warned the Senate Select Committee on Intelligence that al-Qaeda remained determined to strike on American soil and that although in September 2001 it had used conventional weapons, future al-Qaeda terrorists would combine "radicalism and technology" and use nuclear, biological, or chemical weapons to strike the United States on American soil. Iraq's "weapons of mass destruction" have never been discovered, but claims of their existence served as ample justification for invasion.[10]

In the months that preceded the American invasion of Iraq, the U.S.-Canadian relationship descended to its lowest point since the bitterest days of the Vietnam War, perhaps lower. Many Canadians (as did many Mexicans, Europeans, and some Americans) vocally opposed the Bush administration's unalterable course toward war. Liberal Member of Parliament Carolyn Parrish was indiscreet enough to let a television camera catch her saying "Damn Americans! I hate those bastards," although she later explained that she meant only to refer to President Bush and his advisers, not to the American people. Nicholas Kristof put Parrish's angry comment in context for his *New York Times* readers: "When even the Canadians, normally drearily polite, get colorfully steamed at us, we know the rest of the world is apoplectic. After all," he continued, "the latest invective comes on top of the prime minister's spokesman calling George Bush a 'moron' last fall."[11]

The question of how best to respond to the Saddam Hussein regime in Iraq also provided an example of the futility of Mexican-Canadian attempts to constrain their larger North American "partner" the United States. During a state visit to Mexico by Prime Minister Chrétien in February 2003, Mexican president Vicente Fox pledged that

Mexico would use its membership on the UN Security Council to press a Canadian compromise resolution that called for Iraq to disarm by 28 March or face war. The Bush administration ignored the attempted compromise, however, and it never reached a vote; by 28 March the U.S. invasion of Iraq had been underway for a week. The Chrétien government agonized over its position on an invasion of Iraq from the time that President Bush first declared that the United States claimed the right to attack Iraq without specific provocation. Finally, the government announced that Canada would join a U.S.-led coalition against Iraq only if the invasion had formal UN sanction. When U.S. and British forces attacked without that sanction, they did so without a Canadian contingent. Given the small size and the state of the Canadian forces, and other Canadian military commitments in the "War against Terrorism," it is difficult to imagine how Canada could have made an effective contribution to the war in any event. The real significance of Canadian participation, however, would have been symbolic rather than military. When the *New York Times* listed the member nations of the "coalition of the willing" that the Bush administration had patched together, it pointedly noted that "the group did not include the United States' closest neighbors, Canada and Mexico." [12]

Just as they had been divided about the U.S. war in Vietnam three decades earlier, Canadians divided about the U.S. adventure in Iraq. Opinion polls suggested that six Canadians in ten supported their government's decision not to participate. Some of the 40 percent who felt otherwise were motivated by fears that the United States would hinder the $1.3 billion worth of trade that crossed the U.S.-Canadian border each day; this was the main theme of pro-participation statements by the Canadian Council of CEOs and by Conservative provincial premiers Ralph Klein of Alberta and Ernie Eves of Ontario. Vocal supporters of U.S. policy included hockey great Wayne Gretzky, who told a reporter that President Bush was "a great leader." A nameless opponent of the war hung a sign that read "U$ Lackey" on Gretzky's statue in front of the Edmonton hockey arena. Prime Minister Chrétien summed up Canadian ambivalence with his assurance, "Of course, I hope that the Americans will do as well as possible." [13]

The prime minister's comment could have brought little comfort in Washington. More than any other issue, the Chrétien's government's refusal to commit forces to Iraq in 2003 occasioned Bush administration fury with Canada, and unsurprisingly, the Bush administration's response broke all the polite rules of binational diplomacy. Presumably acting on instructions, the U.S. ambassador to Canada, Paul Cellucci, told an audience of businesspeople in Toronto that "there is a lot of disappointment in Washington" over the level of Canadian support for the war effort. He warned that Canada might indeed suffer economically for its impertinence, because U.S. concern for "security will trump trade." Lest any Canadian miss his message, Cellucci repeated the essence of his remarks before similar audiences in Vancouver and in Calgary. As the military phase of the invasion of Iraq ended, the Canadian government attempted to conciliate Washington by promising its vigorous participation in rebuilding Iraq, regardless of whether that rebuilding were a multilateral project of the United Nations or unilaterally directed by the United States. There was no sign that Washington heard or cared. In a message delivered "with the diplomatic version of a bullhorn," the White House canceled a scheduled visit to Ottawa by President Bush. The president did, however, pointedly spend the weekend before the aborted visit at his ranch with Australian prime minister John Howard, whose government had sent a contingent to join the U.S. invasion of Iraq.[11]

The Limits of Cultural Convergence

Political scientist Donald Barry has argued that the Canadian decision not to join the invasion of Iraq was not simply the product of high politics, but that it reflected "the growing divergence between values and worldviews of the Canadian and American publics in the post–cold war era." By 2003, it had become more obvious that very real limits constrained "North American cultural convergence." The predictions of Canadian cultural convergence with the United States, ubiquitous in the 1980s and 1990s, seemed suddenly strange, almost fantastic. Canadians had cast Americans as the "Other" against which they defined their "imagined community" for more than two centuries. Canadian critiques of the U.S. "Other" surged in response to the Bush administration's aggressive international policies. Any U.S. president can infuriate some Canadians all of the time, and some U.S. presidents can infuriate all Canadians some of the time. But George W. Bush seemed uniquely able to infuriate almost all Canadians, almost all of the time. A U.S. immigrant who arrived in Toronto in 2003 was shocked by the "knee-jerk anti-Americanism" she encountered, she wrote in an op-ed in the *Toronto Star*. The Canadians she had met, wrote Jacqueline Swartz, stereotyped Americans as "pushy, self promoting, arrogant, individualistic, greedy, out for yourself, and imperialistic—they want to conquer the world." "Oh yes," she added, "and fat." Swartz had not yet encountered the Canadian stereotypes of Americans as immoral, racist, and hypocritical, but she had only lived in Canada for a short time. Like virtually all Americans, she had been blissfully unaware that she had been playing the villain in the melodrama of Canadian national identity. Like Swartz, many other Americans began to have a heightened awareness of Canada and a sharper sense that Canada was different.[15]

This sense of cultural difference emerged in large part from dramatically different Canadian policy responses to four contemporary North American issues. Canada's seemingly less militant response to the "War on Terror" was magnified by Canada's unwillingness to participate in the U.S. invasion of Iraq. Even before the invasion, Canada had drawn widespread criticism from U.S. conservative commentators for being "soft" on terrorism. When Prime Minister Chrétien mused that "the West" might bear some responsibility for creating the circumstances that breed terrorism, Fox News commentator Bill O'Reilly took his comments as evidence that "Canada shows its true colors." "I expected something like this," O'Reilly opined. "Chrétien is a socialist. . . . His government allows nearly everyone into Canada even if they have false documentation." Even the Royal Canadian Mounted Police became a target for right-wing American journalists. *National Review* ran a photo of the Mounties' Musical Ride, printed over with

"WIMPS" in 30-point type, as the cover to an issue that featured a lead article on "Canada's Whiny and Weak Anti-Americanism." Even the U.S. magazine *Maxim*, aimed at young male readers, lampooned Canada's military weakness in a sophomoric satirical article about a successful "invasion" of Quebec by a small group of its staff members.[16]

The second new U.S. image of Canada was as a country that had a more advanced welfare state than the United States, with a national government-financed health care system as its centerpiece. Americans had been dimly aware of this for many years, but only an infinitesimally small percentage of them had any idea of how the system functioned. The U.S. interest groups that had the largest stake in for-profit medicine spent heavily to make certain that the U.S. public understood the Canadian system only as "socialized" medicine that directed Canadians in need of health care to a government clinic in which aspirin was the most potent wonder drug. In 2003, however, virtually every American became aware that part of the Canadian approach to national health care is government control of the price of prescription drugs. The issue of importing prescription drugs from Canada (and the obvious question "Why can't we have cheaper drugs in the United States?") became a central public policy issue in the United States.[17]

A third source of a new U.S. image of Canada was the decision of the Canadian government to allow the medical use of marijuana and to "decriminalize"—"legalize" was the verb more often used in U.S. descriptions—its recreational use. Prime Minister Chrétien's musing that he might sample legal marijuana drew wide coverage in the United States, as did Canada's decision to introduce government-regulated "safe injection centers" for "hard" drug users and "to treat addiction more as a medical issue and less as one of law enforcement." U.S. government response to both these decisions was near apocalyptic. The comment from a Bush administration official that regulated injection sites were "immoral" and "state-sponsored suicide" ensured even wider news coverage in both countries.[18]

The fourth source of a new U.S. image of Canada followed from the decision of the Canadian Parliament to allow same-sex couples to marry. This was the polar opposite of the policy defined by the U.S.

Defense of Marriage Act of 1996. As with Canada's new approach to drugs, same-sex marriage inspired a cascade of U.S. criticism. "What's happening in Canada is a warning to America," said a spokesman for the Family Research Council. "Unless the American people rise up to defend this indispensable institution, we could lose marriage in a very short time." The Canadian decision also brought praise from U.S. lesbian and gay groups, who allegedly called it "the Canadian earthquake." A year later, the need to defend marriage from homosexuals became a major theme in President Bush's successful reelection campaign against Democrat John Kerry, and Bush promised a constitutional amendment against gay marriage in his 2005 State of the Union address.[19]

"Maurice," a caller to the U.S. National Public Radio program *Wait, Wait, Don't Tell Me!* summed up the new stereotypes of Canada succinctly: "Canada criticizes the U.S. president and American foreign policy, harbors terrorists, allows gay marriage and heroin use, supports open prostitution and a proliferation of Asians and other immigrants claiming amnesty, hasn't taken any leadership since the Suez Canal crisis and is generally a country of whining left-winged [sic] liberals." Maurice's intervention and other specific and general U.S. criticisms of Canada were widely reported in Canadian media. And unlike the old U.S. stereotypes of Canada as a land of ice, moose, and Mounties, these new U.S. stereotypes of Canada were stereotypes that Canadians (most of them, at least) could embrace with pride, heightening their own sense of difference from the United States.[20]

The research of sociologist-pollster Michael Adams seemed to offer quantitative evidence of these U.S.-Canadian differences. In *Fire and Ice: The United States, Canada and the Myth of Converging Values*, published in 2003, Adams used survey data to group Canadians and Americans under four broad categories that he considered values: idealism and autonomy, exclusion and intensity, status and security, and authenticity and responsibility. He argued that his survey results from 1992, 1996, and 2000 indicated that many Americans had moved into the exclusionist category, what he labeled the survival of the fittest category, while Canadians tended to cluster in the idealist sector.

Other polls showed that many Canadians were increasingly hostile to the United States and that some Americans were reciprocating. A *Maclean's* magazine survey released on 3 May 2004 captured that evident tension: 68 percent of Canadians thought that the global reputation of the United States had declined over the previous decade; 49 percent reported that they viewed the United States as arrogant and bullying; 38 percent indicated that their attitudes toward the United States had become less positive since the Iraq war. An Ipsos-Reid Poll the next year of a thousand Americans and a thousand Canadians revealed that attitudes had not warmed. The number of Canadians who viewed their southern neighbor as "Canada's closest friend" had declined from 60 percent in 2002 to 54 percent. Only 14 percent of the Americans surveyed viewed Canada as a significant U.S. ally.[21]

Canadian neoconservative expatriate David Frum wrote in the *New York Times* in 2005 that "many Americans see Canada as a kind of utopian alternative to the United States: a North American democracy with socialized medicine, same-sex marriage, empty prisons, strict gun laws, and no troops in Iraq." Statistics bore out Frum's contention. Gay Americans came to Canada to marry: 1,600 gay couples wed in Toronto between 2003, when same-sex marriage became legal, and 2006. There was a dramatic increase in the number of U.S. visits to the Canadian government's immigration Web site the day following George Bush's reelection: 191,000 hits, six times the usual traffic. Beginning in 2004, the balance of migration between Canada and the United States, six Canadians moving south for every American moving north, shifted in Canada's favor. By 2006, as the illusion of an easy victory in Iraq had soured and the bloody war divided the United States as the Vietnam War had done, the number of Americans moving to Canada increased to 11,000—the largest number since 1977. It was not a return to the migration levels of the 1960s and 1970s; no American has been conscripted to fight in Iraq, and Canadian men are no longer deterred from moving to the United States by the fear of being drafted. Because 24,000 Canadians moved to the United States in 2006, Canada still had a net loss of 13,000 people. But this was a much smaller net loss of population than during the 1980s and 1990s. "The southward brain drain is being narrowed," the *Toronto Star* reported cheerfully. Moving to Canada had become an Internet discussion subject in the United States, the *Star* contended, quoting a U.S. blogger who posted a comment that "If every American who didn't like George W. Bush left the country, there would be no one here but illegal immigrants."[22]

Martin "Manages" the Relationship

When Paul Martin became prime minister on Jean Chrétien's retirement in December 2003, he did his best to discourage such disparagement of President Bush. As Chrétien's minister of finance, Martin had been a voice for calm in a government that sometimes seemed to deliberately provoke the Bush administration. But as prime minister, Martin found that the turbulent relationship with the Bush administration was not so easily smoothed as he had imagined. His best efforts could not curtail such Liberal colleagues as Carolyn Parrish, who announced that "America is completely out of touch with the rest of the free world," and then appeared on the popular CBC comedy program *This Hour Has 22 Minutes* stomping on the head of a George Bush doll. Martin ultimately expelled the unrepentant Parrish from the Liberal caucus. She was not alone in her views; Natural Resources Minister Herb Dhaliwal referred to President Bush as a "failed statesman." Martin's attempts to rebuild the damaged U.S.-Canadian relationship, and to manage it with more skill than had his predecessor, encountered similar obstacles during his twenty-six months as prime minister. A number of academics and public figures sympathized with Martin's goals and lamented what they considered excessive moralizing and a lack of realistic concern for national interests in Canadian policy toward the United States. Martin's Liberal government accordingly moved away from the emphasis that former foreign minister Lloyd Axworthy had placed on "soft" power, in the hope that this would improve the U.S.-Canadian relationship. Public opinion polls underlined the extent to which both Canadians and Americans recognized the need for practical cooperation on such issues as border security and energy. But polls also showed that criticism of President Bush played well with the Canadian public; Parrish's political theater also evoked angry comments from the United States. And despite the best Canadian intentions, serious policy differences continued.[23]

President Bush's visit in December 2004 to Ottawa and then to Halifax, Nova Scotia, meant as part of the mending process, instead demonstrated these policy differences and the way that Bush's style could exacerbate them. In Halifax, the president extravagantly praised the Maritime Provinces for their practical support to stranded U.S. travelers in the aftermath of the 9/11 attacks. But despite this belated effort to salve Canadian sensitivity about his earlier omission of Canada from his list of America's "closest friends and allies," the president couched his gratitude in critical terms, suggesting that by declining to fight in Iraq and by vacillating about joining the National Missile Defense system (a subject Martin's staff had been promised that the president would not raise), Canada had abandoned Mackenzie King's strategy to "meet the enemy before he reaches our shores." Bush's comments left Prime Minister Martin in an embarrassing dilemma. At a press conference following the president's departure, he (correctly) found historical fault with Bush's analogy between Iraq and World War II; on NMD he continued to vacillate. Canada would never participate in the "weaponization" of space, he promised, but he would continue to consult with the Bush administration about NMD "to make sure that there is no weaponization of space." An angry debate ensued in the Canadian Parliament in which New Democratic Party (NDP) leader Jack Layton demanded that "the prime minister say no to the Canadian flag on George Bush's missiles." Martin refused to respond directly, and Canadian participation in NMD remained an open question, to the continuing frustration of the U.S. defense establishment and of Canadian nationalists who wanted him to answer "no." In February 2005, Martin officially rejected a Canadian role in NMD. It was a politically popular decision: a poll showed that a substantial majority in all demographic groups "approved of Canada's stand—from teenagers to senior citizens, men and women, urban and rural dwellers, and a majority of respondents in every single province." It was also, said the *New*

York Times, "a symbolic setback for the Bush administration," a setback that contradicted alleged assurances by Canada's ambassador Frank McKenna that Martin intended to support NMD.[24]

The Canadian rejection of NMD hung over the trilateral North American summit in March 2005, when Martin and Mexican president Vicente Fox met President Bush in Texas. But although Bush-Martin interactions remained formal and without enthusiasm, the summit showed that they could on occasion be productive. At its conclusion they announced the establishment of a Security and Prosperity Partnership of North America (SPP). The nervousness of all three North American publics—especially those of Canada and the United States—about attempts to broaden and deepen NAFTA was evident in the way the Bush administration handled the announcement. They emphasized that the SPP was not treaty or even an agreement, but rather a trilateral "dialogue," a White House–led initiative in which the Department of Commerce had responsibility for economic and trade aspects and the Department of Homeland Security for the security dimensions. It had taken almost four years from the terrorist attacks of 11 September 2001 to reach this modest level of formal trilateral cooperation, and to a considerable degree Canada bore responsibility for that delay. When the foreign ministers of the three countries had met in Washington to discuss the implications of the terrorist attacks on trilateral security relations, Canada's John Manley bluntly told his Mexican counterpart that Canada had a very different institutional relationship with the United States than did Mexico, a relationship untroubled by illegal immigration, drug trafficking, or organized crime. Under the circumstances, Canadian officials intended to work on essentially a bilateral basis with the United States and suggested that their Mexican counterparts do the same; one result was the establishment of separate U.S.-Canadian and U.S.-Mexican "Smart" border agreements. This suggested the weakness of a spirit of trilateralism that allegedly had underlain NAFTA. Over the next four years, however, the three countries had moved slowly toward more positive trilateral measures. The private sector in all three countries urged still greater trilateral collaboration, led by the United States and the Mexican Council on Foreign Relations in cooperation with the Canadian Council of Chief Executives. Former Massachusetts governor William Weld, former Mexican finance minister Pedro Aspe, and, ironically, former foreign minister John Manley of Canada cochaired the initiative. In 2005, the group recommended a common North American defense perimeter and the gradual evolution of NAFTA from simple free trade to a common external North American tariff. None of the three governments, however, was prepared for such bold initiatives. The SPP established working groups to address a range of issues—the movement of goods, energy, the environment, communications technologies, financial services, food and agriculture, transportation, and health—but greater institutional integration of North America would not be among them.[25]

Prime Minister Martin acknowledged after the 2005 trilateral summit that there were differences of approach between Canada and the United States but pointed to successful collaborations, such as the action in Afghanistan, which he described as integral to the defense of North America. When his government issued "Canada's International Policy Statement" in 2005, the first section dealt with "A Strategy for Our North American Partnership." It made only a passing reference to "Human Security," the central theme of the Lloyd Axworthy years, and voiced faint echoes of the Bush administration's *National Security Strategy* document of 2002, reworked in Canadian language: Canada would work to transform NATO, to reinforce democracy across the world, and to control weapons of mass destruction. Some agenda items were uncontroversial, like the promise to address the international challenges of infectious diseases and to build cross-border partnerships to protect the environment. But the document did not evade the most important question that had shaped Canada's relationship with the United States since President Bush assumed office. It stated bluntly that "the United States' more assertive role on the world stage and growing sense of vulnerability at home have implications across the socio-economic, political, diplomatic and defence spectrum . . . developments within the U.S. will profoundly affect Canada for years to come." The text noted that "in many cases we may wish to follow distinct but complementary paths" and cited the case of Afghanistan as an example of those paths.[26]

As had the Chrétien government (and as would the Harper government after February 2006), Martin did not waver in support of the U.S.-led Afghanistan initiative, and most Canadians gave the commitment at least grudging support, unlike their hostility toward the U.S. war in Iraq. There were tensions, however, about the civil rights of alleged terrorists. Canadian troops fought well in the overthrow of Afghanistan's radical Islamist Taliban government—so well that the U.S. magazine *Soldier of Fortune* entitled a cover story "Canuck Snipers Take Out Taliban." When the Taliban retreated to the isolated mountainous terrain of the Pakistan border region to fight a guerrilla war, Canada played a leading military role, especially in the southern Kandahar province. More than two thousand Canadian combat troops and a Canadian commitment to the reconstruction of post-Taliban Afghanistan enabled the United States to move forces to Iraq to relieve pressure on its overstretched forces. Partially in response to public and parliamentary concerns about Canada's military role in the region, the Martin government (and subsequently the Conservative Harper government) stressed the economic and political dimensions of Canada's contribution, which included not only soldiers but also officials from Foreign Affairs and the Canadian International Development Agency, and RCMP officers. Afghanistan became the largest single recipient of Canadian foreign aid, with $616 million (CDN) committed between 2001 and 2009. Former Liberal minister of national defence John McCallum pointed out in 2003 that 14 percent of Canada's land forces were deployed internationally, second only to the United States among NATO members. This was in part a statistical mirage, given the small numbers of the Canadian forces, but McCallum expressed concern that unless all NATO governments made a similar political and military commitment to the Afghanistan mission, the country could fall into chaos or even revert to Taliban control. Domestic criticism of Canadian involvement increased, as opposition parties asked if Afghanistan involved real Canadian national interests or was simply a way to appease the United States for Canadian refusal to send forces to Iraq.[27]

The U.S.-Canadian relationship became unmanageable for Prime Minister Paul Martin when his Liberal Party lost its majority in Parliament in a Canadian national election on 28 June 2004. His minority situation meant that he had to depend on the parliamentary support of the Bloc Québécois and the NDP to remain in power, and both the Bloc and the NDP spoke for those anti-American Canadians least inclined to compromise with, let alone to appease, the Bush administration. By the end of 2005, Martin's promises to fix Canada's broken relationship with the United States and to manage it adroitly had themselves been broken. Asked by the *Globe and Mail* how this had happened, Martin's adviser on relations with the United States, John English, blamed negative Canadian public opinion about the United States, which had "made it a lot harder for Mr. Martin to push his agenda" on bilateral relations. But "the Bush administration has brought some of this down on itself," English concluded; public opinion in Canada had been inflamed by "the U.S. conduct of the [Iraq] war." [28]

The *Globe's* interview with English took place in the midst of a vicious general election campaign in which the Martin Liberals struggled for their political lives. As had desperate Canadian prime ministers in 1891, 1911, 1962, and 1963, Martin played the anti-American card. In televised leaders' debates, he claimed that Conservative leader Stephen Harper would abandon commitment to the Kyoto climate protocol, send troops to support the war in Iraq, join the Bush administration's NMD program, and shrink Canada's social programs to U.S. dimensions. None of Canada's four federal parties pulled any punches in their negative campaign advertisements, and in characteristic Canadian language, each party accused the others of employing "American-style attack ads." An anti-Conservative campaign T-shirt sported the slogans "Canada is not America Jr.—Don't vote Conservative" and "Harper = Bush." The crudest attack against Conservative leader Harper was a Liberal television ad that called him "Bush's new best friend . . . the poster boy for his ideal foreign leader." [29]

Bush's "Ideal Foreign Leader"?

Despite the anti-American venom directed at their leader, however, the Harper Conservatives eked out a 124-seat plurality of the 308 parliamentary seats to end twelve years of Liberal Party government. Canada's multiparty system provides one explanation: Conservative candidates won only 36 percent of the popular vote, but with four competitive parties, this earned them a minority government. *Time* warned readers not to conclude that "Canada is moving . . . in the same direction as, say, the U.S.," because many more Canadian voters had chosen the anti-American and "left-tilting Liberals, NDP or Bloc Québécois." But the Conservative victory was also possible because they had discarded the policies that had made them seem to be pro-Bush. Their national advertising said nothing about their past opposition to gay marriage or to the Kyoto accord on global warming. Harper admitted that he would reconsider Canadian participation in NMD but also stated unequivocally that a Conservative government would not send Canadian troops to join the U.S. war in Iraq. Given the greater ideological affinity between the new prime minister and President Bush—both social conservatives with fundamentalist religious convictions—some pundits predicted that a Harper government in Ottawa would mean a "border thaw" in U.S.-Canadian relations. Others were skeptical of significant change. "It's a delicate balancing act," said James Blanchard, former U.S. ambassador to Canada. "I am sure that Stephen Harper wants good relations with President Bush and the United States, but any Canadian prime minister has to keep a noticeable independence from the United States, or he loses credibility in Canada."[30]

Harper chose the longstanding issue of Arctic sovereignty to establish his credible independence from Washington. What divided the two countries was whether the Northwest Passage was within Canadian national waters or was an international waterway as the United States contended. Asked at his first press conference about a denial of Canadian claims by U.S. ambassador David Wilkins, the new prime minister snapped, "It is the Canadian people we get our mandate from, not the ambassador from the United States." The issue is not as simple as either Harper or Wilkins made it. Criteria for determining sovereignty over the oceans had been established by the 1982 Convention on the Law of the Sea to which Canada but not the United States is a signatory. A nation-state has full sovereignty up to twelve miles from its coast, but if a territorial sea constitutes an international strait that links two major seas, the coastal state cannot prevent international passage. Submarines, however, must travel on the surface, and the coastal state has the right to apply laws and regulations governing the passage, such as to ensure environmental protection. Because the Northwest Passage connects the Atlantic and Pacific via the Labrador Sea and the Beaufort Sea, legal experts maintain that is clearly an international strait. A further issue is control over the sea and the continental shelf within two hundred nautical miles from the coast, issues that will become increasingly significant in the event there is major natural resource exploitation in the area. Canadian governments assert such sovereignty over the Arctic Archipelago in part based on historic title, which requires historically effective occupation and control over territory. The United States could legally challenge Canada's claims to sovereignty, but it is unlikely to do so because it has not accepted the compulsory jurisdiction of the International Court of Justice since it refused to recognize a 1984 decision involving the U.S.-backed Contras in Nicaragua. The dispute is not simply bilateral; other countries, most notably Russia and Denmark, also make polar claims that have strategic, environmental, and resource development (in particular, oil extraction) dimensions. Most of the international transit through the Northwest Passage had been with the consent and knowledge of Canadian authorities, and in many cases with the assistance of Canadian icebreakers; to demonstrate U.S. claims, however, American vessels had made a number of incursions into the Northwest Passage without informing Canada, the most recent with a U.S. Navy submarine in 1995.[31]

The Martin government's 2005 International Policy Statement had called for strengthened Arctic policies; Harper proposed actually doing something to strengthen them. He told the UN General Assembly in September 2006 that Canada would "defend our sovereignty over all our territory, including over the islands, waterways and resources of the High Arctic, even if that conflicts with American claims." Over the next year he provided the details: Canada would build a deep-water port at the eastern entrance to the passage and new polar war-ships, expand its sovereignty patrols, and establish a military base in Nunavut. This "Canada First" defense plan, wrote a defense analyst, "clearly resonates with the public." The U.S. response (and the Danish and Russian response) was not in the least conciliatory. A report com-missioned by Congress recommended an "increasing U.S. presence in international waters of the north." An editorial plea from the *New York Times* called for the United States to sign the Law of the Sea Conven-tion and to allow Arctic issues to "be decided by geologists, lawyers and diplomats." The Toronto *Globe and Mail* suggested that Washing-ton simply back Canada's claims and negotiate a North American solu-tion: "Mr. Bush should recognize that firm Canadian legal control over shipping would be the best protection against foreign adventurism or terrorist incursions." Neither solution seems likely to a problem that has such strategic and economic importance, and such emotional reso-nance in Canada.[32]

In broader security matters outside the Arctic, the Harper govern-ment and the Bush administration maintained a more cordial relation-ship, but there could be little doubt that (other than in Afghanistan) the significance of the U.S.-Canadian defense relationship to the United States remained diminished. In May 2006, Foreign Affairs Minister Peter MacKay and Minister of National Defence Gordon O'Connor, following debate and approval in the House of Commons, announced that Canada and the United States had renewed the NORAD agree-ment. Defense analysts pointed out, however, that there was much less to the renewal of the aerospace defense system than the ministers im-plied. Because Canada had decided not to participate directly in the U.S. National Missile Defense system, "the United States gradually will perform this function more and more on its own, without depend-ing on NORAD." NORAD had survived only because of "benign in-difference on the American side" and as little more than a symbol of the once-close U.S.-Canadian defense relationship. The Conservative government increased Canada's very modest defense budget, but the Canadian forces remained relatively tiny—smaller proportionately, another defense analyst pointed out, than New Zealand's—despite Canada's large and increasingly bloody commitment in Afghanistan. The continuing Canadian efforts against the resurgent Taliban drew bipartisan praise from such different Americans as former president Bill Clinton and Bush defense secretary Donald Rumsfeld. Secretary of State Condoleezza Rice visited Halifax in September 2006 to reiterate the administration's line and to offer further tribute: "we have to fight the terrorists where they are. We can't allow them to group and re-gather, and that work that Canada is doing in Afghanistan is essential to that fight." As casualties mounted, however, the Canadian public's support for the action became more qualified. In a poll in October 2006, 59 percent of Canadians agreed with the statement that their soldiers were "dying for a cause we cannot win"; three-quarters said that "the Bush administration had made the world more dangerous" and that U.S. policy had "contributed to a rise in terrorism." The Harper minority government nonetheless held firm to the Afghan mission. In April 2007, with support from some Liberals, it narrowly defeated an opposition motion that Canada withdraw in February 2009.[33]

U.S. violations of human rights in the conduct of the "War on Terror" alienated Canadians who had been overwhelmingly sympathetic to the United States after the 9/11 attacks, just as it did around the world. The imprisonment and torture of Maher Arar focused this concern and raised Canadian fears that their own government might be complicit in such violations. A Canadian software engineer born in Syria, Arar was detained by U.S. authorities in New York in September 2002 and spirited off on a CIA plane to Syria, where he was incarcerated, interrogated, and tortured for ten months before his release in October 2003. On his return to Canada, Arar demanded an apology and compensation from the Canadian government for wrongful treatment. A judicial enquiry found Arar entirely innocent and discovered RCMP collusion in the original detention. Even had Arar been guilty of a terrorist act, his "rendition" to a Syrian torture chamber clearly violated both international and U.S. law. Most distressing to Canadians was U.S. unwillingness to admit the slightest wrongdoing. In December 2006 Foreign Minister Peter MacKay discussed the case with Secretary of State Condoleezza Rice. Her eventual reply was that the United States placed a high value on counterterrorism cooperation with Canada, but that the two countries had different processes to deal with the antiterrorism issues and those different processes had to be respected. The Harper government announced in early 2007 that Arar would receive $11.5 million CDN in compensation for his treatment, but despite this decision, Arar was banned from entering the United States. When Canadian minister of public safety Stockwell Day pressed the United States to change its position, U.S. ambassador Wilkins replied that the U.S. government, not Canada, would determine who could and who could not enter the United States.[34]

The Arar matter underscored different Canadian and U.S. approaches to reconciling national security with civil liberties. The Antiterrorism Act passed by the Chrétien Liberal government after the 9/11 attacks was subject to mandatory periodic review and required an annual report on the use of its preventive detention provisions. Those provisions have been used very sparingly, in contrast to the Bush administration's detention of several hundred alleged terrorists at its naval base in Guantánamo, Cuba. One of those detainees, Omar Khadr, is a Canadian citizen. He was only fifteen years of age when he was captured in Afghanistan after allegedly killing a U.S. soldier with a grenade. His guilt seems to have come from association: his father was a known al-Qaeda member, and three of his brothers were also combatants in the Afghanistan conflict. By early 2007, Khadr had been held at Guantánamo without formal charge or trial and had been subjected to interrogation for a period of five years. The Globe and Mail blamed Canadian authorities for not being more active in demanding that Khadr be tried or released, in contrast to the position that the British and Australian governments had successfully taken on behalf of their citizens held in Guantánamo. "Odious as the crimes he is accused of committing are," wrote the Globe, "it's time Canada stopped acquiescing by its silence to the abhorrent treatment of Mr. Khadr." In early June 2007, a U.S. military judge ruled that the case against Omar

Khadr was outside the jurisdiction of his court because Khadr had several years earlier been classified as an "enemy combatant" by a military panel, rather than as an "alien unlawful enemy combatant," as required by the Military Commission Act under which he had been imprisoned. Under that act only those classified as "unlawful" enemy combatants can face trial under the military tribunals. Khadr is still incarcerated in Guantánamo Bay detention camp, to the increasing anger and frustration of Canadians. A recent editorial contrasted his treatment by U.S. justice with the valor of Canadian troops in the U.S.-led mission in Afghanistan: "Canada has nothing to be ashamed of in asking for Mr. Khadr to be sent home. It has earned its war-on-terror stripes in fighting terrorists in Afghanistan."[35]

The Largest Commercial Relationship in the History of the Planet

Prime Minister Harper regularly linked Canada's contribution to the "war on terror" in Afghanistan and in North America to difficult bilateral economic issues. Intensified U.S. anxiety about national security has added new impediments to the transborder movement of people and goods necessary for what Harper accurately called "the largest commercial relationship in the history of the planet" to function smoothly. Some of the new U.S. border security measures seem more symbolic than serious, such as arming small Coast Guard vessels on the Great Lakes with heavy machine guns to repel terrorists or (the possibly apocryphal) "Operation Noble Mustang," in which wild horses are trained to be used to patrol the Montana-Alberta section of the forty-ninth parallel. Other border security measures, however, threaten serious economic disruption. Accepting the conclusions of the U.S. 9/11 Commission, Congress required in 2005 that all travelers entering the United States, returning Americans included, have a valid passport.[36] Legislation set the date for implementation as 1 January 2008. Harper addressed this new constraint in his speech at the prestigious Economic Club of New York in September 2006. He reminded the club that Canada's contributions to U.S. security were economic rather than simply military. Canada was an "energy superpower," he continued, the largest energy exporter to the United States and "the only stable and growing producer of this scarce commodity in an unstable world." He urged his business audience to help persuade Congress to postpone the passport requirement until streamlined procedures could be established. Congress did exactly that, delaying the date until June 2009. It is impossible, of course, to know what role (if any) Canadian remonstrations played in the decision.[37]

Harper's New York speech was but one example of his government's determination to address frictions old and new that hindered full implementation of the North America Free Trade Agreement. Although unloved by most of the public in all three countries, for better or worse, NAFTA integrated the U.S., Canadian, and Mexican economies to a degree unimaginable two decades earlier. On NAFTA's tenth anniversary, the *New York Times* prepared an intensive assessment. The report quoted Robert B. Zoellick, the U.S. trade representative, who praised the accord for increasing total North American trade by 109 percent. Pressed by the *Times* interviewer, however, Zoellick conceded that over this same period the U.S. trade deficit with Canada and Mexico had increased nine times, to almost $90 billion U.S. If North American consumers were better off from lower prices for things that they bought, the *Times* pointed out that "The consumers of the United States or Mexico or Canada are also each nation's workers." In manufacturing towns in the U.S. Midwest, the *Times* found that total industrial employment and wages had plummeted. A woman from Indiana complained, "we all feel it's Nafta coming around to bite us in the behind." For Mexico, the report concluded, the benefits of NAFTA had been temporary. *Maquiladoras,* plants located just south of the Mexican-U.S. border that manufactured principally for the U.S. market, had brought 700,000 new jobs to Mexico in the early years of the agreement. After a decade, however, 300,000 of those jobs were no longer there, as Mexico lost its comparative advantage, cheap labor, to China. Did NAFTA leave a winner among "three hugely different economies: the wealthy United States, middle-class Canada and striving Mexico?" The *Times* concluded that it was Canada, "where Nafta helped shape a more com-petitive economy," but where the "growing pains" of transition "were cushioned by a strong social safety net."[38]

Canadians often saw the NAFTA glass as half-empty, however: a veteran Canadian trade negotiator even claimed that the United States was "ripping the heart out of NAFTA." A few well-publicized bilat-eral trade disputes seemed to prove that the United States would ca-priciously impose nontariff barriers, further evidence that Washington insisted on playing by its own rules. These disputes invariably arose and endured because U.S. political institutions enabled them to. An organized group of U.S. producers would lobby representatives and senators vigorously for a hard line against their Canadian competitors. U.S. Great Plains grain farmers contend, for example, that the Cana-dian Wheat Board gives Canadian prairie farmers an international marketing advantage, despite the fact that a significant minority of Canadian farmers would like to abolish the board. A second agricul-tural example came from the U.S. reaction to the discovery of bovine spongiform encephalopathy (BSE), "mad cow disease," in a handful of western Canadian cattle. When a single case of the disease turned up in Alberta in May 2003, the United States banned all imports of Cana-dian beef and live cattle. Prices in western Canada plummeted: cattle that had been worth $1,300 CDN prior to the border closing sold for us little us $159 Canadian beef producers lost an estimated $11 million CDN every day. Then in December 2003 U.S. officials discovered an-other case of the disease in a steer in Washington State that had been born in Canada. Given the virtual integration of the binational cattle industry, experts were unanimous that mad cow disease was a North American rather than a Canada problem, and that the infinitesimal number of sick cattle meant that matters were well in hand. But po-litical pressure from U.S. producers maintained the border closure; Canada did not ban U.S. beef imports. It took two years of hardship for Canada's cattle growers, hundreds of millions of dollars of federal and provincial compensation, and extensive bilateral negotiations before the United States officially lifted the ban in March 2005. The mad cow confrontation eventually had a satisfactory conclusion, argues trade expert Michael Hart, because "regulators on both sides of the border put their heads together to form an integrated approach to regulation, with the result that none of the isolated cases of mad-cow disease since 2005 have led to trade disruptions." [39]

As they grew increasingly politically desperate, Prime Minister Paul Martin and his ministers had warned the United States that Canada might retaliate for U.S. lumber duties by curtailing Canadian exports of oil. The Harper Conservative government has taken a lower-key approach than its Liberal predecessors to such trade imbroglios and has worked hard to depoliticize them. It has (apparently, at the time that this book is written) resolved the longest standing and most acrimonious bilateral trade issue, U.S. harassment of Canadian softwood lumber exports. In July 2006 David Emerson, minister of international trade, announced a framework agreement with the Bush administration that he claimed brought "full revocation of American duty orders, ended years of costly litigation, protects Canadian forestry policies and puts more than $4 billion back into the pockets of Canadian exporters." Prime Minister Harper contended that the agreement, which had been concluded with the participation of the provinces and the industry, "demonstrates that, as two countries, we will disagree at times. But with goodwill and mutual respect, we can resolve our differences in a positive manner for both sides." The agreement requires Canada to disclose on a monthly basis the total volume of softwood lumber shipped to the United States, and U.S. importers to reveal the region and province where each shipment originated. The agreement covers an initial period of seven years; it provides for an end to all litigation and for unrestricted trade as long as lumber prices were over $335 per thousand board feet. When prices fall below that level, Canadian exports would be subject to a combination of export charges or volume limits. The U.S. lumber companies that had brought trade complaints against Canada would receive $500 million (U.S.) in compensation, and an additional $450 million would be provided to fund community assistance programs in lumber-reliant communities allegedly harmed by Canadian imports. Initial Canadian response to the deal that Harper had brokered was at best mixed and in some quarters hostile, although opposition gradually diminished. NDP leader Jack Layton called the agreement "outrageous" and a "sellout." The president of the British Columbia Lumber Trade Council observed, more thoughtfully, that no agreement would be perfect. A spokesperson for the U.S. National Association of Home Builders expressed reservations that that lumber consumers had been adequately consulted. Susan Schwab, the U.S. trade representative, assured David Emerson that concerns over possible U.S. termination of the agreement prior to the agreed expiration were ill-founded. The United States would not take such a step because, like Canada, it had invested substantial political capital to conclude the agreement. In December 2006, Emerson announced that Bill C-24, the Softwood Lumber Products Export Charge Act, 2006, had received Royal Assent. He praised the legislation as "the last step in implementing the Softwood Lumber Agreement between Canada and the United States" and claimed that it represented a "tremendous achievement for Canada's New Government," and that the agreement would enable Canadian softwood lumber companies to "grow their businesses."[40]

These trade disputes need to be understood in the context of the massive trade and investment relationship that continued to grow during the first decade of the twenty-first century regardless of mean-spirited political wrangling. Some 98 percent of U.S.-Canadian bilateral trade flows unimpeded; the 2 percent that does not receives virtually all the media attention and distorts public appreciation of the general success of the economic relationship. Presidential or prime ministerial popularity (or the lack of it) and their mutual good (or ill) will is not the driving force of that relationship. The bilateral trade relationship continued to strengthen under Prime Ministers Chrétien, Martin, and Harper, whatever their personal relationships with (and despite the Canadian public's distaste for) President Bush. By 2006, total annual trade between Canada and the United States was approximately $500 billion (U.S.), more than the combined U.S. trade with the twenty-five countries of the European Union and double the value of the bilateral trade at the time NAFTA was concluded in 1994. Canadian officials tout the success of bilateral trade with the example of the Ambassador Bridge between Michigan and Ontario: the exports that cross

this span are equal to all U.S. exports to Japan. Canada is the leading export market for thirty-nine of the fifty U.S. states. Canada has
also become the largest single foreign supplier of energy to the United
States, accounting for 17 percent of U.S. oil imports and 18 percent of
natural gas demand. There is now a clear recognition of the importance of Alberta's tar sands to the long-range fossil fuel security of the
United States. The two-way flow of direct foreign investment is now
both cause and effect of this massive volume of trade. By the end of
2005, U.S. direct foreign investment (DFI) in Canada was $228 billion,
concentrated in manufacturing, petroleum, chemicals, finance, and
mining, and representing 65 percent of total DFI in Canada. With $235
billion invested in the United States, concentrated in manufacturing,
banking, finance and insurance, and retailing, Canada was America's
sixth largest foreign investor.[41]

As we conclude this fourth edition of *Ambivalent Allies*, the war in
Iraq continues to defy solution. Sectarian violence in the country brings
death daily to Iraqis, and al-Qaeda, which was not in Iraq at the time
of the U.S. invasion, has gained another foothold in the power vacuum
that the war has created. Nor is there an end in sight in the critical war
against the Taliban and its supporters in Afghanistan, where Canada
continues to play a leading role. If al-Qaeda's main goal in its 9/11 attacks on the United States was to destabilize the Western world and,
especially, the United States, the policies pursued by the Bush administration have made it more likely that that goal would be achieved.
Canada, despite reservations and even fervent opposition to the Bush
administration's policies from many Canadians, has sought to be a
good ally and friend to its U.S. neighbor, supportive yet cautious, reserved, and sometimes critical of U.S. actions and policies. Canadian
ambivalence continues.

Epilogue: "Plus ça change . . ."

No other pair of international neighbors can claim as successful and mutually prosperous a relationship as has evolved between the United States and Canada over the past two hundred years. The two countries share not only a continent but also an interwoven cultural, political, and economic heritage. Because it is impossible to depict U.S.-Canadian relations within the framework of a traditional diplomatic narrative, in this fourth edition of *Canada and the United States: Ambivalent Allies*—as in the first three editions—we have thus also considered the political, economic, and especially the cultural and social considerations that inform the bilateral relationship.

Since the third edition appeared, however, the military and diplomatic dimension of the relationship has come to the fore. Since the terrorist attacks on the United States on 11 September 2001, no one has described the border that it shares with Canada as "undefended." Politicians now speak of "smart" borders rather than open borders, and the Bush administration's Western Hemisphere Travel Initiative will require that all entering the United States, including returning Americans, possess and display a passport. This concern with border security is a return to something very old as much as a change to something new. For the first century and a quarter in the bilateral relationship the U.S.-Canadian boundary was anything but undefended. The British used Canada as a base to attack their rebellious American colonists, and the Americans invaded Canada twice, from 1775 to 1776 and again from 1812 to 1814. There has been no subsequent invasion, unless one dignifies the Fenian terrorists, but war seemed likely at other times and imminent at least twice, after the Canadian rebellions and during the U.S. Civil War. As the United States ascended to world might, and Canada became more autonomous from Great Britain, war was relegated to the imaginations of army staff officers. After 1900—probably after 1871—continentalism did not involve overt annexationism among

333

significant groups on either side of the border. With the boundary firmly in place after the Alaska dispute, U.S. ambitions toward Canada were limited to securing strategic advantage, guaranteeing access to natural resources or the security of U.S. investment in Canada, and assuring that Canada did not become a gap in American hemispheric security.

U.S. predominance also colors ("colours", for Canadians) the economic and social dimensions of the relationship. The peoples of the two countries have crossed the shared border in both directions, but nine Canadians have emigrated south for every American who has moved north. In the 1990s, Canadian emigration to the United States reemerged as a significant political issue in Canada; unlike Mexican migration, Americans worried little about arrivals from Canada until 11 September 2001. As an illustration of U.S. apprehension that Canada's more gentle immigration and refugee policies allow terrorists to flourish, in the 2006 U.S. feature film *The Sentinel,* a plot to assassinate the president originates in Toronto! Hollywood's Canada has come a long way since Mounties and Texas Rangers cooperated across the border to capture villains.

These new tensions should not, however, blind us to the extent to which the border has historically been more a symbol than a barrier to the movement of ideas, goods, people, and capital. Since the late nineteenth century, U.S. capital has developed Canadian natural resources, and U.S. manufacturers have built branch plants and sought markets in Canada. Social movements in the United States have often been mirrored in parallel, even dependent, institutional developments in Canada: the North American labor movement, crusades for social reform, scholarly societies and service clubs, professional sports. Since the early twentieth century, American popular culture has rolled across English and French Canada like a tidal wave.

Canadian concern about dependence on the United States has constantly shaped Canada's national policies. Despite the concern of Canadian leaders not to appear to respond to American influences, the Liberal government of Jean Chrétien moved right to appropriate the Clinton Democratic administration's agenda of free trade, balanced budgets, and a diminished welfare state. The Stephen Harper Conservative government's ideological affinity to the George W. Bush administration—both probusiness, socially conservative, cool toward global warming, and hawkish on defense—would seem to bring high politics in Canada and the United States into closer harmony than even during the Reagan-Mulroney years. But Prime Minister Harper understands that President Bush is at least as unpopular in Canada as he is in the United States, and that his government is working with a lame-duck Bush administration that was soundly repudiated in the midterm congressional elections in 2006. Thus, on a visit to Colombia and Chile in July 2007, Harper recommended Canada as a "free-market model that rejects the leftist policies of Venezuela's Hugo Chavez, but is also a clear alternative to George W. Bush's United States." Like Harper's reiterations of his determination to stand up to the United States on Arctic sovereignty, this "third economic option" is a characteristic expression of Canadian ambivalence about the United States. A (mostly fanciful) editorial cartoon in the *Globe and Mail* went so far as to depict Harper dancing a "traditional South American dance" on the American flag![1]

Governments and administrations come and go, as do years in which incompatibilities and tensions between the two countries seem insuperable. Canadian dependence on the United States is tempered by North American interdependence. Canadian natural resources and territorial integrity are critical to U.S. economic viability and national security. Ironically, despite the divisive debate over NAFTA, its effects in many ways drew Americans and Canadians together, mobilized by their common concerns about the environment and potential job losses to Mexico. Neither the worst fears nor the most optimistic predictions about the pitfalls or benefits of NAFTA materialized. In both countries, and in Mexico, anxiety over NAFTA has been supplanted by concerns about the outsourcing of jobs to Third World countries. Economic integration has continued to increase. U.S. direct foreign investment (DFI) in Canada at the end of 2006 was $241 billion, representing 61 percent of total DFI in Canada. Canadian DFI in the United States at the end of 2005 was $235 billion. Their mutual investment has created substantial employment in each country. As former president Bill Clinton told a

Toronto audience: "We're stuck with each other. We can't get a divorce. And that is the ultimate definition of interdependence—we're tied together, rowing in this little boat toward tomorrow."[2]

Clinton's platitude notwithstanding, Canadians continue to protest U.S. indifference and ignorance about their country. As an example of indifference, the August 2007 North American summit in Montebello, Quebec, among Prime Minister Harper, President Bush, and President Felipe Calderón of Mexico dominated Canadian print and electronic media for a week; the *New York Times* did not even send a correspondent. Illinois senator Barack Obama, a leading Democratic presidential contestant, provided the ignorance. When he became president, Obama announced in a U.S. national television debate, he would meet with "the president of Mexico [and] the president [sic] of Canada" to rewrite NAFTA. Canadians respond to U.S. indifference and ignorance with anti-Americanism, which routinely drips from editorial cartoonists' pens and flows from the keyboards of newspaper columnists. "Americans are so viral," complained a columnist in the *Globe and Mail,* one of Canada's *least* anti-American English-language newspapers,

> They come at us in so many ways via their culture (let's be honest and start calling it "peasant" instead of "pop"), their vicious corporate style that has turned their own citizens into serfs, and their faked Republicrat democracy. . . . You wouldn't watch their network news if they read it naked. . . . Their law enforcement is so pathetic they even have serial mass murderers.

But if there is arrogance and ignorance on both sides, the power relationship has been overwhelmingly one-sided, as would be expected given America's greater population, military and economic power, and international influence.[3]

The shared cultural heritage of English Canadians and Americans early on created shared consciousness on a wide range of issues, and similarities are abundant and apparent. Both the United States and Canada, as Robin Winks has noted, are "imagined nations," invented in a remarkably short span of world history. Both countries are made up of immigrants who seized what was, in a sense, a common western frontier from Native North Americans. There were differences in the process of "civilizing" those frontiers, but neither country treated Native peoples in a manner that can be cause for pride in the twenty-first century. Both are capitalist countries grounded in the free market, even though the state played a larger role in Canada than in the United States in the last half of the twentieth century. Both enjoy Liberal-Democratic political systems, and in both countries ordinary citizens grumble about the difficulty of penetrating the political apparatus to make politicians listen to their voices. Both countries are prosperous relative to the rest of the globe, and if the United States has been shaped by self-consciousness as a "people of plenty," there is no reason to assume that similar self-satisfaction has not tinged the Canadian body politic over the last half-century.[4]

But the differences between the United States and Canada are not insignificant, although Americans underestimate them and Canadians overstate them. Canada was born, if not of counterrevolution, at least out of a conscious decision not to break the British connection. Though it has more to do with Canada's difficult northern geography and its fear of the United States than with any collectivist ideology, Canada has been more inclined to accept an enhanced state role in the private sector, from foreign investment review through national health care and the creation of public corporations. It is significant, for instance, that the United States, deeply wedded to the ideology of free enterprise, is the only major oil-producing nation in the world never to have had a state oil company.

The Canadian party system has left more room for divergence from accepted truths; third parties have played a more significant, if never dominant, role. The Canadian national election of January 2006 returned members of four parties to the House of Commons, whereas in the United States third-party presidential candidates remain unable to do more than to act as "spoilers" of the electoral hopes of a Republican or Democratic nominee. Only the rarest third-party candidate has made an impact on congressional representation. As elastic as the Republican and Democratic parties have been, it would be preposterous to contend that the two-party system has prevailed, and third parties died, primarily because Americans of any political persuasion could find an ideological home within one of the two umbrella parties. Alexis de Tocqueville commented on the quest for conformity of belief and behavior in American society, whether in the democratic orientation of clothing noted by historian Daniel Boorstin or in the fear of expressing views beyond the prevailing consensus. This tendency toward homogenization rather than diversity, in spite of the profound American belief in individualism, sustains one of the paradoxes in U.S. history. Scholarship in ethnic studies has demonstrated that the English-speaking majorities of both countries pressed immigrants to conform and assimilate, and that despite this pressure, those immigrants manifested remarkable cultural resilience on both sides of the U.S.-Canadian border. But scholarship little affects national identities: the United States continues to understand itself as a "melting pot" nation, no matter how much the large and increasingly influential "Latin" American sector raises serious questions about the validity of that image. As significant a scholar as political scientist Samuel Huntington can express alarm that the "latinization" of the United States undermined the Anglo-Protestant "values that built the American dream." Canada, on the other hand, has constitutionally enshrined both its French-English biculturalism and its "cultural mosaic," although the accuracy of that image is also open to debate.[5]

The most distinctive tile in Canada's "cultural mosaic" is, of course, the province of Quebec, and the survival and growth of a substantial French-speaking minority stands out as the single most significant difference between the Canadian and the American experiences. Quebec voters rejected a vaguely worded version of "sovereignty" by the narrowest of margins in an October 1995 referendum that attracted unprecedented U.S. interest. U.S. political scientist Charles Doran speculated to a congressional hearing that Quebec's departure might cause Canada to "unravel" into "a series of small, isolated, weak entities," and that "the United States may find that on the threshold of the 21st century, its relations with Canada are far from exceptional." The electoral successes of political parties committed to an independent Quebec suggest that Doran's conjecture cannot be dismissed ten years later: the Bloc Québécois won two-thirds of Quebec's seats in the Canadian Parliament in 2006, and the Parti Québécois, while humbled in the 2007 provincial election, remains a force in Quebec politics.[6]

In terms of U.S. foreign policy, however, what is striking about relations with Canada is how *un*exceptional the "special relationship" has, in fact, been. Neither Canada nor NAFTA partner Mexico, for that matter, was exempted from the U.S. Helms-Burton law with regard to trade with Cuba. Nor have Canada and Mexico escaped heightened American concerns over terrorism and border security. U.S. policy toward Canada conforms to, rather than diverges from, U.S. policy toward the rest of the world. One of the last anomalies in U.S. policy, Canada's inclusion within the State Department's "European and Eurasian Affairs" section, ended in 1998; Canada has been appropriately relocated to the Western Hemisphere for State Department organizational purposes. Unique features to the bilateral relationship undoubtedly remain, most notably the profusion of "clearly discernable, mainly nongovernmental, continental subsystems" (to borrow John H. Redekop's jargon) in categories ranging from entertainment to education and the establishment of bilateral institutions such as the International Joint Commission or the Permanent Joint Board on Defense. But the latter are becoming less unique than Canadians suppose: the United States has long participated in, indeed led, hemispheric defense organizations and has had joint agreements with its other immediate neighbor, Mexico.

The basic pattern of U.S. foreign policy since the early nineteenth century has been self-consciously liberal, capitalist, internationalist, and anticolonial—in the sense that policymakers and political culture have preferred to avoid the formal acquisition of colonies whenever possible. The American approach to Canada has been entirely consistent with these maxims of U.S. policy. For more than two centuries, the United States has balanced a rational consideration for northern strategic security with its desire for an open door for capital and trade in Canada. When Canada has seemed less than secure, or when there has been any perceived threat to that open-door policy, relations have been fractious: during the Kennedy-Diefenbaker and Johnson-Pearson years over Cuba, nuclear weapons, Vietnam and the cold war, and more recently because of Canadian reticence to join in the National Missile Defense System or the invasion of Iraq. Similarly, America responded sharply to Canadian economic nationalist policies during Trudeau's years in power. But the United States never attempted direct colonial control: the integration of Canada into the U.S. system after World War II was, by the standards of international relations, a gentle seduction. Thus, the history of the past two centuries suggests a higher degree of similarity between America's Canada policy and the general characteristics of U.S. foreign policy more than it does any "special relationship."[7]

The rituals of the supposed "special relationship," like the supposed tradition that the Canadian prime minister will be the first foreign leader invited to meet with a new president, have long been without substance, however much Canadians valued them. Yet many Canadians cling tenaciously to the notion that their prime minister should in some unusual way have the president's ear. When the United States barred Canadian cattle because of "mad cow" disease in 2003, the editor of the *Western Wheel*, a weekly in southern Alberta, argued that the U.S. border would have remained open to Canadian beef exports had Prime Minister Chrétien cultivated better personal relations with President Bush! This example suggests that even the overt disagreements that have marked the second Bush presidency have not fully persuaded Canadian policymakers and the public that Canada, to the United States, is just like any other country. Bush's unintended slight in failing to list Canada among U.S. friends in his 19 September 2001 address after terrorist attacks on New York and Washington is only one of many cases in point. But Canada's lack of understanding of this basic truth has been the source of confusion, uncertainty, and wounded sensibilities on the part of Canadians either when Canadian policy has failed to meet a desired American standard, or when Canada has seemingly or actually challenged a U.S. position. Pierre Elliott Trudeau's oft-quoted metaphor of Canada as the mouse and America as an elephant continues to resonate, but it misleads by suggesting that it is only the power relationship between the two that is unequal. Rather, as this study suggests, fundamental differences transcend issues of raw power between the two nations. Some social scientists suggest an increasing convergence in values among all three North American countries; others equally strongly challenge the notion of convergence. Any apparent tendency toward convergence, however, must be viewed through the lens of persistent divergence and ambiguity. More than two centuries of ambivalence must surely suggest that differences of policy and perspective will not disappear in the twenty-first century.[8]

Appendix: U.S.-Canadian Trade

Trade in Goods: U.S. Exports to Canada, 1989–2006

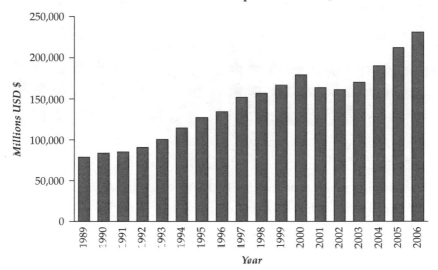

Source: U.S. Census Bureau, Foreign Trade Division, Data Dissemination

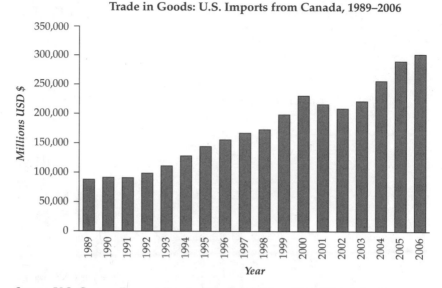

Trade in Goods: U.S. Imports from Canada, 1989–2006

Source: U.S. Census Bureau, Foreign Trade Division, Data Dissemination Branch.

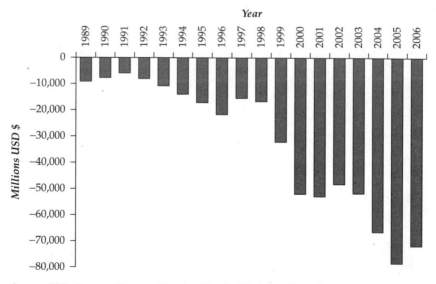

U.S. Trade Balance with Canada, 1989–2006

Source: U.S. Census Bureau, Foreign Trade Division, Data Dissemination Branch.

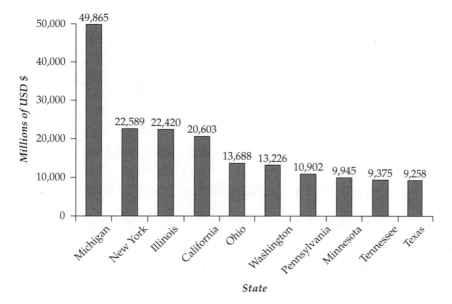

U.S. Imports from Canada by State, 2005

Source: Statistics based on a 2006 study commissioned by the Canadian Embassy in the United States.

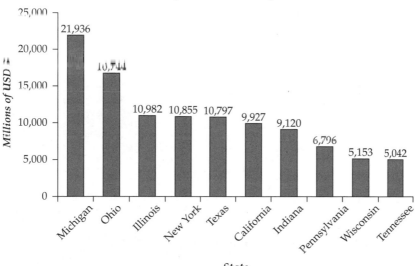

U.S. Exports to Canada by State, 2005

Source: Statistics based on a 2006 study commissioned by the Canadian Embassy in the United States.

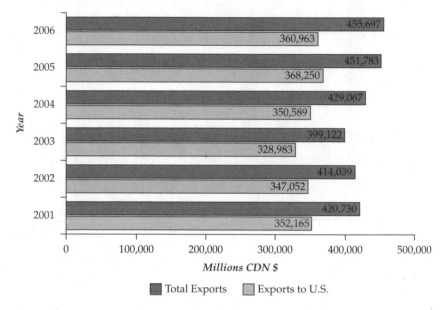

Canadian Exports to the United States in Relation to Total Exports, 2001–2006

2006	455,697 / 360,963
2005	451,783 / 368,250
2004	429,067 / 350,589
2003	399,122 / 328,983
2002	414,039 / 347,052
2001	420,730 / 352,165

Millions CDN $

■ Total Exports   □ Exports to U.S.

Source: Statistics Canada.

Canadian Imports from the United States in Relation to Total Imports, 2001–2006

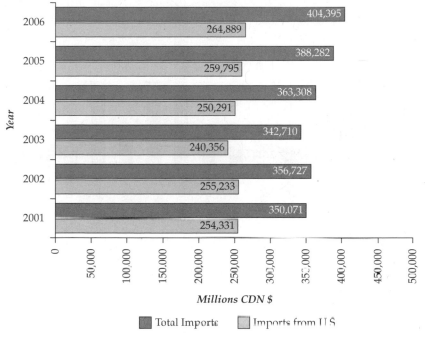

Millions CDN $

■ Total Imports   □ Imports from US

Source: Statistics Canada.

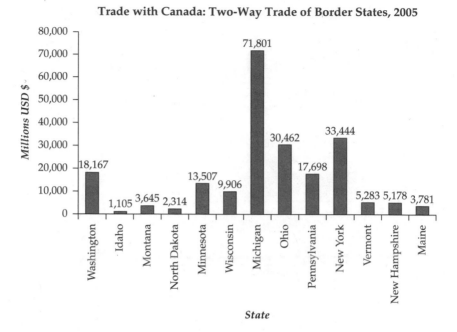

Trade with Canada: Two-Way Trade of Border States, 2005

Source: Statistics based on a 2006 study commissioned by the Canadian Embassy in the United States.

Notes

Abbreviations

ARCS   *American Review of Canadian Studies*
CHCD   Canada, House of Commons, *Debates*
CHR   *Canadian Historical Review*
DCER   *Documents on Canadian External Relations*
DDE   Dwight David Eisenhower Presidential Library
FRUS   United States Department of State, *Foreign Relations of the United States*
Globe   *Toronto Globe* (after 1936, the *Globe and Mail*)
HSTL   Harry S. Truman Presidential Library
JFK   John Fitzgerald Kennedy Presidential Library
LBJ   Lyndon B. Johnson Presidential Library
NAC   National Archives of Canada
NYT   *New York Times*

Unless specified otherwise, all translations from French are by the authors, and all statistics are drawn from *Historical Statistics of Canada,* 2nd edition (Ottawa, 1983), and from *Historical Statistics of the United States* (New York, 1976).

Introduction

1. Stuart Elliott, "Twenty Questions Even a Caveman Can Ask," *NYT,* 29 May 2007.
2. Jeffrey Simpson, "And Nary a Mention of Canada," *Globe,* 22 September 2001.
3. S. F. Wise and Robert Craig Brown, *Canada Views the United States: Nineteenth-Century Political Attitudes* (Seattle, 1967), 18–19.

1. Building North American Nation-States, 1774–1871

1. A. R. M. Lower, *Colony to Nation*, cited in George A. Rawlyk, *Revolution Rejected, 1775–1776* (Scarborough, Ontario, 1968), 9.
2. Hamilton cited in H. L. Keenleyside, *Canada and the United States* (New York, 1929), 9; Philip Lawson, *The Imperial Challenge: Quebec and Britain in the Age of the American Revolution* (Buffalo, 1989).
3. Edmund S. Morgan and Helen M. Morgan, *The Stamp Act Crisis: Prologue to Revolution*, 3rd ed. (Chapel Hill, 1995), 174; Jefferson to John Randolph, 29 November 1775, in *The Writings of Thomas Jefferson*, ed. P. L. Ford (New York, 1892), 1:492; for a similar expression about Nova Scotia, see R. H. Lee to William Lee, 14 May 1778, in *Letters of Members of the Continental Congress*, ed. E. C. Burnett (Washington, 1921–34), 3:236–37; Adams to James Warren, 3 November 1778, in Burnett, *Letters of Members*, 3:476–77; congressional letters are discussed and quoted in Reginald C. Stuart, *United States Expansionism and British North America, 1775–1871* (Chapel Hill, 1988), 11–13; Elizabeth A. Fenn, *Pox Americana: The Great Smallpox Epidemic of 1775–82* (New York, 2001), 62–79.
4. For accounts of the reaction to both the American Revolution and the Quebec Act, see Hilda Neatby, *Quebec: The Revolutionary Age, 1760–1791* (Toronto, 1966), 142–55; Fernand Ouellet, *Histoire économique et sociale du Québec, 1760–1850* (Montréal, 1966), 99–124; Donald Creighton, *The Commercial Empire of the St. Lawrence* (Toronto, 1937); Washington quoted in Stuart, *United States Expansionism*, 13; Generals Wooster and Schuyler quoted in Keenleyside, *Canada and the United States*, 27–28; Bourassa cited in H. Blair Neatby, "Canadianism—a Symposium," *Canadian Historical Association Report* (1956), 74; Gustave Lanctot, *Le Canada et la Révolution américaine* (Montréal, 1965).
5. The classic accounts are J. B. Brebner, *The Neutral Yankees of Nova Scotia: A Marginal Colony during the Revolutionary Years* (New York, 1937), and George Rawlyk, *Nova Scotia's Massachusetts: A Study of Massachusetts–Nova Scotia Relations, 1680–1784* (Montreal, 1973), but Elizabeth Mancke's *The Fault Lines of Empire: Political Differentiation in Massachusetts and Nova Scotia, ca. 1760–1830* (New York, 2005) substantially revises these versions; Gordon Stewart and George Rawlyk discuss the effect of religious revival in *A People Highly Favoured of God: The Nova Scotia Yankees and the American Revolution* (Montreal, 1972).

6. The Treaty of Paris is quoted in John Patrick Diggins, *John Adams* (New York, 2003), 34–35. The most useful account of the negotiations remains Samuel Flagg Bemis, *Diplomacy of the American Revolution* (New York, 1935). Samuel Adams's vehement demand for New England's access to the fisheries is discussed at length in John K. Alexander, *Samuel Adams: America's Revolutionary Politician* (Oxford, 2002), 166–67, 171–72, and the Adams quotations are from A. L. Burt, *The United States, Great Britain and British North America: From the Revolution to the Establishment of Peace after the War of 1812* (New Haven, 1940), 48–53.

7. The estimate of the total number who had loyalist sympathies is from Paul H. Smith, "The American Loyalists: Notes on Their Organizational and Numerical Strength," *William and Mary Quarterly* 25 (1968): 259–77. Simon Schama splendidly brings together the historical literature on "the Revolutionary War's 'dirty little secret' "—massive African-American support for the British cause—in *Rough Crossings: Britain, the Slaves, and the American Revolution* (New York, 2006). The estimate of 60,000 émigrés is from Robert C. Calhoon, *The Loyalists in Revolutionary America, 1760–1781* (New York, 1973), 501; the estimate of 100,000 émigrés is from Wallace Brown, *The Good Americans: The Loyalists in the American Revolution* (New York, 1969), 192; Roger Daniels, *Coming to America: A History of Immigration and Ethnicity in American Life* (New York, 1990), 111; Neil MacKinnon, *This Unfriendly Soil: The Loyalist Experience in Nova Scotia* (Kingston, Ont., 1986), 57–65; W. H. Nelson, *The American Tory* (New York, 1960), 88–91.

8. Loyalist characterizations of America quoted in MacKinnon, *This Unfriendly Soil*, 159; Cartwright quoted in Jane Errington, *The Lion, the Eagle, and Upper Canada: A Developing Colonial Ideology* (Montreal, 1987), 33; Winslow quoted in Ann Gorman Condon, *The Envy of the American States: The Loyalist Dream for New Brunswick* (Fredericton, N.B., 1984), 173–74.

9. Seymour Martin Lipset, *Continental Divide: The Values and Institutions of the United States and Canada* (New York, 1990), 1–18; "Loyalist myth" discussed in Jo-Ann Fellows, "The Loyalist Myth in Canada," *Canadian Historical Association Historical Papers* (1971), 94–111, Murray W. Barkley, "The Loyalist Tradition in New Brunswick: A Study in the Growth and Evolution of an Historical Myth, 1825–1914," *Acadiensis* 4 (1975): 3–45; Norman Knowles, *Inventing the Loyalists: The Ontario Loyalist Tradition and the Creation of Usable Pasts* (Toronto, 1997); S. F. Wise and Robert Craig Brown, *Canada Views the United States*, 22.

10. Tavern sign described in Stuart, *United States Expansionism*, 33; Marcus Lee Hansen and J. B. Brebner, *The Mingling of the Canadian and American Peoples* (New Haven, 1940), 81–86; George Rawlyk, "The Federalist-Loyalist Alliance in New Brunswick, 1784–1815," *Humanities Association Review* 27 (1976): 142–60; Errington, *Lion, Eagle, and Upper Canada*, 38–39.

11. H. G. Nicholas, *The United States and Britain* (Chicago, 1975), 11; the claim of "exceptionalism" is made in Edelgard E. Mahant and Graeme S. Mount, *An Introduction to Canadian-American Relations* (Scarborough, Ont., 1989), 290; Hamilton quoted in Bradford Perkins, *The First Rapprochement: England and the United States, 1795–1805* (New York, 1955), 31, 33–34, 40. Richard White explains the critical role of Indian nations in *The Middle Ground: Indians, Empires and Republics in the Great Lakes Region, 1650–1815* (Cambridge, 1991); and in *Divided Ground: Indians, Settlers, and the Northern Borderland of the American Revolution* (New York, 2006). Alan Taylor explains how the "broad and porous borderlands" that the Indian Confederacy defended became an established international border between the United States and British North America.

12. A. J. Langguth, *Union 1812: The Americans Who Fought the Second War of Independence* (New York, 2006); Walter R. Borneman, *1812: The War That Forged a Nation* (New York, 2006). A synthesis of the traditional consensus is Marshall Smelser, *The Democratic Republic* (New York, 1968), 138–50; scholarly revisionist views include Clifford Egan, "The Origins of the War of 1812: Three Decades of Historical Writing," *Military Affairs* 38 (April 1974): 72–75; J. C. Stagg, *Mr. Madison's War: Politics, Diplomacy and Warfare in the Early American Republic, 1783–1830* (Princeton, 1983); Steven Watts, *The Republic Reborn: War and the Making of Liberal America, 1790–1820* (Baltimore, 1987); Reginald Horsman, "The War of 1812 Revisited," *Diplomatic History* 15 (Winter 1991): 115–24; Calhoun quoted in Donald R. Hickey, *The War of 1812: A Forgotten Conflict* (Chicago, 1989), 44.

13. Quotes from Lewis Hacker, "Western Land Hunger and the War of 1812: A Conjecture," *Mississippi Valley Historical Review* 10 (March 1924): 370, and Julius W. Pratt, *Expansionists of 1812* (New York, 1925), 88; White, *Middle Ground*, 482–83; Stuart, *United States Expansionism*, 54–65; *National Intelligencer*, 8 November 1815.

14. James D. Richardson, ed., *A Compilation of the Messages and Papers of the Presidents* (Washington, D.C., 1899), 2:484–90; Burt, *United States, Great Britain*, 206–316.

15. Jefferson in Richard W. Van Alstyne, *The Rising American Empire* (Chicago, 1960), 88; on the identification of America with Napoleonic France, see Errington, *Lion, Eagle, and Upper Canada*, 80–81, and Condon, *Envy of the American States*, 204–5.

16. A good account of the Anglo-American diplomacy of the period is Bradford Perkins, *Castlereagh and Adams: England and the United States, 1812–1823* (Berkeley, 1965); Brian W. Dippie, *The Vanishing American: White Attitudes and U.S. Indian Policy* (Middletown Conn., 1982), 10–11.

17. For treatment of the War of 1812 treaties and aftermath, see Perkins, *Castlereagh and Adams*; Charles Campbell, *From Revolution to Rapprochement: The United States and Great Britain, 1783–1900* (New York, 1974).

18. On Secord, see Colin M. Coates and Cecilia Morgan, *Heroines and History: Representations of Madeleine de Verchères and Laura Secord* (Toronto, 2002); on Perry see Hickey, *Forgotten Conflict*, 133; New Orleans campaign description from Ward, *Andrew Jackson: Symbol for an Age* (New York, 1955), 6, 16–27; S. F. Wise, "The War of 1812 in Popular History," in *War along the Niagara: Essays on the War of 1812 and Its Legacy*, ed. Arthur Bowler (Youngstown, N.Y., 1991).

19. James A. Henretta et al., *America's History* (Chicago, 1987), 298–303; Mark C. Carnes and John A. Garraty, *The American Nation: A History of the United States* (New York, 2006).

20. The most complete discussion of these American influences in British North America is Fred Landon, *Western Ontario and the American Frontier* (Toronto, 1941), 59–143, 193–204.

21. Allen P. Stouffer, *The Light of Nature and the Law of God: Antislavery in Ontario, 1833–1877* (Montreal, 1992), 216–17; Ryerson quoted in Susan Houston, "Politics, Schools, and Social Change in Upper Canada," *CHR* 53, no. 2 (1972): 263; Bruce Curtis, "Schoolbooks and the Myth of Curricular Republicanism: The State and the Curriculum in Canada West, 1820–1850," *Histoire sociale/Social History* 16 (1983): 305–30; Taché quoted in Jacques Monet, *The Last Cannon Shot: A Study of French-Canadian Nationalism, 1837–1850* (Toronto, 1969), frontispiece; Yolande Lavoie, *L'Emigration des Canadiens aux Etats-Unis avant 1930* (Montréal, 1972), 21, 69–71.

22. William H. Goetzmann, *When the Eagle Screamed: The Romantic Horizon in American Diplomacy, 1800–1860* (New York, 1966), 75, 91; William Goetzmann, *Exploration and Empire: The Explorer and the Scientist in the Winning of the American West* (New York, 1966).

23. For example, William E. Weeks's survey of U.S. continental expansion dismisses Anglo-American conflict over British North America in two pages and concludes that the Rush-Bagot Treaty of 1817 was "the first step in the creation of what eventually became the world's longest undefended border." Weeks, *Building the Continental Empire: American Expansion from the Revolution to the Civil War* (Chicago, 1996), 48–49.

24. Mackenzie cited in Wise and Brown, *Canada Views the United States*, 33; David Mills, *The Idea of Loyalty in Upper Canada, 1784–1850* (Montreal, 1988), 32–51, 93–110; Colin Read, *The Rebellion of 1837 in Upper Canada* (Ottawa, 1985); J. E. Rea, "William Lyon Mackenzie—Jacksonian?" *Mid-America* 50 (July 1968): 223–35.

25. Fernand Ouellet, ed., *Papineau: Textes choisis* (Québec, 1958), 17, 21, 53–58; Wise and Brown, *Canada Views the United States*, 30–32; Jacques Vallee, ed., *Tocqueville au Bas Canada* (Montréal, 1973), 112–13; O'Sullivan and Albany newspaper quoted in Stuart, *United States Expansionism*, 128, 130; Allan Greer, *The Patriots and the People: The Rebellion of 1837 in Rural Lower Canada* (Toronto, 1993), 122–23, 138, 350–51.

26. Arthur and Palmerston quoted in Kenneth Bourne, *Britain and the Balance of Power in North America, 1815–1908* (Berkeley, 1967), 80, 86; Albert B. Corey, *The Crisis of 1830–1842 in Canadian-American Relations* (New Haven, 1941), 27–43; Kenneth R. Stevens, *Border Diplomacy: The* Caroline *and McLeod Affairs in Anglo-Canadian-American Relations, 1837–1842* (Tuscaloosa, Ala., 1989).

27. Campbell, *From Revolution to Rapprochement*; Howard Jones, "Anglophobia and the Aroostook War," *New England Quarterly* 17 (December 1975).

28. Polk in Richardson, *Messages of the Presidents*, 4:398; for comprehensive analyses of the role of the Pacific Northwest in Anglo-American diplomacy, see Frederick Merk, *The Oregon Question: Essays in Anglo-American Diplomacy and Politics* (Cambridge, 1967), and Norman Graebner, *Empire on the Pacific* (New York, 1955).

29. Manifesto cited in L. B. Shippee, *Canadian-American Relations, 1849–1874* (New Haven, 1939), 2; Wise and Brown, *Canada Views the United States*, 46–73; Stuart, *United States Expansionism*, 93–97; support for annexation to offset southern political power was expressed in Henry Dearborn to Daniel Webster, 1830, cited in Charles M. Wiltse, ed., *1830–1834*, vol. 3 of *The Papers of Daniel Webster* (Hanover, N.H., 1977), 18; Garrison, July 1848, cited in W. Merrill, ed., *1841–1849*, vol. 3 of *The Letters of William Lloyd Garrison*

(Cambridge, 1971), 577; Donald F. Warner, *The Idea of Continental Union: Agitation for the Annexation of Canada to the United States, 1849–1893* (Lexington, Ky., 1960), 19–32.

30. D. C. Masters, *The Reciprocity Treaty of 1854* (Toronto, 1963 [1938]); J. M. S. Careless, *The Union of the Canadas, 1841–1857* (Toronto, 1967), 132–49; Senator Jacob Collamer cited in Shippee, *Canadian-American Relations,* 88; A. R. M. Lower et al., *The North American Assault on the Canadian Forest: A History of the Lumber Trade between Canada and the United States* (Toronto, 1938), 123–47; for the role of American interests in Upper Canadian railroad development, see Peter Baskerville, "Americans in Britain's Backyard: The Railway Era in Upper Canada, 1850–1880," *Business History Review* 55, no. 3 (Autumn 1981): 314–33.

31. Colborne cited in Robin W. Winks, *The Blacks in Canada,* 2nd ed. (Montreal, 2000), 155–56; Karolyn Smardz Frost, *I've Got a Home in Glory Land: A Lost Tale of the Underground Railroad* (New York, 2007); John Hope Franklin, *From Slavery to Freedom: A History of American Negroes* (New York, 1947), 361–71; Jason H. Silverman, *Unwelcome Guests: Canada West's Response to American Fugitive Slaves, 1800–1865* (Millwood N.Y., 1985); Joseph Taper to Joseph Long, 11 November 1840, Long Papers, Special Collections, Duke University Library; Fred Landon, "Canadian Negroes and the John Brown Raid," *Journal of Negro History* 6 (April 1921): 174 82; Howe quotations from I. E. Richards, ed., *Letters and Journals of Samuel Gridley Howe* (Boston, 1906–9), 2:447, cited in Winks, *Blacks in Canada,* 270. Franklin and Smardz Frost are much more positive about Euro-Canadians' reception of African-American migrants than are Winks and Silverman.

32. "The Fugitive Slave Case in Canada," *Harper's Weekly,* 9 February 1861, 82; Robin Winks, *Canada and the United States: The Civil War Years* (Baltimore, 1960), 228–29; John A. Williams, "Canada and the Civil War," in *Heard Round the World: The Impact Abroad of the Civil War,* ed. Harold Hyman (New York, 1969), 257–98; Macdonald cited in W. L. Morton, *The Critical Years: The Union of British North America, 1857–1873* (Toronto, 1964), 93; McGee quotation from Hyman, *Heard Round the World,* 283.

33. Palmerston quoted in Bourne, *Britain and the Balance of Power,* 213; Brian Jenkins, *Britain and the War for the Union* (Montreal, 1974), 1:40–43.

34. On "skedaddlers," see Hansen and Brebner, *Mingling,* 148–49; Campbell, *From Revolution to Rapprochement,* 110; on the St. Alban's raid, see Jenkins, *War for the Union,* vol. 2 (1980), 357, 359–60.

35. British strategists quoted in Bourne, *Britain and the Balance of Power,* 218–47; on the Trent affair, see David P. Crook, *The North, the South and the Powers* (New York, 1974), 122–47; Palmerston quotation is from Gordon Warren, *Fountain of Discontent: The Trent Affair and Freedom of the Seas* (Boston, 1981), 135.

36. *Chicago Tribune* cited in the *Toronto Globe,* 17 January 1866, 2; W. C. Ford, ed., *A Cycle of Adams Letters, 1861–1865* (Boston, 1920), 2:254; Potter quoted in Warner, *Idea of Continental Union,* 47.

37. Leon O'Broin, *Fenian Fever: An Anglo-American Dilemma* (New York, 1971); Hereward Senior, *The Fenians and Canada* (Toronto, 1978) and *The Last Invasion of Canada: The Fenian Raids, 1866–1870* (Toronto, 1991).

38. C. P. Stacey, "Fenianism and the Rise of National Feeling in Canada at the Time of Confederation," *CHR* 12, no. 3 (1931): 238–61; Morton, "British North America and a Continent in Dissolution, 1861–1871," *History* 47 (1962): 139–56; F. H. Underhill, *The Image of Confederation* (Toronto, 1964), 4.

39. Grant's message to Congress is from *The State of the Union Messages of the Presidents, 1790–1966* (New York, 1967), 2:1210; Donald Creighton, *John A. Macdonald II: The Old Chieftain* (Toronto, 1955), 74–102; Goldwin Smith [Jr.], *The Treaty of Washington, 1871: A Study in Imperial History* (Ithaca, N.Y., 1941). For Grant and U.S. expansionist ideas toward Canada, see also William McFeely, *Grant* (New York, 1981), 347–48.

2. Canada in the Shadow of Industrial America, 1871–1903

1. The world systems model originated with Immanuel Wallerstein, *The Modern World-System* (New York, 1974) and *The Capitalist World Economy* (Cambridge, 1979), and with Terence K. Hopkins, *World-Systems Analysis: Theory and Methodology* (Beverly Hills, Calif., 1982); Cardwell quoted in Bourne, *Britain and the Balance of Power,* 303–4.

2. "The Fourth of July," *Globe,* 5 July 1876; "Dominion Day," *Globe,* 3 July 1876. Although the "unwanted attention" remained unchanged, Canadian cartoonists' depictions of "Uncle Sam" and "Miss Canada" evolved continuously. For examples, see Charles and Cynthia Hou, *Great Canadian Political Cartoons, 1820 to 1914* (Vancouver, 1997) and *Great Canadian Political Cartoons, 1915 to 1945* (Vancouver, 2002).

3. NAC, Sir John A. Macdonald Papers, Charles Tupper to Macdonald, 1 December 1888; Henry James's review of Francis Parkman's *The Old Re-*

gime in Canada in *The Nation,* 15 October 1874; Shippee, *Canadian-American Relations,* 476–77; *Congressional Globe,* 40th Cong., 2nd sess., 3659; Richard A. Preston, *The Defense of the Undefended Border: Planning for War in North America* (Montreal, 1977), 41–43.

4. *Montreal Evening Star,* 3 July 1876; Douglas Owram, *The Promise of Eden: The Canadian Expansionist Movement and the Idea of the West, 1856–1900* (Toronto, 1980), chapter 4; George F. G. Stanley, *The Birth of Western Canada* (London, 1936) and *Louis Riel* (Toronto, 1963).

5. Donnelly quoted in Warner, *Idea of Continental Union,* 115; W. L. Morton, ed., *The James Wickes Taylor Correspondence* (Winnipeg, 1968); Alvin Gluek Jr., *Minnesota and the Manifest Destiny of the Canadian North West* (Toronto, 1965).

6. Allan Nevins, *Hamilton Fish* (New York, 1937), 388–90; lieutenant quoted in Morton, *Critical Years,* 244.

7. Boat song quoted in Margaret Ormsby, *British Columbia: A History* (Toronto, 1958), 142; California resolution in Warner, *Continental Union,* 135; David Shi, "Seward's Attempt to Annex British Columbia, 1865–1869," *Pacific Historical Review* 47, no. 2 (1978): 217–38.

8. Tina Loo, *Making Law, Order, and Authority in British Columbia, 1821–1871* (Toronto: 1994), chapter 3; Charles John Fedorak, "The United States Consul in Victoria and the Political Destiny of the Colony of British Columbia, 1862–1870," *BC Studies* 79 (1988): 8–15; Barry Gough, *The Royal Navy and the Northwest Coast of North America, 1810–1914* (Vancouver, 1971), 134–41; poem in the *Victoria British Colonist,* 1870, cited in Walter N. Sage, "British Columbia Becomes Canadian, 1871–1901," *Queen's Quarterly* 52, no. 2 (1945): 170.

9. Richard Maxwell Brown, "Law and Order on the American Frontier: The Western Civil War of Incorporation," and R. C. Macleod, "Law and Order on the Western-Canadian Frontier," in *Law for the Elephant, Law for the Beaver: Essays in the Legal History of the North American West,* ed. John McLaren et al. (Regina, Sask., and Pasadena, Calif., 1992), 74–105; Roger D. McGrath, *Gunfighters, Highwaymen and Vigilantes: Violence on the Frontier* (Berkeley, 1985); Paul F. Sharp, "Three Frontiers: Some Comparative Studies of Canadian, American, and Australian Settlement," *Pacific Historical Review* 24 (1955): 373; Stanley D. Hansen, "Policing the International Boundary Area in Saskatchewan, 1890–1910," *Saskatchewan History* 19, no. 2 (1966): 73; Desmond Morton, "Cavalry or Police: Keeping the Peace on Two Adjacent Frontiers, 1870–1900," *Journal of Canadian Studies* 12, no. 2 (1977): 27; Pierre

Berton, *Klondike: The Life and Death of the Last Gold Rush* (Toronto, 1963), makes the classic Canadian case for a nonviolent Canadian mining frontier, but Adele Perry challenges this notion in *On the Edge of Empire: Gender, Race, and the Making of British Columbia, 1849–1871* (Toronto, 2001); David Breen, *The Canadian Ranching Frontier and the Prairie West* (Toronto, 1983); *Harper's Weekly*, 5 August 1876, 630–31.

10. Robert M. Utley, *Frontier Regulars: The United States Army and the Indian, 1866–1891* (New York, 1973), 55–56; on the similarities between U.S. and Canadian institutional frameworks for western settlement and Indian treaty policy, see John Herd Thompson, *Forging the Prairie West* (Toronto, 1998), chapter 4; Roger L. Nichols, *Indians in the United States and Canada: A Comparative History* (Lincoln, Neb., 1998), chapter 8; Jill St. Germain, *Indian Treaty-Making Policy in the United States and Canada, 1867–1877* (Lincoln, Neb., 2001), and Sheila McManus, *The Line Which Separates: Race, Gender, and the Making of the Alberta-Montana Borderlands* (Lincoln, Neb., 2005); Garrick Mallory, "The Indian Systems of Canada and the United States," *Nation*, September 1877, 148; Hana Samek, *The Blackfoot Confederacy, 1880–1920: A Comparative Study of Canadian and U.S. Indian Policy* (Albuquerque, 1987), 33; Mills in John Jennings, "The Plains Indians and the Law," in *Men in Scarlet*, ed. Hugh Dempsey (Calgary, 1974), 53–54.

11. R. C. Macleod, *The North West Mounted Police, 1873–1919* (Ottawa, 1978), 3; L. H. Thomas, *The Struggle for Responsible Government in the Northwest Territories, 1870–1897* (Toronto, 1978), 4–5, 60–61; Samek, *Blackfoot Confederacy*, 29–31, 105–22.

12. S. W. Horrall, "Sir John A. Macdonald and the Mounted Police Force for the Northwest Territories," *CHR* 53, no. 2 (1972): 179–200; Pliney Earle Goddard, "The Indian Problem in Canada," *Red Man*, December 1911, 134; Wallace Stegner, *Wolf Willow: A History, a Story and a Memoir of the Last Plains Frontier* (New York, 1962), 101; Douglas Owram, "'White Savagery': Some Canadian Reaction to American Indian Policy, 1867–1885" (M.A. thesis, Queen's University, 1971); *Nation*, 6 September 1877, 148.

13. The controversy surrounding Sitting Bull is the subject of Gary Pennanen, "Sitting Bull: Indian without a Country," *CHR* 51, no. 2 (1970): 123–40; Christopher C. Joyner, "The Hegira of Sitting Bull to Canada: Diplomatic Realpolitik, 1876–1881," *Journal of the West* 16 (1974): 6–18; and Joseph Manzione, *"I Am Looking to the North for My Life": Sitting Bull, 1876–1881* (Salt Lake City, 1991).

14. Beth LaDow, *The Medicine Line: Life and Death on a North American Border-land* (New York, 2001), chapter 3; Lord Dufferin, governor general of Canada, to Sir Edward Thornton, British minister in Washington, 14 February 1878; R. W. Scott, secretary of state of Canada, memorandum, 11 February 1878; James F. McLeod, commissioner, North West Mounted Police, to Generals Terry and Lawrence, Sitting Bull Commission, Fort Walsh, 17 October 1877; Evarts to Sir Edward Thornton, 17 June 1878, *FRUS* (1878), 344–45, 349–50; Evarts to Thornton, 27 May 1879, *FRUS* (1879), 496–98; Thornton to Evarts, 15 November 1879, *FRUS* (1880), 498; *New York Herald*, 23 October 1877, and *Fort Benton (Mont.) Record*, 28 July 1881, cited in Joyner, "Sitting Bull," 14, 16.

15. Lee Hansen and J. B. Brebner, *The Mingling of the Canadian and American Peoples* (New Haven, 1940); Stuart, *United States Expansionism*, 260–61; Lipset, *Continental Divide*, 172–92; Donald G. Godfrey, "'Canada's Brigham Young': Charles Ora Card, Southern Alberta Pioneer *ARCS* 18, no. 2 (1988): 224–34. Royden K. Loewen's study of two almost identical Mennonite groups that settled in Nebraska and Manitoba in the 1870s concludes that "while the Canadian political and social context encouraged greater [cultural] continuity," after two generations "neither the Canadian nor the American communities were able to remain homogeneous within and separate from the outside society." Loewen, *Family, Church, and Market: A Mennonite Community in the Old and New Worlds, 1850–1930* (Toronto, 1993), 268.

16. The most accessible sources for migration statistics are Leon E. Truesdoll, *The Canadian Born in the United States, 1850–1930* (New Haven Conn., 1943) and R. H. Coats and M. C. Maclean, *The American-Born in Canada: A Statistical Interpretation* (New Haven Conn., 1943), but the best analysis of those statistics is Yolande Lavoie, *Emigration des Canadiens aux Etats-Unis avant 1930* (Montréal, 1972); Goldwin Smith, *Canada and the Canadian Question* (Toronto, 1891), 233; "Boston Is the Promised Land of Canadians," *PEI Magazine* 1 (1899): 82; Bruno Ramirez, *On the Move: French-Canadian and Italian Migrants in the North Atlantic Economy* (Toronto, 1991), 21–33; Hugh Dempsey, *Big Bear* (Lincoln Neb., 1984), 95–105, 112, 122.

17. Lavoie, *Emigration*, 69–71; Yves Roby, "Un Quebec emigré aux Etats-Unis," in *Les rapports culturels entre le Québec et les Etats-Unis*, ed. Claude Savary (Montréal, 1984), 106, 109; *Toronto Globe*, 2 July 1892; P. N. Facktz, *Canada and the United States Compared* (Toronto, 1889), 13–14; "bone and sinew" in John Carr, *Pioneer Days in California* (Eureka, Calif., 1891), cited in Hansen

and Brebner, *Mingling,* 133; "The New President of Cornell University a Canadian," *Toronto Globe,* 23 May 1892, 1.

18. *Annual Report of the Massachusetts Bureau of Statistics and Labor,* 1881, cited in Gerard J. Brault, *The French-Canadian Heritage in New England* (Hanover, N.H., 1986), 68; Yves Roby, *Les Franco-Américaines de la Nouvelle Angleterre, 1776–1930* (Sillery, Que., 1990); Mark Paul Richard, *"Loyal but French": The Negotiation of Identity by French-Canadian Descendants in the United States* (East Lansing, Mich., 2007), chapters 1–3.

19. Randy William Widdis, *With Scarcely a Ripple: Anglo-Canadian Migration into the United States and Western Canada, 1880–1920* (Montreal, 1998), 175–289, 339–51; *Canadian-American, Western British-American,* and *Mining Journal* (Marquette, Mich.), 3 July 1880, cited in Hansen and Brebner, *Mingling,* 205–6, 215 n. 129; Norah Faires, "Leaving the 'Land of the Second Chance': Migration from Ontario to the Upper Midwest in the Nineteenth and Early Twentieth Centuries," in John J. Bukowczyk, Nora Faires, David R. Smith, and Randy William Widdis, *Permeable Border: The Great Lakes Basin as Transnational Region, 1650–1990* (Pittsburgh and Calgary, 2005), 78–119; in *Property and Inequality in Victorian Ontario* (Toronto, 1994), 161–83, Gordon Darroch and Lee Saltow suggest that both English- and French-Canadian farmers who migrated to the United States in the 1860s were less prosperous than other migrant groups; naturalization rates in Alejandro Portes and Ruben G. Rumbaut, *Immigrant America: A Portrait* (Berkeley, Calif., 1990), 120–22; Bernice Webb, *The Basketball Man, James Naismith* (Lawrence, Kans., 1973).

20. J. M. S. Careless, *Brown of the Globe,* vol. 2, *Statesman of Confederation* (Toronto, 1963), 312–22; Allan Nevins, *Hamilton Fish: The Inner History of the Grant Administration,* rev. ed. (New York, 1957), 2:412–13; also Fish to Ambassador Thornton, 11 February 1875, *FRUS* (1875), 653; P. B. Waite, *Canada 1874–1896: Arduous Destiny* (Toronto, 1971), 79–80.

21. Macdonald "coin" comment quoted in C. C. Tansill, *Canadian-American Relations, 1875–1911* (New Haven, 1943), 381 n. 37; speech in *CHCD,* 14 May 1879; *Canadian Monthly and National Review,* May 1876; Tilley story in Waite, *Arduous Destiny,* 101.

22. Michael Bliss, "Canadianizing American Business: The Roots of the Branch Plant," in *Close the 49th Parallel, etc.: The Americanization of Canada,* ed. Ian Lumsden (Toronto, 1970), 26–42; *Monetary Times* cited in Herbert Marshall, Frank Southard Jr., and Kenneth W. Taylor, *Canadian-American Industry*

(1935; repr., Ottawa, 1976), 11–16; on INCO, see Michael Bliss, *Northern Enterprise: Five Centuries of Canadian Business* (Toronto, 1987), 286–87, 302–5; relative DFI (direct foreign investment) estimate from Scott Nearing and Joseph Freeman, *Dollar Diplomacy* (1925; rpt., New York, 1966), 12; Hugh G. J. Aitken, *American Capital and Canadian Resources* (Cambridge, Mass., 1961); an excellent overview of U.S. corporate expansion abroad is Mira Wilkins, *The Emergence of Multinational Enterprise: American Business Abroad from the Colonial Era to 1914* (Cambridge, Mass., 1970).

23. Graham D. Taylor, "Charles F. Sise, Bell Canada, and the Americans," *CHA Historical Papers* (1982), 18, 28–30; the classic revisionist accounts are Walter LaFeber, *The New Empire: An Interpretation of American Expansion, 1860–1898* (Ithaca, N.Y., 1963), and William A. Williams, *The Tragedy of American Diplomacy* (New York, 1962) and *The Roots of the Modern American Empire: A Study of the Growth and Shaping of Social Consciousness in a Marketplace Society* (New York, 1969). See as well LaFeber's subsequent overview of the period, *The American Search for Opportunity* (1993). William Becker disputes the export paradigm in *The Dynamics of Business-Government Relations: Industry and Exports, 1893–1921* (1982). On American finance and overseas investments, see Paul Abrahams, *The Foreign Expansion of American Finance, 1907–1921* (1976), Wilkins, *Emergence of Multinational Enterprise*, and David M. Pletcher, *The Diplomacy of Trade and Investment: American Economic Expansion in the Hemisphere, 1865–1900* (1998).

24. Tansill, *Canadian-American Relations, 1875–1911*, 385–411; NAC, Sir Wilfrid Laurier Papers, G. Amyot to Laurier, 5 August 1887, vol. 2; Ian Albert Hodson, "Commercial Union, Unrestricted Reciprocity and the Background to the Election of 1891" (M.A. thesis, University of Western Ontario, 1952), 129; Richard Cartwright, "The United States and Canada: Speech to the . . . Board of Trade . . . of New York," 21 February 1890.

25. Goldwin Smith, *The Political Destiny of Canada* (Toronto, 1878); "Canada and the United States," *North American Review*, July 1880, 14–25, *Handbook of Commercial Union* (Toronto, 1888), and *Canada and the Canadian Question* (1891; repr., Toronto, 1971); trade statistics from U.S. Department of Commerce, Bureau of the Census, *Historical Statistics of the United States: Colonial Times to 1970* (Washington, D.C., 1976), part 2; Robert Craig Brown, *Canada's National Policy, 1883–1900: A Study in Canadian-American Relations* (Princeton, 1964), 232–35; first Blaine quotation in *Manitoba Free Press*, 20 February 1890, 4.

26. Macdonald's speech reported in *Toronto Empire*, 18 February 1891; "crisis" in *Halifax Morning Herald*, 9 February 1891, and *Regina Standard*, 12 February 1891, both quoted in Patricia Katharine Wood, "'Under Which Flag, Canadian?': Anti-Americanism and the Election of 1891" (M.A. thesis, Queen's University, 1991), 1, 50.

27. Carl Berger, *The Sense of Power: Studies in the Ideas of Canadian Imperialism, 1869–1914* (Toronto, 1970), 4, 153–76, with the Smith quotation on page 98; P. N. Facktz, *Canada and the United States Compared: With Practical Notes on Commercial Union, Unrestricted Reciprocity, and Annexation* (Toronto, 1889), 39–42; Brown, *Canada's National Policy*, 252–56; Warner, *Idea of Continental Union*, 234–41; "Excited Canadians Tear Up Minister's Flag," *New York Times*, 3 July 1892, 1.

28. Margaret Beattie Bogue, "To Save the Fish: Canada, the United States, the Great Lakes, and the Joint Commission of 1892," *Journal of American History* 79, no. 4 (1993): 1429–55.

29. Quotation from *Montreal Evening Star*, 3 July 1876; Alvin C. Gluek, "Canada's Splendid Bargain: The North Pacific Fur Seal Convention of 1911," *CHR* 63, no. 2 (June 1982): 179–201.

30. Brown, *Canada's National Policy*, chapters 2, 4; Briton Cooper Busch, *The War against the Seals: A History of the North American Seal Fishery* (Montreal, 1985), chapter 5.

31. For the abrogation proclamation, see *FRUS* (1885), 466–69; C. P. Stacey, *Canada and the Age of Conflict: A History of Canadian External Policies*, 1:35–38.

32. H. G. Nicholas, *The United States and Britain* (Chicago, 1975), 46; Olney to Thomas F. Bayard, London, 20 July 1895, *FRUS*, vol. 1 (1895), 558; Preston, *Defence of the Undefended Border*, 124–41; *Canadian Military Gazette*, 1 January 1896, quoted in Preston, *Defence of the Undefended Border*, 126; Stacey, *Canada and the Age of Conflict*, 1:48–51.

33. Mahan quoted in Foster Rhea Dulles, *America's Rise to World Power, 1898–1954* (New York, 1954), 27; Graeme S. Mount, "Friendly Liberator or Predatory Aggressor? Some Canadian Impressions of the United States during the Spanish-American War," *North/South: Canadian Journal of Latin American Studies* 22 (1986): 59–76; "impérialism" in *La Verité*, 21 May and 18 June 1898, quoted in Pierre Savard, *Jules-Paul Tardivel, la France et les Etats-Unis* (Quebec, 1967), 363–405; on U.S. expansionism, see Walter LaFeber, *New Empire*, and Robert Beisner, *From the Old Diplomacy to the New, 1865–1900*, 2nd ed. (New York, 1986).

34. Canadian expansionism is discussed in Norman Penlington, *Canada and Imperialism, 1896–1899* (Toronto, 1965); Robert Page, "Canada and the Imperial Idea in the Boer War," *Journal of Canadian Studies* 5 (February 1970): 33–49; Carl Berger, *Imperial Relations in the Age of Laurier* (Toronto, 1969); and Carman Miller, *Painting the Map Red: Canada and the South African War, 1899–1902* (Montreal, 1993). See also chapter 2 in Robert Craig Brown and Ramsay Cook, *Canada, 1896–1921: A Nation Transformed* (Toronto, 1974).

35. William R. Morrison, *Showing the Flag: The Mounted Police and Canadian Sovereignty in the North, 1894–1925* (Vancouver, 1985), 34–35.

36. On Canadian access, Sir Julian Pauncefote, British minister to the United States, to John Day, 18 April 1898, *FRUS* (1899), 320; Bradford Perkins, *The Great Rapprochement: England and the United States, 1895–1914* (New York, 1968), 168–69; Roosevelt to Arthur Lee, 24 April 1901, cited in Calvin D. Davis, *The United States and the Second Hague Peace Conference: American Diplomacy and International Organization, 1899–1914* (Durham, N.C., 1975), 65, and also 62–70; George B. Courtelyou to Secretary of War Elihu Root, 27 March 1902, Root Papers, Library of Congress; for the proclamation and terms of the agreement, see *FRUS* (1903), 488–92; Roosevelt to Root, Lodge, and Turner, 17 March 1903; Roosevelt to Holmes, 25 July 1903, cited in George Mowry, *The Era of Theodore Roosevelt and the Birth of Modern America, 1900–1912* (New York, 1958), 163, for the appointment of the American commissioners, see John Hay to Sir Michael Herbert, 5 March 1903, *FRUS* (1903), 494.

37. Final settlement described in *FRUS* (1903), 478–79; Edward P. Kohn, *This Kindred People: Canadian-American Relations and the Anglo-Saxon Ideal, 1895–1903* (Montreal, 2004), chapter 5; Canadian opinion on the Alaska boundary decision reprinted in *Literary Digest*, 26 (1903): 279.

38. *Toronto Globe*, 2 July 1892; Laurier in *Manitoba Free Press*, 4 July 1906.

3. Beginning a Bilateral Relationship, 1903–1918

1. Daniel T. Rodgers, *Atlantic Crossings: Social Politics in the Progressive Age* (Cambridge, Mass., 1998); Fisher quoted in Samuel F. Wells Jr., "British Strategic Withdrawal from the Western Hemisphere," *CHR* 49, no. 4 (1968): 348; Carman Miller, *The Canadian Career of the Fourth Earl of Minto* (Waterloo, Ont., 1980), 131–55; C. P. Stacey, *Canada and the Age of Conflict: A His-*

tory of Canadian External Policies, vol. 1, *1867–1921* (Toronto, 1984), 121; Bryce quoted in John Hilliker, *Canada's Department of External Affairs* (Montreal, 1990), 30–34.

2. The most important works that discuss this tendency in the United States are Robert Wiebe, *The Search for Order, 1877–1920* (New York, 1968), Alfred Chandler Jr., *The Visible Hand: The Managerial Revolution in American Business* (Cambridge, Mass., 1977), and Ellis Hawley, "The Discovery and Study of a Corporate Liberalism," *Business History Review* 52 (Autumn 1978). These insights have been applied to U.S. foreign policy history by Michael Hogan in "Revival and Reform: America's Twentieth Century Search for a New Economic Order Abroad," *Diplomatic History* 8 (Fall 1984). For Canada, see Tom Traves, *The State and Enterprise: Canadian Manufacturers and the Federal Government* (Toronto, 1979), and Paul Craven, *"An Impartial Umpire": Industrial Relations and the Canadian State* (Toronto, 1980).

3. *Joint Report upon the Survey and Demarcation of the International Boundary between the United States and Canada* (1918).

4. The text of the treaty establishing the IBC is in *FRUS* (1908), 384–97; Bryce quoted in A. C. Gluek Jr., "The Passamaquoddy Bay Treaty, 1910: A Diplomatic Sideshow in Canadian-American Relations," *CHR* 47, no. 1 (1966): 18; *Joint Report upon the Survey and Demarcation of the Boundary between the United States and Canada from the Source of the St. Croix River to the Atlantic Ocean* (1934). See also "Treaty between the United States and Great Britain Relating to the Boundary Line in Passamaquoddy Bay," *FRUS* (1910), 540.

5. For the Boundary Waters Treaty, see *Treaties and Agreements Affecting Canada,* 312–19; *DCER,* vol. 1, 1909–18 (Ottawa, 1967); N. F. Dreisziger, "Dreams and Disappointments," in *The International Joint Commission Seventy Years On,* ed. Robert Spencer, John Kirton, and Kim Richard Nossal (Toronto, 1981), 9, 11; for negotiations, see Peter Neary, "Grey, Bryce, and the Settlement of Canadian-American Differences, 1905–1911," *CHR* 49, no. 4 (1968): 357–79, and Harriet Whitney, "Sir George C. Gibbons, Canadian Diplomat, and Canadian-American Boundary Water Resources, 1905–1910," *ARCS* 3, no. 1 (1973): 66–71.

6. See the *Annual Reports* of the IJC, and for specific examples, see T. J. Streiter to SS, 6 July 1915, and W. S. Hammond to SS, 10 July 1915, *FRUS* (1916), 296. John D. Wirth explores the Trail smelter dispute at length in *Smelter Smoke in North America: The Politics of Transborder Pollution* (Lawrence, Kans., 2000), 1–103.

7. C. Joseph Chacko, *The International Joint Commission* (New York, 1932), 375;
P. E. Corbett, *The Settlement of Canadian-American Disputes* (New Haven,
1937), 51–59; Holmes cited in Spencer et al., *International Joint Commission, 4;*
J. L. Granatstein and Norman Hillmer, *For Better or for Worse: Canada and
the United States to the 1990s* (Toronto, 1991), 40–42; R. Douglas Francis and
Donald B. Smith, *Destinies: Canadian History since Confederation* (Toronto,
1988); Thomas G. Paterson, J. Garry Clifford, and Kenneth J. Hagan, *American Foreign Policy: A History to 1914*, 3rd ed. (Lexington, Mass., 1988).

8. Richard A. Preston, *The Defence of the Undefended Border: Planning for War
in North America* (Montreal, 1977), 142–43; Alvin C. Gluek, "The Invisible
Revision of the Rush-Bagot Agreement, 1898–1914," *CHR* 60, no. 4 (December 1979): 466–84.

9. The best account is Alvin C. Gluek Jr., "Programmed Diplomacy: The Settlement of the North Atlantic Fisheries Question, 1907–1912," *Acadiensis* 6
(1976): 43–70; Taft's acceptance of arbitration in his Message to Congress,
7 December 1909, in *Presidential Addresses and State Papers of William Howard Taft* (New York, 1910), vol. 1, 447–49; Calvin D. Davis, *The United States
and the Second Hague Peace Conference: American Diplomacy and International
Organization, 1899–1914* (Durham, N.C., 1975), 315–16; Minutes of Conferences in Washington, D.C., January 1911, *FRUS* (1911), 271–73.

10. Stacey, *Age of Conflict,* 1:105 n ; Neary, "Settlement of Canadian-American
Differences," 379–80; A. C. Gluek Jr., "Pilgrimages to Ottawa: Canadian
American Diplomacy, 1903–1913," *CHA Historical Papers* (1968), 64–83; Gibbons to Laurier, 11 December 1907 cited in Whitney, "Gibbons," 69.

11. Marvin McInnis, "Migration," *Addressing the Twentieth Century, 1891–1961,*
vol. 3 of *The Historical Atlas of Canada* (Toronto, 1990), plate 27; Bruno
Ramirez, *Crossing the 49th Parallel: Migration from Canada to the United
States, 1900–1930* (Ithaca, N.Y., 2001).

12. Harold Troper, *Only Farmers Need Apply: Official Canadian Government Encouragement of Immigration from the United States, 1896–1911* (Toronto, 1972);
Paul F. Sharp, "When Our West Moved North," *American Historical Review* 55,
no. 2 (1950): 286–300; Grant MacEwan, *Charles Noble: Guardian of the Soil*
(Saskatoon, Sask., 1983); Karel Denis Bicha, *The American Farmer and the Canadian West* (Lawrence, Kans., 1968); David C. Jones, *Empire of Dust: Settling
and Abandoning the Prairie Dry Belt* (Edmonton, Alta., 1987).

13. Janet E. Schulte, " 'Proving Up and Moving Up': Jewish Homesteading Activity in North Dakota, 1900–1920," *Great Plains Quarterly* 10, no. 4 (1990):

240–41; Victor Peters, *All Things Common: The Hutterian Way of Life* (Minneapolis, 1965), 41–49; letter to Du Bois in Harold Martin Troper, "The Creek-Negroes of Oklahoma and Canadian Immigration, 1909–11," *CHR* 52, no. 3 (1972): 286; R. Bruce Shepard, "Diplomatic Racism: Canadian Government and Black Migration from Oklahoma, 1905–1912," *Great Plains Quarterly* 3, no. 1 (1983): 12–13.

14. H. V. Nelles, *The Politics of Development: Forests, Mines and Hydro-electric Power in Ontario, 1849–1941* (Toronto, 1974), 48–107, 307–47; investment statistics from Herbert Marshall, Frank Southard Jr., and Kenneth W. Taylor, *Canadian-American Industry: A Study in International Investment* (Toronto, 1976), 299; Mira Wilkins, *The Emergence of Multinational Enterprise: American Business Abroad from the Colonial Era to 1914* (Cambridge, Mass., 1970), 135–48.

15. Leon Fink, *Workingman's Democracy: The Knights of Labor and American Politics* (New York, 1983); Gregory S. Kealey and Bryan D. Palmer, *Dreaming of What Might Be: The Knights of Labor in Ontario, 1880–1900* (Cambridge, 1982); Fernand Harvey, "Les Chevaliers du Travail, les États-Unis et la société québécoise, 1882–1902," in *Le mouvement ouvrier au Québec* (Montréal, 1980).

16. Miner quoted in Bryan D. Palmer, *Working-Class Experience: Rethinking the History of Canadian Labour, 1800–1991* (Toronto, 1992), 169–70; Gompers and *Herald* quoted in Robert H. Babcock, *Gompers in Canada: A Study in American Continentalism before the First World War* (Toronto, 1974), 36, 110.

17. Jacques Rouillard, *Les Syndicats nationaux au Québec de 1900 à 1930* (Québec, 1979), 74–83; Babcock, *Gompers in Canada*, 210–16.

18. Craig Heron, "Labourism and the Canadian Working Class," *Labour/ le travail* 13 (1984): 45–76; Carlos Schwantes, *Radical Heritage: Labor, Socialism and Reform in Washington and British Columbia, 1885–1917* (Seattle, 1979); Canada, Senate *Debates*, 22 July 1903, 683–91; the bill failed in the House of Commons.

19. Allan Smith, "The Continental Dimension in the English-Canadian Mind," *International Journal* 31, no. 3 (1976): 442–69; *CHCD*, 1907–8, 6989; Lemieux quoted in A. D. Gilbert, "'On the Road to New York': The Protective Impulse and the English-Canadian Cultural Identity, 1896–1914," *Dalhousie Review* 58, no. 3 (1978): 410; reformers cited in John H. Thompson, "American Muckrakers and Western Canadian Reform," *Journal of Popular Culture* (1972): 1063–66; Sir Andrew MacPhail, *Essays in Politics* (New York,

1909), 85; Samuel E. Moffett, *The Americanization of Canada,* introduction by Allan Smith (repr., Toronto, 1972), 9, 114.

20. André Siegfried, *The Race Question in Canada* (1907; repr., Toronto, 1968), 95–103; Wilhelm Cohnstaedt, *Western Canada 1909* (Regina, Sask., 1976), 32; John Foster Fraser, *Canada as It Is* (London, 1905).

21. Laurier quoted in Paul Stevens, "Reciprocity 1911: The Canadian Perspective," in *Canadian-American Free Trade: Historical, Political and Economic Dimensions,* ed. A. R. Riggs and Tom Velk (Halifax, N.S., 1987), 2; *Manitoba Free Press* quoted in D. C. Masters, *Reciprocity, 1846–1911* (Ottawa, 1965), 17.

22. A. K. Weinberg, *Manifest Destiny: A Study of Nationalist Expansionism in American History* (Baltimore, 1935), 367–81; Kendrick A. Clements, "Manifest Destiny and Canadian Reciprocity in 1911," *Pacific Historical Review* 42, no. 1 (1973): 32–52; L. E. Ellis, *Reciprocity 1911: A Study in Canadian-American Relations* (New Haven, 1939), 15, 85–86, 137–38, 191; Richard Gwynn, *The 49th Paradox: Canada in North America* (Toronto, 1985), 37; Robert E. Hannigan, "Reciprocity 1911: Continentalism and American Weltpolitik," *Diplomatic History* 4, no. 1 (1980): 3; Paul Wolman, *Most Favored Nation: The Republican Revisionists and U.S. Tariff Policy, 1897–1912* (Chapel Hill, 1992), xiii–xv; *NYT,* 26 February and 7 March 1911.

23. Robert Craig Brown, *Robert Laird Borden: A Biography,* vol. 1, 1854–1914 (Toronto, 1975), 173–95; Toronto Eighteen Manifesto in *Canadian Annual Review* (1911), 48–49; Foster in *CHCD,* 14 February 1911, 3560–61.

24. Clark in *Congressional Record,* 61st Cong., 3d sess., 14 February 1911, 2520; "bosh" in *NYT,* 28 April 1911; Taft to Roosevelt, 11 January 1911, in Henry F. Pringle, *The Life and Times of William Howard Taft* (New York, 1939), 2:588; Canadian reaction to release of the letter in 1912 quoted in *Literary Digest,* 18 May 1912, 1029–30.

25. John English, *The Decline of Politics: The Conservatives and the Party System, 1901–1920* (Toronto, 1977) 59–60; Borden, Women's League, and election speech quoted in W. M. Baker, "A Case Study of Anti-Americanism in English-Speaking Canada: The Election Campaign of 1911," *CHR* 51, no. 4 (1970): 432, 435; *Le Devoir,* 1 February 1911, 2.

26. Roosevelt in Lawrence Martin, *The Presidents and the Prime Ministers: The Myth of Bilateral Bliss, 1867–1982* (New York, 1982), 75–76; Professor O. D. Skelton cited in John W. Dafoe, *Clifford Sifton in Relation to His Times* (Toronto, 1931), 374; *Varsity* cited in J. Murray Beck, *Pendulum of Power: Can-*

ada's Federal Elections (Scarborough, Ont., 1968), 126; Borden statement in *Canadian Annual Review* (1911) 266.

27. White in *Canadian Annual Review* (1913): 247; Gluek, "Programmed Diplomacy," 69–70.

28. Brown, *Borden,* 1:230–32; Robert Bothwell, "Loring Christie: The Failure of Bureaucratic Imperialism" (Ph.D. diss., Harvard University, 1972), 59–60; White and Walker in *Canadian Annual Review* (1913): 247, 666, 743–45; Donald Page, "Canada as the Exponent of North American Idealism," *ARCS* 3, no. 2 (1973): 34–36.

29. Laurier in *CHCD,* Special War Session (1914), 10.

30. Arthur S. Link, *Woodrow Wilson and the Progressive Era, 1910–1917* (New York, 1963), 148 n. 9; Keenleyside, *Canada and the United States,* 372; NAC, Maj. H. J. Woodside Papers, MG 30, I 11, vol. 15, W. H. Gamble to Woodside, 3 February 1916.

31. "German Organizations in the United States," *Canadian Annual Review* (1916): 221–27; Martin Kitchen, "The German Invasion of Canada in the First World War," *International History Review* 7, no. 2 (1985): 245–60; Gaddis Smith, *Britain's Clandestine Submarines, 1914–1915* (New Haven, 1964); on the *U-Deutschland* and *U-53* incidents, Michael L. Hadley and Roger Sarty, *Tin-Pots and Pirate Ships: Canadian Naval Forces and German Sea Raiders, 1880–1918* (Montreal, 1991), 133–78; *Globe,* 11 October 1916, 6.

32. On American neutrality and entry into the war, see Robert H. Ferrell, *Woodrow Wilson and World War I* (New York, 1985); Ross Gregory, *The Origins of American Intervention in the First World War* (New York, 1971); "Wilson—Democracy's Hope," *Nutcracker* (Calgary), 16 February 1917; Gompers visit in *Canadian Annual Review* (1918): 291–93; Hadley and Sarty, *Tin-Pots and Pirate Ships,* 235–38, 258–64; R. D. Cuff and J. L. Granatstein, *Canadian-American Relations in Wartime: From the Great War to the Cold War* (Toronto, 1975), 3–67; Granatstein and Hillmer, *For Better or for Worse,* 56–59.

33. Borden's letter is in *DCER,* vol. 1 (1909–18), 24–25; Spring Rice to Governor General, 31 January 1918, *DCER,* vol. 4 (1909–18), 30–32; Stacey, *Canada and the Age of Conflict,* 1:230–31.

34. Michael Bliss, "A Canadian Businessman and War: The Case of Joseph Flavelle," in *War and Society in North America,* ed. J. L. Granatstein and Robert Cuff (Toronto, 1971), 34–36; Hearst incident in *Canadian Annual Review* (1918): 260–61; Bryan incident in *NYT* and *Globe,* 1 March 1918; Borden in *Globe,* 2 March 1918; Keenleyside, *Canada and the United States,* 362, 372.

4. A Relationship Matures, 1919–1938

1. Joan Hoff Wilson, *American Business and Foreign Policy, 1920–1933* (New York, 1971).
2. R. A. Preston, *Defence of the Undefended Border*, 213–33; L. H. Larsen, "The U.S. Army's 1919 Contingency Plan to Defend North Dakota against an Unspecified Invader from Canada," *North Dakota History* 43, no. 4 (1976): 22–27.
3. Arthur S. Link, ed., *The Papers of Woodrow Wilson* (Princeton, 1990), 65:505; Wilson to Gompers, 20 June 1919, *Papers of Woodrow Wilson*, 61:39; Ralph A. Stone, *The Irreconcilables: The Fight against the League of Nations* (Lexington, Ky., 1970), 134–35.
4. Borah and Rowell quoted in John Herd Thompson with Allen Seager, *Canada, 1922–1939: Decades of Discord* (Toronto, 1985), 54–56.
5. Dafoe to Sifton, 18 May 1921, in Ramsay Cook, ed., *The Dafoe-Sifton Correspondence*, vol. 2, *1919–1927* (Altona, Man., 1966), 70.
6. John S. Galbraith, "The Imperial Conference of 1921 and the Washington Conference," *CHR* 29, no. 2 (1948): 145–47; Stephen Roskill, *Naval Policy between the Wars* (London, 1968); Michael Hall, "Anglo-American Naval Relations, 1919–1930" (Ph.D. diss., McGill University, 1990); C. P. Stacey, *Canada and the Age of Conflict: A History of Canadian External Policies*, vol. 1, 1867–1921 (Toronto, 1984), 348–55.
7. John S. Galbraith, *The Establishment of Canadian Diplomatic Status at Washington* (Berkeley, 1951), 69–77; Colby to President Wilson, 30 April 1920, and 13 April 1920, in Link, ed., *Papers of Woodrow Wilson*, 65:182, 237; Robert Bothwell, "Canadian Representation at Washington: A Study in Colonial Responsibility," *CHR* 53, no. 2 (1972): 141–48.
8. King in *CHCD*, 1920, 2:2456–60; John Hilliker, *Canada's Department of External Affairs*, vol. 1, *The Early Years, 1909–1946* (Montreal, 1990), 93–95.
9. *NYT*, 13 July 1922; King in Roger Frank Swanson, *Canadian-American Summit Diplomacy, 1923–1973: Selected Speeches and Documents* (Toronto, 1975), 7–10.
10. Philip G. Wigley, *Canada and the Transition to Commonwealth: British-Canadian Relations, 1917–1926* (Cambridge, 1977), 175; Hughes quoted in R. MacGregor Dawson, *William Lyon Mackenzie King: A Political Biography*, vol. 1, *1874–1923* (Toronto, 1958), 434; John A. Schultz, "Canadian Attitudes toward the Empire, 1919–1939" (Ph.D. thesis, Dalhousie University, 1975), 82–84.

11. Massey appointment in Privy Council Order, 10 November 1926, *DCER*, 4, 1926–30, 13–14; Vincent Massey, *What's Past Is Prologue: The Memoirs of Vincent Massey* (Toronto, 1963), 121–32, 144–47; Peter C. Kasurak, "American 'Dollar Diplomats' in Canada, 1927–41," *ARCS* 9, no. 2 (1979): 57; William Phillips, *Ventures in Diplomacy* (London, 1955), 64–70.

12. Winnipeg slogan and *Ladies' Home Journal* quoted in Thompson, *Canada, 1922–1939,* 63–69; *DCER*, vol. 3, 1919–25 and *DCER*, vol. 4, 1926–30, are replete with documents on Prohibition disputes; Richard Kottman, "Volstead Violated: Prohibition as a Factor in Canadian-American Relations," *CHR* 43, no. 2 (1962): 114–23; Stephen T. Moore, "Defining the 'Undefended': Canadians, Americans, and the Multiple Meanings of Border during Prohibition," *ARCS* 34, no. 1 (2004): 3–32.

13. Newspaper quotations from M. Paul Holsinger, "The *I'm Alone* Controversy: A Study in Inter-American Diplomacy, 1919–1935," *Mid-America* 50, no. 4 (1968): 305–13; Laframboise incident in *Globe,* 5 February 1930.

14. Hoover quoted in Arthur M. Schlesinger Jr., *The Crisis of the Old Order, 1919–1933* (New York, 1957), 89.

15. J. A. Guthrie, *The Newsprint Paper Industry* (Cambridge, 1941), 30–59; Carl Weigman, *Trees to News* (Toronto, 1953), 101–12; Trevor J. O. Dick, "Canadian Newsprint, 1913–1930: National Policies and the North American Economy," *Journal of Economic History* 42, no. 3 (1982): 659–87; E. S. Moore, *American Influences in Canadian Mining* (Toronto, 1941), 104; Herbert Marshall, Frank Southard Jr., and Kenneth W. Taylor, *Canadian-American Industry* (1935; repr., Ottawa, 1976), 87–102; David Massell, *Amassing Power: J. B. Duke and the Saguenay River, 1897–1927* (Montreal, 2000).

16. Studebaker quotation in Tom Traves, *The State and Enterprise: Canadian Manufacturers and the Federal Government* (Toronto, 1979), 103; Robert E. Ankli and Fred Frederikson, "The Influence of American Manufacturers on the Canadian Automobile Industry," *Business and Economic History* 10 (1981): 101–13; Provincial Archives of Ontario, William Gray Papers, undated clipping (1923?).

17. Mira Wilkins, *The Maturing of Multinational Enterprise: American Business Abroad from 1914 to 1970* (Cambridge, Mass., 1974) 60–63; Coke in Richard S. Tedlow, *New and Improved: The Story of Mass Marketing in America* (New York, 1990) 63–65.

18. Definitions from Kari Levitt, *Silent Surrender: The Multinational Corporation in Canada* (Toronto, 1970), 58–59; *Journal of the Canadian Bankers' Association* 28,

no. 3 (1921): 367; Irving Brecher and S. S. Reisman, *Canada–United States Economic Relations* (Ottawa, 1957), 100–101.

19. Cf. Gordon Laxer, *Open for Business: The Roots of Foreign Ownership in Canada* (Toronto, 1989); Jose Igartua, " 'Corporate' Strategy and Locational Decision-Making: The Duke-Price Alcoa Merger, 1925," *Journal of Canadian Studies* 20, no. 3 (1985): 97; Peter Kresl, "Before the Deluge: Canadians on Foreign Ownership, 1920–1955," *ARCS* 6, no. 1 (1976): 93–96; Yves Roby, *Les Québécois et les investissements américains, 1918–1929* (Québec, 1976), 81–118; Neil F. Morrison et al., *The Dominion of Canada* (Toronto, 1937), 275–76; *Leader* in Gwenn Ronyk, "The United States in the Twenties as Seen by the Western Canadian Press" (M.A. thesis, University of Regina, 1979), 189–90; Harding in *Canadian Annual Review* (1923), 83–84.

20. IODE cited in *Canada and Her Great Neighbor: Sociological Surveys of Opinions and Attitudes in Canada Concerning the United States*, ed. Henry F. Angus (New Haven, 1938), 236; service clubs in Thompson, *Canada, 1922–1939*, 175.

21. Mary Vipond, "Canadian Nationalism and the Plight of Canadian Magazines in the 1920s," *CHR* 58, no. 1 (March 1977): 43–63.

22. John A. Schultz, "Whose News: The Struggle for Wire Service Distribution, 1900–1920," *ARCS* 10 (1980): 27–35; Paul Rutherford, *The Making of the Canadian Media* (Toronto, 1978), 38–76.

23. William Humber, *Diamonds of the North: A Concise History of Baseball in Canada* (Toronto, 1995); Marshall Wright, "Crossing Borders: The MINT League," in *Dominionball, Baseball above the 49th*, ed. Jane Finnan Dorward (Cleveland, 2005), 50–54; Charles H. Good, "Will U.S. Cash Cripple Hockey?" *Maclean's*, 1 March 1925, 13, 55–56.

24. Allan Smith, "Canadian Culture, the Canadian State, and the New Continentalism," *Canadian-American Public Policy* 3 (October 1990): 10–20; Frank W. Peers, *The Politics of Canadian Broadcasting, 1920–1951* (Toronto, 1969), 3–29; Thompson, *Canada, 1922–1939*, 180–83.

25. John Egli O'Brien, "A History of the Canadian Radio League, 1930–1936" (Ph.D. thesis, University of Southern California, 1964), 58–69; quotations from Margaret Prang, "The Origins of Public Broadcasting in Canada," *CHR* 46, no. 1 (1965): 9–31; Kenneth C. Dewar, "The Origins of Public Broadcasting in Comparative Perspective," *Canadian Journal of Communication* 7, no. 2 (1982): 40–43; Merrill Denison, "Radio in Canada," *Annals of the American Academy of Political and Social Science* (1935): 53–54.

26. Lary May, *Screening Out the Past: The Birth of Mass Culture and the Motion Picture Industry* (New York, 1980), 163–66; Peter Morris, *Embattled Shadows: A History of Canadian Cinema, 1895–1939* (Montreal, 1978), 57–93; Ian Jarvie, *Hollywood's Overseas Campaign: The North Atlantic Movie Trade, 1920–1950* (Cambridge, Mass., 1992), 25–42.

27. R. Laird Briscoe, "What the Censor Saves Us From," *Maclean's*, 1 November 1925.

28. Emily Rosenberg, *Spreading the American Dream: American Economic and Cultural Expansion, 1890–1945* (New York, 1982), 7–8; "Canadian Culture," *NYT*, 7 March 1923, 14; Michael Hogan, *The Marshall Plan* (Cambridge, Mass., 1987), 4–5; Jarvie, *Hollywood's Overseas Campaign*, 50–57, 279; Richard Lowitt, "Ontario Hydro: A 1925 Tempest in an American Teapot," *CHR* 49, no. 2 (1968): 267–74.

29. Maria Tippett, *Making Culture: English-Canadian Institutions and the Arts before the Massey Commission* (Toronto, 1990); *Unionist* cited in Angus, *Canada and Her Great Neighbor*, 225–48; Guildo Rousseau, *L'Image des Etats-Unis dans la littérature québécoise, 1775–1930* (Sherbrooke, Que., 1981); Phillips, *Ventures in Diplomacy*, 70; Randolph Greenfield Adams, *The Foreign Policy of the United States* (New York, 1926), 428.

30. Taschereau in Roby, *Investissements américains*, 141; G. E. Jackson, "Emigration of Canadians to the United States," *Annals of the American Academy* 107 (1923): 28; *HSUS*, series c88–114; Lavoie, *Emigration*, 21.

31. *Canadian Forum*, July 1929; A. R. M. Lower, "The Case against Immigration," *Queen's Quarterly* 37 (1930): 573; W. A. Irwin, "Can We Stem the Exodus?" *Maclean's*, 15 May 1927; Lee Hansen and J. B. Brebner, *The Mingling of the Canadian and American Peoples* (New Haven, 1940), 253–62; Carl Berger, *The Writing of Canadian History* (Toronto, 1976), 142–43.

32. "600 Entry Ports Sought," *NYT*, 7 January 1930, 1, 11; Upjohn case in Leslie Roberts, "Step-Uncle Sam: A Canadian Looks across the Border," *Harper's Magazine*, June 1930, 26–27; Lavoie, *Emigration*, 76–79; Ramirez, *Crossing the 49th Parallel*, 136–37. Over 100,000 Canadians returned voluntarily from the United States between 1930 and 1936, so that the Great Depression turned the balance of binational migration in Canada's favor.

33. "Tariff Panic along the Canadian Border," *Literary Digest*, 27 April 1929, 15–16; Drew Pearson, "High Tariff Diplomacy," *Nation*, 27 February 1929, 250–51; Richard N. Kottman, "Herbert Hoover and the Smoot-Hawley Tariff: Canada, a Case Study," *Journal of American History* 62, no. 3 (December

1975): 609–35; H. Blair Neatby, *William Lyon Mackenzie King,* vol. 2, *1924–1932* (Toronto, 1963), 282–89.

34. Quotations in Thompson, *Canada, 1922–1939,* 202.

35. Ian M. Drummond, *Imperial Economic Policy, 1917–1939* (Toronto, 1974), 191–94, 219–89; Charles Bishop, "Canadian Elections and U.S. Business," *Forbes,* 1 July 1930, 45; branch plant statistics in Wilkins, *Maturing of Multinational Enterprise,* 189–90; Marshall, Southard, and Taylor, *Canadian-American Industry,* 173–75.

36. Swanson, *Canadian-American Summit Diplomacy,* 27–29; Richard N. Kottman, "The Hoover-Bennett Meeting of 1931: Mismanaged Summitry," *Annals of Iowa* 42 (1974), 205–21; *Citizen* quoted in Richard N. Kottman, "Hoover and Canada: Diplomatic Appointments," *CHR* 51, no. 3 (1970): 295.

37. Harvey Levenstein, "Canada and the Suppression of the Salvadorean Revolution of 1932," *CHR* 62, no. 4 (1981): 451–69; Richard N. Kottman, "Herbert Hoover and the St. Lawrence Seaway Treaty of 1932," *New York History* 56, no. 3 (1975), 314–46; William R. Willoughby, *The St. Lawrence Waterway: A Study in Politics and Diplomacy* (Madison Wis., 1961), 133–59.

38. "Canada and the U.S. Election," *Canadian Forum,* December 1932.

39. W. J. McAndrew, "Canada, Roosevelt and the New Deal" (Ph.D. thesis, University of British Columbia, 1973), 84–90; Harriman in *The Liberal Way* (Toronto, 1933), 169, 249–50; NAC, Bennett Papers, Herridge to Bennett, 12 April 1934; Roosevelt in E. S. Greenberg, *Capitalism and the American Political of New Democracy* (Menlo Park, 1985), 9; and Bennett in Alvin Finkel, "Origins of the Welfare State in Canada," in *The Canadian State,* ed. Leo Panitch (Toronto, 1977), 351; Larry Glassford, *Reaction and Reform: The Politics of the Conservative Party under R. B. Bennett, 1927–1938* (Toronto, 1992), 143, 153–54, discounts any direct influence of Roosevelt upon Bennett.

40. King quoted in Thompson, *Canada, 1922–1939,* 273; James H. Gray, "Canada Flirts with Fascism," *Nation,* 9 October 1935, 407; J. A. Stormon, "A History of the International Peace Garden," *North Dakota History* 31, no. 4 (October 1964): 205–15; William E. Leuchtenburg, "The Great Depression," in *The Comparative Approach to American History,* ed. C. Vann Woodward (New York, 1968), 308.

41. David Montgomery, *The Fall of the House of Labor* (Cambridge Mass., 1987), 427–30; *Globe,* 7, 9, 10, 12 October 1929; AFL, *Report of the Forty-Ninth Annual Convention* (Washington, D.C., 1929), 2, 8, 357–59. For general accounts of la-

bor history in this period, with good bibliographies, see Robert H. Zeiger, *American Workers, American Unions, 1920–1985* (Baltimore, 1986), and Bryan D. Palmer, *Working-Class Experience: Rethinking the History of Canadian Labour, 1800–1991* (Toronto, 1992).

42. Sidney Fine, *Sit-Down: The GM Strike of 1936–37* (Ann Arbor, Mich., 1969), 341.

43. Irving Abella, "Canadian Labor: Some Myths and Realities," in *The Influence of the U.S. on Canadian Development,* ed. R. A. Preston (Durham N.C., 1972), 209, Hillman quoted on 214.

44. "Labour Organization," in *Proceeding of the Conference on Canadian-American Affairs* (Boston, 1937), 168–95; "Terror in the Wake of the CIO," *Globe,* 1 June 1937, 1; Irving Abella, *Nationalism, Communism and Canadian Labour: The CIO, the Communist Party and the Canadian Congress of Labour, 1935–1956* (Toronto, 1973), 1–22, Hepburn quoted on 17; Norman Ware, *Labor in Canadian-American Relations* (New Haven, 1937), 70; Craig Heron, *The Canadian Labour Movement* (Toronto, 1989), 74; David Brody, "The Breakdown of Labor's Social Contract: Historical Reflections, Future Prospects," *Dissent,* Winter 1992, 34–36.

45. For a mid-1930s comparison of the two countries, see League for Social Reconstruction, *Social Planning for Canada* (Toronto, 1935), 56, 125, 204–8.

5. World War to Cold War, 1939–1947

1. *Cleveland Plain Dealer* and statistics quoted from Canadian Bank of Commerce, *Monthly Letter,* no. 47 (May 1933), and no. 59 (May 1934); Pierre Berton, *The Dionne Years: A Thirties Melodrama* (Toronto, 1977), 115, 191–97; Wilson in Richard Gwynn, *The 49th Paradox: Canada in North America* (Toronto, 1985), 43; complaint cited in Peter Morris, *Embattled Shadows: A History of Canadian Cinema, 1895–1939* (Montreal, 1978), 232.

2. Carl Berger, "Comments on the Carnegie Series on the Relations of Canada and the United States," in *The Influence of the U.S. on Canadian Development,* ed. R. A. Preston (Durham, N.C., 1972), 32–50; Arthur Lower, *My First 75 Years* (Toronto, 1967), 196–97; survey data in Henry F. Angus, ed., *Canada and Her Great Neighbor: Sociological Surveys of Opinions and Attitudes in Canada Concerning the United States* (New Haven, 1938), 105–8, 272–89.

3. C. P Stacey, *The Military Problems of Canada* (Ottawa, 1936), 29.

4. Bennett in Roger Frank Swanson, *Canadian-American Summit Diplomacy, 1923–1973: Selected Speeches and Documents* (Toronto, 1975), 36; Richard N. Kottman, "The Canadian-American Trade Agreement of 1935," *Journal of American History* 52, no. 2 (1965): 288–96; Marc T. Boucher, "The Politics of Economic Depression: Canadian-American Relations in the Mid-1930s," *International Journal* 41 (1985–86): 3–36.

5. *NYT*, 1 August 1936, 1, 5; *Saturday Night*, 8 August 1936, 1.

6. King in Swanson, *Canadian-American Summit Diplomacy*, 48–50, and in *Canadian Annual Review* (1937–38), 49–52; Tweedsmuir in *NYT*, 2 April 1937; *Evening Standard* (London), 1 April 1937; Victoria M. Wilcox, "Prime Minister and Governor General: Mackenzie King and Lord Tweedsmuir, 1935–1940" (M.A. thesis, Queen's University, 1977), 65–79, 94–98; David Reynolds, *The Creation of the Anglo-American Alliance, 1937–41* (Chapel Hill, N.C., 1982).

7. Speeches in Swanson, *Canadian-American Summit Diplomacy*, 52–62; Chandler Bragdon, "Canadian Attitudes to the Foreign Policy of the United States, 1935–1939" (Ph.D. thesis, University of Rochester, 1961), 163–69; letter to Tweedsmuir in Robert Dallek, *Franklin D. Roosevelt and American Foreign Policy* (New York, 1979), 162–63; Galen Roger Perras, *Franklin Roosevelt and the Origins of the Canadian-American Security Alliance, 1933–1945* (Westport, Conn., 1998), admirably summarizes the ten years of Roosevelt-King interactions.

8. Frank Friedel, *Franklin D. Roosevelt: Rendezvous with Destiny* (Boston, 1990), 300; *The Mackenzie King Diaries* (Toronto, 1973), 20 August 1938; *DCER*, vol. 6 (1936–39), 606–7; Roosevelt to King, 11 October 1938, in *FDR: His Personal Letters, 1928–1945*, ed. Elliott Roosevelt (New York, 1950), 2:816–17; Macphail in *CHCD*, 1937, vol. 1, 254; Richard W. Scott, "Anschluss with Canada?" *American Mercury*, October 1938, 158–65.

9. David Lenarcic, "The Nye Committee Visits the Fire-Proof House: A Comparison of Canadian Non-interventionism and American 'Isolationism' between the Wars" (Ph.D. thesis, York University, 1990); *Mackenzie King Diaries*, 28 October 1938 and 13 September 1938, cited in J. L. Granatstein and Robert Bothwell, "'A Self-Evident National Duty': Canadian Foreign Policy, 1935–1939," *Journal of Imperial and Commonwealth History* 3, no. 2 (1975): 222.

10. *Winnipeg Free Press*, 10, 13 June 1939; Gordon Young, *Voyage of State* (London, 1939), 217–60, Mounties on 260.

11. Dallek, *Roosevelt and American Foreign Policy*, 199.

12. Cf. Edelgard E. Mahant and Graeme S. Mount, *An Introduction to Canadian-American Relations*, 2nd ed. (Scarborough, Ont., 1989), 157.

13. Poll in Robert D. Schulzinger, *American Diplomacy in the Twentieth Century* (New York, 1990), 168.

14. Friedel, *Franklin D. Roosevelt*, 350; "The Canada–United States Permanent Joint Board on Defense, 1940–1945," Dean Acheson Papers, Box 47, HSTL; Dallek, *Roosevelt and American Foreign Policy*, 245.

15. Hugh L. Keenleyside, *On the Bridge of Time*, vol. 2 of *Memoirs* (Toronto, 1982), 49–51; Moffat to Acting Secretary of State Sumner Welles, 14 August 1940, *FRUS*, vol. 3 (1940), 144–45; poll in Stanley Dziuban, *Military Relations between the United States and Canada* (Washington, D.C., 1959), 25; "Defense Plans with Canada," *Chicago Daily Tribune*, 20 August 1940, 10; Welles to Jefferson Caffrey (Brazil), 22 August 1940, *FRUS*, vol. 3 (1940), 146.

16. *CHCD*, 12 November 1940, 55–58; Churchill cited in James Eayrs, *In Defence of Canada*, vol. 2, *Appeasement and Rearmament* (Toronto, 1965), 209–10, and in John W. Dafoe, *Canada Fights: An American Democracy at War* (New York, 1941), 1; on the Royal Navy, C. P. Stacey, *Arms, Men and Governments: The War Policies of Canada* (Ottawa, 1970), 328–32, and *DCER*, vol. 8, 1939–41, 65–97; Reynolds, *Anglo-American Alliance*, 2–3.

17. R. D. Cuff and J. L. Granatstein, "The Hyde Park Declaration: Origins and Significance," *Canadian-American Relations in Wartime* (Toronto, 1975), 69–92; *CHCD*, 28 April 1941, 2286–89.

18. Donald Creighton, *Canada, 1939–1957: The Forked Road* (Toronto, 1976), 42–44; J. L. Granatstein, *How Britain's Weakness Forced Canada into the Arms of the United States* (Toronto, 1989).

19. Roosevelt in Thomas G. Paterson, ed., *Major Problems in American Foreign Policy*, 2nd ed. vol. 2, *Since 1914* (Lexington, Mass., 1984), 209; Robert Divine, *Second Chance: The Triumph of Internationalism in America during World War II* (New York, 1967).

20. Stacey, *Arms, Men and Governments*, 137–80; King to Lord Moran, 9 June 1950, in *Churchill: Taken from the Diaries of Lord Moran* (Boston, 1966), 117 n. 3.

21. Keenleyside, *On the Bridge of Time*, 61–62; "The Canada–United States Permanent Joint Board on Defense, 1940–1945," Dean Acheson Papers, Box 47, HSTL; C. P. Stacey, "The Canadian-American Permanent Joint Board on Defence, 1940–1945," *International Journal* 9 (1954): 105–24.

22. Knox to Hull, 21 July 1941; John D. Hickerson, Assistant Chief, Division of European Affairs, DS, Memorandum of conversation with Hume Wrong, Minister Counsellor, Canadian Legation, 25 July, 1941; Moffat to Hull, 18 August 1941; Hull to Moffat, 16 October 1941, *FRUS* (1941), 3:130–36; Dziuban, *Military Relations between the United States and Canada*, 72–76.

23. *FRUS* (1941), 3:79–83; David Mackenzie, *Inside the Atlantic Triangle: Canada and the Entry of Newfoundland into Confederation, 1939–1949* (Toronto, 1986).

24. Waldo Heinrichs, *Threshold of War* (New York, 1988), 88; Stetson Conn and Byron Fairchild, *The Framework of Hemispheric Defense* (Washington, D.C., 1960), 46, 378; David G. Haglund, "'Plain Grand Imperialism on a Miniature Scale': Canadian-American Rivalry over Greenland in 1940," ARCS 11, no. 1 (1981): 15–36; Michael F. Scheuer, "On the Possibility That There May Be More to It Than That: Professor Haglund, The Documents on American [sic] External Relations Series and the Canadian-American Controversy over Greenland in 1940," ARCS 12, no. 3 (1982): 72–83.

25. Cordell Hull, *The Memoirs of Cordell Hull* (New York, 1948), 2:1128–31; Douglas Anglin, *The St. Pierre and Miquelon Affair of 1941: A Study in Diplomacy in the North Atlantic Quadrangle* (Toronto, 1966); Paul M. Couture, "The Politics of Diplomacy: The Crisis of Canada-France Relations" (Ph.D. thesis, York University, 1981).

26. Hull memorandum of conversation with British Ambassador, 25 April 1942, Ambassador William Leahy (Vichy) to Secretary of State, 27 April 1942, *FRUS* (1942), 2:179–81; Hull, *Memoirs*, 2:1157–58; J. L. Granatstein and Norman Hillmer, *For Better or for Worse: Canada and the United States to the 1990s* (Toronto, 1991), 150, interpret the result as the success of Canadian policy.

27. Conn and Fairchild, *Framework of Hemispheric Defense*, 377.

28. Galen Roger Perras, *Stepping Stones to Nowhere: The Aleutian Islands, Alaska, and American Military Strategy* (Vancouver, 2003), 133–57; George C. Marshall, *The Papers of George Catlett Marshall*, ed. Larry I. Bland, vol. 3, *7 December 1941–May 31, 1943*, 690–91; Hull, *Memoirs*, 2:1182; Dziuban, *Military Relations between the United States and Canada*, 252–59.

29. C. P. Stacey, *Canada and the Age of Conflict: A History of Canadian External Policies*, vol. 2, *1921–1948, the MacKenzie King Era* (Toronto, 1981), 339–41; Pearson quoted in John English, *Shadow of Heaven: The Life of Lester Pearson*, vol. 1, *1897–1948* (Toronto, 1989), 257.

30. Donald Creighton, *Canada's First Century* (Toronto, 1970), 242–43; King cited in James Eayrs, "The Road Past Ogdensburg," *Canadian Forum,* February 1971, 366.

31. S. McKee Rosen, *The Combined Boards of the Second World War* (New York, 1951), 232–33.

32. Winston Churchill, *The Hinge of Fate* (Boston, 1950), 374–77; Dean Acheson, *Present at the Creation* (New York, 1969), 165; Robert Bothwell and William Kilbourn, *C. D. Howe: A Biography* (Toronto, 1979), 168–69, 205.

33. Donald Avery, "Secrets between Different Kinds of Friends: Canada's Wartime Exchange of Scientific Information with the United States and the USSR, 1940–1945," *CHA Historical Papers* (1986), 225–53.

34. Stephen J. Randall, *United States Foreign Oil Policy: For Profits and Security* (Montreal, 1985), 160–65.

35. Worker quoted in Barry Broadfoot, *Six War Years, 1939–1945* (Toronto, 1974), 222; Curtis R. Nordman, "The Army of Occupation: Malcolm MacDonald and U.S. Military Involvement in the Canadian Northwest," and Richard J. Diubaldo, "The Alaska Highway in Canada–United States Relations," both in *The Alaska Highway: Papers of the 40th Anniversary Symposium,* ed. Kenneth Coates (Vancouver, 1985), 83–115; Kenneth Coates and William Morrison, *The Alaska Highway in World War II: The U.S. Army of Occupation in Canada's Northwest* (Norman, Okla., 1992).

36. George Britnell and V. C. Fowke, *Canadian Agriculture in War and Peace, 1935–1950* (Stanford, Calif., 1962), 135–38; Lawrence R. Aronsen, "From World War to Limited War: Canadian-American Industrial Mobilization for Defence," *Revue Internationale d'Histoire Militaire* 51 (1982): 210–16; Robert Bothwell, *Canada and the United States: The Politics of Partnership,* (Toronto, 1992), 23.

37. Danford W. Middlemiss, "Economic Defence Co-operation with the United States, 1940–1963," in *An Acceptance of Paradox: Essays on Canadian Diplomacy in Honor of John W. Holmes,* ed. Kim Richard Nossal (Toronto, 1982), 109; "The Permanent Joint Board on Defense," Box 47, Dean Acheson Papers, HSTL; Robert Bothwell and William Kilbourn, *C. D. Howe: A Biography* (Toronto, 1979), 171–72.

38. R. D. Cuff and J. L. Granatstein, "The Hyde Park Declaration: Origins and Significance," *Canadian-American Relations in Wartime,* 69–92; R. Warren James, *Wartime Economic Cooperation: A Study of Relations between Canada*

and the United States (Toronto, 1949), 394; "49th State?" *Time* Magazine, 23 February 1948, 46; William R. Willoughby, "The Canada-U.S. Joint Economic Agencies of the Second World War," *Canadian Public Administration* 50, no. 1 (1972): 59–73; Alan S. Millward, *War, Economy and Society, 1939–1945* (Berkeley, 1977), 233.

39. Beatrice Bishop Berle and Travis Beal Jacobs, eds., *Navigating the Rapids, 1918–1971* (New York, 1973), diary entry for 18 March 1941, 365; Keenleyside, *On the Bridge of Time*, 91–92.

40. Gary Gerstle, *Working-Class Americanism: The Politics of Labor in a Textile City, 1914–1960* (Cambridge, Mass., 1989), 278–309; Jacques Ducharme, *The Shadows of the Trees: The Story of the French Canadians in New England* (New York, 1943), 217–19; FDR to King, 18 May 1942 in Jean-François Lisée, *Dans l'oeil de l'aigle: Washington face au Québec* (Québec, 1990), 20–23, 454–55.

41. Cf. for the metaphor Seymour Martin Lipset, *Continental Divide: The Values and Institutions of the United States and Canada* (New York, 1990), 172–88; Allan Smith, "Metaphor and Nationality in North America," *CHR* 51, no. 3 (1970): 273; "The Permanent Joint Board on Defense," Box 47, Dean Acheson Papers, HSTL.

42. Roger Daniels, "Japanese Relocation and Redress in North America: A Comparative View," *Pacific Historian* 26, no. 1 (1982): 2–13.

43. *Sporting News* in David Pietrusza, *Baseball's Canadian American League, 1936–1951* (Jefferson, N.C., 1990) 152–54; Richard Collins, *Culture, Communication and National Identity: The Case of Canadian Television* (Toronto, 1990), 59.

44. Michael Hirsh and Patrick Loubert, *The Great Canadian Comic Books* (Toronto, 1971).

45. Broadfoot, *Six War Years*, 215–16, 221, 286, 290; J. L. Granatstein, *Canada's War* (Toronto, 1975), 421–24.

46. Brinton, *The United States and Britain* (Cambridge, Mass., 1945), 222–23; Pearson in English, *Shadow of Heaven*, 257.

47. Department of State, Memorandum for the President, "Visit of Prime Minister of Canada," 28 September 1945, President's Secretary's File, Subject File, Foreign Affairs, Box 172, Truman Papers, HSTL; J. L. Granatstein, *A Man of Influence: Norman A. Robertson and Canadian Statecraft, 1929–68* (Ottawa, 1981); John T. P. Humphrey, *Human Rights and the United Nations* (Dobbs Ferry, N.Y., 1984).

48. Stacey, *Canada and the Age of Conflict*, 2:379, 385.

49. Canadian reaction in report of U.S. ambassador Atherton, 30 October 1945, forwarded to Truman, President's Secretary's File, Subject File, Foreign Affairs, Box 172, Truman papers, HSTL; Pearson in *DCER*, 11, 12 November 1946, 1670–72; Kennan in Thomas Paterson, ed., *Major Problems in American Foreign Policy*, 2:296–97; Acheson, *Present at the Creation*, 150.

50. FBI, "Soviet Espionage Activities," 19 October 1945, President's Secretary's File, Subject File, FBI-A-Communism, HSTL; U.S. Department of War, Intelligence Division, "Soviet Espionage in Canada," 3 October 1946, Naval Aide Files, Alphabetical file, Box 17, HSTL; Central Intelligence Agency, "Canada," 5 May 1950, President's Secretary's File, Intelligence File, CIA Reports, Box 261, HSTL; on Pearson, J. L. Granatstein and David Stafford, *Spy Wars: Espionage and Canada from Gouzenko to Glasnost* (Toronto, 1990), 47–75, esp. 58–60; Truman's speech in *Public Papers of the Presidents, Truman* (Washington, D.C., 1963), 176–180.

51. Department of State, Memorandum for the President, "Visit of Prime Minister of Canada," 28 September 1945, President's Secretary's File, Subject File, Foreign Affairs, Box 172, Truman Papers, HSTL; Theodore Ropp, "Politics, Strategy and Commitments of a Middle Power," in *Canada–United States Treaty Relations*, ed. David R. Deener (Durham, N.C., 1963), 82.

52. Stacey, *Canada and the Age of Conflict*, 2:391.

6. Canada in the New American Empire, 1948–1960

1. Lawrence Aronsen and Martin Kitchen, *The Origins of the Cold War in Comparative Perspective: American, British and Canadian Relations with the Soviet Union, 1941–1948* (London, 1988), 205; T. G. Paterson, *Soviet-American Confrontation: Postwar Reconstruction and the Origins of the Cold War* (Baltimore, 1973) and *Meeting the Communist Threat* (New York, 1988); Gar Alperovitz, *Atomic Diplomacy*, 2nd ed. (New York, 1985); Harry S. Truman, *Memoirs*, vol. 2, *Years of Trial and Hope, 1946–52* (Garden City, N.Y., 1956), 250.

2. Text of NSC-68 in Thomas Paterson, ed., *Major Problems in American Foreign Policy*, 2:310–15.

3. King in Roger Frank Swanson, *Canadian-American Summit Diplomacy, 1923–1973: Selected Speeches and Documents* (Toronto, 1975), 124; Kennan

and State Department memo quoted in David J. Bercuson, *True Patriot: The Life of Brooke Claxton, 1898–1960* (Toronto, 1993), 157, 227.

4. Claxton in James Eayrs, *In Defence of Canada*, vol. 4, *Growing Up Allied* (Toronto, 1980), 45; Colonel G. F. G. Stanley, *Canada's Soldiers: The Military History of an Unmilitary People* (Toronto, 1960), 414.

5. Denis Smith, *The Diplomacy of Fear: Canada and the Cold War, 1941–1948* (Toronto, 1988), 226–36; Lester Pearson, *Words and Occasions* (Cambridge, Mass., 1970), 70, 170; external affairs documents cited in Don Page and Don Munton, "Canadian Images of the Cold War," *International Journal* 32, no. 3 (1977): 585, 587, 595.

6. "Hard and fast" cited in Page and Munton, "Canadian Images of the Cold War," 593 (the conclusion that we draw is at odds with theirs, however); J. W. Pickersgill and D. F. Forster, *The Mackenzie King Record*, vol. 4, *1947–1948* (Toronto, 1970), 192.

7. Claxton memo to King cited in Bercuson, *Claxton*, 164–65; Eayrs, *Growing Up Allied*, 246.

8. St. Laurent in *CHCD*, 29 April 1948, 3449; charter, among many places, in Escott Reid, *Time of Fear and Hope: The Making of the North Atlantic Treaty, 1947–1949* (Toronto, 1977), 264–66.

9. John A. Munro and Alex Inglis, eds., *Mike: The Memoirs of the Right Honourable Lester B. Pearson*, vol. 2, *1948–1957* (Toronto, 1973), 33; Escott Reid, *Radical Mandarin: The Memoirs of Escott Reid* (Toronto, 1989), 267; St. Laurent in *CHCD*, 29 April 1948, 3449.

10. Dwight D. Eisenhower, *The White House Years: Mandate for Change, 1953–1956* (Garden City, N.Y., 1963), 12; statistics in John W. Warnock, *Partner to Behemoth: The Military Policy of a Satellite Canada* (Chicago, 1970), 322.

11. Claxton in Eayrs, *Growing Up Allied*, 200; Acheson in Walter LaFeber, *America, Russia and the Cold War, 1945–1975* (New York, 1976), 100; Truman to King, 5 January 1948; King to Truman, 8 January 1948, White House Central files, Confidential Files, Truman Papers, HSTL; Acheson, *Present at the Creation*, 404–5.

12. Reid, *Radical Mandarin*, 257–66; NAC, Pearson to External Affairs, 6 November 1950, DEA File 50069-A-40, No. 324, cited in Charles M. Dobbs, "Canadian-American Relations and Truman's Decision to Cross the 38th Parallel in Korea: An Analysis," paper prepared for the *Journal of Northeast Asian Studies (n.d.)*; "Diplomats Hope General Ousted," *Globe*, 3 April 1951, 1; Claxton in Denis Stairs, *The Diplomacy of Constraint: Canada, the Korean*

War, and the United States (Toronto, 1974), 212 n. 84; Edelgard Mahant and Graeme S. Mount's conclusion about Canada's influence on U.S. policy in Korea (and on other cold war issues) is expressed in the title of their book: *Invisible and Inaudible in Washington: American Policies toward Canada* (Vancouver, 1999), 34–39.

13. Peyton Lyon, "Quiet Diplomacy Revisited," in Stephen Clarkson, *An Independent Foreign Policy for Canada?* (Toronto, 1968), 34.

14. Quotations from Raymond B. Blake, "An Old Problem in a New Province: Canadian Sovereignty and the American Bases in Newfoundland, 1948–1952," *ARCS* 23, no. 2 (Summer 1993): 183–202; David J. Bercuson, "SAC vs. Sovereignty: The Origins of the Goose Bay Lease, 1946–1952," *CHR* 70, no. 2 (1989), 221.

15. Memorandum from Defence Liaison Division to Undersecretary of State for External Affairs, Canada, 9 July 1952, *DCER*, vol. 18 (1952), 1112–18. Woodward to Acheson, 13 January 1953, Papers of Stanley Woodward, HSTL; Briefing Papers for President's visit to Ottawa, November 13–14, 1953, Box 6, Whitman File, International Series, DDE; James E. Webb, Acting Secretary of State memo for Truman, 2 March 1951, outlining PJBD discussions in 1951 and subsequent correspondence, White House Central files, Confidential Files, Truman Papers, HSTL; White House Central files, PJBD—Canada-U.S. files, Truman Papers, HSTL; Joseph T. Jockel, *No Boundaries Upstairs: Canada, the United States, and the Origins of North American Air Defence, 1945–1958* (Vancouver, 1987), 127.

16. Robert Bothwell and John English, "Canadian Trade Policy in the Age of American Dominance and British Decline, 1943–47," *Canadian Review of American Studies* 8 (1977): 52–56.

17. Howe in *CHCD*, 25 June 1948, 5845; J. L. Granatstein and R. D. Cuff, "Canada and the Marshall Plan, June–December 1947," *CHA Historical Papers* (1977), 196–213—Truman quoted; Willard Thorp Oral History, 118, HSTL; J. L. Granatstein and Norman Hillmer, *For Better or for Worse: Canada and the United States to the 1990s* (Toronto, 1991), 175.

18. Quotations from Robert Cuff and J. L. Granatstein, "The Rise and Fall of Canadian-American Free Trade, 1947–48," *CHR* 57, no. 4 (1977): 469, 473; memo and text of the agreement in *FRUS* (1948), vol. 9, *The Western Hemisphere* (Washington 1972), 406–9.

19. *Mackenzie King Record*, 4:268–69.

20. Bruce Muirhead, "Trials and Tribulations: The Decline of Anglo-Canadian Trade, 1945–50," *Journal of Canadian Studies* 24, no. 1 (1989): 50.

21. Report cited in Lawrence Aronsen, "From World War to Limited War: Canadian-American Industrial Mobilization for Defence," *Revue Internationale d'histoire militaire* 51 (1982): 220; Eisenhower to Diefenbaker, 21 September 1958; Diefenbaker to Eisenhower, 28 October 1958; Eisenhower to Diefenbaker, 7 November, 1958, Whitman File, International Series, Canada (5), Box 6, DDE. On Canadian lead and zinc exports, see also Canadian ambassador to Secretary of State, 29 June 1960, Official File 134-E-7, Lead and Zinc (2), Box 679, Eisenhower Papers, DDE.

22. Paul M. Litt, *The Muses, the Masses, and the Massey Commission* (Toronto, 1992); Paul Rutherford, *When Television Was Young: Primetime Canada, 1952–1967* (Toronto, 1990), 131; Douglas Owram, *Born at the Right Time: A History of the Baby Boom Generation* (Toronto, 1990); Reginald Stuart, *Dispersed Relations: Americans and Canadians in Upper North America* (Washington, D.C., 2007), 49–72.

23. Pierre Berton, *Hollywood's Canada: The Americanization of Our National Image* (Toronto, 1975), 167–200.

24. Department of State Press Release, 8 October 1957, Whitman file, "Dulles–October 1957," Box 7, DDE.

25. Department of State Press Release, 8 October 1957, Whitman file, "Dulles–October 1957," Box 7, DDE; Commission on Foreign Economic Policy, *Report to the President and the Congress* (Washington, DC, January 1954), Eisenhower, *Mandate for Change*, 292–94.

26. Stephen Scheinberg, "Invitation to Empire: Tariffs and American Economic Expansion in Canada," in *Enterprise and National Development: Essays in Canadian Business and Economic History*, ed. Glen Porter and Robert Cuff (Toronto, 1973), 95; Ralph Strauss, special consultant to Undersecretary of State for Economic Affairs, *Expanding Private Investment for Free World Economic Growth* (Washington, D.C., 1959); William Draper, Chairman, President's Committee to Study the U.S. Military Assistance Program, Third Interim Report, July 1959, Staff Series, Council on Foreign Economic Policy, Draper Committee (1), Box 5, DDE; Canadian figures from F. H. Leacy, ed., *Historical Statistics of Canada*, 2nd ed. (Ottawa, 1983), series G191–96.

27. Woodward to Acheson, 13 January 1953, Papers of Stanley Woodward, HSTL; U.S. Chamber of Commerce Resolution, 1953, White House Central files, Official File, Box 868, DDE; Middlemiss, "Economic Defense Cooperation," 86–109.

28. Peter Karl Kresl, "Before the Deluge: Canadians on Foreign Ownership, 1920–1955," *ARCS* 6, no. 1 (1976): 102–16.

29. Randall to Herter, 16 April 1957, Chronological File, Council on Foreign Economic Policy, Box 4, DDE; Randall Memorandum, 15 July 1957, and Department of State, "United States–Canadian Economic Integration," 27 June 1957, Eisenhower Papers, Office Series, Council of Foreign Economic Policy, Box 2, DDE; Dulles to Randall, 25 July 1957, Council on Foreign Economic Policy, Randall Series, Box 2, DDE; Briefing Papers for Eisenhower Visit to Canada, July 1958, International Meeting Series, Whitman File, Box 3, DDE.

30. Dulles Memorandum of conversation with Clarence Randall, 8 August 1957, General Correspondence and Memo Series, Box 1, Dulles Papers, DDE; "Specific Topics for Discussion by the President at Ottawa," Whitman File, International Series, Eisenhower Papers, DDE.

31. Basil Robinson, *Diefenbaker's World: A Populist in Foreign Affairs* (Toronto, 1989), 85–87.

32. Robinson, *Diefenbaker;* Diefenbaker to Eisenhower, 2 July 1960, Whitman File, International Series, Box 6, DDE.

33. Diefenbaker to Eisenhower, 7 June 1960; Herter to Eisenhower, 27 May 1960, Whitman file, International Series, Box 6, DDE; Christian Herter memorandum of conversation with Eisenhower, 8 April 1960, Miscellaneous memoranda, Box 10, Herter Papers, DDE; St. Laurent in Swanson, *Summit Diplomacy,* 138.

34. *Montreal Star,* 26 and 29 June 1959.

7. The Moose That Roared, 1961–1968

1. Kennedy quoted in *NYT,* 25 August 1960, and in William E. Leuchtenburg et al., *Britain and the United States* (London, 1979), 11; Richard Walton, *Cold War and Counterrevolution: The Foreign Policy of John F. Kennedy* (Baltimore, 1973), 9.

2. Knowlton Nash, *Kennedy and Diefenbaker: Fear and Loathing across the Undefended Border* (Toronto, 1990), 60; John Diefenbaker, *One Canada,* vol. 2, *1956–1962* (Toronto, 1977), 165–66, 172; Thomas Reeves, *A Question of Character: A Life of John F. Kennedy* (New York, 1991).

3. CIA, National Intelligence Estimates, "Trends in Canadian Foreign Policy," JFK trip to Ottawa, 5/61 (D), Folder 11, Canada, Security, Box 113, POF, JFK.

4. Basil Robinson, *Diefenbaker's World: A Populist in Foreign Affairs* (Toronto, 1989), 168; *Public Papers of the Presidents, Kennedy, 1961* (Washington, D.C., 1962), 305–6.

5. Robinson, *Diefenbaker's World*, 193–94, 200–201. On Cuba, see Briefing Papers for Kennedy Visit to Ottawa, May 1961, Folder 8, Canada, Security, POF, Box 113, JFK; Randall confidential interview with former DEA official.

6. Kennedy in Roger Frank Swanson, *Canadian-American Summit Diplomacy, 1923–1973: Selected Speeches and Documents* (Toronto, 1975), 200–206; David MacKenzie, "'The World's Greatest Joiner': Canada and the OAS," *British Journal of Canadian Studies* 6, no. 1 (1991), 206–208.

7. Victor Levant, *Quiet Complicity: Canadian Involvement in the Vietnam War* (Toronto, 1986), 107–70; U.S. Department of Defense, *United States–Vietnam Relations, 1945–1967* (Washington, D.C., 1971), book 2, part B, 53–57.

8. James M. Minifie, *Peacemaker or Powdermonkey: Canada's Role in a Revolutionary World* (Toronto, 1960), 126.

9. Diefenbaker, *One Canada*, 2:182–83; Rostow memorandum, 10 May 1963, Canada Security, 1963, Box 113, POF, JFK; "prick" comment cited in Robert Dallek, *John F. Kennedy: An Unfinished Life* (New York, 2003), 388–89.

10. President's Trip to Ottawa, Briefing Papers, 12 May 1961, Canada, Security, Box 113, POF, JFK; *Public Papers of the Presidents, Kennedy, 1961,* 534–36, Robinson, *Diefenbaker's World*, 204, 228–30.

11. Soviet officials claim that there were nuclear warheads in storage in Cuba during the crisis: Randall interviews with Georgy Shahknazarov, adviser to Mikhail Gorbachev, Moscow, March 1992, Calgary, June 1992. The most useful insider's account is Robert Kennedy's *Thirteen Days: A Memoir of the Cuban Missile Crisis* (New York, 1969).

12. Kennedy to Diefenbaker, 22 and 19 October 1962, Canada-Security, POF, Box 113, JFK; Diefenbaker, *One Canada*, 2:171.

13. Jocelyn Maynard Ghent, "Canada, the United States, and the Cuban Missile Crisis," *Pacific Historical Review* 48, no. 2 (1979): 169–70. Significantly, Robert Kennedy's account does not mention NORAD, and his only reference to Diefenbaker is to suggest that the Canadian prime minister was concerned about how to convince the rest of the world of the circumstances in Cuba: Kennedy, *Thirteen Days*, 52; George Ball, *The Past Has Another Pattern: Memoirs* (New York, 1982), 299–300; External Affairs Documents, 1962, 336–38.

14. The most authoritative account is J. L. Granatstein, "When Push Came to Shove: Canada and the United States," in *Kennedy's Quest for Victory: American Foreign Policy, 1961–1963,* ed. Thomas Paterson (New York, 1989), 86–104; Paul Martin, *A Very Public Life,* vol. 2, *So Many Worlds* (Toronto, 1983), 364; Diefenbaker, *One Canada,* 3:80, 82.

15. Nash, *Diefenbaker and Kennedy,* 238–57, press release 243–44; Granatstein, "When Push Came to Shove," 98–99. Ball does not even mention these events in his memoirs, nor does Rusk's biographer: Thomas J. Schoenbaum, *Waging Peace and War: Dean Rusk in the Truman, Kennedy and Johnson Years* (New York, 1988).

16. American Embassy to Department of State, 2 February 1963, Canada General, 1963, POF, Box 113, JFK.

17. Butterworth to Department of State, 12 February 1963, Canada General, 1963, POF, Box 113; William Brubeck, Executive Secretary to Bundy, the White House, 5 April 1963, Canada Security, 1963, Box 113, JFK; campaign quotations in J. Murray Beck, *Pendulum of Power: Canada's Federal Elections* (Scarborough Ont., 1968), 356–57.

18. Berton cited in John English and Norman Hillmer, "Canada's Alliances," *Revue Internationale d'histoire militaire,* no. 51 (1982), 45; Paul Martin, *Public Life,* 2:385–87. Martin also expressed these views to the authors during his terms as a visiting scholar at McGill University in the mid-1980s.

19. Denis Smith, *Gentle Patriot: A Political Biography of Walter Gordon* (Edmonton, Alta., 1973).

20. "Ice" from Douglas LePan quoted in James Eayrs, "The Road from Ogdensburg," *Canadian Forum,* February 1971, 364; David McClellan and Dean Acheson, eds., *Among Friends: Personal Letters of Dean Acheson* (New York, 1980), 250.

21. *Public Papers of the Presidents, Kennedy,* 1963, 673.

22. Diary Backup, Box 3, LBJ; National Security File, Country File, Canada, Pearson visit, LBJ; National Security File, Country File, Canada, Pearson Visit, 1964, LBJ. See also William Brubeck memorandum for the president, 24 January 1964, National Security File, Country File, Canada, Pearson Visit, LBJ.

23. Appointments File, 16 September 1964, Diary Backup, Box 9, LBJ; James Keeley, "Cast in Concrete for All Time? Negotiation of the Auto Pact," *Canadian Journal of Political Science* 16 (June 1983): 281–97; Bruce Muirhead, *Dancing around the Elephant: Creating a Prosperous Canada in an Era of Ameri-*

can Dominance, 1957–1973 (Toronto, 2005), 7, 52, 70–90; Hartke in Levant, *Quiet Complicity*, 35–36.

24. Rusk/Sullivan to Lodge, 1 May 1964, in Swanson, *Summit Diplomacy*, 239–40; Martin, *Public Life*, 2:428–29. The U.S. position on the Seaborn missions is in *Administrative History of the Department of State*, vol. 1, chap. 8, "Vietnam," 242–45, LBJ.

25. Editorial comments in the *Globe* and the *Winnipeg Free Press*, both 4 November 1964; Pearson in Swanson, *Summit Diplomacy*, 251–54. National Security Adviser McGeorge Bundy congratulated Pearson on his award, Bundy to Pearson, 30 March 1965, CO 43, LBJ.

26. Robert Dallek, *Flawed Giant: Lyndon Johnson and His Times, 1961–1973* (New York, 1998), 258–60; Lawrence Martin, *The Presidents and the Prime Ministers* (Garden City, N.Y., 1982), 2:226–27; Richard Gwyn, *49th Paradox: Canada in North America* (Toronto: McClelland and Stewart, 1985), 115; Pearson, *Memoirs*, 3:140–43; Appointments File, Diary backup, Box 15, LBJ.

27. Pearson, *Memoirs*, 3:143–44; Ronning mission in Martin, *Public Life*, 2:437–43, George C. Herring, ed., *The Secret Diplomacy of the Vietnam War: The Negotiating Volumes of the Pentagon Papers* (Austin, 1983), 159–207, and *Administrative History of the Department of State*, 1:249–50. The major Canadian study, Douglas Ross's *In the Interests of Peace: Canada and Vietnam, 1954–1973* (Toronto: 1984) argues that Hanoi was, in fact, unwilling to negotiate without a guarantee of the recognition of the NLF (National Front for the Liberation of South Vietnam) as a legitimate political force in South Vietnam.

28. Ross, *Interests of Peace*, 288–95, 308–9; Martin, *Public Life*, 2:444–45; statistics in John J. Kirton, "The Consequences of Integration: The Case of the Defense Production Sharing Agreements," in *Continental Community: Independence and Integration in North America*, ed. Andrew Axline et al. (Toronto, 1974), 136; Levant, *Quiet Complicity*, 54–56.

29. Brewster Kneen to Moyers, 7 December 1965, CO 43 Canada, LBJ; *Montreal Gazette*, 26 May 1967, 14; *CHCD*, 30 May 1967, 771; Fred Gaffen, *Unknown Warriors—Canadians in the Vietnam War* (Toronto, 1990).

30. U.S. memorandum on Martin's proposal, Appointments File, Box 66, LBJ; *NYT*, 26 May 1967, 1; *Washington Post*, 26 May 1967, A1, A3; *Globe*, 26 May 1967, 1, 6.

31. Pearson, *Memoirs*, 3:146–47.

32. Greg Donaghy, *Tolerant Allies: Canada and the United States, 1963–1968* (Montreal, 2002), argues that the Pearson government "careful[ly] man-

aged" Canada's economic and military-diplomatic relationships with the United States despite "the virulent strain of Canadian nationalism" that the Vietnam War encouraged.

33. They also dated their movement's birth from the U.S. student revolt of 1968: Peter Warrian, "From Colonized to Colonizer," in *The Star-Spangled Beaver,* ed. John H. Redekop (Toronto, 1971), 70–79.

34. William H. Chafe, *The Unfinished Journey: America since World War II,* 6th ed. (New York, 2007), 303; Penny Bryden, *Planners and Politicians: Liberal Politics and Social Policy* (Montreal, 1997); J. L. Granatstein, *Canada 1957–1967: The Years of Uncertainty and Innovation* (Toronto, 1986), 169–97.

35. Seymour Martin Lipset, *Continental Divide: The Values and Institutions of the United States and Canada* (New York, 1990), 39, 50, 136–51; Robert Bothwell, "More than Kin, and Less than Kind: The Political Cultures of Canada and the U.S.," in *North America without Borders?* ed. Stephen J. Randall (Calgary, Alta., 1992), 287, and Robert Bothwell, *Canada and the United States: The Politics of Partnership* (Toronto, 1992), 166 n. 52, 174 n. 39.

36. Stephen J. Whitfield, *The Culture of the Cold War* (Baltimore, 1991).

37. Lawrence Aronsen, "Canada's Postwar Re-armament: Another Look at American Theories of the Military-Industrial Complex," *CHA Historical Papers* (1981), 175–96; Norbert MacDonald, *Distant Neighbors: A Comparative History of Seattle and Vancouver* (Lincoln, Neb., 1987), 138–63; "social security state" is borrowed from Bothwell, "Political Cultures," 291, and "national security state" from Daniel Yergin, *Shattered Peace: The Origins of the Cold War and the National Security State* (New York, 1990).

8. The Ambivalent Ally, 1968–1984

1. John English and Norman Hillmer, "Canada's Alliances," *Revue Internationale d'histoire militaire* 51 (1982): 40–48.

2. "Coming apart at home" is William H. Chafe's description in *The Unfinished Journey: America since World War II* (New York, 2007); "U.S. Society Disintegrating, UAW Official Declares," *Globe,* 12 February 1968, 4; "Jubilant Negroes Take the Death of Dr. King as a Sign to Rampage," *Globe,* 6 April 1968, 9; *Le Devoir,* 9 April 1968, 4; *Winnipeg Free Press,* 6 April 1968, 3, 8 April 1968, 21; *Globe,* 6 April 1968, 6; Ryan, "Tragédie de Los Angeles," *Le Devoir,* 6 June 1968, 4; Burton Cummings and Randy Bachman, "American Woman," on *American Woman* by The Guess Who (1970).

3. Helen F. Eckerson, "United States and Canada Magnets for Immigration," *Annals of the American Academy of Political and Social Science* 316 (1958): 34, 38; Michael Bliss, "Cultural Tariffs and Canadian Universities," in *Star-Spangled Beaver,* ed. John H. Redekop, 88.

4. Clippings, Press Reaction to U.S. Exhibit at Expo '67, 25 May 1967, President's Appointment File, Box 66, LBJ; *NYT,* 28 April 1967; Edgar Z. Friedenberg, *Deference to Authority* (White Plains, N.Y., 1980).

5. James Eayrs, "The Road from Ogdensburg," *Canadian Forum,* February 1971, 365–66; coverage described in *Globe,* 18 November 1970, 1–2.

6. Charles Ritchie, *Storm Signals: More Undiplomatic Diaries* (Toronto, 1983), 114, 129; Kim Richard Nossal, *The Politics of Canadian Foreign Policy* (Scarborough, Ont., 1985), 133–43; J. L. Granatstein and Robert Bothwell, *Pirouette: Pierre Trudeau and Canadian Foreign Policy* (Toronto, 1990), 39; Trudeau in Dale C. Thomson, *Canadian Foreign Policy* (Toronto, 1971), 126.

7. Margaret MacMillan, *Nixon and Mao: The Week That Changed the World* (New York, 2007); Lawrence Martin, *The Presidents and Prime Ministers* (Garden City, N.Y., 1982), 12; Trudeau in Roger Frank Swanson, *Canadian-American Summit Diplomacy, 1923–1973: Selected Speeches and Documents* (Toronto, 1975), 275.

8. "Canada Tied to U.S. Plan for Asian Empire: Nixon," *Globe,* 25 May 1967, 4; John Hagan, *Northern Passage: American Vietnam War Resisters in Canada* (Cambridge, Mass., 2001); "Trudeau Welcomes Draft Evaders," *Christian Century,* 8 April 1970, 414.

9. Douglas Ross, *In the Interests of Peace: Canada and Vietnam, 1954–1973* (Toronto, 1984), 339–68; Granatstein and Bothwell, *Pirouette,* 52–60.

10. Scowcroft in Granatstein and Bothwell, *Pirouette,* 93.

11. John Bullen, "The Ontario Waffle and the Struggle for an Independent Socialist Canada: Conflict within the NDP," *CHR* 64, no. 2 (1983): 188–215; "Nixon Drinks Canada Dry" signified opposition to the plan of the North American Water and Power Alliance, which proposed to divert Canadian water to the U.S. Southwest—see Lynton K. Caldwell, "Binational Responsibilities for a Shared Environment," in *Canada and the United States: Enduring Friendship, Persistent Stress,* ed. Charles F. Doran and John H. Sigler (Englewood Cliffs, N.J., 1985), 215–16.

12. Michael Bliss, *Northern Enterprise: Five Centuries of Canadian Business* (Toronto, 1987), 482–83, 508–13; Kari Levitt, *Silent Surrender: The Multinational Corporation in Canada* (Toronto, 1970); Kim Richard Nossal, "Economic Nationalism and Continental Integration," in *The Politics of Canada's Economic*

Relationship with the United States, ed. Denis Stairs and Gilbert R. Winham (Toronto, 1985), 55–94; Bruce Muirhead, *Dancing around the Elephant: Creating a Prosperous Canada in an Era of American Dominance, 1957–1973* (Toronto, 2005), 95–138.

13. Canada, House of Commons, *Eleventh Report of the Standing Committee on External Affairs and National Defence Respecting Canada-U.S. Relations,* 28th Parliament, 2d Session (Ottawa, 1970); Canada, Privy Council Office, *Foreign Direct Investment in Canada* (Ottawa, 1970).

14. Granatstein and Bothwell, *Pirouette* 64–66; Nixon quoted in John Lewis Gaddis, *Strategies of Containment* (New York, 1982), 280. Paul Kennedy analyzes America's downward direction in the early 1970s in *The Rise and Fall of the Great Powers: Economic Change and Military Conflict, 1500–2000* (New York, 1987), 515–35.

15. Granatstein and Bothwell, *Pirouette,* 67–70. Henry Kissinger, *The White House Years* (New York, 1979). Nixon makes no reference to Canadian problems in his own memoirs.

16. Wallace C. Koehler Jr., "Foreign Ownership Policies in Canada: 'From Colony to Nation' Again," *ARCS* 11, no. 1 (1981): 80–97.

17. Edward Shaffer, *The United States and the Control of World Oil* (London, 1983); Daniel Yergin, *The Prize: The Epic Quest for Oil, Money, and Power* (New York, 1990); Stephen J. Randall, *United States Foreign Oil Policy since World War I (Montreal, 2005);* Department of Defense, *The Oil Import Program* (Washington, D.C., 1970), 37–70, 81, 132; Department of State, *Bulletin,* 7 May 1973; U.S. Senate, Committee on Interior and Insular Affairs, *The Geopolitics of Energy,* Energy Publication No. 95–1 (Washington, D.C., 1977), 9–10. The main author was Melvin Conant, a former member of the U.S. War College.

18. U.S. Congress, Senate, Foreign Relations Committee, Subcommittee on Multinational Corporations, *Direct Investment Abroad and the Multinationals: Effects on the United States Economy* (Washington, D.C., 1975), 27–29; *Multinational Oil Corporations and United States Foreign Policy,* Report (Washington, D.C. 1975), 4, 7–8.

19. Paul Audley, "Book Publishing in Canada," in *Getting It Back: A Program for Canadian Independence,* ed. Abraham Rotstein and Gary Lax (Toronto, 1974), 204, 206; *Time* executive quoted in *Business Week,* 20 October 1975, 52.

20. John Herd Thompson, "Canada's Quest for 'Cultural Sovereignty': Promo-

tion, Protection and Popular Culture," in *NAFTA in Transition*, ed. Stephen J. Randall and Herman W. Konrad (Calgary, Alta., 1996), 393–410.

21. Isaiah A. Litvak and Christopher J. Maule, *Cultural Sovereignty: The "Time" and "Reader's Digest" Case in Canada* (New York, 1974); and "Bill C-58 and the Regulation of Periodicals in Canada," *International Journal* 36 (1980): 70–90; Roger Frank Swanson, "Canadian Cultural Nationalism and the U.S. Public Interest," in *Canadian Cultural Nationalism: The Fourth Lester B. Pearson Conference on the Canada–United States Relationship*, ed. Janice L. Murray (New York, 1977), 54–79.

22. Manjunath Pendakur, *Canadian Dreams and American Control: The Political Economy of the Canadian Film Industry* (Detroit, 1990), 169–221; Martin Knelman, *Home Movies* (Toronto, 1987), 4; Dave Chenowith, "Does the Quantity Equal the Quality?" *Montreal Gazette*, 21 March 1980.

23. Paul Audley, *Canada's Cultural Industries: Broadcasting, Publishing, Records and Film* (Toronto, 1983), 257, statistics 259; Charles Pullen, "Culture, Free Trade, and Two Nations," *Queen's Quarterly* 95, no. 4 (1988): 888; R. F. Swanson, "Canadian Cultural Nationalism and the U.S. Public Interest," in *Canadian Cultural Nationalism*, ed. Janice L. Murray (New York, 1977), 63.

24. Martin, *Presidents and Prime Ministers*, 262–76, Carter quoted 266.

25. Carter to Church, 15 November 1980, National Security Adviser files, Tab 6, Box 7, folder "Canada 10/79 1/81," Carter Presidential Library.

26. Jurgen Schmandt and Hilliard Roderick, *Acid Rain and Friendly Neighbors* (Durham, N.C., 1985), 63; Butler memo for Brzezinski, 28 January 1977, White House Central file, folder Co 28, Box Co-14, Carter Presidential Library.

27. C. Arthur Borg, Department of State, to Brzezinski, 16 February 1977, folder Co 28, Box Co-14, White House Central Files, Carter Presidential Library; State Department Memo, 21 February 1977, dinner toast, talking points, folder Co 28, Box Co-14, White House Central File, Carter Presidential Library. Carter was evidently annoyed by the quality of the background materials he was receiving from the State Department and the National Security Council on the Trudeau visit. He told Brzezinski and others in a memo on 21 February: "Get together and from now on give me *one coordinated* briefing book" (Carter's emphasis).

28. Carter to Trudeau, 23 February 1977, folder Co 28, Box Co-14, White House Central File, Carter Presidential Library.

29. J. Brian Atwood, Department of State, to Senator Patrick Moynihan, 26 No-

vember 1979, National Security Adviser files, Tab 6, Box 7, folder "Canada 10/79–1/81," Carter Presidential Library; National Security council Memo, 9 February 1977; and Adams to Carter, 11 February 1977, folder Co 28, Box Co-14, White House Central File, Carter Presidential Library.

30. Jack Watson, White House, to the President, 18 February 1977, conveying James Schlesinger's suggestions, 17 February 1977, for the meetings with Trudeau; Robert Hunter National Security Council, to Brzezinski, 10 February 1977, folder Co 28, 11/29/77–1/20/81, Box Co-14, White House Central Files, Carter Presidential Library. In the aftermath of the official meeting of the two leaders, Alastair Gillespie, Canadian minister for energy, mines and resources, became the Canadian point person for bilateral energy discussions. He met on 4 March in Washington with Vice President Walter Mondale to discuss energy supply issues. National Security Council Memorandum and State Department briefing paper, 3 March 1977, folder Co 28, 11/29/77–1/20/81, Box Co-14, White House Central Files, Carter Presidential Library.

31. Briefing paper for Mondale meeting with Ambassador Towes, 23 January 1979, folder Co 28, 11/29/77–1/20/81, Box Co-14, White House Central Files, Carter Presidential Library.

32. Brzezinski to Vance, 5 December 1977, folder Co 28, 11/29/77–1/20/81, Box Co-14, White House Central Files, Carter Presidential Library.

33. Department of State memo for Brzezinski, and Joint Communiqué, National Security Adviser files, Tab 6, Box 7, folder "Canada 1/78–9/79," Carter Presidential Library.

34. Jean-François Lisée, *Dans l'oeil de l'aigle: Washington face au Québec* (Montréal, 1990).

35. Central Intelligence Agency, Foreign Assessment Center, *The Canadian Elections,* National Security Adviser, Tab 6, Box 7, folder "Canada 10/79–1/81," Carter Presidential Library. There is some indication in the Carter files that the president telephoned Prime Minister Trudeau in July 1980 on this issue, but at the date of writing, the files had not been declassified. State Department memo for Brzezinski on the May 1979 election, 24 May 1979; Enders to Secretary of State, 20 June 1979, National Security Adviser, Tab 6, Box 7, folder "Canada 1/78–9/79," Carter Presidential Library.

36. Granatstein and Bothwell, *Pirouette,* 219–20; Warren Christopher et al., *American Hostages in Iran* (New Haven, 1982); Carter to Taylor, 5 February

1980, National Security Adviser, Tab 6, Box 7, folder "Canada 10/79–1/81," Carter Presidential Library.

37. Canada, Department of Energy, Mines and Resources, *The National Energy Program, 1980* (Ottawa, 1980); *The National Energy Program, Update 1982* (Ottawa, 1982); Robert N. McRae, "A Major Shift in Canada's Energy Policy: The Policies and Impact of the National Energy Program," *Journal of Energy and Development* 7, no. 2 (1982): 173–98.

38. Stephen Clarkson, *Canada and the Reagan Challenge: Crisis and Adjustment, 1981–1985* (Toronto, 1985), 23–41, 55–82; Edward Wonder, "The US Government Response to the Canadian National Energy Program," *Canadian Public Policy* 8 (1982): 480–93; U.S. House of Representatives, Committee on Government Operations, *The Adequacy of the Federal Response to Foreign Investment in the United States* (Washington, D.C., 1980).

39. U.S. Department of State, "Note on National Energy program to the Government of Canada," 5 March 1981; Reagan press conference, 6 March 1981, *American Foreign Policy, Current Documents, 1981* (Washington, D.C., 1982), 639; Myer Rashish, "Approach to Foreign Economic Issues," *Department of State Bulletin* (October 1981), 40–46. An example of the oil industry response may be seen in the *Oil and Gas Journal* 79 (26 January 1981), which noted that Canadian ownership had been on the increase in the 1970s without such interventionist policies, from 22.4 percent in 1971 to 38.5 percent in 1979.

40. *Globe*, 23 September 1981, 1; Eagleburger, *Department of State Bulletin*, December 1981, 34–37; on Trudeau-Reagan differences over the USSR and NATO, see Canadian ambassador Allan Gotlieb's memoir, *"I'll Be with You in a Minute, Mr. Ambassador": The Education of a Canadian Diplomat in Washington* (Toronto, 1991). Stephen Randall thanks Mr. Gotlieb for sharing, in the fall of 1991, his personal reflections of the Trudeau-Reagan relationship.

41. Granatstein and Bothwell, *Pirouette*, 324–25; Clarkson, *Canada and the Reagan Challenge*, 36–50, 51–114.

42. Randall confidential interview, Toronto, July 1973; *Canadian Annual Review of Public Affairs* (Toronto, 1973), 270–71.

43. Liisa North, *Bitter Grounds: Roots of Revolt in El Salvador* (Toronto, 1981); Clarkson, *Canada and the Reagan Challenge*, 350.

44. Canada, Department of External Affairs, 2 November 1983.

45. Peter C. Newman, *True North Not Strong and Free: Defending the Peaceable Kingdom in the Nuclear Age* (Toronto, 1983), NATO statistic 143.
46. Thomas J. McCormick, *America's Half-Century: United States Foreign Policy in the Cold War* (Baltimore, 1989), 229.
47. Eagleburger in Granatstein and Bothwell, *Pirouette,* 371–72; Gotlieb, *Education of a Canadian Diplomat,* 97; Adam Bromke and Kim Richard Nossal, "Trudeau Rides the 'Third Rail,'" *International Perspectives* (1984): 3–10.
48. John English, review of Granatstein and Bothwell's *Pirouette, Globe,* 25 August 1990, c8.

9. Republicans and Tories, 1984–1993

1. Nelson Michaud and Kim Nossal, eds., *Diplomatic Departures: The Conservative Era in Canadian Foreign Policy, 1984–1992* (Vancouver, 2001).
2. *Weekly Compilation of Presidential Documents* 21 (11 February 1985): 146; George Ball, *The Past Has Another Pattern: Memoirs* (New York, 1982), 486. On Reagan foreign policy, see Michael Schaller, *Right Turn: American Life in the Reagan-Bush Era, 1980–1992* (New York, 2006).
3. Carter in *NYT,* 16 July 1979, 1.
4. "Principled realism" in Department of State, *Bulletin,* June 1988, 33.
5. Mulroney in Michael K. Hawes, "Canada and the United States in a Changing Global Context," *ACS Newsletter* 13, no. 1 (1991): 9.
6. James Rochlin, *Discovering the Americas: The Evolution of Canadian Foreign Policy towards Latin America* (Vancouver, 1994).
7. J. L. Granatstein, *Yankee Go Home? Canadians and Anti-Americanism* (Toronto, 1996), 251.
8. Department of State, *Bulletin,* May 1986, 57; John C. Polanyi, "Time for More 'No' in NORAD?" *Globe,* 2 December 1985; for the case against SDI, see Jerome B. Wiesner, former scientific adviser to the White House, quoted in the *NYT,* 27 March 1983; David Leyton-Brown, "Canada-U.S. Relations: Towards a Closer Relationship," in *Canada among Nations, 1985: The Conservative Agenda,* ed. Maureen Molot and Brian Tomlin (Toronto, 1986), 180, 187–88.
9. Department of State, *Bulletin,* January 1986, 42–45, for Clark-Schultz meeting in Ottawa; Gotlieb provides an insightful and often witty account of

these years in *"I'll Be with You in a Minute, Mr. Ambassador": The Education of a Canadian Diplomat in Washington* (Toronto, 1991); Reagan radio address, 4 January 1986, Department of State, *Bulletin*, March 1986, 10.

10. Lynton K. Caldwell, "Binational Responsibilities for a Shared Environment," in *Canada and the United States: Enduring Friendship, Persistent Stress*, ed. Charles F. Doran and John H. Sigler (Englewood Cliffs, N.J., 1985), 207; Gotlieb, *Education of a Canadian Diplomat*, 61–62.

11. Michael Weisskopf, "Canada Is Still Waiting for the Administration to Do Something," *Washington Post*, 14 December 1987, 31; Gotlieb, *Education of a Canadian Diplomat*, 66–74.

12. Mulroney in *Globe*, 29 March 1988, A10; John Maggs, "Acid Rain Pact 'Codifies' Clean Air Act," *Journal of Commerce*, 10 July 1990, 3A; Hugh Winsor, "Canadian Quits Joint Commission," *Globe*, 10 September 1996, A1.

13. Justine Kaplan, "The Not-So-Great Lakes," *Omni*, February 1989, 32; lip service in *Vancouver Sun*, 13 January 1990; cochairs quoted in *Winnipeg Free Press*, 13 October 1989, 14; radioactive lamprey in *Globe*, 14 October 1989, D6.

14. Donald Barry, "The U.S. Senate and the Collapse of the East Coast Fisheries Agreement," *Dalhousie Review* 62, no. 3 (1982): 495–503; "Sub a Surprise to Scallop Poachers," *Globe*, 24 March 1993; R. Quentin Grafton and Daniel Lane, "Canadian Fisheries Policy: Challenges and Choices," *Canadian Public Policy* 24, no. 2 (1998): 133–47.

15. Bruce Doern and Brian Tomlin, *Faith and Fear: The Free Trade Story* (Toronto, 1991), 2; poll in *Globe*, 24 February 1988, A1, A4.

16. Canada, Department of External Affairs, *Canadian Trade Policies for the 1980's: A Discussion Paper* (Ottawa, 1983); *Globe* and *Maclean's* editorials, both 6 August 1985; Doern and Tomlin, *Faith and Fear*, 24–25, 106, 310 n. 2.

17. *NYT, Durham (N.C.) Morning Herald*, both 5 October 1987, 1.

18. There are comprehensive analyses of the agreement in Duncan Cameron, ed., *The Free Trade Deal* (Toronto, 1988), and in Doern and Tomlin, *Faith and Fear*, 70–99.

19. *Statement of Administrative Action* (Washington, D.C., 1988), 72, 88.

20. *Statement of Administrative Action*, 62–63.

21. Conrad Black, "Our Own Meech Shoot-Out," *Saturday Night*, September 1990, 76.

22. There are many examples of this perspective, but one of the most broadly representative is Ed Finn, Duncan Cameron, and John Calvert, eds., *The*

Facts on Free Trade (Toronto, 1988), which contains short essays by, among others, former cabinet minister Eric Kierans, prominent Canadian author Margaret Atwood, president of the Canadian Labour Congress Shirley Carr, political scientist Stephen Clarkson, economist and women's rights activist Marjorie Cohen, president of the Canadian Auto Workers Bob White, and coordinator of the Coalition Against Free Trade Scott Sinclair.

23. Reagan speech in Department of State, *Bulletin*, December 1988, 23.

24. Colin Mackenzie, "Old Allies Are Nice; Votes Are Essential," *Globe*, 13 October 1993, A10; "Sand in the Wheels of Trade," *Economist*, 10 April 1993, 25–26.

25. On Manning, see the study by his former adviser, Thomas Flanagan, *Waiting for the Wave: The Reform Party and Preston Manning* (Toronto, 1995).

26. *NYT*, 25 February 1993, A10; *Sherbrooke Record*, 25 February 1993; cartoon from the *Victoria Times-Colonist*, reprinted in *Globe*, 26 February 1993; Trillin in *Triangle Comic Review*, September 1992; Storer H. Rowley, "Well-Being of Northern Neighbor Significantly Affects U.S.," *Durham (N.C.) Morning Herald*, 25 October 1992; Robert Karl Manoff and Michael Schudson, *Reading the News* (New York, 1986), 60, 74.

27. William Humber, *Diamonds of the North: A Concise History of Baseball in Canada* (Toronto, 1995), 2–14; Frank Hyland, "Message to Toronto: This Is Our Game," *Atlanta Constitution*, 17 October 1992; Stephen Brunt, "Canadian Fans Forgiving about Their Inverted Flag," *Globe*, 21 October 1992, 1.

28. Robert Pastor, "The Salinas Opening," *Journal of Interamerican Studies and World Affairs* 32, no. 3 (Fall 1990): 1–24.

29. Department of External Affairs and International Trade, *Highlights of the North American Free Trade Agreement* (Ottawa, August 1992).

30. Department of State, *Bulletin*, April 1989, 28.

31. See Stephen J. Randall, Herman Konrad, and Sheldon Silverman, eds., *North America without Borders? Integrating Canada, the United States and Mexico* (Calgary, 1992); Gary Clyde Hufbauer and Jeffrey Schott, *North American Free Trade: Issues and Recommendations* (Washington, D.C., 1992); three volumes by Michael Hart offer insight on shifts in Canadian trade policy: *A North American Free Trade Agreement: The Strategic Implications for Canada* (Ottawa, 1990); *Canadian Trade Policy from Colonialism to Globalism* (Vancouver, 2002); and *Common Borders, Shared Destinies: Canada, the United States and Deepening Integration* (Ottawa, 2001).

32. Henry J. Jacek, "Public Policy and NAFTA: The Role of Organized Business Interests and the Labor Movement," *Canadian-American Public Policy*

19 (1994); Matilde Luna, "Entrepreneurial Interests and Political Action in Mexico: Facing the Demands of Economic Modernization, in *The Challenge of Institutional Reform in Mexico,* ed. Riordan Roett (Boulder, Colo., 1995), 77–94; Fen Osler Hampson and Christopher Maule, eds., *After the Cold War: Canada among Nations, 1990* (Ottawa, 1991), 69; Jeffrey M. Ayres, *Defying Conventional Wisdom: Political Movements and Popular Contention against North American Free Trade* (Toronto, 1998).

33. Testimony to the House Committee on External Affairs and International Trade, fall 1990.

10. A North American Trajectory? 1994–2000

1. David Leyton-Brown and Joseph T. Jockel, Introduction to *Weathering the Calm: The State of the Canada-U.S. Relationship, 1995,* special issue of *American Review of Canadian Studies* (Winter 1994): 449–51; "Mr. Mulroney Steps Down," *NYT,* 25 February 1993.

2. Edward Greenspon, "These Liberals Are Different," *Globe,* 26 October 1996; *Globe,* 5 November 1993; "NAFTA Crumbs," *Saskatoon Star-Phoenix,* 3 December 1993; "Is Free Trade Fair?" *Calgary Herald,* 4 December 1993.

3. "Benefits of NAFTA Far Outweigh the Drawbacks, Study Concludes," *National Post,* 5 June 2001; Department of Foreign Affairs and International Trade, "Five Years of NAFTA: A Scorecard," www.dfait-maeci.gc.ca/nafta, accessed 24 June 2001.

4. William J. Davey, *Pine and Swine: Canada–United States Trade Dispute Settlement—the FTA Experience and NAFTA Prospects* (Ottawa, 1996); Benjamin Cashore, "Flights of the Phoenix: Explaining the Durability of the Canada-U.S. Softwood Lumber Dispute," *Canadian-American Public Policy* 32 (December 1997); Barrie McKenna, "Any Lumber Deal May Be as Risky as Canada Fighting On," *Globe,* 2 November 2001, B12.

5. John Meisel, "Escaping Extinction: Cultural Defence of an Undefended Border," in *Southern Exposure: Canadian Perspectives on the United States,* ed. D. H. Flaherty (Toronto, 1986); Joel Baglole, "Canada Loosens Up to Survive Flood of U.S. Media," *Wall Street Journal,* 8 September 2000.

6. "The Viacom Mirror," *Toronto Star,* 20 December 1994; Joyce Zemans, "And the Lion Shall Lie Down with the Lamb: U.S.-Canada Cultural Relations in a Free Trade Environment," *ARCS* 24, no. 4 (1994): 509–36.

7. Ted Magder, "Franchising the Candy Store: Split-Run Magazines and a

New International Regime for Trade in Culture," *Canadian-American Public Policy* 34 (April 1998): 30–34; Shawn McCarthy, "New Face-off Looms with U.S. on Trade," *Toronto Star,* 26 June 1995; "Back Off, Mickey," *Financial Post,* 27 June 1995.

8. Norman Spector, "You Call That Winning?" *Globe,* 4 June 1999; "What about That Promise?" *Globe,* 13 February 2000; Charlotte Grey, "Donna in the Lion's Den," *Saturday Night,* July/August 1995, 20; Howard Schneider, "Canada's Culture War Questioned," *Washington Post,* 15 February 1997.

9. "Newfoundland Cancels Public Consultations on Bulk Water Exports," *Kitchener-Waterloo (Ont.) Record,* 23 September 2001; *Globe,* 21 July 2001.

10. Ronald F. Inglehart, Neil Nevitte, and Miguel Basañez, *The North American Trajectory: Cultural, Economic, and Political Ties among the United States, Canada, and Mexico* (New York, 1996), 150–51, 171; Alan M. Schwartz, "Canada-U.S. Environmental Relations: A Look at the 1990s," *ARCS* 24, no. 4 (1994): 489–508.

11. Schwartz, "Canada-U.S. Environmental Relations," 499–504; Martin Mittelstaedt, "Reducing Mercury Levels No Easy Task," *Globe,* 28 April 1997; Annette Baker Fox, "Observing the Rules: Canada-U.S. Trade and Environmental Regulations," *Canadian-American Public Policy* 31 (November 1997): 1–17.

12. Peter B. Doeringer, David G. Terkla, and Audrey Watson, "Regulation, Industry Structure, and the Future of the North Atlantic Fishing Industry," *Canadian-American Public Policy* 22 (June 1995): 1–3; Gordon Munro, Ted McDorman, and Robert McKelvey, "Transboundary Resources and the Canada–United States Pacific Salmon Treaty," *Canadian-American Public Policy* 33 (February 1998).

13. "Darn Yankees! Our Fish. Their Nets. Guess Who's Winning?" *Maclean's,* 4 August 1997; *Globe,* 7 July 1995; Ross Anderson, "Coastal Fishermen Wary of U.S.-Canada Salmon Deal," *Seattle Times,* 4 June 1999; Raymond A. Rogers and Catherine Stewart, "Prisoners of Their Histories: Canada-U.S. Conflicts in the Pacific Salmon Fishery," *ARCS* 27, no. 2 (1997): 253–69.

14. Giles Gherson, "Shame May Be Watchdog's Weapon," *Globe,* 23 July 1994; *NYT,* 13 March 1998.

15. E-mail from Dan Abele to John Herd Thompson et al., "Government of Canada Tables Species at Risk Act," 14 April 2000. The CEC's trilingual website is at www.cec.org.

16. Inglehart, Nevitte, and Basañez, *North American Trajectory,* 37; Richard Es-

trada, "The Dynamics of Assimilation in the United States," in *Identities in North America*, ed. Robert Earle and John D. Wirth (Stanford, 1995), 80–101; Jorge Bustamente, "The Mexico-U.S. Border: A Line of Paradox," in Earle and Wirth, *Identities in North America*, 183–85, 189.

17. Robert Bothwell and J. L. Granatstein, *Our Century: The Canadian Journey* (Toronto, 2000) 235.

18. John Herd Thompson and Morton Weinfeld, "Entry and Exit: Canadian Immigration Policy in Context," *Annals of the American Academy of Political and Social Science*, 538 (March 1995): 185–98; U.S. Immigration and Naturalization Service, *Immigration Profiles: Canada* (Washington, D.C., 1991), 3, 8, 13; "Canada Pushed on Several Fronts toward Integration with U.S., *Globe*, 4 June 1999, A2; U.S. Census, 1990, "General Characteristics of the Foreign Born."

19. "The Brain Drain," *Globe*, 8 May 1999; U.S. Immigration and Naturalization Service, *Immigration Profiles: Canada* (1991), 8; Jeffrey Simpson, *Star-Spangled Canadians: Canadians Living the American Dream* (Toronto, 2000).

20. Jeffrey G. Reitz and Raymond Breton, *The Illusion of Difference: Realities of Ethnicity in Canada and the United States* (Toronto, 1994), 125–33; Keith Banting, "The Social Policy Divide," in *Degrees of Freedom: Canada and the United States in a Changing World*, ed. Keith Banting, George Hoberg, and Richard Simeon (Montreal, 1997), 268, 309; Gerald Boychuck, "Are Canadian and U.S. Social Assistance Policies Converging?" *Canadian-American Public Policy* 30 (1997): 28–34; IWGIA, *The Indigenous World, 2000–2001* (Copenhagen, 2001), 50, 63; Michael A. Goldberg and John Mercer, *The Myth of the North American City* (Vancouver, 1986).

21. Bustamente, "Mexico-U.S. Border," 180–94; Michael Adams, *Sex in the Snow: Canadian Social Values at the End of the Millennium* (Toronto, 1997), and *Fire and Ice: The United States, Canada, and the Myth of Converging Values* (Toronto, 2003), quotations from *Fire and Ice*, 4, 9.

22. J. L. Granatstein, *Yankee Go Home? Canadians and Anti-Americanism* (Toronto, 1996), ix–x; Gregory Millard, Sarah Riegel, and John Wright, " 'Here's Where We Get Canadian': English-Canadian Nationalism and Popular Culture," *ARCS* 32, no. 2 (Spring 2002): 11–34.

23. Diana Coulter, "Canucks Are Full of Yuks at Yankee Blunders," *Christian Science Monitor*, 20 June 2001.

24. "A Border out of Patrol," *Seattle Times*, 17 October 1999; Anthony DePalma, "A Laid-Back Place Overdoses on Drug Culture," *NYT*, 20 August 1998;

Timothy Appleby, "Super Pot: B.C.'s Bonanza," *Globe,* 22 January 2000; "Canada Not on Drug Blacklist," *Globe,* 16 November 1999.

25. "Canada Is a 'Sieve,' Critics Charge," *National Post,* 21 December 1999; "America's Guard Is Down on Porous Frontier," *USA Today,* 15 March 2000; Stephen Handelman, "The Ressam Effect," *Time,* Canadian ed., 23 July 2001.

26. U.S. official cited in David T. Jones, "Canada and the United States in the Chrétien Years," *Policy Options,* November 2000, 33–43; Edward Greenspon and Graham Fraser, "On the Fairway of Foreign Policy," *Globe,* 5 April 1997; Stephen J. Randall, "A Not So Magnificent Obsession: The United States, Cuba, and Canada from Revolution to the Helms-Burton Law," *Canadian-American Public Policy* 36 (November 1998): 1–30; *Wall Street Journal,* 11 July 1996 and 17 March 1997; *Globe,* 15 March 1997.

27. Joel Sokolsky, "The Bilateral Security Relationship: Will National Missile Defense Involve Canada?" *ARCS* 30 (2000): 227–53.

28. Christopher Kirkey, "Washington's Response to the Ottawa Land Mines Process," *Canadian-American Public Policy* 46 (2001); *NYT,* 22 January 1997.

29. Joel Sokolsky, "Between 'Pulpit Diplomacy' and the 'Bully Pulpit': The Axworthy Doctrine, Neo-Wilsonianism, and Canada-U.S. Relations," in *Over Here and Over There: Canada-US Defence Cooperation in an Era of Interoperability,* ed. David G. Haglund (Kingston, Ont., 2001), 49–72. For the very critical U.S. assessment of Axworthy by a former political counselor in the U.S. embassy in Ottawa, see David T. Jones, "Canada and the US in the Chrétien Years: Edging toward Confrontation," *Policy Options,* November 2000, 33–43.

11. Playing by New American Rules, 2001–2007

1. The former diplomat was David Jones, writing in "Washington Memo: Waiting for Regime Change in Ottawa," *Policy Options,* May 2003, 25.

2. Kim Richard Nossal, "Canada and American Unilateralism in the Post–Cold War Era," *ARCS* 27, no. 2 (Summer 1997): 179–97; Thomas L. Friedman, "Noblesse Oblige," *NYT,* 31 July 2001; Jeffrey Simpson, "When the U.S Won't Listen to Its Friends," *Globe,* 31 July 2001.

3. *Defense Week* 22 (12 February 2001): 3; Joseph Jockel, "National Missile De-

fence and the Future of Canada-US Defence Cooperation," in *Canada and National Missile Defence*, ed. David Rudd, Jim Hanson, and Jessica Blitt (Ottawa, 2000), 84–89; Canada, Department of National Defence, Directorate of Space Development, "A Canadian Military Space Strategy" (Ottawa, April 1998); *Bulletin of the Atomic Scientists* 56 (July 2000): 12.

4. Roy MacGregor, "Sentimentality, Canadian-Style," *National Post*, 20 September 2001; Rachel Giese, "Will U.S. Remember Global Good Will? *Toronto Star*, 20 September 2001; *MacNeil/Lehrer NewsHour*, PBS, 18 October 2001.

5. Jeffrey Simpson, "And Nary a Mention of Canada," *Globe*, 22 September 2001; Rod Mickleburgh, "Angry Callers Roil Airwaves over 'Slight' by Chrétien," *Globe*, 22 September 2001; Norman Hillmer and Christopher Sands, "Where Does Canada Stand?" *Globe*, 1 October 2001; "Asleep at the Switch," *Globe*, 22 September 2001; Ipsos-Reid poll of 17–20 September 2001 reported in *Globe*, 22 September 2001.

6. "As Canadian Troops Go Off to Do Battle," *Globe*, 10 October 2001; "Canada a Full Partner in War on Terrorism, Insists Eggleton," *Edmonton Journal*, 29 November 2001.

7. David Cole and James Dempsey, *Terrorism and the Constitution: Sacrificing Civil Liberties in the Name of National Security*, 2nd ed. (New York, 2002); William Michaels, *No Greater Threat: America since September 11 and the Rise of the National Security State* (New York, 2002), *The 9/11 Commission Report. Final Report of the National Commission on Terrorist Attacks upon the United States* (Washington, D.C., 2007), 81, 176–78, 182, 187. On the passport issue, see as well CBC News, "Target Terrorism," 26 March 2002, located at www .cbc.ca/disclosure/archives/020326 (accessed 7 April 2002; site now discontinued); Joel Sokolsky, "Northern Exposure? American Homeland Security and Canada," *International Journal* 60, no. 1 (2004/2005): 35–52.

8. Condoleezza Rice, "Promoting the National Interest," *Foreign Affairs* 79 (January–February 2000); *The National Security Strategy of the United States of America* (Washington, D.C., 2002), http://www.whitehouse.gov/nsc/nss .pdf (accessed 13 December 2007).

9. Cited in Elinor Sloan, "Beyond Primacy: American Grand Strategy in the Post–September 11 Era," *International Journal* 58, no. 2 (Spring 2003): 303–20; Sokolsky, "Northern Exposure?" 35–52; "Closer Ties with U.S. Military Threat to Sovereignty, Report Says," *CBC News*, 26 April 2002, http://www.cbc

.ca/news/story/2002/04/26/northcommand_020426.html (accessed 13 December 2007). The report quoted was commissioned by the Liu Centre for the Study of Global Issues, an organization headed by former foreign affairs minister Lloyd Axworthy, and written by Michael Byers, a Canadian who at the time taught international law at Duke University.

10. Bush cited in Richard Falk, "The New Bush Doctrine," *Nation*, 15 July 2002; George Tenet, "Evolving Dangers in a Complex World," testimony delivered to Congress, 11 February 2003.

11. Stephane Roussel, "Honey, Are You Still Mad at Me? I've Changed You Know," *International Journal* 58, no. 4 (Fall 2003). For Parrish's comments, see http://www.cbc.ca/news/story/2003/02/26 (accessed 19 March 2007); Nicholas D. Kristof, "Losses, before Bullets Fly," *NYT*, 7 March 2003. Kristof was mistaken: Chrétien's director of communications Françoise Ducros was in fact a spokes*woman!*

12. Ginger Thompson with Clifford Krauss, "Antiwar Fever Puts Mexico in a Quandary over Iraq Vote," *NYT*, 28 February 2003; Luis Rubio, "The Vote That Wasn't," *Hemisphere Focus* 11, no. 8 (28 March 2003); Elizabeth Bumiller, "U.S. Calls Decision by Hussein His 'Final Mistake'" *NYT*, 19 March 2003.

13. Chrétien quoted in *Globe*, 21 March 2003.

14. Bernard Simon, "Trade Concerns as Canada Sits Out War," *NYT*, 1 April 2003; "Canada Will Help Rebuild Iraq," *Globe*, 10 April 2003; Donald Barry, "Chrétien, Bush, and the War in Iraq," *ARCS* 35, no. 2 (Summer 2005): 229–31; John Ward, Canadian Press, 14 April 2003.

15. Barry, "Chrétien, Bush, and the War in Iraq," 215–16; Benedict Anderson, *Imagined Communities: Reflections on the Origins and Spread of Nationalism*, rev. ed. (London, 1991); 60 percent of Canadians interviewed in a Pew Foundation study attributed their negative feelings about the United States to President George W. Bush. The Pew Research Center poll, May 2003; Jacqueline Swartz, "Toronto the Intolerant," *Toronto Star*, 15 October 2003.

16. Clifford Krauss, "In Antiterror Effort, Canada's Authorities Use Surveillance More Than Arrests," *NYT*, 13 March 2003; Bill O'Reilly, "Canada Shows Its True Colors," Fox News, 12 September 2002; *National Review*, 25 November 2002.

17. Pauline M. Vaillancourt Rosenau, "U.S. Newspaper Coverage of the Canadian Health System: A Case of Seriously Mistaken Identity?" *ARCS* 36,

no. 1 (Spring 2006): 27–58; "Is Canada the Best Way to Cut Your Drug Bill?" *AARP Bulletin*, April 2003; as a measure of the significance of the prescription drugs importation issue, see the *NYT* coverage on 18 March, 4 June, 7 August, and 10 September 2003.

18. Clifford Krauss, "Canada Parts with U.S. on Drugs Policies," *NYT*, 18 May 2003; "Drug Users' Center Opens," *NYT*, 16 September 2003; "CANADA: Premier May Try Marijuana," *NYT*, 10 April 2003; John P. Walters, the White House national drug control policy director, made the comments.

19. Christopher Marquis, "U.S. Gays Who Marry in Canada Face Hurdles," *NYT*, 19 June 2003; State of the Union Address, 2 February 2005, located at http://www.whitehouse.gov/news/releases/2005/02/20050202-11.html (accessed 23 March 2007).

20. *Wait, Wait, Don't Tell Me!* broadcast on National Public Radio, 27 September 2003.

21. Michael Adams, *Fire and Ice: The US, Canada and the Myth of Converging Values* (Toronto, 2003); polls cited in Munroe Eagles, "Canadian-American Relations in a Turbulent Era," *PS: Political Science and Politics* 37, no. 4 (October 2006), PSOnline, http://www.apsanet.org (accessed 23 March 2007). Adams's methodology in *Fire and Ice* has, however, been criticized. Even sociologist Joel Smith, who agrees that Adams's "position is perfectly plausible," and who concurs that "Americans and Canadians probably have been drifting in different directions," has nonetheless concluded that "the book fails to meet the standards of acceptable social science." Smith, review of *Fire and Ice* in *ARCS* 35, no. 1 (Spring 2005): 157–60.

22. David Frum, "Woe, Canada," *NYT*, 19 April 2005; Siri Agrell, "A 40-Year Wait for Wedded Bliss," *Globe*, 31 May 2007; Tim Harper, "More Americans Heading North," *Toronto Star*, 6 August 2007.

23. For Parrish's expulsion from caucus see http://www.cbc.ca/news/story/2003/02/26 and also CBC News Online, 18 November 2004 (accessed 19 March 2007). As examples of the many advocates of Canadian policy rapprochement with the United States, see two lectures at the C. D. Howe Institute: Jack Granatstein, "The Importance of Being Less Earnest: Promoting Canada's National Interests through Tighter Ties with the U.S.," delivered 21 October 2003; and Alan Gotlieb, "Romanticism and Realism in Canada's Foreign Policy," 3 November 2004. Kim Nossal made a similar argument to the Canadian Defence and Foreign Affairs Institute in "'The World We Want?' The Purposeful Confusion of Values, Goals, and

Interests in Canadian Foreign Policy," http://www.cdfai.org/PDF/The%20
World%20We%20Want.pdf (accessed 20 November 2007); Thomas Axworthy (once Pierre Trudeau's principal secretary) made the case in "An Independent Canada in a Shared North America: Must We Be in Love or Will
an Arranged Marriage Do?" *International Journal* 59, no. 4 (2004): 761–82.

24. Dana Milbank, *Washington Post*, 2 December 2004; Clifford Krauss, "Bush
Leaves Canada's Leader with Missile Defense Dilemma," *NYT*, 4 December 2004; Dwight N. Mason, *A Flight from Responsibility: Canada and Missile
Defense of North America* (Washington, D.C., 2005); Decima poll reported in
Alexander Panetta, "Martin Move on Missiles Politically Correct," *Globe*,
22 March 2005; Clifford Krauss, "Canada Says It Won't Join Missile Shield
with the U.S.," *NYT*, 24 February 2005.

25. Office of the Press Secretary, the White House, 31 March 2006, http://
www.spp.gov/security_agenda (accessed 9 October 2007); on SPP Working
Groups, see http://www.spp.gov/prosperity_working (accessed 19 February 2007). See also U.S. Department of Homeland Security, Implementation Report, 27 June 2005; Andres Rosenthal, "The Security and Prosperity
Partnership: An Overview," *International Journal* 61, no. 3 (Summer 2006),
541–45.

26. Martin's statement at http://www.qwhitehouse.gov/news/releases/2005/
03/ (accessed 19 February 2007); Canada, *Canada's International Policy Statement: A Role of Pride and Influence in the World* (Ottawa, 2005).

27. Rob Krott, "Canadian Snipers in Afghanistan," *Soldier of Fortune*, August
2002, 36–39, 77; McCallum, Address to the Royal Institute of International
Affairs, 3 December 2003, http://www.mdn.ca/site/Newsroom (accessed
April 2007).

28. Brian Laghi, "Canada-U.S. Relations: Martin Charts New Course with
U.S.," *Globe*, 16 December 2005.

29. Keith McArthur, "Tories Unveil Scathing New Television Ad," and Roy
McGregor, "As Election Gets Serious, Clothes That Talk Back," both in
Globe, 3 January 2006; Clifford Krauss, "Liberals' TV Ads Bring Some Heat
to Canada's Election Campaign," *NYT*, 12 January 2006.

30. "What Stephen Harper's Victory Really Means for Canada," *Time*, Canadian ed., 6 February 2006; Eagles, "Canadian-American Relations";
Blanchard quoted in Clifford Krauss, "Canada's Shift: To the Right, Gently," *NYT*, 25 January 2006.

31. Wilkins continues, of course, to proclaim the U.S. position, as he did in
February 2007 at the University of Calgary, in an exchange with Dr. Da-

vid Bercuson, director, Centre for Military and Strategic Studies; Harper quoted in *Time*, "What Harper's Victory Really Means," 6 February 2006; Donald McRae, "Arctic Sovereignty: What Is at Stake?" *Behind the Headlines* 64, no. 1 (2007): 12, 14, 15.

32. "Reclaiming Canada's Role as a World Player," *Globe*, 22 September 2006; "Canada Steps Up Fight for the Arctic," *Globe*, 10 August 2007; J. L. Granatstein, "Give O'Connor Credit Where Credit Is Due," *Globe*, 16 August 2007; "To Patrol the North," congressional report cited in *Globe*, 11 July 2007; "The Great Arctic Oil Rush," *NYT*, 12 August 2007; "The U.S. Interest in Canada's Claim," *Globe*, 22 August 2007.

33. News release, 12 May 2006, Foreign Affairs and International Trade Canada, http://wo1.international.gc.ca/MinPub/Publication.aspx?isRedirect=True&Language=E&publication_id=383973 (accessed 1 March 2007); Joseph T. Jockel and Joel J. Sokolsky, "Renewing NORAD—Now If Not Forever," *Policy Options* (July–August 2006): 53–58; J. L. Granatstein, "New Zealand's Lessons for the Canadian Military," *Globe*, 24 July 2007; Clinton quoted in Dean Bennett, "Clinton Thanks Canada for Afghanistan Military Commitment," *Globe*, 10 March 2006, and Rumsfeld quoted in Alan Freeman, "Rumsfeld's Praise," 28 July 2006; Rice interview with Michael Tutton of Canadian Press, 12 September 2006; Decima poll quoted in "MacKay Dismisses Poll Indicating Afghan Mission Lost Cause," *Globe*, 3 October 2006; Christopher Mason, "Canadian Vote Defeats Proposal for Leaving Afghanistan," *NYT*, 25 April 2007.

34. Michael John Garcia, legislative attorney, American Law Division, Congressional Research Service, "Renditions: Constraints Imposed by Laws on Torture," 5 April 2006; Scott Shane, "Torture Victim Had No Terror Link," *NYT*, 25 September 2006; U.S. Department of State, Remarks with Canadian Foreign Minister Peter MacKay, 21 December 2006, http://www.state.gov/secretary (accessed 19 February 2007).

35. U.S. Department of State, Western Hemisphere Overview, http://www.state.gov/documents/organization (accessed 19 February 2007); Paul Koring, "Ottawa Failed Khadr, Lawyer Says," *Globe*, 21 February 2007; William Glaberson, "Judge Throws Out Charges in Guantánamo Prisoner Case," *NYT*, 4 June 2007; "To Release Khadr from Guantánamo," *Globe*, 21 August 2007.

36. *9/11 Commission Report*, 81, 176–78, 182, 187.

37. "Fire on the Water," *NYT*, 21 October 2006; Deirdre McNamer, "Montana's Terror Economy," *NYT*, 5 August 2007; *9/11 Commission Report*, 81, 176–78,

182, 187; Canadian Press, "Harper Tells U.S. Audience 'Canada Is Back,'" *Globe*, 20 September 2006.

38. Tim Weiner, Elizabeth Becker, and Clifford Krauss, "Free Trade Accord at 10: Growing Pains Are Clear," *NYT*, 27 December 2003.

39. Gordon Ritchie, "Ripping the Heart out of NAFTA," *Globe*, 29 September 2005; Dawn Walton, "U.S. Backs Away from Lifting Ban on Canadian Beef," *Globe*, 29 July 2006; Kate O'Neill, "Two Cows Make a Crisis: U.S.-Canada Trade Relations and Mad Cow Disease," *ARCS* 35, no. 2 (Summer 2005): 295–319; Michael Hart, "Don't Let the Border Get in Trade's Way," *Globe*, 23 August 2007.

40. Clifford Krauss, "Canada Warns That U.S. Tariffs on Lumber Could Imperil U.S. Access to Oil," *NYT*, 12 October 2005; 1 July 2006, http://pm.gc .ca/eng/media (accessed 19 February 2007); Emerson to Schwab, undated, http://www.dfait-maeci.gc.ca/eicb/softwood (accessed 19 February 2007); Office of the United States Trade Representative, "U.S, Canada Reach Final Agreement on Lumber Dispute," 1 July 2007, http://ustr.gov (accessed 15 March 2007); CBC News Online, "In Depth: Softwood Lumber Dispute," 27 April 2006, http://www.cbc.ca/news/background (accessed 13 March 2007); news release, 14 December 2006, Foreign Affairs and International Trade Canada, http://wo1.international.gc.ca (accessed 19 February 2007).

41. "United States–Canada Relations: Trade," http://canada.usembassy.gov (accessed 5 April 2007).

Epilogue: "Plus ça change . . . "

1. Alan Freeman, "PM Sells Canada as Third Economic Option," *Globe*, 18 July 2007; "Harper Steps Out," *Economist*, 14–20 July 2007, 41–42; cartoon in *Globe*, 19 July 2007.

2. For DFI figures see U.S. Department of State, "Background Note: Canada," http://www.state.gov/r/pa/ei/bgn/2089.htm (accessed 20 November 2007); Clinton quoted in Dean Bennett, "Clinton Thanks Canada for Afghanistan Military Commitment," *Globe*, 10 March 2006.

3. Obama was quoted more widely in Canada than he was in the United States, as, for example, in Neil Reynolds, "U.S. Protectionists 14; Free Traders 3," *Globe*, 29 August 2007; Heather Mallick, "Americans: Hate 'em or Hate 'em," *Globe*, 11 September 1999.

4. Robin Winks, "Imagining Canada," in *Northern Exposures: Scholarship on*

Canada in the United States, ed. Karen Gould, Joseph T. Jockel, and William Metcalfe (Washington, D.C., 1993), 15.

5. Laura B. Stephenson, Thomas J. Scotto, and Allan Kornberg, "Slip, Sliding Away or *le plus ça change:* Canadian and American Partisanship in Comparative Perspective," *ARCS* 34, no. 2 (Summer 2004): 283–312; Mildred A. Schwartz, *Party Movements in the United States and Canada* (New York: 2006), 204–8; Samuel P. Huntington, "The Hispanic Challenge," *Foreign Policy,* March–April 2004, 30–45.

6. Charles F. Doran, "Will Canada Unravel?" *Foreign Affairs* 75, no. 5 (1996): 108–9; in 2007 the Parti Québécois received its lowest level of support since 1973, but the federalist Liberal Party won a plurality with the smallest popular vote of any party in Quebec's political history.

7. Former ambassador Richard Holbrooke told Stephen J. Randall in March 2007 that when he and his colleagues in the State Department originally broached the idea of shifting Canada from the European division to the Western Hemisphere, the objections came not from U.S. but from Canadian Europhiles; John H. Redekop, "A Reinterpretation of Canadian-American Relations," *Canadian Journal of Political Science* 9, no. 2 (1976): 227–43.

8. *Western Wheel* quoted in John Herd Thompson, "Taking Care of Business: Chrétien and the Americans," *Canada Watch* 9, no. 3&4 (February 2004): 8–9; Ronald Inglehart, Miguel Basanez, and Neil Nevitte offer the strongest argument for convergence in *North American Trajectory,* and the strongest case for divergence is Michael Adams, *Fire and Ice;* Edward Grabb and James Curtis propose a more nuanced argument in *Regions Apart: The Four Societies of Canada and the United States* (Don Mills, Ont., 2004).

Bibliographical Essay

The endnotes to *Canada and the United States: Ambivalent Allies* provide the reader with the sources for specific references in the text, in particular to the archival and government sources that have been used in preparing the four editions of this book. This bibliographical essay will guide those who wish to read more widely on a particular aspect of U.S.-Canadian relations. It is not all encompassing and includes neither M.A. and doctoral theses nor all relevant academic periodical literature.

There is a wide range of general studies of U.S.-Canadian relations, of U.S. and Canadian foreign policy, and of the social, political, and economic relationships discussed in this volume. On the U.S. side, there is no substitute for Thomas G. Paterson, J. Garry Clifford, and Kenneth T. Hagan's *American Foreign Policy: A History* (3rd ed., 1988). The Paterson volume is balanced but inclined toward revisionist scholarship. For a different perspective, consult Norman Graebner's realist interpretations of U.S. diplomacy or Alexander DeConde's *History of American Foreign Relations* (1971). The theoretical underpinnings of this volume, in particular the world systems model, are explored in Michael J. Hogan and Thomas G. Paterson, eds., *Explaining the History of American Foreign Relations* (1991). On world systems analysis, we draw from Immanuel Wallerstein's *The Modern World System* (1974) and *The Capitalist World Economy* (1979), as well as from Terrence Hopkins's *World-Systems Analysis: Theory and Methodology* (1982). More specialized are the volumes in the *American Secretaries of State and Their Diplomacy* series, which began in 1928 under the editorship of Samuel Flagg Bemis and continued under Robert H. Ferrell. Frank Merli and Theodore Wilson, eds., provide a brief interpretive approach to the same subject in *Makers of American Diplomacy* (1974). All students of U.S. foreign policy rely on the documents contained in the Department of State's *Foreign Relations of the United States*, published in annual volumes since the late nineteenth century and now complete into the 1960s. This can be supplemented with the considerably less useful Department of State *Bulletin* and with the *Documents on American Foreign Relations, 1938–1970* (1939–73), published by the Council on Foreign Relations.

The most useful general study of Canadian foreign policy remains C. P. Stacey's two-volume *Canada and the Age of Conflict: A History of Canadian External Policies* (vol. 1, *1867–1921* [1979]; vol. 2, *The Mackenzie King Era, 1921–1948* [1981]), which is impeccably researched, written, and argued. G. P. deT. Glazebrook's *A History of Canadian External Relations* (2 vols., 1950; rpt., 1966) is dated. The five volumes of James Eayrs's thoughtful series *In Defence of Canada* (1964–83) examine Canadian policy from the 1920s to the 1960s. For the period since World War II, general studies include Dale Thomson and Roger Swanson's *Canadian Foreign Policy: Options and Perspectives* (1971) and Peyton Lyon's *Canada in World Affairs* (vol. 12, *1961–1963* [1968]), which is part of the valuable series on Canada in world affairs. The *Canada among Nations* series (1984–2006), produced annually by Carleton University's Norman Patterson School of International Affairs and published by McGill-Queen's Press, remains the most important source until archival materials eventually open to researchers. The Canadian equivalent to the *Foreign Relations of the United States* volumes are the *Documents on Canadian External Relations*, published by the Department of External Affairs, but like the *FRUS* series, *DCER* stops well short of the contemporary period. Those wishing more documentary material on recent Canadian foreign policy should consult the *Annual Review* of the Department of External Affairs, the title of which has varied but nonetheless carries into the 1980s. The *International Journal*, published by the Canadian Institute for International Affairs, is valuable for specialist and generalist alike.

Studies of Canada's relationship with the United States dominate scholarship on Canadian foreign policy, but few historians of U.S. foreign policy specialize in the field. An important exception in this regard is Gordon Stewart's "A Special Contiguous Country Economic Regime: An Overview of America's Canada Policy," *Diplomatic History* 6, no. 4 (1982), and his book *The American Response to Canada since 1776* (1992). Britain's role in U.S.-Canadian relations forms the central theme of John Bartlett Brebner's classic *The North Atlantic Triangle* (1945) and J. L. Finlay's *Canada in the North Atlantic Triangle* (1975). Kenneth Curtis and John Carroll focus on more contemporary issues in *Canadian-American Relations: The Promise and the Challenge* (1983), as does author/diplomat John Holmes in *Life with Uncle: The Canadian-American Relationship* (1981). Two volumes that collect primary and secondary materials for classroom purposes are still useful: Richard Bowles, James Hanley, Bruce Hodgins, and George Rawlyk's *Canada and the U.S.: Continental Partners or Wary Neighbours?* (1973) and Norman Hillmer's *Partners Nevertheless: Canadian-American Relations in the*

Twentieth Century (1989). The best general interpretive study is J. L. Granatstein and Norman Hillmer's engaging *For Better or for Worse: Canada and the United States to the 1990s* (1991). Edelgard Mahant and Graeme Mount provide a synthesis in *An Introduction to Canadian-American Relations* (2nd ed., 1989). Robert Bothwell's study of the post-1945 years, *Canada and the United States: The Politics of Partnership* (1991), combines outstanding synthesis with strongly expressed opinions. John Sigler and Charles Doran, eds., *Canada and the United States: Enduring Friendship, Persistent Stress* (1985) and Doran's *Forgotten Partnership: U.S.-Canada Relations Today* (1984) provide insights into the more recent relationship. The most recent general study reached us as this book was going to press. In *Dispersed Relations: Americans and Canadians in Upper North America* (2007), Reginald C. Stuart stresses the interdependence of Canadians and Americans.

U.S.-British North American relations from the American Revolution to 1871 are thoughtfully described in Reginald C. Stuart's *United States Expansionism and British North America, 1775–1871* (1988). Gerald M. Craig's 1968 study of the eighteenth and nineteenth centuries in *The United States and Canada* remains valuable, as does the first edition of H. L. Keenleyside's *Canada and the United States* (1929). Sidney F. Wise and Robert Craig Brown's *Canada Views the United States: Nineteenth-Century Political Attitudes* (1967) traces Canada's attitudes to the United States back to their ideological roots. Jane Errington's *The Lion, the Eagle, and Upper Canada: A Developing Colonial Ideology* (1987) and David Mills's *The Idea of Loyalty in Upper Canada, 1784–1850* (1988) offer differing interpretations of the role of the United States in an emerging Canadian national identity.

The years from the American Revolution through the War of 1812 have attracted considerable scholarly interest. George Rawlyk's collection of contemporary documents and later historical accounts in *Revolution Rejected, 1775–1776* (1968) is invaluable, as is his *Nova Scotia's Massachusetts: A Study of Massachusetts–Nova Scotia Relations, 1680–1784* (1973). But Elizabeth Mancke's *The Fault Lines of Empire: Political Differentiation in Massachusetts and Nova Scotia, ca. 1760–1830* (2005) finds institutional sources of difference well before the Revolution. William H. Nelson provides the analysis of the Tory experience in the Revolutionary era on which this study relies in *The American Tory* (1960). Among the many important analyses of the Loyalist/Tory migration and adaptation to what remained of British North America are Wallace Brown's *The Good Americans: The Loyalists in the American Revolution* (1969), Leslie Upton's

The United Empire Loyalists: Men and Myths (1967), Robert Calhoon's *The Loyalists in Revolutionary America* (1973), and Neil MacKinnon's *This Unfriendly Soil: The Loyalist Experience in Nova Scotia* (1986). Simon Schama sets black loyalists in an Atlantic context in *Rough Crossings: Britain, the Slaves, and the American Revolution* (2006). Copious histories consider the War of 1812. Pierre Berton's *The Invasion of Canada* (1980) and *Flames across the Border* (1981) are popular accounts from a Canadian nationalist perspective; A. J. Langguth, *Union 1812: The Americans Who Fought the Second War of Independence,* and Walter R. Borneman, *1812: The War That Forged a Nation* (both 2006) do the same from the American perspective. George Stanley's *The War of 1812: Land Operations* (1983) and William Dudley, ed., *The Naval War of 1812: A Documentary History* (1985) are scholarly histories. Kenneth Bourne's *Britain and the Balance of Power in North America, 1815–1908* (1967) examines the century in meticulous detail. Students seeking a short overview might consult C. P. Stacey's brief Canadian Historical Association booklet, *The Undefended Border: The Myth and the Reality* (1962).

The years of manifest destiny, westward expansion, and continentalism have evoked passionate interest among historians. Reginald C. Stuart's *United States Expansionism and British North America,* mentioned above, is best on the U.S.-Canadian relationship, but readers should also be aware of important studies of American expansionism in which Canada receives little direct attention. These include William H. Goetzmann's *Exploration and Empire: The Explorer and the Scientist in the Winning of the American West* (1966) and Michael Hunt's study of American ideology in these years, *Ideology and U.S. Foreign Policy* (1987). Anglo-American rivalry on the Pacific coast receives its due in Frederick Merk's *The Oregon Question: Essays in Anglo-American Diplomacy and Politics* (1967), as well as in his *Manifest Destiny and Mission in American History.* The continentalist theme is explored in Donald F. Warner's *The Idea of Continental Union: Agitation for the Annexation of Canada to the United States, 1849–1893* (1960). More general but thorough is Lester B. Shippee's *Canadian-American Relations, 1849–1874* (1939).

Cross-border intellectual, political, and economic issues during the late Jacksonian era and the rebellions in Upper and Lower Canada are treated in a wide range of sources. Wilson Shortridge provides an early account in "The Canadian-American Frontier during the Rebellion of 1837–1838," *Canadian Historical Review* 7 (1926); more recent is Gerald M. Craig's "The American Impact on the Upper Canadian Reform Movement before 1837," *Canadian Historical*

Review 29, no. 4 (1948); more narrowly focused is Colin Read's study *The Rising in Western Upper Canada, 1837–38: The Buncombe Revolt and After* (1982). Important work on the debate over American cultural influences include Susan Houston, "Politics, Schools, and Social Change in Upper Canada," *Canadian Historical Review* 53, no. 2 (1972); and Bruce Curtis, "Schoolbooks and the Myth of Curricular Republicanism: The State and the Curriculum in Canada West, 1820–1850," *Histoire Sociale/Social History* 16 (1983). The economic dimension is explored by Arthur M. Lower et al., *The North American Assault on the Canadian Forest: A History of the Lumber Trade between Canada and the United States* (1938). On reciprocity, one must still consult D. C. Masters, *The Reciprocity Treaty of 1854* (1937); Lawrence Officer and Lawrence Smith, "The Canadian-American Reciprocity Treaty of 1855 to 1866," *Journal of Economic History* 30, no. 2 (1970); and Graeme S. Mount, "Maine and the End of Reciprocity in 1866," *Maine Historical Society Quarterly* 26, no. 1 (1986). Western contacts are thoroughly treated by George F. G. Stanley's *The Birth of Western Canada* (1936) and *Louis Riel* (1963).

The standard accounts of the impact of the American Civil War on the trilateral relationship remain Robin Winks's *Canada and the United States: The Civil War Years* (1960) and the two volumes by Brian Jenkins, *Britain and the War for the Union* (1974, 1980); Winks's study *The Blacks in Canada* (1971; 2nd ed., 2000) is also important for the Civil War years and before, as is the collection *The Black Abolitionist Papers*, volume 2, *Canada 1830–1865* (1986). Karolyn Smardz Frost, *I've Got a Home in Glory Land: A Lost Tale of the Underground Railroad* (2007) uses one fugitive family's experience to bring a larger story to life. More general studies of the period include David P. Crook's *Diplomacy during the American Civil War* (1975) and *The North, the South and the Powers, 1861–1865* (1964). John A. Williams's "Canada and the Civil War," in Harold Hyman, ed., *Heard round the World* (1969), recognizes the critical importance of the war to Canada. Two works on the Trent Affair warrant attention: Norman B. Ferris's *The Trent Affair* (1977) and Gordon Warren's *Fountain of Discontent: The Trent Affair and Freedom of the Seas* (1981). The Fenians receive their due and more in Hereward Senior's *The Fenians and Canada* (1978) and Charles Stacey's "Fenianism and the Rise of National Feeling in Canada at the Time of Confederation," *Canadian Historical Review* 12, no. 3 (1931). Like many Canadian historians, they and others underline the importance of fear of U.S. aggression as a stimulus to British North American confederation to form the Dominion of Canada. See in this connection Donald Creighton's classic *The Road to Confederation* (1964) and C. P.

Stacey's "Britain's Withdrawal from North America, 1864–1871," *Canadian Historical Review* 36, no. 3 (1955), which emphasizes Canadian vulnerability during and after the Civil War. The Treaty of Washington in the aftermath of the Civil War is the focus of an analysis by late nineteenth-century continentalist Goldwin Smith [Jr.], *The Treaty of Washington, 1871: A Study in Imperial History* (1941). Also useful for this topic and period are Donald Creighton's biography of John A. Macdonald, *The Old Chieftain* (1955), and Allan Nevins's biography of Grant's secretary of state, *Hamilton Fish: The Inner History of the Grant Administration* (1936). Lawrence Martin's useful *The Presidents and the Prime Ministers: The Myth of Bilateral Bliss, 1867–1982* (1982) is well written and provides many exciting leads but is unfortunately scantily documented.

In the period from the Treaty of Washington to the Alaska boundary dispute of 1903, the United States emerged as a major world player, and Great Britain turned its attention away from the Western Hemisphere. Walter LaFeber's *The New Empire: An Interpretation of American Expansion, 1860–1898* (1963) has the best discussion of Canada's place in American policy during the period when the United States changed (in James G. Blaine's words) from "annexation of territory" to "annexation of trade." A. K. Weinberg's *Manifest Destiny: A Study of Nationalist Expansionism in American History* (1935) stretches from the eighteenth to the twentieth century and has much discussion of Canada. Several other authors provide the important context in which American policy toward Canada was formulated; among such studies are William A. Williams's *The Roots of the Modern American Empire* (1969) and Mira Wilkins's *The Emergence of Multinational Enterprise: American Business Abroad from the Colonial Era to 1914* (1970). Very useful for trade policy is Tom Terill's *The Tariff, Politics, and American Foreign Policy, 1874–1901* (1973). The transformation of Anglo-American relations, which so affected Canada, is skillfully traced in Kenneth Bourne's *Britain and the Balance of Power in North America, 1815–1908* (1967) and Charles S. Campbell's *From Revolution to Rapprochement: The United States and Great Britain, 1783–1900* (1974).

Continued cross-border contacts are discussed by Alvin C. Gluek Jr. in *Minnesota and the Manifest Destiny of the Canadian Northwest* (1965) and brilliantly analyzed in Douglas Owram's *The Promise of Eden: The Canadian Expansionist Movement and the Idea of the West, 1856–1900* (1980; rpt., 1992). Three well-done comparative studies look at U.S. and Canadian relationships with Native North Americans: Roger L. Nichols, *Indians in the United States and Canada: A Comparative History* (1998); Jill St. Germain, *Indian Treaty-Making Policy in the*

United States and Canada, 1867–1877 (2001); Hana Samek's *The Blackfoot Confederacy, 1880–1929: A Comparative Study of Canadian and U.S. Indian Policy* (1987). Joseph Manzione's *"I Am Looking to the North for My Life": Sitting Bull, 1876–1881* (1991) narrates the flight of Sitting Bull and the Sioux into Canada. Beth LaDow, *The Medicine Line: Life and Death on a North American Borderland* (2001) and Sheila McManus, *The Line Which Separates: Race, Gender, and the Making of the Alberta-Montana Borderlands* (2005) set boundary making into a broad social history context. The National Policy's role in the construction of a Canadian national consciousness is ably analyzed in Robert Craig Brown's *Canada's National Policy: A Study in Canadian-American Relations, 1883–1900* (1964). Richard A. Preston provides a military dimension to the same process in *The Defense of the Undefended Border: Planning for War in North America, 1867–1939* (1977).

Many books treat migration to and between the United States and Canada. Walter Nugent's *Crossings: The Great Transatlantic Migrations, 1870–1914* (1992) provides a thoughtful comparative overview of European migration to Canada and to the United States. Marcus Lee Hanson and John B. Brebner's *The Mingling of the Canadian and American Peoples* (1940) remains useful, but Randy William Widdis's *With Scarcely a Ripple: Anglo-Canadian Migration into the United States and Western Canada, 1880–1920* (1998) and the chapters in John J. Bukowczyk, Nora Faires, David R. Smith, and Randy William Widdis, *Permeable Border: The Great Lakes Basin as Transnational Region, 1650–1990* (2005), and in Bruno Ramirez, *Crossing the 49th Parallel: Migration from Canada to the United States, 1900–1930* (2001), are cutting-edge scholarship. *Permeable Border* has a comprehensive community-specific building tally. Much more has been written about French-Canadian migration to the United States: Yolande Lavoie's *Emigration des Canadiens aux Etats-Unis avant 1930* (1972), Bruno Ramirez's *On the Move: French-Canadian and Italian Migrants in the North Atlantic Economy* (1991), Gerard Brault's *The French-Canadian Heritage in New England* (1986), Yves Roby's *Les Franco-Americaines de la Nouvelle Angleterre, 1776–1930* (1990), and Tamara K. Hareven and Randolph Langenbach's *Amoskeag: Life and Work in an American Factory-City* (1978) all deserve mention.

The beginnings of the Canadian branch-plant economy with the migration of U.S. capital are traced in several texts: Hugh G. J. Aitken, *American Capital and Canadian Resources* (1961); Michael Bliss, *Northern Enterprise: Five Centuries of Canadian Business* (1987); Bliss, "Canadianizing American Business: The Roots of the Branch Plant," in Ian Lumsden, ed., *Close the 49th Parallel* (1970); Mira Wilkins, *The Emergence of Multinational Enterprise*, noted earlier; and

Scott Nearing and Joseph Freeman's Marxist analysis, *Dollar Diplomacy* (1925). H. V. Nelles's *The Politics of Development: Forests, Mines and Hydro-electric Power in Ontario, 1849–1941* (1974) is a splendid study of one province's development strategy vis-à-vis U.S. capital.

The debate over continentalism and imperialism on the Canadian side is considered in Carl Berger's *The Sense of Power: Studies in the Ideas of Canadian Imperialism 1869–1914* (1971). Norman Penlington examines Canadian external policy in the period of American expansionism in *Canada and Imperialism* (1965). The literature on the U.S. side of the debate over global expansion is very rich, although there is a striking lack of attention to turn-of-the-century views toward Canada. Bradford Perkins provides the larger context of Anglo-American relations during the Alaska boundary dispute in *The Great Rapprochement: England and the United States, 1895–1914* (1968). Norman Penlington's *The Alaska Boundary Dispute: A Critical Reappraisal* (1972) is the best study of the dispute, but Charles Tansill's *Canadian-American Relations, 1875–1911* (1943) remains useful. Edward P. Kohn, *This Kindred People: Canadian-American Relations and the Anglo-Saxon Ideal, 1895–1903* (2004) looks at Anglo-Saxon ideology as a transatlantic imperial discourse, and one of its most effusive proponents was President Theodore Roosevelt. The most useful studies of the foreign policies of Theodore Roosevelt include Howard K. Beale's *Theodore Roosevelt and the Rise of America to World Power* (1956), David H. Burton's *Theodore Roosevelt: Confident Imperialist* (1968), Frederick Marks's *Velvet on Iron: The Diplomacy of Theodore Roosevelt* (1979), and Raymond Esthus's *Theodore Roosevelt and the International Rivalries* (1970).

Volume 1 of Charles Stacey's *Canada and the Age of Conflict* mentioned earlier is the best survey of Canadian foreign policy in the early decades of the twentieth century. Volume 2, *The Mackenzie King Era, 1921–1948*, is essential for the years after World War I. The best sources for the study of U.S. foreign policy with relevance to Canadian-American relations in the period between the Alaska boundary dispute and the 1920s include works by Beale and Burton noted in the previous paragraph; the eight volumes of Elting R. Morison, ed., *The Letters of Theodore Roosevelt* (1951–54); Walter and Marie Scholes, *The Foreign Policies of the Taft Administration* (1970); and Ralph Minger, *William Howard Taft and United States Foreign Policy* (1975). The multivolume edition of Woodrow Wilson's letters and papers by Arthur Link is indispensable, as are several volumes by Link that focus on Wilson's career and diplomacy. See, for instance, *Wilson the Diplomatist* (1960); *Woodrow Wilson: Revolution, War, and Peace*

(1979); and Edward Buehrig, ed., *Woodrow Wilson's Foreign Policy in Perspective* (1957). Robert D. Cuff and J. L. Granatstein survey U.S.-Canadian relations in two world wars in *Canadian-American Relations in Wartime* (1975) and *War and Society in North America* (1971). For important specific topics in Canadian-American relations in these years see Robert Spencer, John Kirton, and Kim Richard Nossal, eds., *The International Joint Commission Seventy Years On* (1981); and Alvin C. Gluek, "The Invisible Revision of the Rush-Bagot Agreement, 1898–1914," *Canadian Historical Review* 60 (December 1979). Broader treatment of the environmental issue and the IJC is provided by John E. Carroll in *Environmental Diplomacy: An Examination and a Prospective of Canadian-U.S. Transboundary Environmental Relations* (1983). John D. Wirth's *Smelter Smoke in North America: The Politics of Transborder Pollution* (2000) is trilateral North American environmental history that sweeps across a century; would that it inspires other studies like it.

Post-1900 migration between the two countries is discussed by Harold Troper in *Only Farmers Need Apply*. Migration is only a sideshow for Pierre Berton in his study of the Klondike Gold Rush, *Klondike: The Life and Death of the Last Great Gold Rush* (1963). There are now two excellent studies of plains settlement in the United States and Canada. Royden Loewen's prize-winning *Family, Church, and Market: A Mennonite Community in the Old and the New Worlds, 1850–1930* (1993) is a brilliant study that compares Anabaptist migrants to Nebraska and Manitoba; John W. Bennett and Seena B. Kohl's *Settling the Canadian-American West, 1890–1915* (1995) starts with the assumption that the settlement process was essentially the same on both sides of the U.S.-Canadian border.

Canadian-U.S. commercial relations are the subject of a number of studies, including those that focus on the contentious election of 1911, such as Peter Neary, "Grey, Bryce, and the Settlement of Canadian-American Differences, 1905–1911," *Canadian Historical Review* 49, no. 4 (1968); L. Ethan Ellis, *Reciprocity 1911* (1939); Paul Stevens, ed., *The 1911 General Election* (1970); W. M. Baker, "A Case Study of Anti-Americanism in English-Speaking Canada: The Election Campaign of 1911," *Canadian Historical Review* 51, no. 4 (1970); and R. E. Hannigan, "Reciprocity 1911: Continentalism and American *Weltpolitik*," *Diplomatic History* 4, no. 1 (1980). Paul Wolman's *Most Favored Nation: The Republican Revisionists and U.S. Tariff Policy, 1897–1912* (1992) reinterprets the U.S. decision to seek reciprocity with Canada. J. L. Granatstein's *Yankee Go Home? Canadians and Anti-Americanism* (1996) is a comprehensive study of how the relationship with the United States has shaped the Canadian psyche; it offers insight on the Canadian perspective of virtually any aspect or period of the U.S.-Canadian relationship.

Binational labor and working-class history has been graced with suggestive studies by Robert H. Babcock, *Gompers in Canada: A Study in American Continentalism before the First World War* (1974), and Carlos Schwantes, *Radical Heritage: Labor, Socialism and Reform in Washington and British Columbia, 1885–1917* (1979), but the field cries out for more such comparative work.

Aspects of Canadian-U.S. relations in the aftermath of World War I and Versailles and the course of the 1920s are covered by a variety of authors, although there remains no thorough overview of the period except Stacey's general history of Canadian external relations. James Eayrs's *In Defence of Canada*, volume 1, *From the Great War to the Great Depression* (1964) was written before much of the archival record was available. On American statesmen in the 1920s, a good starting point would be Norman Graebner's essays on Secretaries of State Charles Evans Hughes, Frank Kellogg, and Henry Stimson in *An Uncertain Tradition* (1961). Dexter Perkins is most helpful on the most important secretary of state in the period in *Charles Evans Hughes and American Democratic Statesmanship* (1956). Robert Bothwell discusses early diplomatic relations in "Canadian Representation at Washington: A Study in Colonial Responsibility," *Canadian Historical Review* 53, no. 2 (1972), as do Richard Kottman in "Hoover and Canada: Diplomatic Appointments," *Canadian Historical Review* 51, no. 3 (1970), and a half-dozen other articles cited in our notes to chapter 4. John S. Galbraith treats the Canadian role in the breakdown of the Anglo-Japanese naval alliance in "The Imperial Conference of 1921 and the Washington Conference," *Canadian Historical Review* 29, no. 2 (1948).

Ian Drummond's *Imperial Economic Policy, 1917–1939* (1975) is useful for the international economic history of the 1920s. U.S. accounts of the 1920s, however, even of such major issues as international trade and investment, tend to ignore relations with Canada. The tariff receives attention from Richard N. Kottman in *Reciprocity and the North Atlantic Triangle, 1932–1938* (1968) and in the same author's "Herbert Hoover and the Smoot-Hawley Tariff: Canada, a Case Study," *Journal of American History* 50, no. 3 (1975). For a firsthand account of early diplomatic relations, see the memoir of William Phillips, *Ventures in Diplomacy* (1952), and the one by Canada's first minister in Washington, Vincent Massey, *What's Past Is Prologue* (1963). There is brief reference to Canada and oil resources in Stephen J. Randall's *United States Foreign Oil Policy* (1985);

Mira Wilkins treats Canadian developments in *The Maturing of Multinational Enterprise: American Business Abroad from 1914 to 1970* (1974). Joan Hoff Wilson's *American Business and Foreign Policy* (1971) is important for understanding American foreign economic policy in the 1920s, although it does not address relations with Canada. Especially important for its interpretation is Ellis Hawley, ed., *Herbert Hoover, Secretary of Commerce, 1921–1928* (1981). The development of the branch-plant automobile industry in Canada is the concern of Tom Traves in *The State and Enterprise: Canadian Manufacturers and the Federal Government, 1917–1931* (1979). David Massell's *Amassing Power: J. B. Duke and the Saguenay River, 1897–1927* (2000) looks in close detail at an American capitalist's investments in Canadian resources.

The 1920s were a decade of at least official Prohibition, a source of considerable traffic between Canada and the United States. That dimension is the subject of C. W. Hunt's *Booze, Boats and Billions* (1988) and·Richard Kottman's "Volstead Violated: Prohibition as a Factor in Canadian-American Relations," *Canadian Historical Review* 43, no. 2 (1962). In "Defining the 'Undefended': Canadians, Americans, and the Multiple Meanings of Border during Prohibition," *ARCS* 34, no.1 (2004): 3–32, Stephen T. Moore brings a new cultural perspective to the issue.

Mary Vipond documents Canadian concern about U.S. popular culture in "Canadian Nationalism and the Plight of Canadian Magazines in the 1920s," *Canadian Historical Review* 58, no. 1 (1977), a theme she pursues more fully in *The Mass Media in Canada* (1989) and for radio in *Listening In: The First Decade Canadian Broadcasting, 1922–1932* (1992). Peter Morris's *Embattled Shadows. A History of Canadian Cinema, 1895–1939* (1978) and Ian Jarvie's *Hollywood's Overseas Campaign: The North Atlantic Movie Trade, 1920–1950* (1992) offer very different explanations of U.S. dominance of Canadian movie screens. All of these things are considered in a wonderful Ph.D. dissertation that should have become a book, John Weaver's "Imperilled Dreams: Canadian Opposition to American Empire, 1918–1930" (Duke University, 1973). For a broader understanding of U.S. foreign policy and cultural expansion, see Emily Rosenberg's *Spreading the American Dream: American Economic and Cultural Expansion, 1890–1945* (1982); Rosenberg's near-exclusion of Canada is astonishing, given its primary importance as a consumer of "American dreams."

The abrupt transition from prosperity to depression and then world war in U.S. foreign policy and Canadian-American relations is discussed in several of the studies noted earlier including Kottman, Bothwell, Wilkins, and Stacey.

Historians of the Hoover presidency and foreign policy, Kottman excepted, pay much less attention to Canada than Hoover did: Robert H. Ferrell's *American Diplomacy in the Great Depression* (1957) and McGeorge Bundy and Henry Stimson's *On Active Service in Peace and War* (1948). An important biography of Hoover is Joan Hoff Wilson's *Herbert Hoover, Forgotten Progressive* (1975), as is Martin Fausfold's *The Presidency of Herbert C. Hoover* (1985).

The Franklin Roosevelt era continues to fascinate. The standard account of Roosevelt's foreign policy is Robert Dallek's *Franklin D. Roosevelt and American Foreign Policy, 1933–1945* (1979), although its strength lies in narrative rather than analysis. The older account by James McGregor Burns, *The Lion and the Fox* (1956), is still valuable, as are the multivolume biographies by Frank Friedel, *Franklin D. Roosevelt* (1953–73), and Arthur Schlesinger Jr., *The Age of Roosevelt* (1957–60). Although William Becker and Samuel Wells, eds., *Economics and World Power* (1984), neglects Canada, the book is important to an understanding of economic policy.

There is no standard account of Canadian-U.S. relations in the 1930s. The most perceptive one-volume study is C. P. Stacey's *Mackenzie King and the Atlantic Triangle* (1976), which should be read in conjunction with Stacey's larger study of Canadian foreign policy noted earlier. Robert Bothwell and Norman Hillmer, eds., have provided an excellent introduction to various facets of Canadian foreign policy prior to the onset of World War II in *The In-Between Time: Canadian External Policy in the 1930s* (1975). Canadian historians have given excellent attention to the trade and economic relationship with the United States in the 1930s, notably Ian Drummond and Norman Hillmer in their book *Negotiating Freer Trade: The United Kingdom, the United States, Canada and the Trade Agreements of 1938* (1989) and Marc Boucher in his extremely useful article "The Politics of Economic Depression: Canadian-American Relations in the Mid-1950s," *International Journal* 41 (Winter 1985–86). Galen Perras traces the evolution of a U.S.-Canadian defense partnership in *Franklin Roosevelt and the Origins of the Canadian-American Security Alliance, 1933–1945* (1998). Stacey provides a thorough account of Canadian wartime policies, including relations prior to Pearl Harbor, in *Arms, Men, and Governments: The War Policies of Canada, 1939–1945* (1970), and Stanley Dziuban focuses on the military aspects of Canadian-American cooperation in *Military Relations between the United States and Canada, 1939–1945* (1959).

Dziuban's study, combined with Stacey's study of the Mackenzie King era and Robert Dallek's work on Roosevelt foreign policy, provides a good understanding of the wartime relationship between the two North American countries. Valuable studies of the Roosevelt administration and World War II include Robert Divine's *Roosevelt and World War II* (1969), Gaddis Smith's *American Diplomacy and the Second World War* (1985), Stephen Ambrose's *The Supreme Commander* (1970), and James McGregor Burns's *The Soldier of Freedom* (1970). Cordell Hull's *Memoirs* (1948) has little insight for Canadian affairs. More useful personal accounts of the war and early cold war years by Americans are Adolph Berle's memoirs, *Navigating the Rapids* (1973), edited by Beatrice Bishop Berle and Travis Beale Jacobs, and Dean Acheson's *Present at the Creation* (1969). Given the importance of lend-lease in the Anglo-Canadian–U.S. economic relationship, see Warren F. Kimball's *The Most Unsordid Act: Lend-lease, 1939–41* (1969). David Reynolds's *The Creation of the Anglo-American Alliance, 1937–41* (1969) provides the major context in which Canada had to develop its relations with the United States.

Robert D. Cuff and J. L. Granatstein's *Canadian-American Relations in Wartime* (1975) is the only solid analysis of the economic impact of the war, and their *American Dollars, Canadian Prosperity: Canadian-American Economic Relations, 1945–1950* (1978) follows the discussion into the early cold war years. S. J. Randall's *United States Foreign Oil Policy* provides a brief discussion of the Canol oil project. Kenneth Coates, ed., *The Alaska Highway* (1985), and Coates and William Morrison's *The Alaska Highway in World War II: The U.S. Army of Occupation in Canada's Northwest* (1992) discuss the American wartime presence in the Canadian North. *The Mackenzie King Record*, in four volumes (1960–68), is drawn from King's diary and covers the years from 1939 through 1948. John Holmes effectively links war and postwar Canadian policy in his two-volume *The Shaping of Peace: Canada and the Search for World Order, 1943–1957* (1979, 1982). Robert Bothwell (with William Kilbourn), J. L. Granatstein, and David J. Bercuson provide biographical studies of three figures important to the development of Canadian defense, economic development, and statecraft in, respectively, *C. D. Howe: A Biography* (1979), *A Man of Influence: Norman A. Robertson and Canadian Statecraft* (1981), and *True Patriot: The Life of Brooke Claxton, 1898–1960* (1993). Danford Middlemiss's "Economic Defense Cooperation with the United States, 1940–1963," in Kim Richard Nossal, ed., *An Acceptance of Paradox: Essays in Honour of John Holmes* (1982), links the war and cold war years.

General Canadian accounts of the transition from war to cold war and into the 1950s include the several volumes in the *Canada in World Affairs* series.

The pertinent volumes for these years are Frederic Soward, *From Normandy to Paris, 1944–1946* (1950); Robert Spencer, *From UN to NATO, 1946–1949* (1967); and Donald Masters, *Canada in World Affairs, 1953–1955* (1959). James Eayrs has contributed *Growing Up Allied* (1980), volume 4 of *In Defence of Canada*; Denis Smith's *The Diplomacy of Fear: Canada and the Cold War, 1941–1948* (1988) and Lawrence Aronsen and Martin Kitchen's *The Origins of the Cold War in Comparative Perspective: American, British and Canadian Relations with the Soviet Union, 1941–48* (1988) also provide information on this subject.

John L. Gaddis provides the best postrevisionist overview of U.S. cold war policies in *The United States and the Origins of the Cold War, 1941–1947* (1972), and his more recent overview *The Cold War: A New History* (2006). Canadian official perspective on the cold war and after is provided by John A. Munro and Alex Inglis, eds., in *Mike: The Memoirs of the Right Honourable Lester B. Pearson* (1973), which covers the 1948–57 years, and by the Mackenzie King diaries noted earlier, whereas Harry Truman's insights are put forth in *Years of Trial and Hope, 1946–1952* (1956), volume 2 of his *Memoirs*. For the subsequent presidency, see Dwight Eisenhower's *The White House Years: Mandate for Change* (1963). On Eisenhower and Dulles, the better studies are by Stephen Ambrose, *Eisenhower the President* (1984); Ronald Pruessen, *John Foster Dulles* (1982), which deals with the pre–secretary of state period; and Townsend Hoopes, *The Devil and John Foster Dulles* (1973).

Lawrence Aronsen has contributed two important articles on cold war Canada: "Canada's Postwar Re-armament: Another Look at American Theories of the Military-Industrial Complex," Canadian Historical Association, *Historical Papers* (1981); and "Imperialism and Dependency: Some Reflections on Canadian-American Economic Relations, 1945–1957," *Bulletin of Canadian Studies* 4, no. 1 (1990). Two other important unpublished papers by Aronsen are "A Leading Arsenal of Democracy: American Re-Armament and the Continental Integration of the Canadian Aircraft Industry, 1948–1953" (1991); and "An Open Door to the North: The Liberal Government and the Expansion of American Foreign Investment, 1945–1953" (1991). Robert Cuff and J. L. Granatstein address similar issues of bilateral free trade possibilities in "The Rise and Fall of Canadian-American Free Trade," *Canadian Historical Review* 58 (December 1977). A major development in Canadian-U.S. economic relations, the St. Lawrence Seaway, is discussed by William Willoughby in *The St. Lawrence Waterway: A Study in Politics and Diplomacy* (1961). The ongoing saga of the

Columbia River treaty in the 1950s is treated fully and fairly by Neal Swainson in *Conflict over Columbia: The Canadian Background to an Historic Treaty* (1979). Joseph Jockel explains the origins of NORAD in *No Boundaries Upstairs: Canada, the United States and the Origins of North American Air Defence, 1945–1958* (1987), but William Willoughby's *Joint Organizations of Canada and the United States* (1979) is also worth consulting.

The sensitive issues of espionage, Communist subversion, and anticommunism are discussed in Robert Bothwell and J. L. Granatstein, eds., *The Gouzenko Transcripts: The Evidence Presented to the Kellogg-Taschereau Royal Commission of 1946* (1982), and in Reg Whitaker and Gary Marcuse, *Cold War Canada: The Making of a National Insecurity State, 1945–1957* (1994). Richard Freeland's *The Truman Doctrine and the Origins of McCarthyism* (1971) analyzes the important relationship between domestic anticommunism and cold war foreign policies, which contributed to the significance of the Gouzenko affair in U.S.-Canadian relations. For the Marshall Plan and NATO, see Timothy P. Ireland's *Creating the Entangling Alliance* (1981), Lawrence Kaplan's *The United States and NATO* (1984), Escott Reid's *Time of Fear and Hope: The Making of the North Atlantic Treaty, 1947–1949* (1977) and *Radical Mandarin: The Memoirs of Escott Reid* (1989), Michael Hogan's *The Marshall Plan* (1987), and Immanuel Wexler's *The Marshall Plan Revisited* (1983).

On Korea, the standard Canadian account is Denis Stairs's *The Diplomacy of Constraint: Canada, the Korean War and the United States* (1974), which states its thesis in its title. Robert S. Prince casts serious doubt on the sincerity and effectiveness of Canada's attempts at "constraint" in "The Limits of Constraint: Canadian-American Relations and the Korean War, 1950–51," *Journal of Canadian Studies* 27, no. 4 (1992–93). Edelgard Mahant and Graeme S. Mount's conclusion about Canada's influence on U.S. policy in Korea (and on other cold war issues) is expressed in the title of their book: *Invisible and Inaudible in Washington: American Policies toward Canada* (Vancouver, 1999).

On John Diefenbaker's foreign policy, see Basil Robinson's *Diefenbaker's World: A Populist in Politics* (1989); Diefenbaker's somewhat unreliable memoirs, *One Canada: The Memoirs of the Right Honourable John G. Diefenbaker* (1976); and Knowlton Nash's *Diefenbaker and Kennedy: Fear and Loathing across the Undefended Border* (1990). J. L. Granatstein provides the best account of the implications for Canada of the Cuban missile crisis in "When Push Came to Shove," in Thomas Paterson, ed., *Kennedy's Quest for Victory* (1989). The best insider's account from a U.S. perspective is Robert Kennedy's *Thirteen Days: A Memoir of the Cuban Missile Crisis* (1969); Canada again is absent from the crisis. Two recent studies of the 1950s and 1960s have added insight to our understanding of bilateral relations in the cold war years: Bruce Muirhead, *Dancing around the Elephant: Creating a Prosperous Canada in an era of American Dominance, 1957–1973* (2005), and Greg Donaghy, *Tolerant Allies: Canada and the United States 1963–1968* (2002).

John English's fine two-volume *Life of Lester Pearson* (1989, 1992) has importance for the U.S.-Canadian relationship from the 1920s until his prime ministership in the 1960s. Pearson himself provides a useful account of his views on Vietnam in volume 3 of his memoirs, as does Paul Martin in volume 2 of *A Very Public Life* (1983). The best secondary account of the Vietnam War and Canada is Douglas Ross's *In the Interests of Peace: Canada and Vietnam, 1954–1973* (1984), but one should also consult Peter Stursberg's *Lester Pearson and the American Dilemma* (1980), James Eayrs's *Indochina: Roots of Complicity* (1983), and Charles Taylor's polemic *Snowjob: Canada, the United States, and Vietnam* (1974). See also George C. Herring, ed., *The Secret Diplomacy of the Vietnam War: The Negotiating Volumes of the Pentagon Papers* (1983). James Keeley addresses another major development of the 1960s, the Autopact, in "Cast in Concrete for All Time? Negotiations of the Auto Pact," *Canadian Journal of Political Science* 16 (June 1983).

Robert Bothwell and J. L. Granatstein's *Pirouette: Pierre Trudeau and Canadian Foreign Policy* (1990) is a brilliant scholarly synthesis, well written and based on original research. Charles Doran's *Forgotten Partnership: U.S.-Canada Relations Today* (1984) remains useful. Stephen Clarkson provides a vigorous critique of U.S. policy toward the National Energy Policy and foreign investment controls in the final Trudeau government in *Canada and the Reagan Challenge: Crisis and Adjustment* (1982; rev. ed., 1985). See also Edward Wonder's "The U.S. Government Response to the Canadian National Energy Program," *Canadian Public Policy* 8 (1982), and a collection of essays edited by E. Erickson and Leonard Waverman, *The Energy Question: An International Failure of Policy* (1974). A more comprehensive study is Denis Stairs and Gil Winham, eds., *The Politics of Canada's Economic Relationship with the United States* (1985). A useful study of Canada's most influential economic nationalist is Denis Smith's *Gentle Patriot: A Political Biography of Walter Gordon* (1973). Richard Nixon provides no insights into his views of Canada during his troubled presidency, although Henry Kissinger, perhaps because of his own relationship with Pierre Trudeau, is more forthcoming in his memoirs; see *Years of Upheaval* (1982) and *The White House Years* (1979). On the early Reagan presidency, see Robert Dallek's *Ronald Reagan: The Politics of Symbolism* (1984) and David Schwartz's *NATO's Nuclear Dilemmas* (1983).

Unfairly overlooked in Canadian-U.S. relations and indeed in world affairs is the Jimmy Carter presidency. These years are given their due in Bothwell and Granatstein's *Pirouette*, noted earlier. Zbigniew Brzezinski's *Power and Principle* (1985) demonstrates in its neglect of Canadian affairs that the former secretary of state had transcended his Polish-Canadian background and his McGill University education.

Stephen Clarkson's study *Canada and the Reagan Challenge*, noted earlier, provides insights into the Pierre Trudeau–Brian Mulroney transition, as well as into Reagan's presidency. Michael Schaller's more recent study, *Right Turn: American Life in the Reagan-Bush Era, 1980–1992* (2006), provides excellent context for an understanding of the particular America with which Canada had to deal in those Republican years. The most useful collection of essays on Canadian policy in the same period is Nelson Michaud and Kim Nossal, eds., *Diplomatic Departures: The Conservative Era in Canadian Foreign Policy, 1984–1992* (2001).

Canadian ambassador Allan Gotlieb's memoirs of the 1981–89 years, *"I'll Be with You in a Minute, Mr. Ambassador". The Education of a Canadian Diplomat in Washington* (1991), is truly indispensable, given the recent nature of these events and the lack of solid historical evidence. The *Canada among Nations* series must suffice for the moment on the Canadian side for general accounts of the period. Among the best of those volumes are Maureen Molot and Brian Tomlin's compilation on 1985 (1986), and Fen Osler Hampson and Christopher Maule, eds., *Canada among Nations, 1990–91: After the Cold War* (1991). The emergence of trilateralism with Mexico is evident in Michael Hart's *A North American Free Trade Agreement: The Strategic Implications for Canada* (1990) and in the essays in Stephen J. Randall, Herman Konrad, and Sheldon Silverman, eds., *North America without Borders? Integrating Canada, the United States, and Mexico* (1992), and the subsequent volume, *NAFTA in Transition* (1995). For the negotiation of the Free Trade Agreement between Canada and the United States, see Bruce Doern and Brian Tomlin's *Faith and Fear* (1991) and Michael Hart et al., *Decision at Midnight: Inside the Canada-U.S. Free-Trade Negotiations* (1994). Other volumes by Hart are equally important for an understanding of the nature and evolution of Canadian trade policy: *Canadian Trade Policy from Colonialism to Globalism* (2002); *Common Borders, Shared Destinies: Canada, the United States and Deepening Integration* (2001). Marci McDonald's *Yankee Doodle Dandy: Brian Mulroney and the American Agenda* (1995) captures Canadian nationalist resentment of Mulroney's rapprochement with the United States.

On Canadian cultural nationalism, see Isaiah A. Litvak and Christopher J. Maule, *Cultural Sovereignty: The* Time *and* Reader's Digest *Case in Canada* (1974); Janice L. Murray, ed., *Canadian Cultural Nationalism* (1977); Paul Audley, *Canada's Cultural Industries: Broadcasting, Publishing, Records and Film* (1983); D. H. Flaherty, ed., *Southern Exposure: Canadian Perspectives on the United States* (1986); and David Flaherty and Frank E. Manning, eds., *The Beaver Bites Back? American Popular Culture in Canada* (1993). Richard Collins's *Culture, Communication and National Identity: The Case of Canadian Television* (1990) takes a skeptical look at the history of Canadian television policy, while Manjunath Pendakur does the same for Canadian feature film policy, albeit from a very different perspective, in *Canadian Dreams and American Control: The Political Economy of the Canadian Film Industry* (1990). The notes to John Herd Thompson's "Canada's Quest for Cultural Sovereignty: Promotion, Protection and Popular Culture" in Helen Holmes and David Taras's *Seeing Ourselves: Media Power and Policy in Canada* (1992) will provide references to other scholarly articles. Two recent studies of popular culture and demographics in the cold war years are especially noteworthy: Douglas Owram, *Born at the Right Time: A History of the Baby Boom Generation* (1990); and Reginald Stuart, *Dispersed Relations: Americans and Canadians in Upper North America* (2007). For the United States in these years, Ronald Reagan provides a rare presidential perspective on Canadian relations, brief as it may be, in *An American Life* (1990). On the contentious issue of the Strategic Defense Initiative (SDI), see Sidney Drell, ed., *The Reagan Strategic Defense Initiative* (1985). The almost consuming Reagan administration involvement in the Central American crisis and the Canadian position are outlined in Walter LaFeber's *Inevitable Revolutions: The United States in Central America* (1983). Liisa North's *Bitter Grounds: Roots of Revolt in El Salvador* (1981) contains an article by Tim Draimin that provides Canadian perspective: "Canadian Foreign Policy and El Salvador." For a more general analysis of the emergence of Canada as a factor in the inter-American system, see James Rochlin's *Canada as a Hemispheric Actor* (1992).

NAFTA and the developing trilateral U.S.-Canadian-Mexican relationship dominate scholarship on the 1990s. One of the most important assessments of NAFTA is Sidney Weintraub, ed., *NAFTA's Impact on North America: The First*

Decade (2004). Gustavo del Castillo and Gustavo Vega Cánovas's *The Politics of Free Trade in North America* (1995) considers the agreement in detail, while the essays in Stephen J. Randall and Herman W. Konrad's *NAFTA in Transition* (1995) look at social and cultural as well as economic implications. Frederick W. Mayer's very useful *Interpreting NAFTA: The Science and Art of Political Analysis* (1998) focuses primarily on the passage of the agreement in the United States. Jeffrey M. Ayres's *Defying Conventional Wisdom: Political Movements and Popular Contention against North American Free Trade* (1998) examines popular opposition to NAFTA and speculates about the prospects of transnational resistance to North American economic convergence. David G. Haglund, ed., *Over Here and Over There: Canada-U.S. Defence Cooperation in an Era of Interoperability* (2001) will bring readers up-to-date quickly with the evolving military relationship. Robert A. Pastor, a distinguished U.S. academic interpreter of Mexico, has considered Canada as well in *Toward a North American Community* (2001). Perhaps this is a sign that NAFTA will persuade other American scholars to consider Canada.

The contributors to Robert L. Earle and John D. Wirth, eds., *Identities in North America: The Search for Community* (1995) speculate about the effects of regional integration on national and subnational "identities." In their ambitious *The North American Trajectory: Cultural, Economic, and Political Ties among the United States, Canada, and Mexico* (1996), Ronald Inglehart, Miguel Basanez, and Neil Nevitte argue that values are converging and nationalism is in decline in all three countries. Their arguments are emphatically rebutted by Michael Adams in *Fire and Ice: The United States, Canada and the Myth of Converging Values* (2003). In *After the Fifth Sun: Class and Race in North America* (1994), James W. Russell attempts an ambitious synthesis of the historical experiences of the three North American nation-states. Anthony DePalma, former *New York Times* correspondent in Canada and in Mexico, has done it better in *Here: A Biography of the New American Continent* (2001). Another talented journalist, the *Globe and Mail*'s Jeffrey Simpson, has written *Star-Spangled Canadians: Canadians Living the American Dream* (2000), a splendid book about Canadian migration to the United States.

George W. Bush's troubled presidency has produced a growing body of literature on relations with Canada as well as on the Bush presidency itself. The annual volumes in the *Canada among Nations* series consistently provide insightful analyses of the bilateral relationship. The 2005 volume edited by Andrew Cooper and Dane Rowlands, *Split Images* (2006), was especially useful for the fourth edition of *Ambivalent Allies*. The evolving Canadian government's search for a viable foreign policy is reflected in its latest foreign policy review, *Canada's International Policy Statement: A Role of Pride and Influence in the World* (2005). The specific impact of 9/11 on the bilateral relationship is effectively addressed in a number of more recent articles and monographs, including the following: Stephane Roussel, "Honey, Are You Still Mad at Me? I've Changed You Know." *International Journal* 58, no. 4 (2003); Joel Sokolsky, "Northern Exposure? American Homeland Security and Canada," *International Journal* 60, no. 1 (2004/2005); Thomas Axworthy, "An Independent Canada in a Shared North America: Must We Be in Love or Will an Arranged Marriage Do?" *International Journal* 59, no. 4 (2004). Especially useful studies on the evolution of U.S. policy in the Bush years include Stephen Flynn, "America the Vulnerable," *Foreign Affairs* 81 (2002); David Cole and James Dempsey, *Terrorism and the Constitution: Sacrificing Civil Liberties in the Name of National Security*, 2nd ed. (2002); William Michaels, *No Greater Threat: America since September 11 and the Rise of the National Security State* (2002); Elinor Sloan, "Beyond Primacy: American Grand Strategy in the Post–September 11 Era," *International Journal* 58, no. 2 (2003). Condoleezza Rice provides an election-year vision of what would become the Bush foreign policy in "Promoting the National Interest," *Foreign Affairs* 79 (2000). Former Mexican foreign minister Andres Rosenthal provides an introduction to the controversial trilateral security plan in "The Security and Prosperity Partnership: An Overview," *International Journal* 61, no. 3 (2006). Stephen J. Randall's *United States Foreign Oil Policy since World War I* (2005) includes a discussion of the Alberta tar sands in U.S. policy during the Bush years. More detailed analysis of the tar sands development and its relevance to U.S. energy policy can be found in Paul Chastko, *Developing Alberta's Oil Sands, from Karl Clark to Kyoto* (Calgary, 2004).

Finally, two scholarly periodicals merit special mention for students of the U.S.-Canadian relationship. The *American Review of Canadian Studies*, the journal of the multidisciplinary Association for Canadian Studies in the United States, annually publishes a special Thomas Enders issue on the U.S.-Canadian relationship, and almost every issue includes excellent individual articles on the historical and the contemporary U.S.-Canadian relationship. Since 1990, the University of Maine has published *Canadian-American Public Policy*, an outstanding quarterly. Each issue contains a single long article about a U.S.-Canadian question.

Index

sim, 223, 226, 231, 236, 257, 339; Bomarc
missiles and, 197; cold war and, 175;
Cuban missile crisis and, 198, 206,
208, 209; defense relations with U.S.
and, 202, 266; Kennedy, John F., and,
200–207; nationalism of, 195; NORAD
and, 186, 196; nuclear weapons and, 195,
196, 197
Dionne quintuplets, 135, 136
Diplomatic relations, establishment of,
103–6, 126, 158
Disney, Walt, 163, 226
Distant Early Warning Line (DEW Line),
184
Dollar crisis (Canada), European recov-
ery and, 186–87,
Dominion Day (Canada), 42, 55, 62, 70
Doran, Charles, 338
Doukhobors, 52
Drew, George, 226
Du Bois, W. E. B., 81
Dulles, John Foster, 194, 195, 197
Dumbarton Oaks, 167
Duplessis, Maurice, 132

Eagleburger, Lawrence, 256, 260
East Coat Fisheries Agreement, 248, 270
Eayrs, James, 231–32
Economic integration, 107–8, 194–95, 272;
impact of World War II on, 194
Economic nationalism, 236–37, 238–39,
240–41, 255, 256
Eden, Anthony, 166
Education, 27, 62, 81, 136
Eggleton, Art, 304, 306
Eisenhower, Dwight D., 153, 174, 179, 198,
204, 226; NORAD and, 185; nuclear
weapons and, 197; OAS and, 204; trade
policies with Canada and, 189, 191, 192,
193, 195, 280; visits of, to Canada, 185
Eisenhower Doctrine, 197

El Salvador, 126, 257, 258, 265
Elections: Canada 1891, 61; Canada 1908,
88; Canada 1911, 91–92, 124, 188; Canada 1930, 124; Canada 1974, 241; Canada
1979, 252; Canada 1984, 262, 264; Canada 1988, 7; Canada 1993, 7; Canada,
2000, 8; Canada 2004, 321; Canada 2006,
8, 337; U.S. 1972, 235; U.S. 2000, 8, 302,
303
Emerson, David, 330, 331
Energy policy: in Canada, 250, 255; in
Carter administration, 392n30; Nixon
administration and, 240; in U.S., 241,
248, 255
Environmental issues, 63, 64, 75, 76; acid
rain, 248, 265, 267–69, 292; free trade
and, 271, 282, 290–91
Erie Canal, 27
Ethnic diversity, 81–82, 160–62, 294, 296
European Recovery Plan. *See* Marshall
Plan
Exceptionalism, 18–19
Expo '67, Montreal, 222, 230

Fallen Timbers, battle of, 18
Fenians (Irish Republican Brotherhood),
38–39, 40, 333
Film industry, 117, 118, 119, 120, 121, 190,
191, 287; during 1970s, 242, 245, 246;
during World War II, 163. *See also* Cultural relations; Hollywood
Fine, Sidney, 130, 131
First Nations, 157. *See also* Indians
Fish, Hamilton, 40, 45, 49, 56
Fisheries, 10, 186; agreements on, 78–79,
92, 104, 270; disputes over, 39–40, 62–63,
64, 73, 99, 186, 250, 251; fishing rights
and, 23, 33, 62; trade and, 87, 291–92;
Treaty of Ghent and, 24; Treaty of Paris
and, 15
Ford, Gerald, 3, 228, 241, 243